D0277986

IRELAND
The 20th Century

Charles Townshend
Professor of International History, University of Keele

A member of the Hodder Headline Group
LONDON • SYDNEY • AUCKLAND
Co-published in the United States of America by
Oxford University Press Inc., New York

1123235

First published in Great Britain in 1999 by
Arnold, a member of the Hodder Headline Group,
338 Euston Road, London NW1 3BH

http://www.arnoldpublishers.com

Co-published in the United States of America by
Oxford University Press Inc.,
198 Madison Avenue, New York, NY 10016

© 1998 Charles Townshend

All rights reserved. No part of this publication may be reproduced or
transmitted in any form or by any means, electronically or mechani-
cally, including photocopying, recording or any information storage
or retrieval system, without either prior permission in writing from
the publisher or a licence permitting restricted copying. In the United
Kingdom such licences are issued by the Copyright Licensing Agency:
90 Tottenham Court Road, London W1P 9HE.

The advice and information in this book are believed to be true and
accurate at the date of going to press, but neither the author nor the
publisher can accept any legal responsibility or liability for any errors
or omissions.

British Library Cataloguing in Publication Data
A catalogue entry for this book is available from the British Library

Library of Congress Cataloging-in-Publication Data
A catalog record for this book is available from the Library of Congress

ISBN 0 340 66336 7 (hb)
ISBN 0 340 66335 9 (pb)

1 2 3 4 5 6 7 8 9 10

Production Editor: Wendy Rooke
Production Controller: Priya Gohil
Cover Design: Terry Griffiths

Typeset in 11/13 Janson by Saxon Graphics Ltd, Derby
Printed and bound in Great Britain by MPG Books Ltd, Bodmin

What do you think about this book? Or any other Arnold title?
Please send your comments to feedback.arnold@hodder.co.uk

24 MAR 1999

Contents

List of maps, figures and tables   vi

Abbreviations   viii

Glossary   ix

Preface   xi

1. The state of the Union, 1900   1

2. The national question   19

3. Cultures and civilizations: the struggle for Ireland's soul   38

4. Home Rule and the British crisis, 1905–1914   52

5. World war and rebellion, 1914–1919   68

6. The first republic and the Anglo-Irish war, 1919–1922   87

     108

7. Civil war and nation-building, 1922–1932   132

8. The dominion of Eamon de Valera, 1932–1948   159

9. The second republic and modernization, 1948–1968   178

10. The Stormont regime: Northern Ireland, 1920–1969   203

11. The thirty years' crisis, 1968–1998   235

Notes   250

Biographical notes   254

Chronology   264

Select bibliography   271

Appendix 1   272

Appendix 2   274

Index

List of maps, figures and tables

Maps and figures

1.1 The effect of the Land Acts, 1881–1909   16

2.1 Irish speakers, 1851–1961   22

5.1 Dublin 1916: the Easter rising   78

6.1 IRA operations, 1919–1921   95

7.1 The pro-treaty/anti-treaty split in the IRA, 1922   112

7.2 The anti-treaty vote in the 1922 general election   114

8.1 Development, approximate size and participation in government of political parties in the Irish Republic, 1918–1994   135

8.2 The average size of farms, 1936   139

8.3 Predominant type of farming   140

10.1 Belfast riots, 1857–1980   182

10.2 The proportion and distribution of Catholics in Northern Ireland   188

11.1 The annual and cumulative death-toll from political violence, 1969–1990   224

Tables

1.1 Numbers of Roman Catholics in selected professions
      (1861–1911)   9
10.1 Wards and local-government election results,
       Derry/Londonderry, 1967   190
10.2 Religion and occupational class, 1971   193

Abbreviations

ACA	Army Comrades Association
CDB	Congested Districts Board
DUP	Democratic Unionist Party
EC	European Community
EU	European Union
INTO	Irish National Teachers' Organization
IRA	Irish Republican Army
IRB	Irish Republican Brotherhood
ITGWU	Irish Transport and General Workers' Union
PIRA	Provisional IRA
RIC	Royal Irish Constabulary
RTE	Radio Telefís Éireann
RUC	Royal Ulster Constabulary
SDLP	Social Democratic and Labour Party
TD	Teachta Dála (member of Dáil Éireann)
UDA	Ulster Defence Association
UDR	Ulster Defence Regiment
UIL	United Irish League
UN	United Nations
USC	Ulster Special Constabulary
UUP	Ulster Unionist Party
UVF	Ulster Volunteer Force
UWC	Ulster Workers' Council
VUPP	Vanguard Unionist Progressive Party

Glossary

árd-fheis	national convention
Bunreacht na hÉireann	constitution of Ireland
Ceann Comhairle	speaker of Dáil Éireann
Dáil Éireann	national assembly of Ireland
Gaeltacht	Irish-speaking area
Oireachtas	parliament
Ogláich na hÉireann	Irish volunteers
Saorstát Éireann	Irish Free State
Seanad Éireann	senate of Ireland
Tánaiste	deputy prime minister
Taoiseach	prime minister

Preface

*M*odern Irish history has often been told as 'the story of a people coming out of bondage'. In that story, the decisive moment was the struggle for political independence between 1916 and 1922. The history of Ireland in the twentieth century has indeed been shaped to some extent by the effort to remove British control, to 'break the connection' as the republican Theobald Wolfe Tone urged 200 years ago. Some Irish political thinkers have insisted that modern Ireland is a post-colonial society, profoundly marked by the ambiguous experience of liberation, having more in common with the third world than the western European norm. Ireland's experience has not been 'normal', but it is wrong to lay too much stress on its abnormality. The idea of a simple western norm is too crude to be of much use.

Ireland's bondage was certainly more complicated than simple colonial control. Tone's claim that the British connection was 'the never-failing source of Ireland's ills' points to a kind of neurotic defensive reaction, which early in this century took shape as an introverted nationalism, another kind of bondage, perhaps harder to recognize or confront. External influences were treated with hostility or at best suspicion. Only in the last quarter of this century could Ireland begin to come finally out of this collective autism, and engage freely and equally with the wider world. The turning-point in this process, that perhaps began with Ireland's entry into the United Nations, was its membership of the European Community in 1973, which laid the basis for a dramatic (if long-delayed) economic growth and a new kind of cultural confidence.

British domination affected Ireland over a very long period – famously 'eight hundred years of oppression' in nationalist rhetoric –

but it was not consistent in its aims and methods. It was only erratically 'colonial'. The primary logic of British control was always
strategic, from the time of Henry II's original intervention in the
twelfth century. The Union, through which Ireland was governed
from 1801 to 1922, was essentially a final effort to 'pacify Ireland', in
Gladstone's famous phrase. There was thus an irony in the decision of
the Irish republicans in 1916 to launch their rebellion in the midst of
a major war, when the threat to British security made any political
concessions unlikely. Both world wars of the twentieth century re-
emphasized the sensitivity of the strategic relationship between the
two islands, but between the First and the Second a dramatic change
had taken place in British assumptions about the relationship. The
defining moment in this change was the Anglo-Irish agreement of
1938 which settled the vexed issue of British control of Irish ports.
Britain had reached the conclusion that, however severe the security
threat, it could never envisage using military force against the Irish
state. Britain's declarations in the 1990s that it had 'no selfish strategic
interest' in Ireland were a logical consequence of this, only delayed by
the fear of antagonizing the Protestant loyalists who still acted as a
(now superfluous) British garrison.

The question whether the Union could have been made to work is
still an important one. In the early twentieth century a group of Irish
Home Rulers seem genuinely to have believed that Irish autonomy
could have been reconciled with membership of the British Empire. If
they were right, Britain's inability to devise and enact an appropriate
Home Rule measure represents a major governmental failure. But
could such a measure really have been devised? It seems likely, in retrospect, that no normalization of Irish-British relations would have
been possible until the British Empire, and Britain's own ideas about
its international role, had changed to an extent that was hardly
thinkable in the early years of the century. Ireland played a vital part
in this evolution, which was in a sense reciprocal.

The aim of this book is to provide an account of the central political
and social processes that have brought Ireland to its millennial liberation. It is intended to be straightforward enough to be useful to those
with no previous knowledge of Irish history. The opening chapters
reach back into the nineteenth century to analyse the context of the
early twentieth-century confrontation between the British state and
the various forms of Irish national consciousness. The rest follow a
chronological path. It may be a truism to say that one cause of British-
Irish misunderstandings has been that one side forgets, while the other

remembers, too much. But there does seem to be an imbalance, and I hope this book may help in some degree to rectify it by enlarging access to the findings of a generation of historians who have recently transformed the study of Irish history. It will be clear to those who have laboured in this field how heavily I have drawn on their work.

CT
August 1998

1

The state of the Union, 1900

*I*n June 1900 Queen Victoria paid her second and last visit to
Ireland. The United Kingdom was almost exactly a century old.
Since 1801 British governments had tried to establish a workable
administrative system for Ireland. The royal visit to the sister island
might be seen as the culminating point of a hundred years of state-
building. The progress of the antique monarch through her Irish
capital was observed by a precocious Dublin teenager, James Joyce.

> Along the way were arrayed the little English soldiers, and behind this
> barrier stood the crowd of citizens. In the decorated balconies were the
> officials and their wives, the unionist employees and their wives, the
> tourists and their wives. When the procession appeared, the people in the
> balconies began to shout greetings and wave their handkerchiefs. The
> Queen's carriage passed, carefully protected on all sides by an impressive
> body of guards with bared sabres, and within was seen a tiny lady, almost
> a dwarf, tossed and jolted by the movements of the carriage, dressed in
> mourning, and wearing horn-rimmed glasses on a livid and empty face.
> Now and then she bowed fitfully, in reply to some isolated shout of
> greeting. ... The English soldiers stood respectfully at attention while
> their patroness passed, and behind them, the crowd of citizens looked at
> the ostentatious procession and the pathetic central figure with curious
> eyes and almost with pity, and when the carriage passed, they followed it
> with ambiguous glances.

Although this time, unlike on her first visit, there were no bombs or
cabbage stalks, 'the old Queen of England entered the Irish capital in
the midst of a silent people'.[1]

Joyce's insinuation that the only royal enthusiasts were government employees and tourists was probably overdone. Certainly
his vision differed from that of *The Times*, which reported that the
crowds thronging the streets greeted the Queen with 'cheers and
blessings', and that even nationalists 'cheered themselves hoarse'.[2]
But Dublin's City Marshal, John Parnell, had to endure a storm of
nationalist criticism for taking part in a civic welcome, even though
he maintained that his late brother, the great Charles Stewart
Parnell, would have done the same. Joyce's 'ambiguous glances'
reflect the fact that this was an event experienced in opposite ways
by opposing groups. It came in the midst of the South African War,
in which two small but much-admired Irish Brigades were fighting
alongside the Boers against Britain. In the Irish countryside, the
United Irish League (UIL) agitation was at the height of its power.
The League itself had been formed to commemorate the centenary
of the 1798 rebellion, and was only the biggest of a welter of
patriotic groups that multiplied around the turn of the century. One
of the events marking the official celebration of Queen Victoria's
visit was a picnic for 5000 children in Phoenix Park, near the resi-
dences of the Irish Viceroy and Chief Secretary. The famous actress
and activist Maud Gonne, 'the most beautiful woman in Ireland',
stung by the press's applause for the royal gesture, formed a committee to organize a counter-demonstration, the Irish Patriotic
Children's Treat. Funds were raised, and 30,000 children were
enrolled for the picnic: though nothing like this number actually
appeared, the nationalist Arthur Griffith claimed that 'Dublin never
witnessed anything so marvellous' as their procession to Clonturk
Park on 1 July. Unionists disputed the numbers claimed by Griffith
and Gonne, and mocked the fact that the patriotic act took so long
to get together, but they were unwise to do so. Maud Gonne's Treat
committee took permanent form as a nationalist women's organization, Inghinídhe na hÉireann (Daughters of Ireland). The mobilization of separatist opinion was still fragmentary, but it formed a
potent undercurrent. After he went into self-imposed exile in 1904,
James Joyce remarked that whatever the legal situation might be, 'a
moral separation already exists between the two countries'; he could
not recall ever having heard 'God save the Queen' (or after 1901,
King) sung in public 'without a storm of hisses, shouts and shushes
that made the solemn and majestic music absolutely inaudible'. The
attempt to create a United Kingdom stood on the brink of open
failure.

The British state project in Ireland

Although by the beginning of the twentieth century 'Unionism' was acquiring a distinctly negative tone – stridently expressed in loyalist slogans like 'We will not have home rule!', 'No surrender!', 'Not an inch!', and 'Ulster says No!' – it began a hundred years earlier with strong positive aspirations. The bloody mayhem of the 1798 United Irish rebellion, and the ferocious Protestant mobilization to suppress it, convinced Prime Minister William Pitt that political reform in Ireland – essentially, the granting of civil rights to Catholics – was vital, and that the Protestants who controlled the Irish parliament would never carry it out. Only unification, merging the Irish into the British parliament, could open up the possibility of 'Catholic emancipation'. The logic that underlay the 1801 Act of Union was to remain directly relevant to Irish politics in the twentieth century: it was that within the larger framework of the United Kingdom, Catholics would be a less threatening minority, which the dominant majority could tolerate.

This perception was right in principle, but in the event failed to guarantee that even as a minority the Catholics would not still provoke the same intense fears as they had in the past. In fact the persistence of anti-Catholic prejudice in Britain itself led to a significant and probably fatal delay in the granting of Catholic emancipation. For nearly 30 years after the Act of Union, Tory governments shelved the issue. Only the formidable mobilization of the Catholic Association under the leadership of Daniel O'Connell in the 1820s forced a resolution. In 1829 Catholic emancipation was conceded. Thus the British state had provoked a major resistance movement, and then after ensuring maximum confrontation given way to its pressure. This was a baleful precedent for British policy in Ireland. O'Connell himself was a lawyer who believed in the emancipatory potential of the British constitution, and who was dedicated to reason and moral force (he was an admirer of the utopian anarchist William Godwin) rather than violence. Even he came to think, by the 1840s, that the Union must be reversed. His repeal agitation brought together many nationalists with more radical ideas about the liberation of Ireland. Long before the Great Famine of the late 1840s the Union faced a formidable range of opposition.

There was more to the British state project in Ireland than Catholic emancipation. Its (more or less unspoken) agenda was a wider attempt to bring Ireland into line with Britain. To the British official mind, this could only mean bringing the benefits of progress pioneered by Britain to a country whose biggest problem was economic backwardness. British prosperity was believed to be the product of free-market capitalism, *laissez-faire*, and Ireland was a prime example of the kind of restrictive traditional society that needed to be swept away if progress was to follow. Several markers of the British effort to 'normalize' Ireland in its own image stand out: the attempt to impose the rule of law through more efficient policing in the 1830s, the attempt to create a non-denominational education system, and the attempt to replace custom by contract law in Deasy's Act of 1860. But although the general drift of the project is clear enough, its development was spasmodic and inconsistent. Ireland was usually a low priority in UK politics – in effect British politics. William Parnell's gloomy verdict in 1805 that 'the English Ministry have no sort of knowledge of affairs in Ireland' was to remain all too true in future. Still more so was his observation that they had little wish to learn: 'it is a dispiriting task to endeavour to interest English ministers, and the English parliament, in the welfare of Ireland'. At root, the performance of the Union as a political structure was marked by permanent tension between the notional unity of the United Kingdom and the actual treatment of Ireland as a special entity, with a curious status somewhere between a sub-state and a colony.

Governance

The irregularity of Ireland's position was etched in the institutions of government. The Act of Union swept away most of the earlier state structure; the single outstanding exception was the Supreme Court of Judicature, though even that was also eventually reconstructed in 1877. The most conspicuous casualty, of course, was the Irish parliament. Under the Union, the 300 members of the parliament on College Green in Dublin were replaced by 100 (out of nearly 600) Westminster MPs. These remained exclusively Protestants until O'Connell defied the law and stood for parliament in Clare in 1828. After the 1829 reform, Catholics could legally stand for parliament, but the Catholic electorate was actually reduced (from over 100,000 to 16,000) by the abolition of the 40-shilling freeholder franchise. Major expansions of the electorate followed in 1850 and 1884, but Irish representation never delivered the responsiveness that the English believed to be the hallmark of 'representative government'.

Irish MPs at Westminster were distant from the quasi-autonomous adminstration that controlled Ireland from Dublin. The only political

connection between the two capitals was a single government minister, the Chief Secretary for Ireland. He was responsible to parliament for Irish affairs, but he had no ministry as such, no executive
apparatus. The Irish Office in London was only a small clerical unit.
The Chief Secretary had to be at Westminster while parliament was in
session, and in Dublin during recess. Over the period of the Union,
the power of this minister in Ireland and within the government was a
variable function of his own political clout and that of his notional
superior, the Viceroy. Although on paper he was the Chief Secretary
to the Viceroy, he was invariably appointed by the Prime Minister, and
towards the end of the century was assured of Cabinet rank.

The Chief Secretaryship was not inevitably a graveyard of political
reputations, but few ministers found that it helped them to rise. The
shining exceptions were Robert Peel in the 1810s and Arthur James
Balfour in the 1880s. More typical was a string of second-rankers like
W. E. Forster, G. O. Trevelyan, John Morley, Gerald Balfour and
George Wyndham, some of whom might have been more effective if
they had stayed longer in post. As it was, a senior police officer at
Dublin Castle later wryly noted, 'each Chief Secretary did little more
than disorganise the system established by his predecessor'.[3] The
besetting weakness of the administration was lack of sustained political
impulse; its most characteristic stance was 'drift'. Most of the time it
was reactive rather than active. This was very marked at the start of the
century, when the first Chief Secretary held office for six months, and
the next eight averaged 16 months apiece. The natural result was, as a
leading historian of the administrative system put it, concentration on
'routine problems rather than large-scale reorganisation'.[4] The Union
did not bring progress. The basic structure persisted until the end.

The agencies of government, mostly centred in Dublin Castle, were
supervised by the Under-Secretary, whose role was thus significantly
bigger and more publicly prominent than that of equivalent civil servants in Whitehall. Even he, however, did not have direct control over
all the agencies, 'the ramshackle collection of boards and councils that
did duty for an Irish administration' (in the words of F. S. L. Lyons).[5]
Disraeli labelled it 'the weakest executive in the world', and with due
allowance for rhetorical exaggeration, he had a point. Little co-ordinating power lay in the hands of the nominal head of the Irish
Executive, the Lord-Lieutenant, usually called the Viceroy. The
splendour of the title, and the Viceregal Lodge in Phoenix Park,
created a somewhat jarring colonial image, at odds with the restrained
vagueness of the Viceroyal function. In 1905 the Prime Minister

likened it to that of a constitutional monarch, but this missed the point that the Viceroyalty was a political post, which was sometimes occupied by Cabinet-rank politicians (such as Lord Spencer in the 1880s and Cadogan in the late 1890s), as well as by many political nonentities. Such powers as Viceroys could exercise were not monarchical, except in the ceremonial sense of holding court for Dublin 'society'. Indeed nothing is more emblematic of the half-baked nature of the British administration than the fact that the Viceroyalty was widely recognized as anomalous, and yet was never altered. Suggestions that it be abolished, or, alternatively, occupied by a royal figure like the Prince of Wales, got nowhere.[6]

Law and order

The pacification of Ireland, the vindication of law and order in the interests of state security as well as public safety, was the underlying imperative of all British action. Catholic emancipation and other reforms were intended to secure this objective. Unfortunately they did not. W. E. Gladstone's ringing declaration in 1867, 'my mission is to pacify Ireland', underlined how badly the project had so far fared. The high-profile reforms that followed – the disestablishment in 1869 of the official Anglican church (the Church of Ireland), and the first Land Act in 1870 – were no more successful. Resistance to the law seemed to be endemic in Ireland, and whole counties could fall under the terrorist sway of 'secret societies' for months or even years at a stretch. Tenants threatened with eviction by their landlords would be backed up by the intimidatory machinery of the agrarian 'associations' under the names of Whiteboys or mythical leaders like Captain Moonlight. Law officers such as sheriffs and process-servers were attacked, the crops and livestock belonging to landlords or tenants who took over farms from which others had been evicted were destroyed, witnesses and jurors were threatened and occasionally assassinated. Though the government talked of agrarian 'outrage' and terrorism (suggesting that ordinary law-abiding people were intimidated into illegal activity), these secret societies were effective because they were part of their local communities. The 'unwritten law' they enforced was seen by many as more legitimate than British statute; and it seemed to be easier to enforce. As one British judge sardonically remarked of the rent strikes at the height of the 'land war' (see ch. 2), 'a very small amount of shooting in the legs will effectively deter an immense mass of people from paying rents which they do not want to pay'.[7]

To deal with endemic agrarian crime, and the occasional episodes of open insurrection, as well as the rather different sectarian battles of the Orange Order, a hefty apparatus of law enforcement was constructed. A battery of special powers were taken under temporary 'Insurrection Acts'; once or twice habeas corpus was suspended, and even martial law was declared. In the first half-century of the Union, Ireland was free of emergency legislation for only five years. Eventually, in 1887, Balfour replaced the sequence of temporary laws with a permanent special powers statute, the Crimes Act, or Criminal Law and Procedure (Ireland) Act. Part of the problem was the weakness of the legal infrastructure in Ireland. The local gentry who made the magistracy such a formidable instrument of control in England were unreliable in Ireland, and had to be stiffened by a corps of 60 paid ('stipendiary') magistrates. But even these resident magistrates could not replicate their English models. The texture of Irish rural society was different. The famous 'Irish R.M.' stories written by Somerville and Ross at the turn of the century (and still more their novel *The Real Charlotte*) acutely reflected its artificial and stilted hierarchical structure.

The true musculature of British control in Ireland, and the British state's most substantial innovation there, was the police force. The first local Peace Preservation Forces set up by Robert Peel in 1814 were followed by an increasingly hefty national structure; an Inspector-Generalship for each of the four provinces merged in 1836 to form a single force, the Irish Constabulary. After the suppression of the Fenian rising of 1867 the title 'Royal' was added in recognition of the fact that the force had done what was expected of it. By that time it had become a distinctive organization, developing on visibly different lines from the English police. It was armed, centrally controlled – by an Inspector-General under ministerial authority – and quasi-military in dress, training and ethos. Its 10,000–12,000 constables, in recognition of the pervasiveness of secret-society intimidation, were posted outside their home counties in local stations called 'barracks'. Such features enabled nationalists to denounce the Royal Irish Constabulary (RIC) as an 'army of occupation', but they fostered a strong tradition of service and *esprit de corps*. The force was, in another nationalist tag, 'the eyes and ears of Dublin Castle': throughout most of the country it was the sole representative of the state. By the turn of the century the 'peelers' were part of everyday life, perhaps tolerated rather than respected, their semi-military style steadily becoming more a hindrance than a help to their normal function. A respected French writer on Ireland at the beginning of the twentieth century may have exaggerated a little in saying that 'the spirit in which the police are inspired by those in command is one of a deplorable and arbitrary provocativeness',[8] but the force certainly carried with it a heavy history of confrontation which it could never quite shake off.

The forces of law mirrored an aspect of the Union which remained fundamental at the beginning of the twentieth century. Catholics, three-quarters of the population of Ireland, were markedly under-represented in responsible positions. While some 90 per cent of police constables were Catholics, scarcely 10 per cent of the district inspectors and county inspectors were. Only 251 out of 1272 justices of the peace appointed between 1895 and 1902 were Catholics, and 19 out of 68 resident magistrates. In 1906 the *Irish Catholic* pointed out that only nine out of 44 benchers of the King's Inns were Catholics, and insisted that Protestants swamped Catholics by seven to one in appointments to local judicial posts. It noted sardonically that 'Religion is never inquired into when making these appointments. Why should it? – when all the Law Officers of the Crown, as far back as the eye can see, are of the dominant creed. At their head you have an Attorney General and a Solicitor General, both remarkable for their hostility to Catholics ...'. Over three years later it still counted seven Catholic to 12 Protestant county court judges, and 22 to 43 resident magistrates.[9]

The structured thwarting of legitimate ambition was ultimately fatal to the Union. Its result was the alienation of a Catholic elite that should have been the easiest segment to integrate.[10] As Roy Foster has noted, Catholics might have become 'a safely diluted minority within the United Kingdom' if they had been 'given access to the spoils system of the political nation'.[11] But since the Union remained incomplete, they were driven to find another route.

The state and the economy

A key assumption of the Union was that English 'political economy' would spread to Ireland and eradicate the backwardness that had produced the Irish problem. Not until halfway though the Union's life, in the late 1860s, did the conviction that what was good for England would be good for Ireland begin to falter. But even before this, there was a major difficulty in exporting *laissez-faire* economic ideas. Free-trade political economy was (and is) inherently hostile to state regu-

lation, yet the weakness of the Irish economic infrastructure made it unlikely that rapid progress would occur without substantial state intervention.[12] Some historians, notably Oliver MacDonagh, have suggested that as a result Ireland became a kind of economic and social laboratory in which the future expansion of state action was tested (distantly prefiguring the welfare state). By contrast, Joseph Lee maintains that state action was usually limited and short-term in vision, and that the suggestion of a larger strategy is grossly exaggerated.[13]

One of the most significant indicators of the underlying logic of the policy process was the 1838 Poor Law. This was imposed in defiance of the recommendations of an Irish Poor Law Commission, which had concluded rather forcefully that the English model would not work in Ireland. Its recommendation of more extensive state commitment, including state-sponsored employment, was unceremoniously set aside in favour of an English-style workhouse system supported by a locally levied rate. The intention was straightforwardly to force the unemployed out on to the labour market.[14] The fact that this policy did not make sense in Ireland, where labour supply dwarfed demand, testified to its ideological basis – but not to any idea of careful experimentation. Ideological momentum was maintained even after the Great Famine: liberal reformers like Lord John Russell in the 1850s remained committed to pressing large-scale social change in Ireland.

The Famine was a human disaster which cast a grim shadow over subsequent Irish life, and called the Union itself into question. Although many modern historians contend that an independent Irish government would have followed essentially the same policy as the British, there can be no doubt that the Union was widely held responsible for the scale of the catastrophe. Britain presided over a drastic demographic reversal in Ireland, whose population had peaked in the mid-1840s at over 8.5 million. Though the rate of growth was probably falling after 1800, the quadrupling of the population since the famine of 1740–41 was remarkable by European standards, and unique in a country which was not experiencing large-scale urbanization. The Irish economy remained overwhelmingly agricultural, and productivity was sharply restricted by the prevalence of very small-scale farming in the west. The spirit of these smallholders was pithily expressed by a writer in 1838: 'the farmer who always grows plenty of potatoes will never be broke'.[15] The Famine broke that spirit. Its economic impact is still disputed, but it clearly pushed forward a general shift from tillage to pasture, and a gradual increase in farm sizes, accompanied by the virtual eradication of the most marginal

rural class, the 'cottiers', who became landless labourers or, more frequently, emigrants. Emigration, already a noticeable trend before the
Famine, accelerated dramatically; the marriage rate fell equally dramatically. The total population went into a free-fall that only slowed
up in the early twentieth century as it levelled out at around 4.5
million. Thus it was almost halved in two generations.

The Famine appeared to do the brutal work needed to realize the
British vision of a more 'normal' Irish economy. In 1860 the keystone of
the British structure was added in the form of 'Deasy's Act', which
expressly Anglicized landlord–tenant relations by declaring that the
contractual rights of landlords must outweigh the customary rights of
tenants. Within a few years, however, the whole project changed
direction. In 1868 the great liberal political economist John Stuart Mill
recognized that the 'normalization' of Ireland was not succeeding:
Ireland's own norms needed to be understood and accommodated. Two
years later Gladstone's first Land Act brought the unBritish idea that
landlord–tenant relations should be regulated by law. The famous 'three
Fs', fixity of tenure, fair rent, and free sale, certainly did not give Irish
tenants all they wanted, but they signalled the new readiness of the
liberal state to intervene. Gladstone's second Land Act in 1881 was an
even more dramatic demonstration that Ireland was to be treated differently from England. The official adjudication of rents on the basis of
a national valuation decisively terminated the free market in land tenure,
creating a kind of 'dual ownership'.

Education and society

Potentially the most fruitful contribution to the viability of the Union
lay in the sphere of education. In 1831 Chief Secretary E. G. Stanley
founded an 'Irish national system of education', with the aim of establishing primary schools throughout the country. An unpaid Commission
of National Education was set up to advance grants for school-building,
to pay teachers' salaries, and to issue lists of approved textbooks. By
1833, 789 schools had been established, with 107,042 children enrolled.
At mid-century the totals were 4547 schools and 511,239 children; by
1870 (when a national education system was eventually established in
Britain) there were nearly a million children in 6800 schools. The bare
statistics were quite impressive, but some aspects of the system were less
edifying. Each National School was controlled by a manager with practically arbitrary power. Teachers had no right of appeal against dismissal

until the end of the century. More seriously, the government's agenda for creating a uniform and secular system came unstuck at a very early stage. Stanley's original instructions to the commissioners urged them to 'look with particular favour' on applications for managerial posts made jointly by Protestant and Catholic clergy, or Protestant and Catholic laymen, or clergy of one denomination and laymen of the other. But few such convenient pairs came forward in the early years, and in order to get the system going the commissioners accepted applications from anyone of good standing. In practice, these were, overwhelmingly, Catholic clerics. By mid-century, less than 4 per cent of schools were under joint managership, while 75 per cent were managed by clergy of a single denomination.

The ecumenical project was stymied in the classroom as well. The attempt to introduce model schools for teacher training in the early 1860s ran into determined clerical opposition, and the model schools were soon deserted in favour of the spreading Christian Brothers schools.[16] According to Donald Akenson's calculation, in 1867 a Catholic manager appointed a Protestant teacher or vice versa in less than 7 per cent of schools. By 1870, he concludes, 'the national system had become denominational in fact, even if still nondenominational in theory'.[17] In 1900 the bishops concluded (in their synodal pastoral letter) that the 'system of National education ... is now in fact, whatever it is in name, as denominational almost as we could desire.'[18]

This certainly represented a failure of state policy, but policy itself played only a relatively small role in the process by which segregated schools emerged. The simple geographical distribution of the two religious groups practically dictated the outcome, as J. J. Lee points out – tartly adding that there is in any case little evidence that co-education would have achieved its founder's aims. 'Schools reflected rather than created community sentiments, and proved powerless against the blind hatred lovingly inculcated in the bosom of the Christian family.'[19] But the schools undoubtedly increased access to education, even if the extent of the increase cannot be precisely measured.[20] They also delivered another crucial component of modernization, mass literacy: illiteracy rates fell from 53 per cent in 1841 to 14 per cent in 1901. Beyond the primary level, the project stalled. Intermediate education was neglected, and the state's insistence on secularism in higher education ensured that the establishment of a publicly funded Catholic university would be delayed for two generations after Peel's proposed non-denominational Queen's Colleges of 1845 were denounced by the Catholic bishops as 'Godless'. The *Dublin Review* put the Catholic attitude trenchantly in

1874: 'it is simply undeniable that the absence of higher education is a powerful preservative against apostasy ... the Church's interest is not in higher education as such, but in Catholic higher education'.[21] Even A. J. Balfour, probably the most successful Chief Secretary of the nineteenth century, indeed of the whole Union period, met with an uncharacteristic failure when he tried to push a Catholic university proposal through in 1889. It foundered not only on the Catholic Hierarchy's reservations but also on opposition from Protestant Unionists.

'Home rule' or 'constructive unionism'?

Towards the end of the nineteenth century there were signs that the Union was beginning to be re-thought, or at any rate re-formulated. The logic of Gladstone's reforms pointed to increasing recognition on Britain's part of Irish differences. The over-complex second Land Act of 1881 was clearly not a final answer. The growing strength of the demand for 'home rule' backed by the agrarian violence of the 'land war', led to the emergence of a powerful political party under Charles Stewart Parnell (see ch. 2). This dinned in the argument that Ireland's special needs could only be efficiently dealt with by some kind of devolution of power. In 1884 one leading member of Gladstone's Cabinet, Joseph Chamberlain, took up the idea of semi-representative local government (the 'central board scheme'), probably to undercut rather than to meet the aspirations of Irish nationalism. Gladstone went much further in 1885, accepting that home rule, the creation of an Irish parliament, could work as a means of reconciling Ireland to the Union. He insisted that it would, indeed, strengthen the Union. But this argument struck Conservatives – and some Radicals like Chamberlain himself – as absurd and dangerous. When Gladstone pushed ahead with a Home Rule Bill in 1886 he broke his own party and triggered a major political crisis. The elections of 1885 and 1886, under the new universal franchise of 1884, dramatically recast the political face of Ireland. The virtual elimination of the Liberal party from Irish politics prefigured a tacit undermining of the Union at a fundamental level.[22] From then on, no 'mainland' British parties would organize in Ireland.

At the same time Unionists became a much more sharply defined and coherent grouping, joining English Conservatives with Chamberlain's Liberal Unionists and a new Ulster Unionist movement – indeed the preservation of the Union became a cause evoking a political passion rare in Britain. A second crisis followed when Gladstone's last government got a second Home Rule Bill through the House of Commons in 1893, only to see it fall to the entrenched Unionist majority in the House of Lords. The negative side of this Unionist campaign was potently expressed by the great constitutional lawyer A. V. Dicey after the second crisis: 'once let the necessity of repelling the separatists fall out of view and our position becomes a weak one'. On the back of this call for resistance, a major mobilization of Unionist forces went ahead at street level in north-eastern Ulster. But for other Unionists this relentless nay-saying was not enough. After the crushing Unionist victory in the election of 1895, a conservative Dublin newspaper pointedly asked whether 'the creed of the unionist party begins and ends in saying "no" to home rule'.[23]

There was, perhaps, an alternative: the policy that came to be labelled 'constructive unionism'. The Unionist governments led by Lord Salisbury and his nephew Arthur James Balfour, holding power for most of the 20 years after 1885, gradually put together a set of reforms that had a more far-reaching effect than Gladstone's. These were mainly economic rather than constitutional, reflecting Salisbury's belief that the Irish question was a 'knife and fork' question, material rather than ideological. The traditional landlord party had reached the conclusion that only land purchase offered a way out of the disorders of the nineteenth century. The struggles of the land war, and the imposition of rent adjudication by Gladstone's second Land Act, had made the position of landlords intolerable. If they could sell their land to their tenants, the Irish countryside would be filled with 'peasant proprietors' with all the conservative instincts of peasants the world over. The prospect of peaceful stability offered consolation for the loss of landlord ascendancy. It would make the Union safe. The problem was how to square the purchase price required by landlords (usually 25 years' rent) with what the tenants could or would pay (usually 15 years' rent). The answer was low-interest loans.

Liberal reluctance to use state money in this way meant that all the significant initiatives were taken by Conservative administrations. The pace was hardly rapid. The Ashbourne Act in 1885 made £5 million available for 49-year loans at 4 per cent. In 1888 another £5 million was added; in 1891 another £33 million, but with complicated restrictions. Arthur Balfour's Chief Secretaryship also produced constructive measures in local government, education, and transport – notably the Light Railways Act of 1889 which helped to 'open up' the west of Ireland, though to what was less clear. The Congested Districts Board

(CDB) of 1891 was a remarkable initiative aimed at developing the backward west. The 'congestion' it set out to deal with was the persistence of tiny farms on marginal land (a congested area was initially defined as one in which total rateable value divided by the number of inhabitants was less than 30 shillings per capita: altogether some 2.5 million acres with a population of half a million in 1891). Its task was to improve the quality of agriculture and industry by technical instruction and limited subsidies, to develop the transport infrastructure by building roads, bridges and piers, and also to foster the amalgamation of uneconomic holdings and help farmers to move to bigger farms. Over time this land transfer function vastly outweighed the other contributions of the CDB, for instance in fishery control and development.[24] By 1912 most of its budget, up from the original £41,000 to £530,000, was dedicated to this, and the redefinition of congested districts had doubled the area in which it operated.[25]

The CDB was far from perfect. A recent historian has pointed to the erratic effects of its unlimited ambitions combined with complete lack of financial discipline. He judges it rather severely: 'as a development agency it was hopeless; as a symbol of what Unionism could do for Ireland it was irrelevant'.[26] But it was undeniably popular, and it was a striking innovation. Its meticulous investigations produced far more accurate information than governments had previously had, and its responsiveness to popular demands made it more attractive to the ordinary people than to the Treasury. It certainly appeared to offer a blueprint for an enlightened Unionist policy, which seemed to be emerging towards the end of the century. During the Chief Secretaryship of Gerald Balfour, Arthur's younger brother, between 1895 and 1900, three major reforms, a new Land Act in 1896, the Local Government Act of 1898, and the creation of the Department of Agriculture and Technical Instruction in 1899, had the appearance of a comprehensive project designed, in Gerald Balfour's famous phrase, to 'kill Home Rule with kindness'. Undoubtedly the reforms were significant, above all the dramatic introduction of a new local government structure based directly on the new and surprisingly democratic English model. The first elections to the new councils swept away the last vestiges of traditional landlord domination of local power in Ireland.

But Balfour came to regret his all-too-memorable slogan, which enshrined the negative side of Unionism (and was clearly intended to secure support from the formidable die-hard right wing). Modern historians have also doubted whether the policy was as consistent or positive as it suggested. Arthur Balfour praised Gerald's Land Act, for instance,

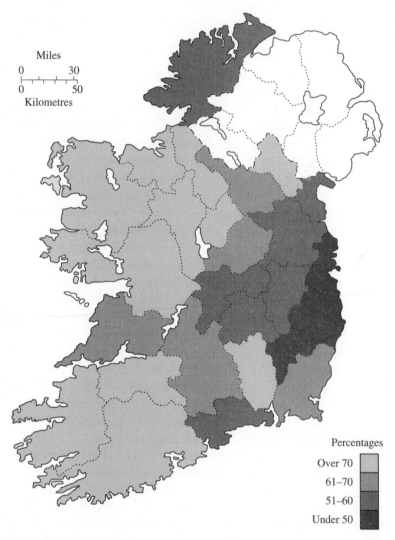

Fig 1.1: The effect of the Land Acts 1881–1909 (percentage of acreage of each county sold to tenants by 1923)
Source: Report of the Irish Land Commission (1951)

because it would avert pressure to bring in a more substantial measure. Certainly the policy ultimately fell sadly short of the vision of progress and harmony propounded by the most outspoken of all 'constructive unionists', Horace Plunkett. It was Plunkett who kick-started the reform process in 1895 when he discovered to his dismay that the government, sitting on its landslide majority, had no plans for major Irish legislation. Plunkett, an aristocrat and one-time Wyoming rancher, was a Unionist who believed that the Union was in danger precisely because it had operated in a negative spirit. He believed that Unionists would be making a suicidal mistake 'if they don't take the great – perhaps the last – opportunity they will have of making a Unionist settlement of the Irish question'.[27] In his view the basic cause of the problem was underdevelopment, both economic and social, and the key to solving it was modernization. Plunkett believed that a co-operative agricultural movement could begin to regenerate the Irish economy at the same time as building the groundwork of co-operative politics, bringing nationalist and Unionist together. He made impressive strides towards his first objective, but failed to get near his second.

From the establishment of the first co-operative creamery in 1889 to the foundation of the Irish Agricultural Organization Society in 1894, the idea of co-operation seemed to be taking off. In 1895 he set up a journal, the *Irish Homestead*, under the unlikely but successful editorship of the poet and mystic George Russell, known as Æ, to preach technical improvement. (Equally improbably, Russell was suggested to Plunkett by his fellow poet-mystic W. B. Yeats.) Next year his cross-party parliamentary recess committee focused the government's mind on the opportunity for a progressive policy, and his efforts seemed to be crowned with success with the creation of the Department of Agriculture and Technical Instruction in 1899, with him as Vice-President. After that, Plunkett's own career began to fall apart. He responded to losing his parliamentary seat in the 1900 election by writing a pungent and pugnacious tract, insisting on the need to push modernization ahead in the mental as well as the physical sphere. *Ireland in the New Century* (1902) pulled no punches in denouncing the flawed 'Irish character' that had been produced by generations of political confrontation and intimidation – 'the lack of initiative and shrinking from responsibility, the moral timidity in glaring contrast with the physical courage'. The building up of collective civic responsibility, he urged, had to accompany the development of industry and commerce. Irish political leaders 'ought to have known that the weakness of character which renders the task of leadership in Ireland comparatively easy is in reality the quicksand of Irish life, and that neither self-government nor any other institution can be enduringly built upon it'.[28] Nationalists in Ireland read this finger-wagging as a sign of the old ascendancy spirit breaking through, rather than as a rallying call for a fraternal Irish future.

Unfortunately for the survival of the Union, Plunkett's assumption that the Irish land question had changed, as he tirelessly argued, from a problem of tenure to a problem of technique proved to be wrong. Even before the Department of Agriculture and Technical Instruction was set up, a new land agitation had begun. The UIL re-started the land war (see ch. 2, pp. 341–6, and made parts of Ireland seem ungovernable again. It was under this pressure that in 1902 an all-party Land Conference urged a massive land purchase scheme, and the culmination of the Conservative land policy, George Wyndham's 1903 Land Act, precipitated the final transfer of landownership. As well as advancing more funds on more favourable terms, Wyndham encouraged landlords to sell not only individual farms but entire estates if three-quarters of their tenants wanted to buy. Eleven million acres changed hands between 1903 and the end of the Union. It was a definite triumph of constructive unionism, but it was followed by a political setback. By 1904 traditional Toryism was reasserting its hostility to progressive policies, and Wyndham had become isolated. When his Under-Secretary, Sir Antony MacDonnell, became involved with the negotiations of the Land Conference group to plan a semi-elected advisory council to press the co-operative development of Irish resources, he precipitated a significant political crisis. Nationalists denounced the council as a device to neutralize the Home Rule demand, while hardline Unionists saw it as Home Rule by stealth. The 'devolution crisis' of 1904 revealed just how heavily such hardliners outnumbered Unionist moderates, and how ready they remained to see Irish government in zero-sum terms. A Catholic gain must be a Protestant loss. Nationalism, in their view, could not be compromised with or accommodated. Constructive unionism may have lived for a moment in reality as well as in Plunkett's imagination, but it was dead long before Wyndham's resignation. The Union remained the rule of force; it could survive only as long as its nationalist opponents remained too weak to overthrow it.

|2|

The national question

The *leitmotiv* of nineteenth-century Irish public life was resistance to the Union. This was not a purely political issue. Four distinct dimensions can be traced over time. First, demands for change in political status; second, demands for change in land law, ownership and distribution; third, demands for institutional structures incorporating the outlook of the overwhelming Catholic majority; and fourth, calls for cultural authenticity. In varying configurations these dimensions formed the 'Irish question', which, as the Conservative leader Benjamin Disraeli famously remarked, always seemed to be changing – 'it is the Pope one day and potatoes the next'. Disraeli's ignorant bafflement on Irish matters was, as we have seen, sadly characteristic of British statesmen. Still, it was not easy to work out which if any aspect of Irish discontent was fundamental.

Elements of Irish nationalism

The demand for 'Catholic emancipation', or in modern political parlance 'recognition', was the oldest one. It included not only the formal (and impeccably liberal) requirement of civil and political equality, but also the demand for complete liberty of religious self-expression (which would tend to produce, in Ireland, an extension of ecclesiastical power which fitted less comfortably with liberal ideas). It generated, indeed, Europe's most impressive mass political movement of the early nineteenth century, the Catholic Association led by Daniel O'Connell in the 1820s. But could Catholic aspirations be said to be more fundamental than the need for land? Irish society was quintessentially agrarian in the sense that the status of its members was determined by possession of land. Farming was not just a means of survival, much less a way of making money; it was a way of life. The land struggle took shape long before the Union. Rural secret societies like the Whiteboys, Rockites, and 'Captain Moonlight' had been using similar kinds of violence to protect Catholic peasants from rack-renting – the deliberate raising of rents to drive tenants off the land – or eviction since at least the mid-eighteenth century. The most intense 'agrarian' action by such Catholic peasant organizations was directed against Protestant tenants, rather than landlords themselves, or even their agents. It was small-scale, targeted violence, and it was effective because it was seen by the people not as a series of private vendettas but as the enforcement of a broadly accepted 'unwritten law'.[1] Nationalists pointed to this popular refusal of legitimacy to British law as evidence of the underlying Irish claim to separation. And indeed in the form of organizations such as the Defenders in the 1790s and the Ribbonmen of the nineteenth century, local secret societies straddled the divide between unpolitical agrarian action and what has been well called a 'visceral kind of politics'.[2]

Nationalists, however, saw the formal political demand for separation – 'freedom' – as the most fundamental issue. To them, the land problem was a by-product of British power, and would be solved by the achievement of national independence. This was the essence of the United Irish demand, in the deathless phrase of the great republican Wolfe Tone, to 'break the connection, the never-failing source of Ireland's ills'. Yet nationalism itself was the most recent of all these patterns of resistance. The demand for a sovereign republic was modelled directly on the example of the American and French revolutions. But what was the basis of the claim to independence? Two distinct forms of justification appeared. The first 'republican' demands were clearly shaped by the Enlightenment rationalism of the eighteenth century. The Protestant-led United Irishmen saw Ireland as a natural entity which self-evidently required its own government. Following American and French democratic ideas, the 'nation' was invoked on the basis of common citizenship: being born in Ireland made people Irish.[3]

This inclusive view of nationality was deliberately invoked by Wolfe Tone in his insistence that old divisions should be transcended; Catholic, Protestant and Dissenter should merge in 'the common name of Irishman'. The very depth of those old enmities made it the more essential to forge a new collective identity. This imperative was movingly argued by a leading nationalist of the following generation, Thomas Davis, in the 1840s:

> I was brought up in a mixed seminary where I learned to know, and knowing, to love my Catholic countrymen. ... Dissension, alas, has destroyed our country for centuries. ... Will you take the boys of Ireland in their earliest youth and deepen the differences between them? Will you sedulously seclude them from knowing the virtues, the genius, the spirit, the affections of each other? If you do, you will vainly hope that they who were carefully separated in youth will be united in manhood, and stand together for their country.[4]

Alongside the Enlightenment belief in the emancipatory power of knowledge which Davis so simply expressed in his phrase 'knowing, to love', there was an equally frank recognition that the persistence of entrenched religious identities would prevent unity.

Like Tone, Davis was a Protestant. To him it was self-evident that Irish identity had to incorporate both Protestants and Catholics, 'planters' as well as 'Gaels'. 'The elements of Irish nationality are not only combining, they are growing confluent in our minds', he optimistically suggested. Irish nationality must contain the 'races' of Ireland – 'it must not be Celtic, it must not be Saxon' – and must embrace 'both the Brehon Law and the maxims of Westminster'.[5] Yet Davis had to acknowledge that Ireland lacked the primary badge of nationality proclaimed by apostles of nationalism in Europe, such as Herder, Fichte and Mazzini. To these thinkers, language was the key to the inner unity of a truly distinct nation. In the first half of the nineteenth century the Irish language was in precipitate decline: whereas possibly half the population were monoglot Irish speakers at the time of the Union, by the mid-nineteenth century a mere 5 per cent spoke only Irish, and less than a quarter could speak it at all. Though it could be argued that this transition was a remarkable self-modernizing achievement on the part of the Irish people, Irish nationalists have almost all seen it as a disaster. No less an authority than Mazzini (who unlike many European nationalists did not make a fetish of language) pronounced that Ireland did not have a sufficiently distinct shared historical experience to make the Irish a political nation. Davis recognized that 'to have lost the national language is death'; but as a non-Irish speaker himself he believed that there was an equally potent source of identity. The land itself created the sense of belonging and

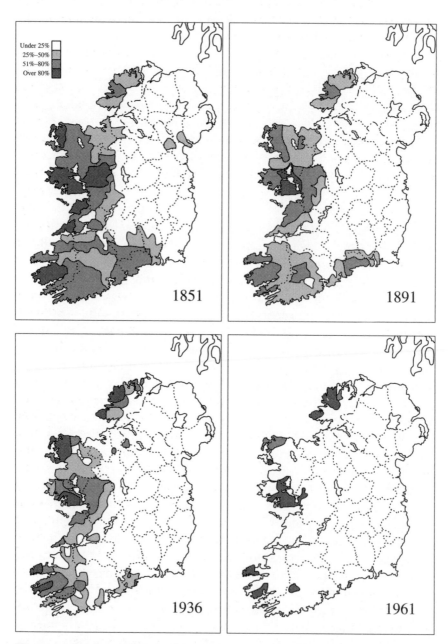

Fig 2.1   Irish speakers, 1851–1961
Source: Based on Brian Ó Cuiv (ed.) *A View of the Irish Language* (Dublin 1969)

common inheritance – 'a union of all Irish-born men'. The intensity of his own love of Ireland suffused his attempt to write a national literature in English, 'racy of the soil'.

If emotion could move mountains, Davis would have triumphed. But he grievously misread the solidity of religious allegiance; his hope that it could be transcended was crushed by the Catholic reaction to Peel's attempt to establish non-denominational Irish universities in the 1840s, branded by the Church as 'Godless colleges'.[6] Although Daniel O'Connell was an impeccable liberal in constitutional terms, he was not an ideological pluralist, or secularist. For him religious conviction was a keystone of liberty. When his Repeal Association, which rested on the simple proposition that repealing the Act of Union would create the basis for a viable political structure, collapsed after 1845, it signalled a slow but steady process of recognition that Irish national consciousness rested on agrarian Catholicism. National liberation requires a people with a strong enough sense of unity to make collective mobilization possible. O'Connell's own commitment to 'moral force' as against violent rebellion imposed a stringent test on this cohesion magnifying the role of Catholic conciousness. Later nationalist attempts to halt or reverse this process managed only to sidestep it.

Moral and physical force

O'Connell's rejection of political violence was unequivocal. In 1843 he declared: 'The principle of my political life, and that in which I have instructed the people of Ireland, is that all ameliorations and improvements in political institutions can be obtained by persevering in a perfectly peaceable and legal course, and cannot be obtained by forcible means, or if they could be got by forcible means, such means create more evils than they cure ...'.[7] In practice the 'monster meetings' that were the hallmark of his great agitations for Catholic emancipation and repeal always contained the threat of violence, and gained some of their effect from it. But there could be no doubt that O'Connell believed that constitutional methods could work. Other nationalists were not so sure. The Young Ireland group split from O'Connell when he demanded a pledge never to resort to rebellion. They were hardly bloodthirsty apostles of violence, but they refused to rule out the possibility of using it as a last resort.

In fact, after the split some of them went on to work out a sophisticated blueprint for modern rebellion, most impressively in James

Fintan Lalor's idea of local resistance. Lalor believed that Irish revolutionaries could avoid the disasters that had wrecked earlier, usually
premature rebellions, if they adopted a grass-roots strategy, which he
labelled 'moral insurrection', building gradually on the energy of the
agrarian struggle. This was a prophetic sketch of what would, a
century later, come to be known as guerrilla warfare, or 'protracted
war'. Unfortunately for Young Ireland its plans were overwhelmed in
their infancy by the tragedy of the Famine, which drove them into
precipitate action. In a desperate situation, amidst starvation and mass
emigration, the appeal of old-fashioned military resistance was irre-
sistible. In July 1848 William Smith O'Brien led the newly established
Irish Confederation in an attempt to rouse the people. It failed within
a few days.

Nationalists were temporarily stunned by the impact of the Famine,
and the failure of the '48 rising. When a revived nationalist movement
reappeared in the late 1850s, under the name of the Phoenix Society,
it was uncompromising about both ends and means. Soon renamed
less gnomically the Irish Republican Brotherhood (IRB), and widely
known as the Fenians, the organization was committed to the establishment of an independent Irish republic, and to the use of force to
achieve it. This principled dedication to physical force was to exert a
profound influence on the national movement from then on. Fenians
rejected constitutionalism (or 'moral force') on several grounds. First,
that it could never achieve independence, since Britain would never
voluntarily concede this: in the words of Jeremiah O'Donovan Rossa,
'I don't believe the Saxon will ever relax his grip except by the persuasion of lead and cold steel'. Second, participation in the Union
electoral system tacitly recognized the legitimacy of British rule in
Ireland. Third, it embroiled nationalists in English politics and led to
corruption, betrayal and compromise. Lastly, even if it were to succeed
in persuading Britain to make 'concessions', these would be
demeaning: only the use of physical force could give Ireland self-
respect. Ireland's freedom was not in the gift of another country – it
had to be grasped by its own strength.

The demand for formal independence, which O'Connell had
thought unnecessary as well as unrealistic, had unforeseen implications. It required a redefinition or rethinking of the nation itself. The
kind of cohesion and discipline that would be needed to reach this
radical objective depended on a more concrete sense of national
identity – an ethnic rather than simply territorial sense – than had so
far existed. This was to be achieved only slowly, but its consequences

were far-reaching, and the Fenians themselves were not to play a central role in this process.

Fenianism

The IRB was a tightly organized, oath-bound secret society, modelled by its founder, James Stephens, on the underground revolutionary groups that proliferated in early nineteenth-century Europe. The need to guard against penetration by aggressive political police forces led to the adoption of a cellular structure with masonic grades of initiation. Recruits were carefully vetted, and the full scale and aims of the organization were only revealed at a high level. Stephens called the IRB cells 'circles', each run by 'centres'; he himself was 'head centre'. The elaborate secrecy was justified by the weakness of earlier revolutionary groups. It gave the IRB both its strength – it survived over 60 years to launch the Easter rebellion in 1916 – and its limitations. It was simply too small to achieve its aim of hurling the British out of Ireland by force. Like other European insurrectionists, the most famous of whom was the French communist Auguste Blanqui, the Fenians believed that the people were ready to rise up against tyranny if only they were given an effective lead. The function of the revolutionary organization was to raise the flag and strike the first blow: the masses would follow.

Fenianism scored a real propaganda triumph by turning the funeral of the exiled Young Ireland 'forty-eighter' (i.e. veteran of the 1848 rising) Terence Bellew McManus in 1861 into a well-publicized national demonstration, so establishing one of the most consistently effective methods of republican consciousness-raising. The IRB prepared for insurrection intelligently. The aggressive infiltration of Irish regiments in the British army, masterminded by John Devoy, was plausibly expected to provide an instant trained force capable of overthrowing the state. Even more tempting prospects seemed to open up in the mid-1860s, with the ending of the American civil war in which thousands of Irish-Americans had fought. Here was virtually an Irish army. But finding a way of using this potential military power against Britain proved difficult. Under Devoy's leadership the American Fenian organization, the Clan na Gael, twice attempted to invade Canada (in 1867 and 1870). Action in Ireland was stymied by Stephens's indecision and the vigorous anti-Fenian purge conducted by the army command. The best the IRB could manage in 1867 was another military fiasco, which gained its real impact later with the attempts to rescue Fenian prisoners in Manchester and to blow up the wall of Clerkenwell prison. The 'Manchester Martyrs' and the Clerkenwell bomb added to the Fenian repertoire two more powerful modes of revolutionary propaganda, the cult of sacrifice and the strategy of terrorism.

After the failure of 1867 the IRB was reorganized, and its Supreme Council accepted that future action would need mass support. But it remained committed to open insurrection and a purely political vision of independence. The President of the Supreme Council, Charles Kickham, wrote one of the most popular Irish novels of the century, *Knocknagow*, but he was no populist in his attitude to social questions, especially the land struggle. He saw agrarian terrorism as sordid and cowardly, demeaning to the national cause. And whilst Kickham was, like almost all his fellow Fenians, a devout Catholic, he was an outspoken opponent of clerical influence in politics. This was partly a matter of principle, to maintain the non-sectarian United Irish ideal, but more viscerally a reaction to the Church's condemnation of oath-bound secret societies (Cardinal Cullen, the leader of the Catholic Hierarchy, had been present during the Mazzinian onslaught of 1848 when Garibaldi had driven the Pope from Rome). In rural Ireland such views were not the basis for a mass mobilization. Terrorism too, which offered a short cut to enlarging the impact of the secret organization, was rejected by the Supreme Council under Kickham's control. Only maverick groups like O'Donovan Rossa's 'Skirmishers', and the Irish-American Clan na Gael dynamiters, really embraced the potential of the urban bomb to shock Britain and dramatize the national cause.

Yet for all its dogmatic inflexibility, secrecy and numerical weakness, the Fenian movement was more representative of the mainstream Irish public outlook than might appear. Indeed, Archbishop Croke, one of the members of the Hierarchy who distanced himself from Cardinal Cullen's condemnation of the Fenians, thought that 'the great bulk of our Irish Catholic people are Fenian in heart or sympathy'.[8] The insurrectionist purism of the Fenian leadership was less stern in the organization's lower circles, where everyday concerns like the land agitation, the newly emerging interest in preserving the Irish language and culture, and even parliamentary politics, were accepted as valid activities. And the real importance of Fenianism lay less in its ideas than in its attitude (with a capital A, as it were): it embodied an inspirational sense of character-building, a posture of self-respect, and the repudiation of servility. The Fenian, even without an actual rebellion, was a mental revolutionary.

The organization was noticeably stronger in the towns than in the countryside, but if this modern slant was initially a weakness, in the long run it enhanced its influence when the movement began to diversify its agitational lines in the 1870s. The leading role in this seminal process was played by Michael Davitt, a classic 'Irish felon' who emerged from his statutory prison term with a readiness to go beyond conventional IRB notions of correctness. Crucially, he picked up Lalor's perception that the land issue was the key to mobilizing the people, and launched the most formidable agrarian organization yet to appear. In 1878 he met John Devoy in America to agree a wider campaign, the 'new departure'. In the spring of the following year he took up a local agitation for rent reductions at Irishtown, Co. Mayo, and pushed it on to the national stage as an assault on 'landlordism' in general. The rapid growth of the Land League of Mayo, which became the National Land League in the autumn of 1879, demonstrated that a vast reservoir of hostility was waiting to be tapped, accelerated by visceral fear. The failure of the 1879 harvest brought the threat of famine closer than it had been for a generation. In October the Wicklow MP Charles Stewart Parnell was elected President of the Land League, and issued the electrifying call to 'keep a firm grip of your homesteads'.

Land war

The Irishtown meeting was a decisive moment, pointing the way to a new kind of national movement. 'It was unprecedented', as T. W. Moody wrote, 'for so much solidarity to be shown not only among farmers but between farmers and townspeople; for such effective cooperation to be realised between local leaders and national politicians; and for such a popular front to be wholly organised by the laity'.[9] The role of the clergy became more prominent as the struggle intensified: priests acted as trustees holding the rents that were kept back from landlords, and sometimes even as agitators. The scale of the mobilization was impressive. The League became a kind of alternative state, enforcing its own land tenure laws through a combination of traditional agrarian violence with a distinctly modern form of civil resistance – ostracism or 'boycotting' – whose eponymous victim, Captain H. C. Boycott, the land agent for Lord Erne's estate in Lough

Mask, Co. Mayo, endured the first organized campaign of ostracism (including the withdrawal of harvest labour) in the autumn of 1880.

Michael Davitt himself wrote a large-scale narrative of the Land League mobilization under the grandiloquent title *The fall of feudalism in Ireland*. Modern historians, by contrast, have echoed the critique of the movement written by Parnell's sister Anna under the more jaundiced title *The tale of a great sham*. Anna Parnell and her Ladies' Land League took over the running of the movement when Parnell and other leaders were imprisoned in 1881–82, and became acutely aware of its internal divisions and inconsistencies.[10] Davitt himself realized all too quickly that the tenant farmers did not share his own theory of 'landlordism'. To Davitt, it was not only the existence of alien or absentee landlords that was the problem; following Henry George, the radical American economic philosopher, he believed that the whole tenurial system should be swept away and replaced by collective ownership, the nationalization of land. As good Catholics, Irish farmers abhorred such socialistic ideas; they wanted to own the land. A 'peasant proprietary' meant that everyone could become a little landlord. To Parnell, as to the Conservatives in Britain, this was the guarantee of social and political stability for the future.

Modern historians have also cast doubt on whether landlordism was the unmitigated evil that Davitt and other nationalist writers alleged. The charge that most landlords were absentees, for instance, strenuously propagated by nationalists, was challenged by the research of Barbara Solow in the late 1960s, together with the popular belief that 'rack-renting' was enforced by eviction. Solow demonstrated that surprisingly few of the eviction processes initiated by landlords were ever completed. W. E. Vaughan has proposed a more complex view of rent levels, suggesting that landlords actually raised rents by less than the general increase in the level of agricultural output.[11] But the myth of the bad landlord is likely to remain far stronger than any academic revision. Its primal potency is akin to the strength of the Land League itself, which fused and blurred particular and general, private and public, local and national issues. The question whether the land question was separable from the 'national question' was ultimately rendered irrelevant. The League's unprecedented success in linking the farmers' grievances to the previously abstract demand for self-government produced a political mobilization that was imposing in scale and permanent in its effect.[12] Ireland led the world in mass party politics.

Parnellism

The motor of this political transformation was the simultaneous emergence of a national land agitation and a dynamic nationalist parliamentary party. The fusion was achieved through the unique leadership qualities of Charles Stewart Parnell. Before Parnell, parliamentary politics were conducted very much in the respectable way that led Fenians to denounce them so fiercely. Successive attempts to put together a coherent nationalist grouping in parliament fell apart, most notoriously when John Sadleir and John Keogh, successful Catholic businessmen and leaders of the 'independent party' of 1852 (a group of Tenant League and Catholic Defence Association MPs who had pledged to vote together) accepted minor office in the Whig administration. Sadleir and Keogh became bywords for selling-out, symbols of the corrupting power of British patronage.

Isaac Butt, who took the process of building an organization further than anyone before, was a rather different proposition. A supporter of the Fenian Amnesty movement after 1867, he was impervious to the lure of office. But he was a lawyer, and he accepted (as had O'Connell) the essential decency of the British constitutional system. The procedural rules of the House of Commons, in particular, had become for many liberals almost sacred conventions of democracy. Yet it was precisely these rules that some Irish MPs, first the Fenian Joseph Biggar and then, more strikingly, the Anglo-Irish landlord Parnell, seized on as a way of putting direct pressure on the British elite. The technique of parliamentary obstruction was a deliberate slap in the face of British assumptions – and also a kind of physical assault. 'Filibustering' (a term borrowed from irregular naval warfare) was organized to spin out debates to intolerable lengths. In the epic session of 25 July 1877, Parnell and his colleagues kept the House going for 45 hours. Butt was genuinely distressed, arguing that such behaviour 'must tend to alienate our truest and best English friends. ... It must expose us to the taunt of being unfit to administer even the forms of representative government ...'. Parnell's counter-argument was brutal: 'England respects nothing but power', and 'What did they ever get in the past by trying to conciliate them? They would never gain anything from England unless they trod upon her toes'.[13]

But just what were they aiming to gain from England? (Significantly, neither of them spoke of Britain.) Butt reformulated O'Connell's demand for repeal of the Union in a more positive, if somewhat flat idea – Home Government, or Home Rule. The careful moderation of this concept reflected Butt's anxiety to make it acceptable to Unionists, even Orangemen. It meant devolution rather than independence, but it was quite radical enough for English tastes in calling for the transfer of responsible parliamentary government to Ireland. It was Parnell's pugnacity that turned it into a weapon in a real conflict. Parnell's gift was to put a fighting edge on an essentially moderate programme. He brilliantly trod a fine line between forceful rhetoric and outright incitement to violence, making skilful use of satisfying quasi-Fenian words like 'retaliate' and 'punish'; for instance, 'If they care for retaliation … the Irish members can help the Irish people to punish the Englishmen who have shown themselves utterly unable to govern this country'. If this was sublimation rather than incitement, it was all the more effective for that.

In Parnell's mouth the objective could sound as aggressive as the means. 'We are determined', he declared in October 1880, 'to take the power of governing Ireland out of the hands of the English Parliament and people, and transfer it to the hands of our own people.' Thus he headed off the old Fenian charge that parliamentary politics meant asking for favours from England. In his shadow Home Rulers could stand tall. His political ideas were vague, perhaps even inconsistent. He was a Protestant Anglo-Irish/American landlord, whose most sustained enthusiasm was for mining and developing his Wicklow estate; his rhetoric was aggressively anti-English but he was hardly a democrat or a social reformer (Paul Bew calls him a 'class conservative'), nor indeed an enthusiast for demotic culture, despite his readiness to support Catholic control of education. Beyond the restoration of 'Grattan's parliament' – in strict terms a meaningless archaism – his speeches presented no concrete vision of a future political system. This vacuum, however, enhanced the personal ascendancy that created the phenomenon of 'Parnellism'.

Parnellism was to leave a potent legacy. Its hallmarks were the leader's almost dictatorial central control of the national organization, and strict party discipline (the 'pledge') for MPs. By 1882 the party, generally called the Irish Nationalist Party or Parliamentary Party (its constituency organization was the National League, later the United Irish League), was a tightly controlled machine. It burgeoned with the extension of the franchise in 1884, and hit its peak with the election of 86 pledged members – the celebrated '86 of 86' – in 1886, the year of the first Home Rule crisis. This crisis demonstrated both the strength and the potential weakness of the constitutional strategy: it could make or break governments but it remained locked in the dynamics of

British politics. Although Parnell's party broke the spirit of the English constitution, it never abandoned parliamentarism altogether. Parnell toyed with the option of abstention from Westminster and withdrawal to Ireland, but does not seem to have taken it seriously. His talk of 'the hands of our own people' did not imply a mass mobilization. To him Home Rule offered a path to class harmony, the resolution of landlord–tenant conflict, even perhaps the restoration of aristocratic leadership in Ireland. For him, Paul Bew suggests, the Irish nation was not an imperative. In this sense he was an enlightened rationalist rather than a modern nationalist.[14]

It is hard to specify the nature of Parnell's extraordinary personal ascendancy over the fairly loose (he said 'hollow') national movement in the decade 1879–89. He was more than a leader – an icon. Unlike O'Connell, whose reputation he equalled and perhaps eclipsed, he was no crowd-rousing orator. The cult of personality that enveloped him – to some extent fostered deliberately – made him an impossible act to follow. But the fetish of autocratic leadership could be and was transmitted via his successors. Parnellism signified not only rigid quasi-military discipline and unswerving loyalty to the Chief, but also the spirit of aggression, risk-taking and brinkmanship. The charge levelled by *The Times* that Parnell had directly incited violence was investigated in impressive depth by the so-called 'Parnellism and Crime' Special Commission of 1888–89, which identified many murky links between the Land and National Leagues and the traditional agrarian terrorist groups. Indeed Conor Cruise O'Brien persuasively suggests that nothing other than this deep ambiguity could have held so potentially fissiparous a movement together.

Parnellism was, Bew suggests, unexpectedly modern in its public stance and style. Even at the height of the land struggle the Land League and its successor organizations were 'remarkably free of anti-urban, *Narodnik* [peasant-populist] or overtly sectarian Catholic sentiments'. But all these came flooding back in the campaign against Parnell led by Tim Healy after the O'Shea divorce case.[15] In his personal life, Parnell took one big risk too many in carrying on a long and semi-public affair with Katherine O'Shea, wife of a mediocre Irish Party hack whom Parnell recklessly foisted on a western constituency. The crash when it came was sudden and stupefying. Tightly disciplined unity gave way to the bitterest infighting, as the party broke up into Parnellite and anti-Parnellite factions. The venom of the 1891 election campaign was deadly, in a literal sense – it killed the exhausted Parnell himself. The split smashed the prospects of Home Rule at a stroke, at least for a generation, and perhaps forever. It destroyed the fabric of the parliamentary party and injected a lethal worm of doubt into the whole project of constitutionalism itself. But the question whether Home Rule could ever have worked remains. If it had, it would certainly have produced a very different Irish polity from anything that actually followed. The future Finance Minister of the Irish Free State, Ernest Blythe, was to argue that – because Parnell was not truly a nationalist – the split was a blessing in disguise, and to suggest mischievously that 'in some quiet side-street, Dublin should have a monument to Kitty O'Shea as the woman who unwittingly saved Irish Nationality'.[16]

Church and nation

Recognition of the Catholic identity of the vast majority of Irish people was the most fundamental, if potentially problematic, dimension of the national case. The problem was that it was two-edged. On the one hand, Catholic 'emancipation' could be seen not only by nationalists, but even by liberal Unionists as a precondition for any pluralist democratic society. But on the other hand the heightening of Catholic consciousness during the emancipation struggle pointed towards a less liberal or pluralist outcome – the identification of the Catholic community as the nation. The movement towards what elsewhere in Europe was called 'integral' or cultural nationalism, the pressure to ground the character of the nation in a single, exclusive cultural or even racial community rather than a plural, inclusive, civic grouping, was very clear in the nineteenth century. As one leading historian has put it, 'By 1914 Irish and Catholic had not only become interchangeable terms, but Catholic had come to be the inclusive term'.[17] The clash between O'Connell and Young Ireland was a turning-point. After it, not only was the salience of Catholicism more openly emphasized, but the effective limits of the national group were more sharply etched. Protestant nationalists became ever rarer (maybe rarer even than Catholic Unionists).

Statistically, Catholics were declining as a proportion of the total population – from 77.7 per cent in 1861 to 74.2 per cent in 1901 – but the very fact that this relative decline was caused by the differential impact of famine and emigration provided the fuel for a heightening of Catholic identity. At the same time there was a remarkable resurgence in Catholic organization and piety, what the leading historian of the

Church has called the 'Devotional Revolution'.[18] At the turn of the century Louis Paul-Dubois, a perceptive commentator, wrote that 'No-one can visit Ireland without being impressed by the intensity of Catholic belief there, and by the fervour of its outward manifestations'.[19] The establishment of the seminary at Maynooth in 1795 prepared the way: by the 1850s nearly all the Irish bishops and over half the local clergy had been educated there. After 1850 Cardinal Cullen (Archbishop of Armagh 1849–52 and of Dublin 1852–78) led the process of bringing the Irish priesthood up to the standards he had learnt in Rome. The old tolerance of folk-religion, which had accommodated traditional (and semi-riotous) communal festivals such as 'patterns', was now swept away.[20] A spectacular upsurge of church-building, however aesthetically dubious in the eyes of later intellectuals, testified to the reassertion of Catholic self-confidence.[21] (This reassertion was, almost inevitably, viewed by many Protestants as aggression.)

The result was sharpened religious division. 'By the middle of the century the bloodshed and repression of the 1790s, the tensions created by the Second Reformation, and the fears and passions aroused by the new style of political agitation had combined to produce a deep religious division at all social levels'.[22] Catholic resistance to mixed marriage was made very plain in reaction to reform of the marriage law in the 1870s, and was tightened by the papal decree *Ne temere* (1907) requiring that children of mixed marriages be brought up as Catholics. At the end of the century a Church of Ireland bishop reflected that the disestablishment of his Church had not, as had been hoped, killed jealousy and drawn all Christians together: 'the very opposite has been the case'.

The organizational power of the Catholic Church, coupled with the reach of its spiritual mission, gave it formidable social and political significance. Its social role reinforced the patterns of discipline necessary for the survival of family farms. As K. T. Hoppen acutely observes, the stress on celibacy and all the clerical denunciations of immodest dancing, company-keeping, and fleshly sins in general, were 'a kind of invited repression'. The priesthood was no longer opposing so much as 'moving *with* the grain of social and economic development'.[23] Catholic values might be seen by Protestants as anti-modern, but they were projected into the commercial as well as the agricultural sphere; indeed, as the Catholic Commercial Club was told by a speaker in 1901, 'religion must be the dominant influence in every sphere of life'.[24] Clerical control of education formed a vital hinge between social and political influence. By the 1880s that control was more or less absolute, and it was effectively established that the power of priests in the national schools derived from the bishops rather than from the National School Board. The extension of higher education went ahead only when the Hierarchy's requirements were met.

The extension of clerical social influence was undoubtedly democratic, even if perversely so in the liberal view. Clerical influence in politics is impossible to measure with any accuracy, but it was similarly reciprocal. The Church played an essential part in the growth of O'Connell's Catholic Association, the first modern mass movement to achieve major political change. By the same token, lack of Church backing fatally undermined O'Connell's campaigns for repeal of the Union in the 1830s and 1840s. Even before Cullen's ascendancy, the Church was naturally anti-revolutionary, and especially hostile to secret societies, which it saw as a violent threat to social order (despite the fact that even Fenians, republicans and secularists in political terms, were almost all Catholics – and observant ones, with little sympathy for the real anticlericalism of the model modern republic France).

But even the Hierarchy did not play the state game either, holding out for control of 'national' education and mounting an increasingly strident defence of rural Irishness against Saxon materialism. The lower clergy sometimes embraced a more radical nationalism, especially through the land agitation (acting as League organizers, holding rents during rent strikes).[25] The Hierarchy gradually moved towards a historic realignment when Parnell committed his party to supporting denominational education in 1884. The result was a formidable conservative anti-socialist alliance, which looked unassailable until the divorce scandal which destroyed Parnell's career. On the Parnellite side, the Church was blamed for the disaster, but once again it seems likely that clerical influence confirmed rather than created public opinion.[26] Some recent historians have been scathing in their verdict on what Oliver MacDonagh calls 'the systematic political ambivalence of the Irish [Catholic] Church', though MacDonagh himself suggests that its limitations should be more sympathetically understood – not just as a product of the fact that 'the priests were but the population writ large', but rather of the distortion created by a semi-colonial condition. 'Dependency enjoined at once conformity and defiance'.[27]

The United Irish League

The Parnell split prostrated the Irish political nation in a welter of internecine conflict. Though the majority of the parliamentary party held together under the leadership of John Dillon, its authoritarian streak became still more deeply etched, and more stultifying, under the continuous sniping of breakaway groups. Parnellites continued to nurse the cult of the lost leader, the hero betrayed by an unholy combination of English blackmail and clerical jealousy. On the clerical side, the vicious anti-Parnellite campaign spearheaded by T. M. Healy heralded a long-drawn-out attempt to assert 'democratic' local power against the centralized party leadership. In Healyite language, the call for democracy meant a more overtly Catholic party. The pressure to assert a Catholic Irish nationality had already played its part in generating a kind of political partition, since the Unionist counter-mobilization on vocally Protestant grounds took firmer shape in the 1890s. There was, however, one last attempt to revive the old United Irish ideal, led by William O'Brien at the centenary of the 1798 rebellion.

O'Brien, the chief organizer of the Plan of Campaign in the late 1880s, grasped the potential for a 'really big 98 celebration' to re-energize the land agitation in tandem with the national party, the explosive cocktail that had originally fuelled the mobilization of the 1880s. The West Mayo United Irish League was inaugurated at Westport, Co. Mayo, in January 1898. Its 4000 members represented the land-hunger of the 'congested districts' of the west, where popular resentment focused on 'landgrabbers', and the big graziers rather dramatically labelled 'ranchers'. Despite its local roots and largely local concerns (above all, the demand for land redistribution), the UIL spread rapidly across the country. Though it weakened as it moved east, with only a nominal membership in Dublin and Ulster (as against 84 branches in Mayo and 73 in Limerick by 1901), its combative leadership and gift for publicity turned it into the most imposing national organization since the Land League. Like the old League it was able to establish its credentials as a kind of counter-state or rival government. O'Brien called the UIL Executive the 'tribunal of the delegates of the people', and invited anyone with a grievance to bring it for settlement. Between October 1899 and October 1900 more than 120 'cases' were brought before UIL branches, some of them charging 'contempt of court' when parties failed to appear or judgments were ignored. This was a serious challenge to the state.

Like the Land League, too, the UIL contained a substantial IRB presence, and deployed a finely balanced mixture of rhetorical persuasion and violent intimidation. Violent rhetoric abounded; even the staid John Dillon revived memories of the Plan of Campaign by calling for the raising of parish forces to mobilize by day or night.

Open violence was rare, because the machinery for communal pressure (through public meetings, resolutions published in the local press, and so on) was by now very sophisticated. The British state had played its part in this by raising the literacy rate. The prestige of the UIL was enhanced by inept and ineffective police confrontational tactics; O'Brien won a battle of nerves when he openly challenged the government to arrest him, and it backed down. According to the Inspector-General of the RIC, people submitted 'rather than do anything to bring themselves into antagonism to the general feeling'. As a result, reporting crime to police became rare and Ireland was once more – by police criteria – ungovernable. By early 1902 the level of interference with individual liberty was 'unparalleled in any civilized country at the present time'.[28]

But for all its success as a rival government, the UIL made no attempt at a revolutionary seizure of power, or even to displace the parliamentary party as the focus of the national movement. O'Brien's aim was to revitalize and reunite the movement, holding out an 'olive branch' (the title of one of his campaigning books) for a truly inclusive United-Irish style political organization. This grand ambition was too much. What he achieved was remarkable enough. In 1900 the bitterly divided party was at last reunited under the leadership of John Redmond, leader of the Parnellite faction. The UIL, like the Land League before it, was eventually neutered by being turned into the national parliamentary constituency organization, though this time not completely under party control (the party disposed of 25 per cent of its funds as against 75 per cent with Parnell's National League). The euphoria of reunification was magnified by the excitement of opposition to the Boer war, but in the process the alienation of Unionists was driven a step further.

O'Brien was profoundly conscious of the partial nature of his achievement. He found the reborn party too Parnellite by far, authoritarian, and hostile to his dreams of reconciliation with those who did not recognize themselves in the now dominant Gaelic image of the Irish nation. His remarkable political career began a long decline when he resigned from the new executive in 1903 and eventually from the party. Giving up the attempt to promote his 'all-for-Ireland' idea within the party, he formed a new organization, the All For Ireland League. But his magic touch had deserted him. Like Davitt before him, he found that his idea of the Irish nation did not mesh with that of the mainstream. With him the party lost a vital source of vision and dynamism, and was set on its way to decline and ultimate extinction.

Monolithic, vampiric in its drive to suck in every rival embodiment of the national spirit, yet inflexible in attitude, it would have difficulty in responding to the challenge of a group which was now devising a far richer and more vibrant national ideology, together with a strategy fusing both constitutional and republican methods with a radically new idea of popular politics. Within a few years of the reunification of the parliamentary party, such a grouping began to emerge. Sinn Féin, as it would become, was ultimately to pose a fatal threat to the Irish nationalist party as well as to the Union.

3

Cultures and civilizations: the struggle for Ireland's soul

*A*round the turn of the century, the trajectory of Irish nationalism shifted in a decisive way. A new focus on cultural identity
radically altered the meaning of Irishness itself. Up until then,
nationality had been conceived politically – the central issue for
nationalists was to break the political connection with England. The
island of Ireland was assumed to be a natural political unit, and its
inhabitants formed the Irish people. Ireland's problems were caused by
English political control. Political sovereignty (or even, as with Home
Rule, mere legislative autonomy) would solve the Irish problem. Now
a much more strenuous and far-reaching aim emerged, under the
slogan 'de-Anglicization' – the rooting-out of all English influence,
mental as well as economic and political. Both linguistic and moral
issues came to mark out a more strenuously defined cultural nation.
Irishness was to become a subjective rather than an objective quality,
and the Irish people became something more – and something less –
than simply the inhabitants of Ireland.

The Gaelic language had not, as Vincent Comerford has emphasized, been one of the 'subjects that fuelled the intense political ani-
mosities of nineteenth-century Ireland'. It is significant that the
leading-edge nationalist paper, *The Nation*, was able to do without a
Gaelic font for 10 years after 1848. As late as 1876, when the Society
for the Preservation of the Irish Language was established, the
eponymous objective was seen as entirely unpolitical, if not indeed
merely antiquarian. Within a decade, however, clear signs of a sense of
cultural crisis can be read. English cultural as much as political power
began to be seen as a threat. There was a mounting concern that the

Irish sense of identity was in danger of erosion, perhaps even of disappearance. By the end of the century it was more than an intellectual concern, it was an open fear. 'By 1900', to quote Comerford again, 'Irish revivalism was an idea whose time had come'.[1]

De-Anglicization

The remarkable fusion of moral, aesthetic and physical resistance that went to generate the Irish revival was succinctly formulated by the Archbishop of Cashel, Thomas Croke, in December 1884. Croke wrote of 'the ugly and irritating fact that we are daily importing from England not only her manufactured goods ... but together with her fashions, her accents, her vicious literature, her music, her dances, and her mannerisms, her games also and her pastimes, to the utter discredit of our own grand national sports'.[2] England's 'fantastic field sports', the bishop averred, were 'not racy of the soil but rather alien to it'. His conclusion was blunt: if Ireland were to go on like this for another 20 years 'we had better abjure our nationality'. He raised this alarm as he was giving his blessing to the newly established Gaelic Athletic Association, founded in Thurles, Co. Tipperary, with the apparently innocuous aims of drafting 'new rules to aid the revival of ancient pastimes' and devising 'schemes of recreation for the bulk of the people, especially the poor'. Only its demand that Irish sport should be organized 'by Irishmen, not Englishmen' hinted at the more pugnacious line it would soon follow in promoting games like hurling and Gaelic football.

The potent identification of foreignness with immorality that framed Archbishop Croke's view of England was further heightened by the growth in nationalist discourse of a distinctive imagery of disease. When *United Ireland* lamented in 1891 that 'the blight is upon us all of English manners and English sway', the resonance of the term for post-Famine Ireland was profound. The vocabulary of contamination implied the existence of an original, organic Irish culture. The need to purify it was trenchantly announced by Douglas Hyde in 1892. In his presidential address to the newly founded Irish National Literary Society, 'On the necessity for de-Anglicizing the Irish People' (25 November 1892), Hyde opened up a revolutionary perspective that reversed traditional nationalist political logic. Independence would follow from, rather than secure, Irish identity. Hyde's leading argument was openly Mazzinian: 'in Anglicizing ourselves wholesale we have thrown away with a light heart the best claim we have upon the world's recognition of us as a separate nationality. What did Mazzini say? ... That we ought to be content as an integral part of the United Kingdom because we have lost the notes of nationality, our very language and customs.' Hyde cast his analysis in the form of an urgent warning: 'just at the moment when the Celtic race is about to largely recover possession of its country, it finds itself deprived and stript of its Celtic characteristics, cut off from the past, yet scarcely in touch with the present'. Yet he seemed to draw no precise connection between this cultural analysis and the political issue facing Ireland, ending with an 'appeal to everyone whatever his politics – for this is no political matter – to do his best to help the Irish race to develop in future upon Irish lines'.

Hyde's talk of 'race' here was in the traditional sense of soil-rootedness (as in the French *race*, or Davis's 'racy of the soil') but it was a word whose biological significance was becoming politically explosive elsewhere in Europe in the 1890s. Unintentionally, it seems, Hyde was opening up a potential rift in the people to which he, as an Anglo-Irish Protestant, believed himself to belong. The next political generation saw the working-out of the far-reaching implications of the call for de-Anglicization.

Gaelicism

The founding of the Gaelic League in 1893 was a response to the most urgent issue identified by Hyde, who became its President: 'we must at once arrest the decay of the language'. The League acted to focus a sense of disquiet, especially amongst the middle class, which may at least indirectly have been related to the political crisis of the Parnell split. There was a widespread sense that there was a 'political vacuum' after Parnell's fall, in which 'culture became a surrogate for politics'.[3] Conor Cruise O'Brien, writing of the famous suggestion made by W. B. Yeats (speaking to the Swedish Academy on receiving the Nobel Prize for Literature in 1925) that 'a disillusioned and embittered Ireland turned from parliamentary politics; an event was conceived and the race began, as I think, to be troubled by that event's long gestation', suggested that few historians would challenge that famous account of the process.[4] More recently, however, Roy Foster has warned us against taking it too literally:[5] Yeats repeatedly reworked that passage in his autobiography where he traced the impact of the three great 'events' (or 'public controversies') which had 'stirred his imagination profoundly' – the first and seemingly most traumatic of which was the fall of Parnell.[6] It is not necessary, however, to go so far as to argue that political activity ceased after 1891 – which it plainly did not – to suggest that the poisonous rancour of the split, the 'frenzy of detraction' as Yeats put it, did have an impact not only on Yeats himself but on the wider political public.

The infighting of the political split worsened through the decade of the 1890s, while the Gaelic League gradually expanded. From a mere 43 branches established in its first four years, the total burgeoned to nearly 600 by 1904. Much of its organizational dynamism was supplied by returned emigrants, and other 'energetic and moderately successful men whose careers provided inadequate scope for their talents and ambitions'.[7] The crucial year was 1900, when the League reached out beyond the narrow educated group ('respectable, suburban, bourgeois – and also tiny', as Foster notes) to a wider public, formed in part by revulsion against the violent jingoism of Britain's struggle to subjugate the Boer farmers of the Transvaal. The Boer war catalysed a mood of national self-awareness. Within a few years the League had changed 'from a coterie to a mass organisation', albeit still heavily over-represented in Munster generally and Cork in particular.[8] By that time the League was into its second newspaper, *An Claidheamh Soluis* (The Sword of Light), edited by the organization's co-founder Eoin MacNeill, and later by Patrick Pearse. MacNeill was a northern Catholic (from Antrim) and a pioneering historian of pre-Norman Ireland, who became the first Professor of Early and Medieval Irish History in the new University College, Dublin, in 1909. His inspirational account of *Celtic Ireland*, originally delivered as a series of lectures in 1904, put encouraging flesh and blood on the Gaelic ideal, showing the strength of indigenous social and legal (if not political) structures. MacNeill drew explicit contrasts between the bases of power in Irish and British legal culture: 'a modern landlord may measure his degree of dominion by power to evict; an ancient Irish noble measured his by power to restrain his tenants from leaving him'. The failure of earlier legal historians to understand the Gaelic culture he attributed to 'the fundamentally barbarous and noxious character of English theoretical jurisprudence'.[9]

Pearse, his successor as editor of the *Claidheamh Soluis* in 1903, was if possible still more aggressive in pushing the campaign of 'militant Gaeldom'. For Pearse, whose father was English, and who grew up in an urban, English-speaking environment, the language issue underpinned all others. 'While other causes are borne along by it as the water-fowl is carried by the current, it alone is our inspiration.' In particular he distanced himself, at this stage, from political activity, asserting that 'Political autonomy can be lost and recovered. ... It is an accidental and an external thing – necessary, indeed, to the complete working out of a national destiny, but not in itself an essential of nationality'.[10]

The League became a formidable pressure group for the introduction of Gaelic into the school curriculum, and also in more symbolic places like street names and signposts. Its most striking practical achievement was the decision of the newly founded National University (1908) to make Irish a compulsory matriculation subject. The campaign for compulsory Irish was not straightforward, however, and revealed some rifts in the nationalist movement. Francis Sheehy Skeffington held that it was the League's failure to 'arouse the enthusiasm of the country' that had driven it to 'resort to the weapon of despair – coercion'. Sheehy Skeffington was a rare radical, almost a party of one, but confirmation of his view came from a much larger and more conventional group, the clergy. The regularization of Catholic practice, such as confirmation, depended on the use of English. As the writer Liam O'Flaherty later caustically noted, 'It may sound ridiculous that Gaelic, supposedly a Catholic language, should be inimical to the spread of Catholic teaching, while English, eminently a language hostile to our holy faith, should have the opposite effect. Such, however, seems to be the truth'.[11] The Hierarchy refused to endorse the League campaign, arguing with deadly realism that separate Gaelic colleges would be better, because making Irish compulsory would risk 'driving [Catholic] boys and girls into Trinity and Belfast' to avoid it.[12] Here an interesting divergence of ultimate good appeared: the Church battling for the individual soul, while the League battled for the soul of the nation.

In the end, either the voluntary or compulsory revival of a dying language proved to be a Herculean, if not Sisyphean task; the reasons for the language's decay are still not fully understood, and were certainly misdiagnosed then. State power was not the sole or even the primary agency. The League's efforts may have marginally slowed the abandonment of the language, but in the process (especially when compulsion was brought in) the language issue was turned from a politically neutral interest to a loaded symbol of polarization. Unionists who did not share Hyde's love of the language could no longer simply tolerate or ignore it; they had to oppose it. The process of polarization and exclusion was also increasingly evident in the methods of the Gaelic Athletic Association, which expelled anyone who played 'English games'. This confrontational sense of struggle was most pungently expressed in the sardonic journalism of David Patrick Moran, who set up the *Leader* in 1900 to encourage the Gaelic League to embrace more ambitious goals than simple language revival and more progressive visions than the romanticization of the peasantry. Moran discovered the Irish language at a Gaelic League class in London, and realized it was the key to his unfocused sense of difference. 'Well damn them for Sassenachs', was his first reaction – 'here is one thing we have got that they haven't!'[13] For Moran, difference was vital, and what he called 'the battle of two civilizations' was indeed a life-and-death struggle. In the spate of articles he published in the Jesuit-run University College journal *New Ireland Review*, issued in book form as *The Philosophy of Irish Ireland* in 1905, he pursued more relentlessly than anyone yet the real political significance of cultural identity. It was Moran, above all, who swept away the lingering blur of meanings between race and nation.

The battle of civilizations

As late as the 1890s advanced nationalists could still hang on to the old United Irish notion of nationality. Eoin MacNeill, for instance, thought of the nation as 'a brotherhood of adoption as well as blood', while William O'Brien combined talk of 'a Celtic race ruled by its spiritual instincts' with talk of national 'heart equally large and equally warm for Protestant and Catholic'. But D. P. Moran remorselessly confronted United Irish fudges. In a characteristically hard-hitting formulation he insisted, 'the foundation of Ireland is the Gael, and the Gael must be the element that absorbs. On no other basis can an Irish nation be reared that would not topple over by force of the ridicule it would beget.'

Who were his 'Gaels'? They could hardly have been defined by use of the Gaelic language, since according to a recent calculation only 13 per cent of those born in Ireland between 1861 and 1871 were native Irish speakers. By 1901 a bare 0.5 per cent were monolingual Gaelic speakers, and 14 per cent could speak it. Moran (who himself failed, like many of his urban contemporaries, to acquire fluent Irish) did not flinch from identifying other sources of identity. A nation meant, he suggested, 'a self governing land, developing its own manners and

customs, creating its own literature out of its own distinctive consciousness, working to their fullest capacity the material resources of
the country, inventing, criticising, attempting and doing'.[14] The
nation must share some fundamental code, and Moran was not afraid
to identify it. In his trademark no-nonsense manner he remarked that
'when we look out on Ireland we see that those who believe, or may
be immediately induced to believe in Ireland as a nation are, as a
matter of fact, Catholics'. The bottom line was that 'the Irish nation
is *de facto* a Catholic nation'.

Out of this apparently pragmatic sociological observation – cast in
his aggressively common-sense style – he posited a *volksgeist* as mys-
tical as any German romantic philosopher. Catholicism in Moran's
imagery became more than a code that happened to be practised by
Irish people. The historical experience of defending their religion had
become a vital binding force, and Catholicism expressed in some sense
the core of what it meant to be Irish. Moran was not exactly a romantic
nationalist himself. He denounced the simplistic ('hand to mouth')
thinking behind clichés like 'the spirit of nationality is eternal', and
recognized that a big difficulty underlying the 'Irish revival' was 'the
length of time we have to go back before we arrive at any mode of life
that may with truth be termed distinctively Irish'.[15] For him, a new
Irish way of life would be forged by the emerging Catholic middle
class. Though he assaulted the corruption engendered by Saxon materialism as ferociously as any priest, he always insisted that industry
would play a key part in this new way of life. He mounted a 'Buy Irish'
campaign, and tirelessly preached the boycotting of English manufactured goods. His progressivism indeed led him into conflict with the
Church. One of his pioneering achievements was the establishment of
a new Catholic Association in 1902 to foster a new lay Catholic culture
and promote the opening of career opportunities for Catholics in
Protestant-dominated trades and professions. Shortly after its first
great success, an agitation impelling the Great Southern and Western
Railway Company to introduce competitive examinations, the
Association was violently denounced by Archbishop Walsh of Dublin
in a pastoral letter for its 'evil work which is doing such grievous harm
to Catholic interests and exposing the Catholic religion itself to
unmerited obloquy'.[16] The Hierarchy detected a Protestant backlash
that might, amongst other things, threaten the hoped-for settlement
of the university question.

Moran has been portrayed as a racist and even a proto-Nazi, but in
trying to identify the essence of Irishness he was hardly going beyond

conventional notions about 'good stock'.[17] Whether it militates in favour of his ideas to say, as Boyce does, that 'any racial undertones were ones that he recognised, not ones that he invented', is perhaps open to question.[18] Likewise Patrick Maume's recent comment that while Moran was 'a bigot', he 'had a sense of humour', and 'never quite reached the level of the hate-filled diatribes published by "Sceilg" [J. J. O'Kelly] and Father Timothy Corcoran in the *Catholic Bulletin*' is faint praise.[19] Moran's characteristic method was less to identify distinctive Irish qualities than to assault Irish people who aped 'Saxon' ways. His bitter sarcasm etched derogatory terms like *Seoinín* (English-loving), 'West Briton', 'Castle Catholic', and 'sourface' (for Protestants) into the nationalist vocabulary. Though he had no qualms about excluding the patron saint of Irish republicanism (and more to the point, of United Irish denominational integration), Wolfe Tone, from membership of the Irish nation, on the grounds that he was a Frenchman born of English parents, his nationalism was not biologically exclusivist. What he was after was, as he put it in a famous phrase, a real, substantial foundation of nationality as against idealistic delusion. He implicity accepted the logical consequence of all this, that Ireland might be partitioned, and one of his closest associates, Arthur Clery, explicitly accepted it.

The *Leader* group naturally pitched into the struggle for a Catholic university, which encapsulated many dimensions of the cultural division in Ireland at the turn of the century. Persistent clerical opposition to secular colleges during the nineteenth century had left Trinity College, the bastion of Unionism, in splendid isolation. The Royal University was no more than an examining body, lacking (as one of its senators protested in 1890) a physical 'centre of light and culture for the teaching and research of our students'.[20] Trinity ostentatiously refused to adapt to the new nationalism, its abrasive Provost, Mahaffy, brutally dismissing the teaching of Gaelic as 'perfectly useless'. Moran in turn dismissed Trinity as simply irrelevant to Ireland, but this merely heightened his anger at what he saw as Britain's failure to solve the 'university problem'. To him, the question suggested by that problem was 'Not – How best can we convince England, but – How can we hit her?'[21] Rhetorical though this may have been, it indicated the possibility of a shift from cultural contention to something more physical.

The university question changed significantly in the early years of the century, when the Church, recognizing the depth of British liberal determination, softened its insistence on an explicitly Catholic university. When the Liberal James Bryce took over as Chief Secretary in 1905 he accelerated moves towards the creation of a new college free, in his words, 'from all theological tests and restrictions'. But this was certainly to be a college for Catholics, and it ran into a formidable defensive action from the University of Dublin. A 'Hands off Trinity' campaign succeeded in stalling the whole project, demonstrating that the battle of two civilizations was more than a figment of Moran's imagination.

The literary revival

The ebullience of the 1890s was heightened by a remarkable literary movement, 'a kind of goldrush towards a true national culture'.[22] A sense of epic historical change informed the work of a striking array of writers. William Butler Yeats, an indisputably great poet of exceptional self-awareness (and a dedicated occult astrologer), saw the challenge as to 'seal with the right image the soft wax before it began to harden'. Yeats and Augusta Gregory, founders of the Irish Literary Theatre in May 1899, believed they could create a literature of world significance, written in English but essentially Irish – drawing on folk consciousness (and in Lady Gregory's case a constructed dialect), but transcending political localism. Yeats was drawn early into salon nationalism, possibly joining the IRB after meeting the venerable Fenian John O'Leary (whom he later apotheosized as his lost ideal of 'romantic Ireland'), and throwing himself more enthusiastically into radical nationalism after he became involved with the débutante-actress Maud Gonne. But his path was always his own. He turned quickly from the disturbingly radical project of de-Anglicization to a more aesthetic revolution, which he cruelly labelled 'de-Davisization'.

Davis was an appropriate symbol of the divergence that was to come. His poetry was bad – though as Boyce charitably remarks, no worse than a huge raft of Victorian heroic balladry – but it was transparently heartfelt and still hugely popular. The Literary Theatre's mission, which took more concrete shape with the establishment of the Abbey Theatre (financed by the distinctly un-national tea heiress Annie Horniman) in 1904, was soon identified by Moran as the most dangerous threat to real Irish nationality – more dangerous than Trinity College or even the British government because more subversive. To Moran, Yeats's 'Celtic note' was a glaring fraud. Most damningly, the *Leader* declared that Yeats 'never wrote a line to touch an Irish heart'.

The crucial divergence between Irish-Irelanders and Yeatsians came over the issue of whether, or how, 'national art' should support the nation. Lady Gregory's (steadily popular, and perhaps underestimated) dramas did this in a quiet way, and Seán O'Faolain's testimony to the impact on him of Lennox Robinson's workmanlike rather than brilliant play *Patriots* probably goes for many other advanced nationalists.[23] Yeats and Gregory provided one transcendent demonstration of how it could be done to the satisfaction of both aestheticians and politicians with their *Cathleen ni Houlihan* (1902), a play with tremendous symbolic force, achieved in part by its brevity, and in part by an unforgettable opening performance by Maud Gonne in the title role. But three years earlier Yeats had produced a play with a more ambivalent message, *The Countess Cathleen* (1899), which confronted the shocking possibility that destitution might have induced Catholics to abandon the faith. 'What is the meaning of this rubbish?', demanded the nationalist Frank Hugh O'Donnell, 'How is it to help the national cause?'

The issue was most squarely joined once Yeats and Gregory found a more natural dramatic genius in John Millington Synge, who became the third pillar of the Abbey Theatre. Yeats immediately recognized Synge as the perfect exemplar of the new theatre – maybe almost as much for his gentlemanly personal qualities as for his dramatic gift.[24] But in any case the latter was beyond dispute. Synge immediately achieved what Yeats, as his biographer says, struggled for: 'unstagey heroics, real passion, the expression of combative individuality', in a word the 'saltiness' of reality.[25] His plays were great works of art that ran into public hostility because they did not fit the national self-image. The first confrontation, over *In the Shadow of the Glen* (1903), saw the battle lines drawn up. Synge's unsentimental portrayal of marital infidelity and financial rapacity outraged not only nationalists but even the *Irish Times*, while Yeats delivered the first of his magisterial rebukes to the critics under the none-too-subtle title 'The National Theatre and Three Sorts of Ignorance'. Yeats aimed his counter-attack at the failure of imagination, the failure to grasp that great literature could not be shackled by programmatic requirements. But his attitude could look perilously close to traditional Protestant dismissals of Catholic obscurantism. The crisis came when Synge's *The Playboy of the Western World* (1907) provoked actual rioting in Abbey Street. The National Theatre was denounced as irreligious (a 'loathsome brood of apostates' in the characteristic language of the Catholic University College students) and treacherous, reinforcing defamatory foreign stereotypes of the Irish.

Unfortunately the increasingly embattled leaders of the literary revival failed to dispel such hostility; all three of the Abbey's dominant trio (Yeats, Gregory and Synge) were Anglo-Irish Protestants, who looked – and in private sounded – not a little condescending to the Catholics. It seemed that there was no way out for these people who, as Moran condescendingly said, 'meant well': if they tried to search for common ground between Protestant and Catholic by looking back to an original pre-Christian Irishness, they were denounced as Pagans.[26]

Sinn Féin

Moran's hostility to the Anglo-Irish literary movement was predictable, but still more damaging in the long run was the criticism of the other outstanding nationalist polemicist of the time, Arthur Griffith. A year before Moran, Griffith also set up his own paper, the *United Irishman*, with the exiguous capital (about £50) he had built up as a jobbing printer in Dublin and South Africa – where he was temporarily driven by the depression of the mid-1890s, and formed a friendship with the founder of the Irish Brigade, John MacBride. At that time, in 1899, he was close to Yeats as well as to MacBride's future wife, Maud Gonne, leading pro-Boer demonstrations (in which MacBride became an icon of resistance to British imperialism) and attending meetings of the Pan-Celtic Society. Even then, however, a telling incident adumbrated their different paths. When, in the wake of the 1900 royal visit, a Dublin society magazine alleged that Maud Gonne was a British spy, Griffith publicly assaulted its editor, with enough violence to break a rhinoceros-hide cattle whip (sjambok) he had brought back as a souvenir from the Transvaal. Griffith later left the IRB and embraced non-violence, but as a political strategy only. He was still in essence a physical-force man, an activist.

Griffith was always cautious about the National Theatre: his early criticism was mild, merely saying that the plays Yeats promoted 'can never be popular. They are too far above the people's heads.' But after the *Countess Cathleen* he shifted his ground, declaring that while he knew Yeats to be patriotic, 'he has exhibited a startling misconception of the character of his countrymen'. After this his criticism sharpened, until by the time of the *Playboy* fracas he was in full cry against un-national art. Unlike Moran, who insisted (whether he really thought this or not) that Yeats was not a great poet, Griffith recognized his stature, but became all the more fiercely embattled against his mistaken direction. For Griffith there could be no question of art transcending nationality: 'nationality is the breath of art'.

Arthur Griffith was by some measure the most original and potent Irish political strategist of the twentieth century. To evaluate him as a political thinker perhaps misses the mark; he did not spend much time worrying about the nature of the ultimate Irish political system. He remained a Fenian in his general acceptance that separation and sovereignty would be unproblematic, and his underlying political ideas were largely those of conventional Victorian liberalism – he assumed some form of representative democracy, and a functional pluralism. Griffith's liberal credentials are often impugned nowadays by historians who point to the strong tinge of anti-Semitism that marks his political commentaries (though it hardly differs from the – admittedly deplorable – British norm of the time), and his robustly capitalist-nationalist dislike of socialism. His defenders point to his claim that he sought 'to increase not only the wealth of the country, which is not prosperity, but the just distribution of that wealth, which *is* prosperity'.[27]

Griffith was to die on the threshold of the ultimate political test, real executive power – he succeeded Michael Collins at the head of the Provisional Government of the Irish Free State for a fortnight in 1922 – and it is probably fruitless to guess how his ideas would have been translated into policy. But in the year before his death he was to make a permanent contribution to the entrenchment of democratic political culture in Ireland. His most distinctive achievement was the transformation of revolutionary method: to mesh the Irish-Ireland redefinition of nationality with a distinctive political strategy. For Griffith, as for Moran, independence meant more than mere separateness; it required the substance that only moral self-assurance and real economic development could generate. To him, 'the Anglicisation of the Irish mind is best exhibited in its attitude to economics'.[28] He found a congenially anti-British model of economic development in nineteenth-century Prussia, where Friedrich List had constructed two attractive arguments: that nations were natural economic units, and that free trade operated to prevent late-starters from ever catching up with countries like Britain. Griffith rhetorically suggested that there should be a copy of List's *The National System of Political Economy* in every Irishman's hand. There was, Griffith held, not only no chance but also no point in getting political independence if Ireland remained economically dependent. Moreover, significant steps could be taken to impose a kind of protective tariff right away, by popular action rather than by the state; everyone could support Irish industry by buying Irish and boycotting British goods. The Listian idea of autarchy could be extended beyond the purely economic sphere, and merged naturally with the new emphasis on cultural autonomy. (This connection was nicely illustrated in the mid-1890s by the Rathkeale solicitor who told one of Horace Plunkett's co-operative organizers that 'every pound of butter made in this creamery must be made on nationalist principles, or it shan't be made at all!'.[29]

The idea of autarchy also echoed into the political sphere, where Griffith's writing gave substance to a third way between constitutionalism and physical force – self-reliance. Independence would come from within: from the strength of the Irish sense of identity on which a campaign of civil resistance could be founded. He found the model, again, in central Europe. In 1904 he published a remarkable historical study, *The Resurrection of Hungary*, which was an immediate sensation. It was accurately described at the time as 'the largest idea contributed to Irish politics in a generation', and has been recognized as 'one of the seminal documents of Irish history'.[30] To Patrick Pearse, it marked 'an epoch, because it crystallises into a national policy the doctrines which during the past ten years have been preached by the apostles of the Irish Ireland movement'.[31] In itself a skilful account of the Hungarian achievement of autonomy (in the form of the *Ausgleich* which established a dual Habsburg monarchy) in 1867, its impact in Ireland was not due to any sudden public interest in central European history but to its careful articulation as a model – as its subtitle *A Parallel for Ireland* made plain.

Griffith drew the parallel with sufficient vividness to overcome the apparent irrelevance of Hungary, offering the tantalizing assertion that if Ireland had had a leader in 1867 with half the qualities of the Hungarian statesman Deák's, it could have become free at that moment. He added the masterly construction that 'if Hungary declared herself a republic tomorrow, Austria would not fight, because she could not'.[32] (This had the cunning, if tendentious implication that under a similar dual-monarchy arrangement, England would be weakened as much as Austria had been.) He sidelined aspects of the Hungarian achievement that were less attractive to liberals – the dominance of the landed aristocracy, for instance, and the ruthless programme of Magyar cultural imperialism against minority ethnic groups. The key process identified by Griffith was political abstention: the nation's elected representatives should refuse to sit in the imperial parliament, but should constitute themselves as a separate national assembly and defy the imperial power to suppress them. In the twentieth century, Griffith believed, old-fashioned military repression could be stymied by a widespread public passive resistance movement. Indeed, Britain had handed to Ireland a powerful mechanism for shaping civil resistance in the local government system of 1898.

Not everyone was persuaded by the exotic Hungarian analogy; Moran mockingly compared 'the Green Hungarian Band' not with revolutionary leaders like Déak and Kossuth but with 'the Blue Hungarian Band', a group of musicians then purveying Danubian chic to the polite society of Dublin. How to organize political action was another problem. Griffith's abstentionist theory did not obviously sit well with the business of creating a political party, and for several years he hesitated to take this step. After the *Resurrection* was published, however, a decisive event occurred: the fringe grouping that had formed around him adopted a potent name for the self-reliance project, and launched a political movement. The National Council, formed in Harcourt Street in 1904, took Griffith's project 'off the back streets', as his biographer put it, and in 1905 the party was launched as Sinn Féin.

|4|

Home Rule and the British crisis,
1905–1914

*I*n the decade before the outbreak of the Great War in Europe, the
United Kingdom experienced its most severe crisis in modern
times. Around the constitutional struggle over the reform of the
House of Lords, and the political struggle over Irish Home Rule,
welled up more diffuse but no less serious conflicts over the rights of
workers and women. The word 'crisis' may have been over-used in this
century, but at the time many people had a sense that the simultaneous
eruption of these multiple conflicts was more than a coincidence.
George Dangerfield labelled this 'the strange death of Liberal
England', but the point was that it stretched beyond England itself.
There seemed to be some kind of 'systemic' crisis, in which all old
assumptions and institutions were being challenged. (The Prime
Minister at the turn of the century, Lord Salisbury, brooded pes-
simistically on 'disintegration'.) The intensity of Unionist resistance
to Home Rule was heightened by this sense of general crisis. A fore-
taste of this atmosphere had come with the 'devolution crisis' that
shook the Conservative government in 1904, when a fairly modest
administrative proposal provoked a ferocious reaction (p. 17 above).

The Liberal tide

The 1906 general election was a Liberal landslide. With a crushing
majority (356) in the House of Commons, the Liberal programme
looked unstoppable. But there was no sign of Irish Home Rule in that
programme. It was not just that the party did not need Irish support;

the Gladstonian commitment to Home Rule had atrophied during a decade's stocktaking, in which the party had reassessed the effect of its Irish policy – 20 years of Tory domination. Few shared the undying enthusiasm of John Morley, Gladstone's acolyte, for Home Rule as the 'one big idea' that gave political shape to the party. In the eyes of the Roseberyite group of 'Liberal imperialists' who controlled the party in 1905, Home Rule was not a vote-winning idea; indeed it threatened the party's ability to deliver social reforms and thus to outbid the nascent Labour party for working-class support. The so-called 'Relugas compact', a policy planning summit just before the election, showed that a key group of Liberal leaders – Sir Edward Grey, R. B. Haldane and H. H. Asquith – thought that no Home Rule legislation should be proposed for the next parliament (then a seven-year term). The subject was duly sidelined in the 1906 election campaign, a fact which would come home to roost with a vengeance when the crisis eventually broke in 1910. The implication, tacitly admitted by Liberal strategy, and later trumpeted by Unionists, was that Home Rule did not have the support of British public opinion.

In spite of this, it was not entirely without backing in the new Liberal administration. The Prime Minister, the veteran 'pro-Boer' Sir Henry Campbell-Bannerman, thought that something should be done. The earlier devolution idea was repackaged as the Irish Council Bill, transferring responsibility for education, local government and agriculture to a part-elected, part-appointed Representative Council. 'C-B' described this ingratiatingly as 'a little, modest, shy, humble effort to give administrative powers to the Irish people'. Was this the start of 'Home Rule by instalments', as Unionists feared? Or was it the opposite, a device to appeal to moderate Irish opinion over the heads of the parliamentary party leadership – the sort of strategy that had been tried in India to undercut the claim of the Indian National Congress to represent the Indian people? It may have combined both these aims. The first Irish Secretary in the Liberal Cabinet, James Bryce (a distinguished constitutional lawyer), immediately saw the danger that the Bill could weaken the Irish constitutional movement by exposing it to damaging criticism from radical nationalists. The 'ultra party, fenian dregs, Sinn Féin men etc etc', as Bryce called them, could put Redmond's leadership of national opinion in a tight spot. So he and his successor, Augustine Birrell, expanded the representative segment of the proposed Council, to the point where Redmond was able to give the Bill a cautious welcome in the House of Commons. But he changed his mind when he got back to Ireland, and came out against it. He may have exaggerated the danger from his radical flank, since some Gaelic League activists (including both Pearse and MacNeill) later said that the Council might have offered a real empowerment of Irish democracy; but his caution was an important warning that the parliamentary party was not invulnerable. Birrell was obviously aware of this, but the warning was lost on subsequent British governments.

Thwarted in their 'humble effort', the Liberals were reduced to less contentious reforms, such as the Evicted Tenants Act and the 1908 Education Act. The reform that from the government's own point of view was most necessary, however, the strengthening of the Irish Executive, remained unachieved. Birrell drew up proposals, but retreated in face of Redmond's objection that administrative reform would give the impression that Home Rule was not imminent.

Nationalism on the edge

The nationalist movement that was to be the supposed beneficiary of Liberal largesse was no longer the monolithic structure that Parnell had once dominated. The rebuilding of the parliamentary party on the back of the UIL agitation was no mean achievement, in the light of the divisions of the 1890s, but the party led by Redmond was confronted by a situation even more unstable than the land war. The land struggle, in fact, was only temporarily abated by the effect of Wyndham's Land Act. Dramatic changes did follow in many areas, and some 317,000 holdings (out of 600,000) were transferred in the first five years. The Congested Districts Board also significantly expanded its land purchase programme immediately after the 1903 Act, but the pace of its activity was noticeably slackening by the time the Liberals returned to power. Birrell struggled in vain to prise more funds out of the Gladstonian-minded Treasury. For nationalist political orators, the 'failure' of the Wyndham Act became a major theme. On 14 October 1906, Laurence Ginnell of the parliamentary party stepped up the agitation when he addressed a big anti-grazing meeting in Co. Westmeath and urged a new form of resistance, cattle-driving. The first cattle-drives began during the winter, and by mid-1907 the midlands and west of Ireland were engulfed in a full-scale 'ranch war'. By the end of the year, there had been yet another general collapse of the legal system.[1]

The parliamentary party took a public lead in organizing the new agitation, presenting it as a public response not only to the failure of the land reform, but also to the fiasco of the Council Bill. But the party was showing signs of strain. The rapid growth of the misleadingly-named Ancient Order of Hibernians, a new Catholic self-help organization, gave unwelcome prominence to the sectarian dimension of the national movement. In stressing Catholic identity it 'represented an entirely different emotional and intellectual conception of what Irish nationality meant' from that advanced by Sinn Féin.[2] It gave a powerful constituency to the dominant Belfast nationalist politician, Joe Devlin, who used the AOH to run the party – sometimes by physical force. Devlin violently attacked every threat to party unity, whether Parnellite, Healyite, or O'Brienite. Healy (who knew about Catholic populism) denounced the demagoguery of this 'pocket demosthenes'. Another warning note was sounded by younger liberal parliamentarians such as Tom Kettle and Francis Cruise O'Brien, who saw Devlin's mastery of American-style machine politics as dangerous. Devlin's personal fiefdom in Ulster can be seen, in retrospect, to have unwittingly prefigured the eventual separation of the North-east. He was too useful, however, for the party to push him aside.[3] It is clear that it felt, perhaps for the first time, under real pressure from more radical groups than itself – in particular Sinn Féin, which was becoming an umbrella group for the reinvigoration of other, still more shadowy organizations. The key figure in this was Bulmer Hobson, a Belfast Quaker who had founded the Protestant National Society and a nationalist boy scout movement, the Fianna Éireann, in 1903. It was characteristic of him to set up two organizations at the same time: he was a natural and gifted weaver of structures, who not only 'meant well' (as D. P. Moran patronizingly said of Protestant nationalists) but who acted to give practical potential to the ideas sketched out by Arthur Griffith. In 1904 he joined the IRB and immediately established, together with Denis McCullough, a new republican group, the Dungannon Club (named after the original Volunteer Convention of 1792), which quickly spread across the country. This had a far more modern and open cast than the moribund IRB, and by the time Hobson joined the IRB's Supreme Council he was pushing the old oath-bound conspirators into a more public engagement with practical methods of resistance. The full-time organizer he appointed for the Dungannon Clubs movement, John (Seán) MacDermott, was to loom large in the history of militant republicanism. In 1907 Hobson became Vice-President of Sinn Féin, and took the new concept across to America. In 1909 the West Belfast branch of Sinn Féin published his civil resistance 'handbook', *Defensive Warfare*, which brilliantly demonstrated the wide scope that existed for passive opposition to the British state. Arguing that for the people 'to recognize an aggressive government is national suicide', Hobson pointed out that Ireland was governable only as long as people obeyed. 'They need not obey, and they need not be governed one day longer than they wish.'[4] This sophisticated notion of resistance, which was later to find a famous echo in Mahatma Gandhi's idea of *satyagraha*, was to make Sinn Féin a global pioneer of twentieth-century revolution. If the constitutional nationalist movement failed to come up with the goods, its position would be increasingly imperilled.

The return of Home Rule

The marginalization of the Irish party at Westminster was ended dramatically by the Liberal struggle against the House of Lords over the so-called 'People's Budget' prepared by Chancellor Lloyd George in 1909. The budget itself was hardly attractive to the Irish party; in particular its powerful backers in the distilling industry were angered by the new liquor duty. But the Lords' reckless resistance precipitated two general elections in 1910 which put the Irish party in a position superficially like Parnell's pinnacle in 1886: the Liberals ended up with 272 seats, exactly the same number as the Unionists (including 17 Ulster Unionists); Labour had 42, the Irish party 84. Even though there could be no question of Redmond threatening to support the Unionists, the position of Campbell-Bannerman's successor, Asquith, was obviously altered. When he restated the Liberal commitment to Home Rule in a speech at the Albert Hall in 1910 he was, in Unionist eyes, unashamedly bidding for Irish support.

The Liberal view was of course somewhat different. Whereas Home Rule had been an impossible legislative project (which had wrecked two Liberal governments) in the past, it now became feasible once the veto power of the House of Lords was swept away by the 1911 Parliament Act. Two years and two parliamentary circuits, on the second of which the Lords could only make 'suggestions', not amendments, would suffice to see Home Rule on the statute book. The government now had the capacity to deliver the party's historic commitment. A third Government of Ireland Bill was duly prepared, and introduced in April 1912.

In drawing up the Bill, the Cabinet did not seem troubled by the possibility of serious resistance outside the House of Lords. Nor did it appear to be passionately concerned with the terms of the Bill. A fairly leisurely drafting process in 1911 brought the Gladstonian Bill up to date (though one or two references to Her Majesty the Queen lived on in the remoter schedules). The Gladstonian model was adopted 'largely by default': only Birrell and Morley seem to have believed it good in itself. Others leaned vaguely towards the fashionable idea of UK federalism, or 'home rule all round', and indeed Asquith hinted at this when he introduced the Bill as the 'first step towards a wider devolution'. But nothing serious was done to take things on in this direction. The Bill set up a bicameral Irish parliament with a nominated Senate (40 members) and an elected House of Commons on the English pattern, with powers to legislate for the 'peace, order and good government of Ireland'. Certain powers were reserved to Westminster (where Irish representation would be cut to 42, although on a strict population basis this should have been 64): the Crown, war and peace, treaties and trade (i.e. foreign policy), defence – so far following the 1893 Bill, though a shorter list – with the addition of new government commitments like land purchase, old age pensions, and national insurance. Control of the police was reserved in the first instance, to be transferred later – presumably, though this was not clarified, on the basis of good behaviour.

The main progress beyond the 1893 Bill was in the area of Ireland's financial relations with the Treasury. The new scheme, worked out by financial wizards Sir Henry Primrose and Herbert Samuel, was 'so complicated that it defeated the comprehension of most of [Samuel's] colleagues' in the government.[5] It was incorporated into the second draft Bill in December 1911, at which point it was shown to Redmond for the first time, with the astonishing proviso that it was 'not the result of serious consideration, but had been thrown together hurriedly'; it did not represent 'the settled view of the Cabinet'. Nothing could be more eloquent of the British attitude. Frantic detail revision followed in preparation for the parliamentary launch on 11 April 1912.

The Unionist rebellion

The storm of resistance began to break even before the Bill appeared. Unionist opposition to the earlier Home Rule proposals had become increasingly well organized. The original Irish Loyal and Patriotic Union of 1885 had been followed by the Ulster Loyalist Anti-repeal Union of 1886, the Ulster Convention League of 1892 and the Ulster

Defence Union of 1893. The Unionist Clubs movement began then, and remained active through to 1905 when the Ulster Unionist Council added a permanent electoral organization for all Ulster constituencies. It is clear enough that the subsequent Unionist portrayal of Ulster militancy as a reaction to the Liberal 'corrupt bargain', as in Ronald McNeill's 1922 history *Ulster's Stand for Union*, understated the pre-existing readiness to do battle.[6]

The election of Edward Carson as leader of the Irish Unionists in 1910 set the seal on preparations for political mobilization. The Unionist party had until then been a rather dull grouping that had made little public impression. His predecessor as leader, Walter Long, was a hard-bitten but uncharismatic Tory backwoodsman (though he had been in the Cabinet as Irish Secretary under Balfour, and would return to it as Colonial Secretary in the Lloyd George coalition). The Dublin-born barrister Carson, by contrast, was one of those public figures with a mysterious capacity to focus and amplify popular will, and to inspire public trust. He had made his reputation as a barrister by his destruction of the most charismatic of all Irish figures of the *fin de siècle*, Oscar Wilde, in a celebrated immorality case. In politics he projected an absolute commitment to fight to the finish to resist Home Rule. As a Dubliner, he insisted that his one motivation was 'my love of Ireland'.[7] His absolutism – more extreme in rhetoric than any to be found outside the IRB itself – was to radicalize the struggle and take it to the brink of civil war.

The paramilitary style of the Unionist challenge was established at a large-scale demonstration held on 23 September 1911. Some 50,000 men from Orange lodges and Unionist Clubs across the North met in the centre of Belfast and marched out to Craigavon, the seat of Carson's deputy Sir James Craig. There Carson issued his defiant and inspirational call – 'We must be prepared … the morning Home Rule passes, ourselves to become responsible for the government of the Protestant Province of Ulster'. Two days later, 400 Ulster Unionist Council delegates met and appointed a committee to prepare a constitution for a provisional Ulster government. This threat of a unilateral declaration of independence may have been intended by Carson himself as a decisive move against Home Rule for any part of Ireland, but it accurately struck a vital chord in the resistance movement. The solidity of a sense of Ulster identity, rooted in the Protestant 'way of life', was the key to the threat. Although there were other arguments in play against Home Rule, mainly focused on the economic benefits of the British and imperial link, it was the belief that Irish nationalism was essentially a Roman Catholic movement, that Home Rule would be 'Rome Rule', that generated the kind of political community capable of mounting credible resistance.

The grass-roots enthusiasm was brilliantly stage-managed for maximum political impact. Unlike its later twentieth-century forms, this loyalism chimed with a powerful strain of imperial patriotic sentiment in Britain itself. On Easter Tuesday 1912, another vast meeting was held in Belfast at the Agricultural Society showgrounds; over 100,000 men marched past Carson, and assembled to pass a resolution against Home Rule. As the vote was taken the biggest Union flag ever woven, 48 feet by 25, was broken out from a 90-foot mast. Even this theatrical event was topped by the mounting of a whole series of meetings on 'Ulster Day', 28 September, when nearly half a million people signed the Ulster Solemn League and Covenant. This skilful evocation of seventeenth-century religious war declared that Home Rule would be a 'calamity', 'disastrous to the material well-being of Ulster ... subversive of our civil and religious freedom, destructive of our citizenship, and perilous to the unity of the Empire', and committed its signatories to 'using all means which may be found necessary to defeat the present conspiracy to set up a Home Rule parliament'.[8] That evening a torchlit procession of men armed with dummy rifles paraded past Carson in Lisburn, looking to *The Times* correspondent like the sea with a storm brooding over it.[9]

Just how serious the storm might be, is a question that goes to the heart of twentieth-century Irish history. Were the loyalists in real earnest in their determination to resist Home Rule, or were they bluffing? Could a more skilful approach have undermined their resistance? The government certainly underestimated Unionist resolution at the start. When the new leader of the Conservative party, Andrew Bonar Law, heightened the atmosphere of tension in his speech at Blenheim in July 1912, Liberals dismissed his rhetoric as political opportunism. Bonar Law's language was certainly unmeasured, not to say hysterical: he called the government 'a revolutionary committee which has seized upon despotic power by fraud', and declared that 'if an attempt were made to deprive these men [i.e. Irish Unionists] of their birthright, they would be justified in resisting by all means in their power, including force'. To this barely veiled threat of civil war he added another dimension by pledging 'I can imagine no length of resistance to which Ulster can go in which I should not be prepared to support them'.[10]

Redmond's party encouraged the government's assumption that all this was no more than bluster. Nationalists simply could not believe

that anyone would push resistance to Home Rule to the point of violence. Modern historians tend to stress nationalist neglect of the
Ulster question as a kind of failure of imagination, rooted in the fixed
belief in the unity of Ireland and the existence of a single 'Irish
people'. It is also important to note that Redmond himself went
further than most twentieth-century Irish nationalists in accepting a
high-profile role for Ireland in the British Empire. This was a genuine
commitment on his part, and one which should have reassured
Unionists.[11] But throughout 1912 and 1913, while the Home Rule Bill
rolled through the parliamentary circuit, evidence was accumulating
that Ulster resistance was deadly serious. After the Craigavon rally, at
which a group of Co. Tyrone Orangemen had caused a minor sensation by demonstrating military drill, a drilling craze swept the
province. A loophole in the Unlawful Drilling Act permitted men to
drill with the permission of two JPs if their purpose was to uphold the
constitution, 'to make them more efficient citizens'.[12] That was exactly
what Unionists (including most magistrates) believed they were doing.
This dangerous trend was accelerated and concentrated in January
1913 when local groups coalesced into the Ulster Volunteer Force
(UVF), a citizen militia organized on strict military lines. By
September, 75,000 signatories of the Covenant had enrolled, and the
number went on to top 100,000. All that was lacking was rifles. The
Unionist leadership were apprehensive about turning the UVF into a
real rather than a stage army, but their reluctance was overwhelmed by
grass-roots pressure from the regiments that were fed up with dummy
guns. In early 1914 preparations were made for a major purchase and
shipment of arms.

At the same time, an equally fateful development was occurring, as
nationalists began to imitate the UVF and set up their own drilling
bands. On 1 November 1913 the Gaelic League pioneer and
University College, Dublin, history professor Eoin MacNeill published an ironic essay hailing the UVF as a Home Rule army. 'The
North Began' was followed by a more ominous essay on 'The Coming
Revolution' by his fellow-Leaguer Patrick Pearse, which declared 'we
must accustom ourselves to the thought of arms, to the sight of arms,
to the use of arms'; 'bloodshed is a cleansing and a sanctifying thing,
and the nation which regards it as the final horror has lost its
manhood'. In the last week of that month the Irish Volunteers were
founded at a Dublin meeting, and within a few weeks had equalled or
exceeded the size of the UVF. MacNeill became President of the
Volunteer Executive, still a fairly civilian-sounding outfit. Like the

UVF, this was conceived (at least by MacNeill) as a pressure group, to hold the government steady on the Home Rule course. But as Joseph Lee has pointed out, this was a case in which moral force rested rather directly on the threat of physical force.[13] And once these militias were in existence, they could change the agenda. Alongside MacNeill were the Sinn Féiner Bulmer Hobson, and a strong IRB presence. The republicans were at last getting the army they had dreamed of for so long.

Class war

A third militia also appeared in Ireland in November 1913. The Irish Citizen Army, formed by the socialist leaders James Larkin and James Connolly, was a grand name for a thousand or so veterans of the biggest industrial struggle that had yet taken place in Ireland. The 1913 Dublin lockout was the culmination of a sudden and dramatic mobilization of the Irish working class, which seemed to open up the possibility that the traditional pattern of nationalist politics would be transformed. The appalling conditions of work and housing in Irish cities, which had been tacitly ignored by the middle-class parliamentary party, briefly joined land and nationalism at the top of the public agenda.

'Big Jim' Larkin arrived in Belfast from Scotland in January 1907, as the representative of the National Union of Dock Labourers. Within a few months he had recruited almost 3000 members, and his characteristic brand of aggressive confrontational tactics led to a full-scale industrial struggle. Larkin accused the Belfast Steamship Company of trying to 'smash the union' by replacing workers who had walked out on 6 June in protest against two non-union men. Refusing to accept anything short of full recognition of the union in pay negotiations, he denounced the company chairman as an 'obscene scoundrel'. The atmosphere of class war generated by his charismatic leadership was powerful enough to neutralize traditional sectarian divisions, and unite both Protestant and Catholic workers. Larkin's version of European syndicalism, the idea of organizing 'one big union', was pushed forward by remorseless use of sympathetic strike action.

Larkin was both an asset and a liability to the Irish working-class movement. His larger-than-life presence, and ferocious hostility to those employers he singled out for attack, inspired a fierce fighting spirit amongst his followers: one of the most remarkable of them, the Anglo-Irish aristocrat Constance Markievicz (born Gore-Booth, married to a Polish papal count), felt that 'the great elemental force that is in all crowds had passed into his nature for ever'.[14] It also provoked an equally fierce resistance, and a determination never to recognize his unions or negotiate with him. 'Larkinism' became a bogey which spurred the employers into creating the formidable cartels which eventually broke his attempts to organize a revolutionary general strike. In Belfast in 1907, the big-union project broke up when rioting began in August, and relapsed into sectarian battles. But in 1908 the foundation of the Irish Transport and General Workers' Union (ITGWU) signalled Larkin's determination to organize the disparate 'general labourers' around his idea of decisive confrontation. 'Larkinism' triggered labour militancy throughout Ireland – leading to two major dock strikes in Galway and Limerick in 1912–13, and two local 'general strikes' in Galway and Sligo in 1913, as well as the intensifying series of disputes in Dublin (30 separate strikes, lockouts, and sympathetic strikes between January and August 1913). Larkin's 'unique achievement was to give unskilled Irish workers the tactics to fight, and above all the will to struggle'.[15]

James Connolly, who returned from America in 1910, added a powerful theoretical edge to the labour movement, which took it into a closer relationship with nationalism. While classical Marxism rejected nationalism as a bourgeois device to delude and divide the international working-class movement, Connolly anticipated Lenin (and the Second Communist International's 1915 Zimmerwald conference doctrine) in accepting that the force of nationalism might begin the revolution which could ultimately open the way for socialism. Before there could be a workers' republic, there had to be a republic. Connolly held that socialists and nationalists could combine to destroy imperialism, and wrote a tendentiously impressive historical study, *Labour in Irish History* (1910), to elaborate the message. He even argued, in *Labour, Nationality and Religion*, published about the same time, that there was no necessary conflict between socialism and Catholicism.[16] None of this, however, did much to endear the labour movement to the suspicious Catholic middle class who dominated the nationalist mainstream. Nor, indeed, to the radical nationalists of Sinn Féin; Griffith denounced the Irish labour movement as the puppet of English trades unionism, inflicting misery on the artisans of Dublin.[17]

Connolly was not merely an impressive revolutionary theoretician and a philosopher of history, he was also an organizer at least as capable as Larkin. The two of them provided the labour movement with a formidable leadership. It developed a social as well as a purely industrial dimension. Larkin's ringing assertion 'I have raised the morals and sobriety of the people. ... I am careful about my conduct because I know this cause requires clean men' reflected his battle against the squalor of tenement life. A total abstainer and passionate temperance campaigner, he set up an 'Irish Workers' Choir' and dancing classes at the Irish Women Workers' Hall; an Irish language class and the Irish Workers' Dramatic Company at the ITGWU headquarters, Liberty Hall; and he bought a three-acre property outside Dublin to provide a recreation centre (and later a rifle range for the Citizen Army). But the bid to turn the wave of Dublin industrial disputes in 1913 into a full-scale class war was premature. Ireland remained an agricultural economy, and the industrial proletariat was small. Larkin made up for this by aggression and skill in deploying the weapon of the sympathetic strike, and his quasi-dictatorial power over the Dublin working class was cemented by victory over the City of Dublin Steam Packet Company in a strike lasting from January to April 1913. His next target, the Dublin United Tramway Company, was a harder nut to crack. Its chairman, William Martin Murphy, was Ireland's leading businessman, and perhaps the classic exemplar of Moran's vision of a new Catholic middle class. A former nationalist MP, but a staunch Healyite during the Parnell split, Murphy had brilliantly exploited the growth potential of both the physical and verbal communications businesses.[18] He was absolutely determined to fight 'Larkinism' to the death, and as the proprietor of both the successful national daily *Irish Independent* (which he founded in 1905) and the Dublin *Evening Herald* (the first evening paper to pass the 100,000 sales mark), he was well placed to retaliate against the typically extravagant denunciation of his character ('a soulless, money-grubbing tyrant', 'a blood-sucking vampire') in the pages of the *Irish Worker*.

Indeed it might be said that throughout the great struggle of 1913 the initiative was always held by Murphy. He forced the ITGWU into strike action by his declaration that the Tramway Company would never recognize 'Larkin or his Union', and went on to counter each additional strike action with a lockout. Despite Larkin's belligerent assertion that 'we can smash the Tramway Company in a few days', the dispute escalated for months. By 22 September when the timber and cement merchants locked their men out, some 25,000 were out of work – so that 100,000 already impoverished people were dependent on strike pay, donations from British unions, and charity. As winter approached, a human tragedy threatened.

At this dangerous stage, Larkin's leadership began to create fatal problems. The decision to send starving children to temporary homes in England seemed a natural one to him, but it provoked a dismaying reaction from the Catholic clergy of Dublin, who not only denounced the scheme as dangerous to the children's faith, but physically prevented groups of children leaving Dublin by boat and rail. Besides testifying to the astonishing strength of the continuing fear of proselytism, this distressing confrontation went a long way to refuting Connolly's belief in the compatibility of socialism and Catholicism. Sad as this was, it was not so fatal to the endurance of the workers as Larkin's alienation of the British unions which contributed over £100,000 to support the strike. Larkin's relationship with the British unions had been problematic ever since he had been removed from the Dockers' Union at the end of 1908 by its General Secretary for his reckless commitment of union resources in Belfast. His creation of the ITGWU was a riposte to this, and his attitude to the British unions during the 1913 strike was hardly less aggressive than his attitude to the employers. The conflict boiled up at the Trades Union Congress (TUC) in London on 9 December, when Larkin impugned the democratic credentials of union leaders like J. H. Thomas, and offered to go out and fight them in the street. The withdrawal of British financial support was almost immediate and catastrophic.

In formal terms the outcome of the great strike was perhaps a draw, since neither side achieved all its aims. The *Irish Times* complained in February 1914 that even if Larkin himself had been successfully 'smashed', 'that is very far from being the same thing as "smashing Larkinism"'. Most importantly, the strike militarized the worker movement. The government contributed to this by unwisely arresting Larkin on charges of seditious libel and conspiracy, and in late October he was imprisoned for seven months. Seventeen days later, on 14 November, an embarrassing climbdown in the face of public protest saw him released – an ambivalent triumph, perhaps, since he immediately set off for England to carry his 'fiery cross' to the British unions. But this was a heady mobilization, and it was rapidly given sharper focus. On the day of Larkin's release Connolly addressed a huge demonstration with the words 'Listen to me. I am going to talk sedition. The next time we are out for a march, I want to be accompanied by four battalions of trained men with their corporals and sergeants.'[19] Within days a new militia was forming, first delicately named the Citizen League, then on 23 November given the resonant title Irish Citizen Army. As the strike petered out over the following weeks, the Citizen Army shrank from a strength of over a thousand to a few hundred, but under Connolly's control it was to make up for its size in its unswerving commitment to violent insurrection. If Carson and MacNeill might have been bluffing, Connolly was not.

The political showdown

The government did its best to appear unruffled by the sequence of ominous moves in Ireland. Not until late 1913 did any minister suggest that controls on the importation of arms into Ireland should be tightened up. The Home Rule Bill rolled on through parliament unaltered, although the idea of excluding some northern areas from Home Rule had appeared as early as August 1911, when Birrell suggested to his Cabinet colleague Winston Churchill that 'were the question referred to Ulster county by county', only Antrim and Down might refuse to accept it. They could be allowed a 'transitional period, say 5 years' after which there would be a second referendum. 'If this was done, there could be no Civil War.'[20] It is clear that Birrell at least saw the possibility of civil war, and was prepared to go to so unBritish a length as holding a referendum to head it off. Churchill and Lloyd George supported the idea of exclusion at a Cabinet meeting in February 1912, but Morley and Lord Crewe opposed it. No other ministers offered any opinion. Asquith opted to do nothing.

Asquith's 'wait and see' strategy has had its defenders, but its ultimate effect was to hand over the initiative to increasingly radical grass-roots forces in Ireland. The impression of governmental ineffectiveness mounted as it became clear that the promise of Home Rule had raised expectations that could not be fulfilled. When Asquith eventually offered a six-year exclusion for some Ulster counties, Carson's celebrated rejection of this 'sentence of death with a six-year stay of execution' further damaged Liberal credibility. And when the government eventually began to take direct action to counter the threat of Ulster resistance, its belated initiative blew up in its face.

Early 1914 brought an increase in the stridency of Unionist rhetoric, and signs of real preparation for armed action. The professional-looking Special Service Forces of the UVF were established early in the year, and several trial mobilizations were mounted – and well publicized by the sympathetic military correspondent of *The*

Times. In March the government decided to move some troops from
the central military base at the Curragh to strengthen the garrisons of
arms depots and official installations in Ulster, to forestall the possibility of a UVF coup. (In fact a UVF plan entitled 'The Coup'
envisaged a 'sudden, complete and paralysing blow' involving the
capture of 'all depots of arms, ammunition and military equipment'.[21])
Through the special prism of Unionist perception, this preparation
was seen as the key move in a Cabinet 'plot' to provoke the UVF into
a rising, which would turn British public opinion against the loyalists
and enable the government to crush them. Tory leaders in Britain, like
Leo Amery and Walter Long, who spoke of 'a deliberate plan ... to
attack Ulster', saw the appointment of Major-General Nevil Macready
to command the troops in Ulster, with a dormant commission as military governor of Belfast, as proof that the operation was far more
ambitious and sinister than merely safeguarding arms depots.

What is certain is that the government's attempt to head off the possibility of political dissent within the army over the move to Ulster
backfired spectacularly and disastrously. In an extraordinary departure
from normal British assumptions about the automatic obedience of the
army to any government, the government agreed to the idea (proposed
by an apprehensive Commander-in-Chief in Ireland, Sir Arthur Paget)
that officers whose homes were in Ulster would be permitted to 'dis-
appear', without prejudice to their careers, for the duration of the
expected crisis, in order to prevent any conflict of loyalty.[22] General
Paget's over-dramatic way of presenting this option to his officers at the
Curragh (the central military base in Ireland) triggered a mass resignation threat, often called the 'Curragh Mutiny', which was then
bought off by a damaging political concession – the Secretary of State
for War agreed that the army would not be used 'to crush political
opposition to the policy or principles of the Home Rule Bill'.[23] At this
point, the government was almost as effectively paralysed as it would
have been by the imagined UVF coup. King George V was seriously
alarmed by the possibility that the army would break up (a fear deliberately fomented by Unionist officers in Britain), and stepped into the
political arena to secure all-party talks. When Asquith eventually
agreed to the Buckingham Palace Conference in late July, it merely
revealed how completely unnegotiable the deadlock had become. 'I
have rarely felt more hopeless in any practical affair', Asquith dismally
admitted: 'an impasse, with unspeakable consequences'.[24] Two days
after the conference broke up on 24 July, three people were killed in
Dublin as the Irish Volunteers ran in a shipment of guns.

The gun-runnings of April and July 1914 represented another and maybe penultimate lurch towards civil war. The asymmetry of the two events has often been noticed. The cargo brought into Larne for the UVF on the night of 24 April by Major Fred Crawford consisted of over 20,000 fairly modern service rifles, with 3 million rounds of ammunition. To a world that had not yet witnessed the 'storm of steel' on the western front, this was sufficiently impressive. Equally impressive, perhaps, was the efficiency of the staff work, organized by Wilfred Spender, by which the arms were got away from the port and distributed. Unsurprisingly, in the light of their demoralization (long disputes over pay and conditions) and the hands-off policy of the authorities, the police stood by and watched. The cargo brought in to Howth, just outside Dublin, by Erskine Childers in his own sailboat on 26 July was much smaller – 900 distinctly long-in-the-tooth single-shot Mauser rifles with 29,000 rounds of ammunition. (Another 600 rifles and 20,000 rounds were run in to Kilcoole, Co. Wicklow, in another small boat sailed by Conor O'Brien.) To compensate for this, the Irish Volunteers defiantly staged the Howth landing in daylight, and marched the guns openly towards Dublin. Even the police drew the line at this, and the Assistant Commissioner of the Dublin Metropolitan Police (without the permission of his superiors) called out troops in an attempt to disarm the Volunteers. After a verbal confrontation between the police and the Volunteer leaders, during which most of the rifles were spirited away across the fields, the frustrated troops were marched back to their barracks in Dublin accompanied by jeering crowds. In Bachelors Walk they turned on their tormentors and opened fire, killing three people and wounding 30.

To Birrell and Asquith, this disaster showed that they had been right to soft-pedal; to their Tory critics, it demonstrated the humiliating paralysis the government had imposed on the Irish authorities. A senior police officer recorded that the outcome 'thoroughly disheartened every police official in Ireland'.[25] But nobody could doubt that the result was a disaster. The threat of serious violence loomed large, and it is hard to see how a dramatic escalation could have been avoided, but for the yet more dramatic escalation of conflict in Europe. The Bachelors Walk affray coincided with the culmination of the 'July crisis': two days afterwards, Austria-Hungary declared war on Serbia. A week later, Britain was at war with Germany. Irish policy was once again to be swept aside by other priorities, this time the all-conquering demands of the 'war effort'.

|5|

World war and rebellion,
1914–1919

'The First World War', Roy Foster suggests, 'should be seen as one of the most decisive events in modern Irish history'.[1] A proposition like this would hardly be controversial in the history of most European countries. In Ireland, however, the memory of the war was for a long time marginalized. A kind of collective amnesia discarded it as a British experience, dwarfed by an event that was, in physical comparison with the titanic battles on the western and eastern fronts, tiny. The Easter rebellion in 1916 has been commonly acknowledged as the turning-point in the evolution of modern Ireland – the moment when, as W. B. Yeats saw, 'all changed, changed utterly'. (What changed, for him, was his opinion of the executed leaders of the rising, but his reverberant phrase took on a wider resonance.) A thousand of the Irish Volunteers and Irish Citizen Army held the centre of Dublin for six days. The suppression of the rebellion triggered a mass desertion of public opinion from the Irish parliamentary party towards Sinn Féin, culminating in the virtual elimination of the old nationalist movement in the general election of 1918.

Participation in the war

The triumph of Sinn Féin created a dominant interpretation of Ireland's war experience which smothered all alternatives – such as John Redmond's belief that by committing itself to the war Ireland would vindicate its claim to autonomy; or the argument of moderate Irish Volunteer leaders that violence was unjustified, because the pressure of war would force Britain to impose conscription and alienate Irish opinion. Irish rejection of Britain's imperial war came to appear natural and inevitable, and the function of the 1916 rebellion in inspiring and mobilizing a new national allegiance indisputable. The fact that over 200,000 Irishmen enlisted in the British army (voluntarily, since conscription was never applied in Ireland), and that in 1916 many times more Irish soldiers were serving on the western front than came out in the Easter rising, was to be an inconvenient memory for the independent Ireland established after the war.[2]

The flow of recruits into the British army in the first year of the war suggests that Irish opinion did not wholly reject Britain's claim to be fighting for the survival of small nations (and 'Catholic Belgium' in particular). The day before Britain declared war on Germany, Redmond committed himself to the war effort by offering the services of the National Volunteers to defend Ireland and allow the British military garrison to be sent to France. This gesture was not as spontaneous as it looked. It was made in the expectation that Asquith would push through the Home Rule Act despite the crisis it had provoked; and Asquith duly did so in September.[3] In formal terms this was indeed a moment of triumph for the Home Rule party. But the rhetorical aspect of Redmond's pledge was not answered by Britain, which was disinclined to give military recognition to the Volunteers. In a speech at Woodenbridge, Co. Wicklow, on 20 September Redmond went much further, committing the Volunteers to serve 'wherever the firing-line extends'. This was too much for the founding fathers of the Volunteers, and the old Provisional Committee led by Eoin MacNeill and The O'Rahilly broke away, repudiating 'the claim of any man to offer up the blood and lives of the sons of Irishmen and Irishwomen to the services of the British Empire while no National Government which could speak and act for the people of Ireland is allowed to exist'.[4] The rhetoric of 1916 was clearly prefigured here, but the scale of the breakaway movement remained small.

Redmond's Woodenbridge speech is often seen as the beginning of the end for the parliamentary party. His belief that the common cause would bury old suspicions and enmities was surely not an extravagant one, by European standards, in the heady atmosphere of 1914, but even so it outran the limits of Irish politics.[5] Certainly Redmond's fraternal support was ill requited by the British authorities. The refusal of the War Secretary, Lord Kitchener, to offer any kind of symbolic welcome to Irish recruits, by way of establishing a distinctive Irish corps, carried cussedness to the point of political subversion. Redmond himself may have miscalculated when he turned down Asquith's offer of a Cabinet seat, which would have balanced the position taken by Carson when Asquith transformed his Liberal government into a war coalition in 1915. This may not have seemed so important as it looks in retrospect: like most people, Redmond assumed that the war would be over within months, and he could hardly have foreseen the crushing impact that long-drawn-out postponement would have on the apparent triumph of 1914. But his refusal was also in part a tribute to the continuing potency of the old fear of a sell-out, and showed how conscious he was of possible threats to his position. Still, for the time being that position remained outwardly strong. His party won all five contested by-elections in Ireland between the outbreak of war and the Easter rebellion. Support for the Home Rule policy held up well, though there was clear evidence of growing weakness in the United Irish League's local structure.[6] In January 1915 the UIL General Secretary reported with muted but audible alarm that a 'considerable' number of branches had not paid their affiliation fees in 1914, a novel symptom which was to become still more marked in the next year.[7]

Although there was nothing like the upsurge of patriotic sentiment that greeted the war in Britain, outright opposition to the war was rare at first. David Fitzpatrick's vivid analysis of opinion in the west suggests that Irish people initially supported the war in principle, as long as they were not called upon to participate. Redmond's initial pledge 'at first provoked applause, then mutterings, then resentment'.[8] The National Volunteer organization began to suffer as time went by. When the Provisional Committee broke away from Redmond in September they took with them (on most calculations) a bare tenth of the rank and file, but the majority group had a much weaker sense of commitment and purpose, and began to melt away rapidly. Recruitment to the British army was fairly well sustained through 1915 (in Ulster it exceeded the British rate, in the rest of Ireland it ran at nearly two-thirds of it), but collapsed in 1916. The process of radicalization predated the Easter rebellion. Even the optimistic Augustine Birrell felt a change of atmosphere from his study of the local press in late 1915 – 'an increasing *exaltation of spirit* and a growth in confidence. ... I feel the Irish situation one of actual menace.'

The germination of rebellion

Just what kind of menace existed could not, however, have been grasped by anyone outside a tiny group within the Irish Republican Brotherhood. Throughout 1915 a quiet power struggle was going on amongst the breakaway Irish Volunteers. IRB activists had been at the heart of the Volunteer movement from its inception, sharing control with leaders who had made their reputations in the Gaelic League. The IRB had, traditionally, a simple attitude to an event like a European war: it would create 'England's difficulty', and thus 'Ireland's opportunity'. But there was no simple Fenian way of grasping that opportunity. The men who ran the IRB Supreme Council before 1914, Bulmer Hobson and Denis McCullough, took the IRB constitution seriously and maintained that the lives of its members should not be risked unless there was a real prospect of success. For Hobson, as for MacNeill outside the IRB, it made sense to wait for Britain to make a false move (historically, a virtual inevitability) and then use the Volunteers to mobilize the people for a campaign of mass resistance. As J. J. ('Ginger') O'Connell, the one member of the Volunteer Executive with military experience (acquired in South Africa), put it, the government was 'in a cleft stick'. Others, led by the conspiratorial traditionalist Tom Clarke, wanted to seize the day and strike, whatever the risk. The key adherent of this view was not the ageing Clarke but the 30-year-old Sean MacDermott (MacDiarmada), who had been picked out by Hobson as a gifted and utterly committed organizer, and whose fearsome energy survived a crippling poliomyelitis attack in 1912.

It was MacDermott who brought into the IRB the man who was to lead the rebellion and, vitally, to give it its unique moral cast – Patrick Pearse. Pearse made his reputation as a Gaelic League enthusiast and an educational reformer. For him, as for other cultural nationalists, the British 'national school' system was anything but national: it was the 'murder machine' engineered to kill the Irish language and the national spirit with it. He set up a series of experimental schools, each hovering on the brink of bankruptcy but energetically projecting an ethos of heroic struggle. His last and most successful school, St Enda's, was saturated with the spirit of the legendary warrior Cuchulainn, whose dark-age boast 'I care not if I live but one day and one night, if my fame and my deeds live after me' was enshrined in stained glass over the door.

Pearse uniquely fused Cuchulainn's triumphal violence with Christ's sacrifice to produce a Gaelicized and aestheticized kind of muscular Christianity. His message was propounded in a growing torrent of essays and poems in which the incitement to violence was all but direct – as in the peroration of the 1912 poem *Mionn* (Oath),

an imposing litany of apostolic figures from Christ, Mary and St
Patrick through to Tone, Emmet and 'the Famine Corpses', pledging

> That we will free our race from bondage,
> Or that we will fall fighting hand to hand
> Amen[9]

Most people, including perhaps even Pearse's loyal ex-pupils like the
poet Thomas MacDonagh, thought that this ferocity was rhetorical
rather than practical. But Pearse was building a profound moral basis
for direct action, which could not only inspire and legitimize
rebellion, but redefine the notion of success. This was to cast a long
shadow over the twentieth century in Ireland.

Pearse's reaction to the European war was not exactly the stuff of
traditional Fenianism, but it brilliantly served the purposes of Clarke
and MacDermott. To Pearse, the 'millions of lives given gladly for love
of country' were an inspiration – 'the most august homage ever offered
to God'. Nowhere in the literature of nationalism has the divine
purpose of the nation been more directly attested. Pearse became a
member of the unofficial 'military council' of the IRB – unknown to
either the President of the Supreme Council or the Irish Volunteer
Executive – which began to plan a military strike. Early in 1915 he
became Director of Military Organization on the newly established
Headquarters Staff (formerly Executive) of the Volunteers. In August
he was chosen to deliver the graveside address at a great Fenian event,
the funeral of the old 'skirmisher' Jeremiah O'Donovan Rossa. Here
he gave the motif of sacrifice its most direct political expression: 'from
the graves of patriot men and women spring living nations'; 'the
Defenders of the Realm think thay have ... foreseen everything, think
that they have provided against everything, but the fools! the fools! the
fools! – they have left us our Fenian dead ...'. The impression he made
was literally unforgettable. As one onlooker wrote, 'the people of
Dublin never heard quite such speeches as he gave them'.[10]

The Rossa funeral served notice of the IRB's intentions to anyone
with eyes to see. And indeed it was not only Augustine Birrell but also
Eoin MacNeill who became a little alarmed at this stage. In
September MacNeill went to a Volunteer review in Limerick, and was
taken aback to find that some of the local commanders had received
private instructions from Pearse to make certain 'definite military dis-
positions in the event of War in Ireland'.[11] In January 1916 he held a
meeting to try to assess the seriousness of the warlike noises coming

from a very different direction, James Connolly's Marxist newspaper the *Workers' Republic*. As late as December 1915 Connolly was still angrily denouncing Pearse's bloodthirsty rhetoric ('the world is sick of such teaching', he wrote),[12] but he was also moving towards an embrace of specifically Catholic nationalist symbols.

This shift may in part have been caused by recognition of labour's industrial weakness and the futility of its syndicalist ideas, in the wake of the failure of the 1913 strikes. Connolly widened his focus from the working class to the nation, aiming to use his Citizen Army to launch a revolt that would mobilize the Irish people as a whole. Although he had long castigated the ideological bankruptcy of the separatist 'physical force party', he certainly believed in the power of secular martyrdom to energize a social movement – witness his brilliant commentary on the IRB 'Manchester Martyrs' in November 1915: he could not respect their intelligence or political judgement, but celebrated their 'heroic souls'. 'How beggarly appear words before a defiant deed!'[13] He still cast his increasingly Fenian approach in Leninist terms, as an anti-imperialist (i.e. anti-capitalist) struggle, but by February 1916 he was writing 'we recognize that of us, as of mankind before Calvary, it may truly be said "without the shedding of blood there is no redemption"'.[14] The iconic force of the convergence of Connolly and Pearse was conveyed by Yeats in his potently symbolic poem 'The Rose Tree':

'But where can we draw water,'
Said Pearse to Connolly,
'When all the wells are parched away?
O plain as plain can be
There's nothing but our own red blood
Can make a right rose tree.'

Whether, in the process, Connolly abandoned and betrayed the labour movement is a question that has been fiercely debated ever since.[15] If labour did indeed lose its way, the course had been set some time before, when (as Roy Foster has pointed out) the ITGWU itself had become as much a nationalist as a labour organization.

Although Pearse, like most nationalists, disliked or feared socialism as an ideology, he was able to add a sentimental socialist tincture to his vision of national harmony. He gave this resonant, if sketchy, expression in his 1916 proclamation of the Republic, declaring 'the right of the people of Ireland to the ownership of Ireland', and asserting that the Republic 'guarantees equal rights and equal opportunities to all its citizens, and declares its resolve to pursue the happiness and prosperity of the whole nation and of all its parts, cherishing all the children of the nation equally'. But Pearse was clearly thinking more of the Protestants than the working class, and the means of realizing his benign vision remained the old-fashioned Fenian way, of simply removing the English: the new Republic would be 'oblivious of the differences carefully fostered by an alien government, which have divided a minority from the majority in the past'.

The rising: plans

Was the 1916 rebellion conceived as a heroic gesture, a blood sacrifice, or did its planners have a real expectation of success – that is, the actual establishment of an independent Irish republic? This is perhaps the question most often asked about the events of 1916. The evidence remains ambiguous. The secret military council's plans drawn up by Joseph Plunkett can be read both ways. They certainly had a defeatist look, at least in retrospect. By concentrating the limited forces available in Dublin, and seizing a handful of salient buildings, the rebels put themselves on the defensive and handed the operational initiative to their enemy. In the event they ensured that the rebellion would be a brief blaze of glory, just enough to lift the rising above the level of past failures. As Pearse told his forces, they had 'redeemed Dublin from many shames, and made her name splendid'.[16] The defensive approach, however, was not necessarily suicidal: it could also be seen as enshrining the best military wisdom. Plunkett was an amateur student of Clausewitz, whose insistence on the inherently greater strength of the defensive posture now appeared to have been overwhelmingly confirmed by the numbing trench battles on the western front in 1915. Connolly was a strong advocate of 'street fighting' as a way of maximizing the effect of small forces, and driving up the financial cost of repressive action (indeed he affected to think that capitalist governments would blench at destroying property on the scale that would be required). For Connolly, certainly, there was the lingering hope that a really dramatic insurrection could trigger a mass response. Ireland was a 'powder keg' of discontent.

Those who took a cooler view of the explosive potential of the Irish people argued that effective defiance of Britain would require extensive preparation, and a longer-term strategy of building up popular resistance. Whereas Connolly was prepared, when the crunch came, to come out and fight whatever the chances of success – as he said on Easter Monday morning, 'We are going out to be slaughtered' – MacNeill believed that a hopeless rising would be both immoral and counter-productive: it would set the national cause back a generation. It was MacNeill's disapproval that drove the conspirators to keep their plans secret, and this deception eventually produced an open conflict on Easter weekend, creating confusion that sharply reduced the number of Volunteers who joined the rising. After a series of discussions in early 1916, MacNeill approved the idea of pre-emptive action on the assumption that a large shipment of arms, obtained by Sir Roger Casement in Germany, would arrive in time to give the Volunteers a realistic fighting chance. The consignment – a rather miserly 20,000 captured Russian rifles, indicating German scepticism about the enterprise – was indeed despatched, but the ship was intercepted and scuttled. To keep MacNeill up to the mark, the military council concocted a fake 'Castle document' ordering the arrest of the Volunteer leadership (a policy actually advocated by the Lord-Lieutenant, but never implemented). When MacNeill discovered that the rising was planned to go ahead, with or without the German guns, on the Volunteers' national field day on Easter Sunday, he issued his famous 'countermanding order' cancelling the manoeuvres.[17]

This sequence of events strongly suggests that the leaders of the rising had, as Connolly so bluntly admitted, given up any real hope of military success. The carelessness of the arrangements made to receive and distribute the German arms shipment seems to bear this out. The German ship actually arrived off the Kerry coast on schedule after successfully running the British blockade, but the IRB leadership had unilaterally changed the landing date, too late for the captain to be told. If their failure to grasp the limits of German communications may possibly be understood, the failure to keep watch in the bay on the original date passes understanding. So does the fact that when the Dublin leaders decided to go ahead in spite of the countermanding order, they did not make any effort to involve the provincial forces. An alternative strategy was available. Both J. J. O'Connell in the Volunteers and Michael Mallin, deputy commander of the Citizen Army, had written thoughtfully about 'hedge fighting' and guerrilla warfare, a style of operations that would have meshed well with the longer-term planning favoured by Sinn Féin in Bulmer Hobson's pamphlet *Defensive Warfare*. It would have allowed the rebels to hold on to the initiative, and to minimize the effect of their numerical and technological inferiority: above all to survive. But it was a style that did not appeal to old-fashioned Fenians like Clarke and MacDermott, and certainly did not fit the apocalyptic vision of Pearse himself.

Easter week: the clash of arms

Arthur Griffith, who was not involved in planning the rising, but who knew enough about the grip of Fenianism on the national imagination to go out and get himself arrested, later put the events of 1916 in perspective, when he said that it was the British who saved Pearse from ultimate failure. British errors were a key dimension of the rising from start to finish. Although the 'Castle document' was a forgery, the policy it purported to announce should have been implemented in the week before Easter. In the event, MacNeill's countermand seemed to take the pressure off the authorities. Amazingly, the Commander-in-Chief took (unauthorized) home leave on Easter weekend, and most of his officers went off to the Fairyhouse races on Monday. When the insurgents came out on the streets of Dublin that morning, they were practically unopposed. About 1300 Irish Volunteers (belonging to the four battalions of the Dublin Brigade) and 219 of the Citizen Army seized five groups of large buildings, including Jacob's Biscuit Factory (2nd Battalion), Boland's Mill (3rd Battalion), the South Dublin Union (4th Battalion) and St Stephen's Green (Citizen Army). A half-hearted attempt to capture Dublin Castle was quickly aborted, despite the fact that the premier symbol of British rule was almost ungarrisoned.[18] A scratch force, subsequently but misleadingly called 'Headquarters Battalion' (including a group of recently returned emigrants, one of whom was Michael Collins), occupied the General Post Office on Sackville (O'Connell) Street, where James Connolly became military commander, and Pearse read the proclamation of the Provisional Government of the Irish Republic (Poblacht na hÉireann). His justly celebrated opening sentence trumpeted three crucial elements of nationalism, divine sanction, historical continuity, and elitism: 'In the name of God and the dead generations from which she receives her old tradition of nationhood, Ireland, through us, summons her children to her flag and strikes for her freedom'.

The defensive positions taken up by the insurgents were inherently strong, but were too far apart to allow mutual support or any flexible response to British counter-measures. Plunkett's original plan was evidently – though no complete copies of it have survived – made on the assumption that at least the full strength of the Dublin Brigade would be available; in the event, barely one-third turned out. The strength of each battalion was a product of chance, not planning. Thus the potentially impregnable South Dublin Union position was held by only 60 rebels. No command machinery existed to redeploy forces or supplies to areas where they were needed, so that the strong 2nd Battalion in Jacob's factory was practically inactive for the whole of the rising. Food supplies were a matter of chance and the voluntary efforts of Cumann na mBan, the women's nationalist organization in which Countess Markievicz was a leading light. There was no reserve force to dispute the gradual British isolation of the rebel positions. The most serious British setback, the slaughter of the newly arrived, inexperienced reinforcements advancing into Dublin at Mount Street Bridge, could easily have been avoided, since the Volunteers were unable to defend the nearby approaches to the city: the British commanders simply refused to take a detour. In this dogmatic rigidity, to the point of bone-headedness, the fight at Mount Street Bridge was a small but none the less ghastly precursor of the battle of the Somme three months later.

The British authorities could have relaxed at a fairly early stage, as soon as the numerical weakness of the rebels, and the fact that there was not going to be any German landing, became clear – as it was by Tuesday. In the event the reverse was the case. British military action became more intense and violent, peaking in the unnecessarily lethal (to their own raw recruits) assault on Mount Street Bridge and the artillery bombardment of Liberty Hall and the General Post Office. On Wednesday night the much-admired radical pacifist Frank Sheehy-Skeffington was taken out into the countryside and murdered by a deranged British officer. Less horrific but almost equally damaging assaults multiplied; as British troops tightened the cordon around the rebel positions, they found it fatally easy to confuse rebels and innocent civilians (their orders encouraged them to be suspicious). The truth was that the military plan 'for the prompt suppression of the existing disturbances' was carried out without any political advice or restraint. Whether the security objective justified the political costs was simply never discussed. The prestige of the civil government, which had underrated the risk of rebellion and refused to risk trying to disarm the militias, was overthrown. Birrell did his best to argue that the government should not over-react, but his only real option was resignation. The army was the only state department with an agenda during Easter week.

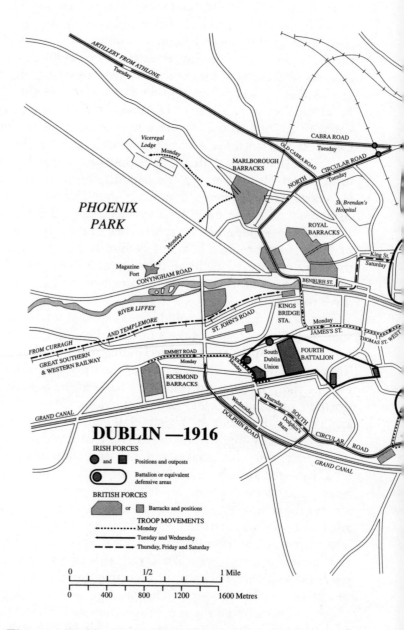

Fig 5.1 Dublin 1916: The Easter rising

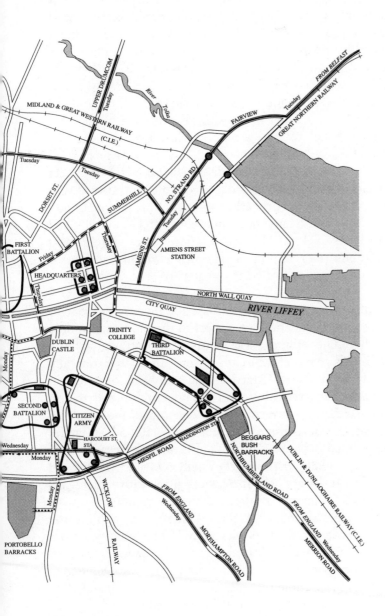

In strictly military terms the rising was doomed to defeat once it was clear that the country would not 'rise up'. Nearly all the provincial Volunteer units stayed at home. The most significant exception, giving a dramatic hint of what might have been (and would in future be), was the ambush carried out on Friday at Ashbourne, Co. Meath, by the Fingal Volunteers led by Thomas Ashe and Richard Mulcahy. A small RIC column surrendered after losing 10 dead and 18 wounded. (The problem of what to do with his prisoners might have troubled Ashe if the rebellion had gone on.) More typically, the two companies of Wexford Volunteers who turned out on 25 April joined up, waited for orders for a day, and then dispersed; Galway Volunteers assembled to attack a police barrack, but set up a camp instead. On Saturday Pearse surrendered. Altogether some 450 people, including 116 soldiers, had been killed, and 2600 injured. Central Dublin looked unnervingly like Ypres or Arras. The destruction had permitted mass looting by the Dublin poor, and brought down a wrathful chorus of middle-class condemnation on the heads of the Provisional Government.

Even now it might not have been too late for the government to attempt a gesture of reconciliation, an appeal to the moderate middle class. But British public opinion was predictably outraged by the treason of the rebels. Military measures went ahead without any political restraint or guidance. Martial law had been declared in Dublin at the start of the rebellion, and the Viceroy's proclamation was enlarged by the British government to encompass the whole of Ireland – even areas where there had been no outbreak. General Maxwell was appointed Military Governor. But since it became clear that (as Maxwell complained) the government had no intention of allowing martial law to be applied, these were provocative rhetorical gestures. After Pearse's surrender a large-scale programme of arrests was mounted 'to arrest dangerous Sinn Féiners' throughout the country, and some 3500 people were picked up.[19] This was even more provocative: 1500 of them were released within a few days. Of the rest, 160 were tried and convicted by court-martial (under the Defence of the Realm Act, but most people thought of it as martial law) and 1841 were interned. Between 3 and 12 May 15 of the leaders, including all the signatories of the Provisional Government proclamation and all the battalion commanders except Eamon de Valera (who had US citizenship), were shot. All these figures looked small in the shadow of the war in Europe, but the shock effect in Ireland grew larger day by day. Asquith woke up to the situation in time to save Countess Markievicz from death, and commissioned his most able minister, Lloyd George, to reopen the question of Home Rule.)

The legatees: Sinn Féin

The government may have had an inkling of the danger that the rising represented, but its freedom of manoeuvre had already been largely removed by its acceptance that Ulster's refusal of Home Rule would have to be respected. Lloyd George displayed all his famous negotiating skills in attempting to stitch together a compromise, or rather a fudge, over partition (telling Redmond it would be temporary and Carson it would be permanent) during the summer of 1916, but even these were not enough.[20] The impossibility of compromise had still not dawned on ministers. Henry Duke, Birrell's Conservative successor as Chief Secretary for Ireland, shared their ingrained belief that 'honest and intelligent men can always agree on some solution for a question'. Hence the Irish Convention, which opened in July 1917 under the chairmanship of Horace Plunkett. The shortsightedness of the British approach, and the depth of British misunderstanding of the situation in Ireland, was starkly displayed in the comment of the influential Geoffrey Dawson, editor of *The Times* – 'every day it sits is a day gained'.[21] The reverse was the case. Months of debate served only to underline the fact that Ulster resistance could not be fudged, and also that the claim of the old Irish parliamentary party to represent the nationalist position had been fatally subverted. Sinn Féin, which refused to attend the Convention, was poised to deliver it a death blow.

The government's damage limitation exercise was like British policy in Ireland as a whole, flawed both in conception and in execution. The increasingly desperate cries for help from the parliamentary party were ignored. Martial law was seen as a way of encouraging the law-abiding majority to support the state. Instead it alienated them. The release of the internees around Christmas 1916 (an as yet obscure Volunteer captain from the Headquarters Battalion, Michael Collins, was released on 21 December), 'instead of exciting gratitude', as the government hoped, drove the process on. The Inspector-General of the RIC lamented that 'their release is by ignorant country folk regarded as proof that they were interned without any just cause'.[22]

Collins and his fellow internees had used their time in prisons and camps like Frongoch to lay the foundations for the reorganization of the national movement. The key to this was the linkage of the Volunteers to Sinn Féin, a party which could supply them with a distinctive political platform and strategy. Collins himself pushed this fusion ahead as soon as he returned to Ireland, first campaigning for Count Plunkett (Joseph Plunkett's father) who won the Roscommon by-election as an independent Sinn Féiner in February, and next going on to put up one of the Volunteers' own men still imprisoned in Lewes gaol, Frank McGuinness, for the Longford by-election in May. To do this he had to overcome the traditionalist Fenian resistance of the prisoners' leader, Eamon de Valera, the 3rd Battalion commandant during the rising, and the sole commandant to survive, who pronounced the idea 'extremely dangerous from several points of view' and advised McGuinness not to stand. One danger was of course that he might lose; Collins's vigorous electoral tactics, including the famous slogan 'Put him in to get him out', and probably some creative use of the electoral roll, ensured that this did not happen.[23]

During 1917 Sinn Féin was transformed into a coherent political movement that rapidly picked up the support that was melting away from the old parliamentary party. The process of transformation was not wholly straightforward. As late as March a well-informed journal could say that 'there is no such thing at present as a Sinn Féin party'.[24] Count Plunkett made an attempt to use his early success as a springboard for remodelling Griffith's party around himself. Griffith saw this challenge off – Plunkett agreed to the merging of his Liberty Clubs into Sinn Féin in May – but then faced the prospect of a bruising struggle to retain control of the rapidly enlarging movement against the most prestigious of the 1916 veterans, de Valera. On his release from Lewes in June, de Valera immediately and effortlessly achieved the status of a national icon. Like Parnell before him, he had a potent charisma that was not easy to explain, but impossible not to recognize. He possessed real political substance as soon as he embarked on his long career of carefully constructed verbal formulae. His triumph in the East Clare by-election in August 1917 was a vital moment in the emergence of Sinn Féin as a major political force. Characteristically, he campaigned on a fierce but flexible platform: 'we want an Irish republic ... but if the Irish people wanted to have another form of government, so long as it was an Irish government, I would not put in a word against it'.

Sinn Féin's profile was insistently raised over the summer of 1917. The hostile *Freeman's Journal* noted ominously that 70 Sinn Féin clubs were formed in the first fortnight of June; the police counted 336 branches by the end of July.[25] The grass-roots growth can be followed from townland to townland as each new club encouraged its comrades in neighbouring areas. Irish Volunteer stalwarts abandoned any lingering traces of Fenian suspicion, and revelled in the sheer excitement of political activism and electioneering. The culminating point in the process was the national convention (Ard-fheis) held on 25 October, attended by some 1700 delegates representing some 1000 clubs – virtually one for each Catholic parish in the country. Griffith retained strong support, but stood aside to allow de Valera to be elected unopposed as President (Priomh-aire), the multi-layered title that would be so closely associated with him through the next five years. Here the recognizably Valeraesque formulation of the party's policy was agreed: Ireland must become independent, but 'having achieved that status the Irish people may by Referendum freely choose their own form of government'.

The growth of Sinn Féin as a truly national movement was made possible by the participation of the Volunteers in politics, and was finally to be cemented by the approval of the Church. The symbolic turning-point was the death of Thomas Ashe, hero of Ashbourne, head of the IRB, and de Valera's only rival in terms of prestige. Arrested for a 'seditious' speech in July, he demanded political status, and died in Mountjoy gaol under clumsy force-feeding after a hunger strike that electrified the country. His funeral on 30 September became (predictably, by all but the government) a major national event; thousands of uniformed Volunteers from all over Ireland assembled in Dublin to escort his body to Glasnevin cemetery, where a volley was fired over his grave. Michael Collins, Ashe's successor as head of the IRB, delivered a laconic funeral address – a single sentence declaring that the rifle volley that had just been fired 'is the only speech it is proper to make over the grave of a dead Fenian'. The fusion of elegiac and violent tones was arresting; and perhaps more threatening to the government than even this chilling drama was the fact that for the first time a Fenian funeral procession was accompanied by a Catholic bishop.

The crisis of 1918

The government was no longer in touch with the situation in Ireland, and its vacillating policy was the despair of the endangered Redmondite party. The tough reaction to the hunger strike was followed by a hasty retreat in the face of public outrage at Ashe's death. His fellow hunger-strikers were released, but then re-arrested. The general belief that Ireland was being kept under martial law steadily alienated moderate public opinion, and the protracted discussions of the Convention looked ever more pointless in the absence of Sinn Féin. Even so, some hope for the constitutional party remained, and in early 1918 it was still strong enough to win three by-elections in a row. If 1916 had changed everything utterly, the full extent of that change was not finally revealed until the British government took the fatal step of announcing that compulsory military service would at last be implemented in Ireland. In March 1918 the German army broke through the British front, and the decisive moment of the long trench war seemed to be imminent. Estimates of the military value of imposing conscription varied; some experts forecast that the number of troops extracted would barely exceed the number required to enforce the law in the face of organized resistance. In any case, they would not be available in time to affect the German offensive. The key issue for the government was British public opinion, or the patriotic press, which refused to tolerate Irish shirking.

The impact of the Military Service Bill (10 April 1918) on Irish public opinion was, as MacNeill and Hobson had always predicted, deadly for the Union. Lloyd George's accompanying promise of Home Rule was inept and implausible. An unprecedented coalition of nationalists rallied to the Sinn Féin banner to repudiate what the Hierarchy denounced as an 'oppressive and inhuman law'. Barely a month after the broken John Redmond had died of heart failure, the parliamentary party at last walked out of the House of Commons and returned to Ireland, the labour movement mounted a one-day national strike, and the Church held masses of intercession across the country. On 17 April the Hierarchy declared that 'the Irish' had the right to resist conscription 'by every means that are consonant with the laws of God'. Even this proviso was subtly dissolved in the pledge taken at church doors the following Sunday 'to resist conscription by the most effective means at our disposal'.

The government responded by appointing Field-Marshal Lord French as Viceroy – a gift to nationalist propagandists. Ironically, French, who was generally believed to be a 'military governor', could not get the government to agree to the use of martial law. As so often, the authorities thus reaped the maximum odium for the minimum effect. He proceeded to arrest the Sinn Féin leadership under the Defence of the Realm Act on the basis of a 'German plot'. Sadly enough, the intelligence services did not simply invent this plot as a convenient excuse for disposing of their opponents, they actually thought that it existed. Their understanding of Sinn Féin was already minimal, and their ability to penetrate the reborn Volunteer organization was limited, both by the decline of the police intelligence system, and by the strength of commitment of the new nationalist movement. By the time of the 'German plot' arrests, Michael Collins was already capable of getting advance warning of police plans, and he went into hiding. De Valera and Griffith preferred to be arrested. Thus the leadership of Sinn Féin passed into the hands of a more vigorous and extreme-republican younger generation, probably not the result intended by Lord French. The dynamic Harry Boland, working closely with Collins, doubled the number of Sinn Féin branches (*cumainn*) – whose total membership rose from 66,270 to 112,080 – between May and the general election in December. In June the head of the RIC reported that in parts of the country there was 'a fairly wide estrangement of the people from law and order, and a contempt of authority' which made it useless to imagine that arresting a few leaders would stop the rot.[26]

The end of the Great War in November 1918 precipitated a seismic political upheaval in Ireland. The Irish situation remained marginal to Lloyd George's concerns when he went to the country next month, but in 'a bitter and ugly election, with no holds barred on either side', as Lyons describes it, Sinn Féin virtually annihilated the great party of Parnell and Redmond. The 'sides' fighting it out were not nationalist versus Unionist, but separatist versus Home Rule nationalist. Labour, in what came to seem a serious miscalculation, chose not to contest the election, and missed its chance to appeal to the newly enfranchised younger electorate. Between the new and old nationalist parties there was no such generosity. Only in Ulster, where Joe Devlin's tightly controlled domain held together, and where almost all of the surviving Home Rulers sat, did Sinn Féin stand aside in their favour. The old party plunged from 68 seats to 6; Sinn Féin leapt from 7 to 73. Only in two constituencies (Joe Devlin's Belfast and William Redmond's Waterford) did Home Rulers successfully fight off a Sinn Féin challenge (the other four survived by electoral pacts with Sinn Féin). As one political scientist has recently emphasized, this 'was one of the greatest electoral landslides in western Europe in the twentieth century'; in particular, the virtual annihilation of a major party is almost unique.[27] Implicit in the destruction of the constitutionalist party was the destruction of the United Kingdom. Sinn Féin candidates often played down the party's republican commitment, to an extent that may undermine the claims of present-day republicans about the mandate delivered by the election, but even the dual-monarchist aim of Griffith's conservative wing of Sinn Féin was far more radical than anything Britain had yet been prepared to consider. By the end of December it had become, as the doughty old Tory Walter Long warned his uncomprehending Cabinet colleagues (more concerned with the stupendous problems of postwar reconstruction and European peacemaking), 'a fair and square fight between the Irish Government and Sinn Féin as to who is going to govern the country'.[28]

|6|

The first republic and the Anglo-Irish war, 1919–1922

The shots fired at Soloheadbeg, Co. Tipperary, on 21 January 1919, killing two RIC men guarding a cartload of gelignite on its way to a quarry, are generally taken to have opened hostilities in what has come to be called the Irish War of Independence. More colloquially, and revealingly, it is the 'Tan War', remembered as a bitter conflict that brought out the worst on both sides. The Irish Volunteers abandoned the Fenian dream of open war, in favour of a guerrilla campaign of ambush and assassination; the British unleashed the 'Black and Tans' to plunge into the murky depths of counter-terrorism. Something like the original Sinn Féin strategy of civil resistance was also implemented, though often at gunpoint as much as by conviction. The result was the last, and most decisive, paralysis of British governing capacity in Ireland.

Sinn Féin, Dáil Éireann, and the IRA

By chance, the Soloheadbeg ambush happened on the same day that the victorious Sinn Féin members of parliament – at least the half of them who were not in jail (de Valera stayed in Lincoln jail until Collins and Boland staged a famous escape on 3 February) – met in the Dublin Mansion House to constitute themselves the Irish national assembly, Dáil Éireann, and issued a Declaration of Independence. 'We solemnly declare foreign government in Ireland to be an invasion of our national right which we will never tolerate, and we demand the evacuation of our country by the English Garrison.' The Tipperary

Volunteers had been trying to mount their ambush for some time, but as other guerrilla fighters would soon discover, such things could not be timed with precision. By killing policemen they deliberately raised the stakes, intending to ensure that the Sinn Féin political leadership could not sell out or compromise the republican demand.

The deep-set Fenian distrust of the political process endured, despite the fact that many of the new members of the Dáil (officially named 'Deputies' in English, Teachtai Dála in Irish – colloquially Anglicized as 'TDs') were themselves Volunteers. Sinn Féin had mushroomed too swiftly to be an entirely coherent body. Arthur Griffith's original idea of abstention and passive resistance leading to the establishment of a dual monarchy still had real force, both as a method and as an objective. Griffith himself retained great prestige, but his decision to make way for de Valera indicated the tendency of the enlarged Sinn Féin to favour more radical aims and more violent means. The acting Speaker (Ceann Comhairle) of the Dáil at its first meeting was an unblinking republican die-hard, Cathal Brugha, who confirmed the unanimous vote in favour of the Declaration of Independence with the terse words, 'Deputies, you understand from what is asserted in this Declaration that we are now done with England'.[1]

The Dáil was an unselfconsciously Catholic assembly; it opened with a prayer read in Irish by Father Michael O'Flanagan, the Vice-President of Sinn Féin. It adopted a Democratic Programme (albeit one noticeably toned down from the original draft composed by the Labour leaders Thomas Johnson and William O'Brien) declaring 'the right of every citizen to an adequate share of the produce of the nation's labour', and promising to abolish the 'odious, degrading and foreign poor-law system', to develop Irish industry and 'ensure the physical as well as the moral well-being of the nation'. Labour's reward for standing aside in the general election was all too modest.[2]

The Dáil also issued a 'Message to the Free Nations of the World', as part of its bid to secure a hearing at the Paris Peace Conference, on which many of Sinn Féin's hopes rested. (The hard-bitten veteran parliamentarian Tim Healy witheringly recorded a meeting with youthfully enthusiastic Sinn Féin leaders – including Collins – who 'blithered of the gorgeous precedents of the Yugo-Slavs and the Shugs Blabs and the Boobo Kalves'.[3]) The Message specified that 'nationally, the race, the language, the customs and traditions of Ireland are radically distinct from the English', and referred to 'the existing state of war between Ireland and England', which 'can never be ended until

Ireland is definitely evacuated by the armed forces of England'. This was the nearest the Dáil came to a declaration of war as such, but the Volunteers' journal *An tOglach* made it clear that they were justified in 'treating the armed forces of the enemy – whether soldiers or policemen – exactly as a National Army would treat an invading army'. This deftly elided the question whether the Volunteers actually were the national army. They were never formally proclaimed as such, and it was not until April 1921 that de Valera as President of the Dáil publicly took responsibility for their actions. Cathal Brugha, as Minister for Defence in de Valera's Cabinet, proposed that all Volunteer units should take an oath of allegiance to the Dáil, but this was only erratically administered. Also erratic, but more enthusiastic, was the adoption by most Volunteer units of a new title, Irish Republican Army (IRA): oddly, not the Army of the Irish Republic, and a title never rendered in Irish. Essentially there were still two nationalist organizations in operation, closely intertwined but with distinct core values. Eventually this was to help trigger a political catastrophe. But in 1919 the confluence of political and military forces was dynamic and creative; for the first time, as Connolly might have said, the physical force party had a brain. The virtual republic of Dáil Éireann was a real political triumph.

The Dáil counter-state

The idea of a unilateral declaration of independence was the key to Sinn Féin strategy, but little thought had been given to how the rebellious national assembly should make good its claim to be the *de jure* government of Ireland. Inspirational works of Sinn Féin propaganda such as Darrell Figgis's *The Gaelic State* (1917) argued for the local devolution of power, but implied that the precise forms of an authentic Irish government could not be established until the people had recovered their 'surety of intuition' by returning to their national language. This postponed things for some time, and in 1919 something had to be done immediately. Griffith's notion of civil resistance involved subverting the functions of government by establishing alternative structures, and this impelled the would-be revolutionaries towards direct duplication, and in effect imitation, of British administrative structures. So a Cabinet was set up (using the British title), with ministers responsible for internal and external affairs (Griffith and Plunkett), defence (Brugha), finance (Collins), local government

(W. T. Cosgrave), labour (Countess Markievicz), and industry (Eoin MacNeill). There was also a Director of Publicity, and a Director of Trade and Commerce, and in June 1919 two further ministers, for fisheries and for 'the national language' (to which was later added, as an afterthought, education).[4]

The paradoxical Britishness of so much of the system set up by these crusading de-Anglicizers has often been noted, but lacks a wholly satisfactory explanation. British tropes and habits pervaded the republican structure. The Declaration of Independence itself was constructed in a quintessentially English style – 'Whereas ... Whereas ... Whereas ... Now we ...' – and while some (recognizably English) functionaries, such as the Speaker, were instantly and permanently re-labelled with Gaelic titles (Ceann Comhairle), many (like the Chief Clerk, a pivotal figure) were not. The reasons put forward for this incongruity, even by critics of 'our marked tendency to imitate British precedent', focus on the pressure of events and circumstances in 1919–21. Joseph Lee, for instance, suggests that 'the leaders had no time to meditate at leisure on the constitutional arrangements of other countries, or to think through the deeper implications of their own behaviour. They were virtually under siege.'[5] But so, of course, have been many if not most revolutionaries in history. Many of them, however, took power already equipped with a theory of revolution and a blueprint for a new social and political order. The Irish revolution seems to lack just that theoretical impulse and control, reflecting, surely, the long-standing simplicity of Fenian assumptions about sovereignty. Even the more intellectual Sinn Féin had no administrative blueprint for the future. As a result, pragmatism would triumph over idealism time and again – most weightily, as will be seen later, in the eventual survival of both the British legal system and civil service.

On 17 June, by which time there was some public speculation about what the Dáil was up to, the ministry presented its 'constructive programme', involving the establishment of a consular service abroad, the promotion of fisheries and forestry, land redistribution fostered by arbitration courts, and a commission of inquiry into national resources. This was a fairly ambitious programme for an administration with little experience and few resources, whose difficulties were dramatically increased when Dáil Éireann was proclaimed an illegal association on 11 September, followed in late November by Sinn Féin, the Irish Volunteers, Cumann na mBan, and, for good measure, the Gaelic League. From then on this was an underground counter-state, and the extent to which its departments could achieve real results depended on the skill and determination of individual min-isters. The co-ordinating power of de Valera was hardly exerted before it was removed. Suddenly and surprisingly, after a bare three months spent in hiding in Ireland, de Valera decided to go to the USA to press Ireland's case for recognition. It became clear in May that the Irish case was not going to get a hearing at the Paris Peace Conference, and de Valera's trip was intended to be brief. In the event he stayed in the USA until December 1920, leaving the acting presidency of the Dáil to Griffith. The effect of this is hard to calculate; Griffith was hard-working and meticulous in attending meetings and handling corre-spondence, but despite his forceful character, strong views and great prestige, he seems to have made surprisingly little impression on the process of policy-making.[6]

What is plain is that in de Valera's absence, the career of Michael Collins blossomed. He was easily the most dynamic minister, and combined his civil function with a central role in the direction of the IRA (nominally as Director of Intelligence, but effectively a virtual commander-in-chief). He launched a loan scheme designed to raise £250,000, against bonds repayable by the future independent Irish state. This was a key idea because it tied fund-raising into the legit-imacy of the Dáil's claim to be the government of Ireland. Collins threw himself into the task with his habitual energy, and exploitation of his own charisma: he invested £600 in commissioning a short film of himself receiving applications, and used the Volunteers to get it shown in cinemas across the country (a pioneering move that should have disposed of the myth that only one photograph of Collins was available to the British authorities). The experience of conducting the loan was invigorating but also a bruising one for Collins, who wrote to Harry Boland 'I never imagined there would be so much cowardice, dishonesty, hedging, insincerity, and meanness in the world as my experience of this work has revealed'.[7] Despite this unflattering view of Irish patriotic spirit, Collins raised the not unimpressive total of £371,848 from around 150,000 people by the closure of the loan on 17 July 1920.

Other crucial aspects of the counter-state were developed by the department of local government, which fostered a dramatic seizure of local power in the course of 1920, when Sinn Féin came to dominate the urban councils (elected in January) and the county councils (June), many of which ostentatiously severed their connection with the Dublin Castle Local Government Board. Perhaps the most important of all these developments were the arbitration courts foreshadowed on the constructive programme. The idea was not new; it stemmed from the courts set up by the Land League and the United Irish League, with still deeper pre-echoes in the tradition of peasant 'midnight courts'. Griffith pointed to examples in Cavan and Kerry early in 1919, but neither he nor his successor as Home Minister, Austin Stack (whose erstwhile friend Collins eventually rounded on him with the charge 'your department is just a bloody joke'), did anything about it. As with so many of the most effective policies, it was local initiative that took advantage of the work of the Dáil Land Commission headed by Kevin O'Shiel to multiply arbitration courts in the spring of 1920. Once they began, these tribunals were dramatically successful in taking business away from the British court system. The *Manchester Guardian* commented on 10 May that they were the 'natural result of the strong common will for independence and national responsibility', while a *Daily Mirror* reporter attending a court in Galway described it as 'an extraordinary exhibition of despatch, efficiency, and, if the truth be told, a fairness bordering on Quixotism'.

On 29 June 1920 the Dáil met for the first time in eight months, and resolved to establish a national court system: instead of arbitration courts, these would have the theoretical power of original jurisdiction. The system blossomed in the summer as hastily recruited judges and court officials improvised procedures whose spontaneity offered the fleeting prospect of a truly popular legal system. The legal professionals looked at it askance, but while solicitors soon followed their clients into the illegal courts, barristers refused to – the Bar Council ruled it professional misconduct – so the revolutionary prospect of a non-adversarial system opened up. The dreams of Gaelic scholars who had rediscovered the old Brehon law seemed suddenly to be practicable. By late 1920 there were three elected judges in each parish, and each Dáil constituency had a District Court with five judges, elected by the parish justices. The jurisdiction of parish courts was limited to minor criminal cases and civil cases involving claims of less than £10; more serious cases were handled by the District Court on thrice-annual circuit. A Supreme Court, of four professional judges (paid £750 a year from August 1920), was given unlimited jurisdiction. It is possible, indeed, that the 'Dáil courts' offered the most substantial possibility of a real Irish revolution, but this possibility was gradually to be choked off. In the end, the weight of the old British structures proved too heavy for these anarchic shoots to break through. Lawyers were strongly represented in the republican leadership, and the Cabinet like most governments preferred the coercive regularity of the system it knew. Increasingly the Volunteers were used as 'republican police', rules became stricter and more comprehensive, the adversarial system returned, and the legal professionals co-opted the new courts.[8]

The guerrilla struggle

In tandem with the construction of the republican government went the steadily escalating military campaign of the Irish Volunteers. Dramatic events like Soloheadbeg remained sporadic in 1919, but they were straws in the wind; in June a district inspector of the RIC was shot dead in broad daylight; in September the North Cork Brigade of the IRA attacked a platoon of soldiers marching to church on Sunday and captured all their weapons. All the time, the more energetically led units were training, raiding big houses for guns, and sniping at police stations. The police were the principal targets of the first phase of the guerrilla campaign: their ubiquity and small numbers made them obvious targets, and the organization of a public boycott helped the Volunteers to extend their local networks. The political branches of both the RIC and the Dublin Metropolitan Police came under particularly intense attack, with Collins organizing his famous 'Squad' to systematically assassinate the Special Branch in Dublin. Collins and Richard Mulcahy, who became Chief of Staff in the revamped General Headquarters of the IRA, laboured ceaselessly to centralize the command and control of the local Volunteers. The two of them shared the functions of overall command, as far as it could be exerted, and other GHQ staff pushed the development of training, organization, engineering, and so on. An elaborate organizational structure existed on paper, with one or two brigades to each county – three in the most active, such as Cork and Tipperary – but the source of the movement's vitality remained local, the companies and battalions that had grown up around the Sinn Féin clubs.

By early 1920 a noticeable gap was opening up between the most active units, which were beginning to attempt attacks on bigger RIC barracks, and those which had scarcely managed to acquire a handful of modern weapons. The IRA's weapon supply was always tenuous, and a sense of inferiority clearly paralysed many units in areas where there was no tradition of local resistance. Attacking the RIC, even in its declining state, required some nerve. In May, Mulcahy issued a general order prohibiting unauthorized action, explaining that 'This order is not intended to restrict the "imperturbable offensive spirit" of our forces, but rather to preserve this spirit by preventing it running riot in hasty action to its own detriment'.[9] This was a careful way of saying that discipline left much to be desired, and that planning was too often unsystematic. To local complaints about shortages of guns, or overwhelming enemy strength, he replied that intelligent planning could overcome such problems. The 'offensive against communications', for instance, was a way of neutralizing the British advantage in motor transport by cutting roads and restricting military and police patrols to routes offering good ambush prospects. Despite all such chivvying, however, the most consistent IRA success was against softer but politically sensitive targets. The burning of abandoned police stations and big houses always seized public attention, and the intimidation of witnesses and jurors not only safeguarded the Volunteers themselves from arrest and prosecution but also humiliated the British state by demonstrating the impotence of its legal machinery. During the 1920 summer assizes the circuit judges were repeatedly handed the white gloves, symbolizing the absence of criminal cases, even in areas of less intense IRA activity.

A major shift in the impact of the IRA campaign followed in the autumn, partly as a result of their success in bringing the British courts to a standstill. The IRA remained a part-time, often nocturnal fighting force, but draconian repressive legislation (the Restoration of Order in Ireland Act, below p. 100) forced many active Volunteers to give up their day jobs and go 'on the run'. Forming these men into permanent 'Active Service Units' was a way of helping them to survive, as well as of increasing the IRA's ability to mount serious ambushes and tackle hard military targets. In the autumn of 1920 some of these 'flying columns' began to pose a significant threat to British patrols and convoys, even to the more formidable mobile forces then appearing, especially the Auxiliary Division of the RIC. The most spectacular IRA actions came in November. On the 21st, 'Bloody Sunday', Collins's Squad and the Dublin Brigade Active Service Unit killed a dozen suspected British secret intelligence officers. A week later the West Cork flying column commanded by Tom Barry, an ex-soldier with a need to demonstrate his republican ruthlessness, annihilated an Auxiliary patrol at Kilmichael. After a fierce fight, all survivors were shot.[10]

But it is possible that the republican action which did most to radicalize Irish opinion in the autumn of 1920 was the hunger-strike of Terence MacSwiney, who had become Lord Mayor of Cork when his

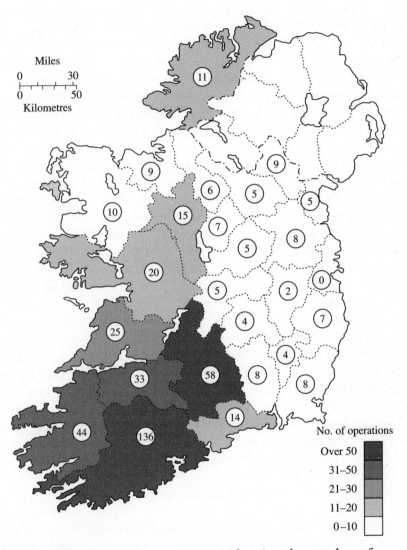

Fig. 6.1 IRA operations, 1919–1921 (showing the number of significant operations in the periods 1 Sept 1919–30 June 1920 and 1 January–30 April 1921, omitting Dublin city and county; information for Northern Ireland not available)

Source: Chronology of the Bureau of Military History 1913–1921 (Dublin)

old Volunteer comrade Thomas MacCurtain was assassinated in March 1920. MacSwiney and MacCurtain had surrendered the Cork Volunteers' weapons to the authorities during Easter week, baffled by the confusion of the orders they had received. MacSwiney celebrated the execution of Sir Roger Casement after the rising as a nationalist victory, saying that he joined 'the long heroic line of martyrs to English misrule'.[11] After release from internment, MacSwiney became a typically polymorphous republican activist, serving simultaneously as commandant of an IRA battalion, Sinn Féin branch organizer, Dáil deputy, writer of idealistic political essays ('there are moral horrors worse than any physical horror, and freedom must be had at any cost of suffering'[12]), and finally Mayor of Cork. Mayor MacCurtain's death was popularly blamed on the police, and a coroner's jury brought in a spectacular verdict of murder against the local RIC, the Inspector-General, and the Prime Minister. MacSwiney's arrest in August 1920 gave him the opportunity to demonstrate the strength of his own belief that 'victory is won not by those who can inflict the most but by those who can endure the most'. His refusal to recognize the court martial that tried him ('Facing our enemy we must declare an attitude simply. We see in their regime a thing of evil incarnate') and his 73-day hunger strike in Brixton prison became a national and even international epic. Though other republican prisoners were also on hunger strike, and two died in Cork gaol, MacSwiney's fast ensured his immortality. When he died on 25 October he took his place in that line of martyrs whose inspirational power he had so clearly recognized, and powerfully projected into the future.[13] Even more than Thomas Ashe, MacSwiney symbolized the all-consuming dedication evoked by the republican cause.

A nation in arms?

The republican publicity organization which formed an integral part of the Dáil government was extremely effective in building up a picture of full-scale national mobilization behind the counter-state and its army. The litany of British atrocities in the *Irish Bulletin*, a mimeographed underground fortnightly edited by Desmond FitzGerald and later Erskine Childers, with the help of many of the Sinn Féin leaders, helped to convince public opinion in countries like France and the USA, and to some extent even in Britain, that Irish resistance was unanimous.[14] The *Bulletin* was a great propaganda triumph, but modern historians have been more sceptical of the image it projected. While the IRA certainly could not have operated as effectively as it did if Irish public opinion had been hostile, the rebels themselves were acutely conscious of widespread indifference. The regional variations in the intensity of guerrilla action were never ironed out; in some counties hardly a shot was fired during the whole conflict. Even in a strongly republican area like north Cork, many nominal revolutionaries were – at least in the opinion of the IRA commander – 'an absolute failure ... if anything they were a burden on the Army'.[15] Historians have also tended to stress the salience of social divisions in postwar Ireland, the growing incidence of strikes in 1919, and the marked conservatism of the Sinn Féin mainstream. This was a middle-class revolution. Arthur Griffith, the printer and self-taught journalist, was the archetype of his party. Two-thirds of the Dáil, and a larger proportion of the ministry and local leadership, were urban professionals – journalists, clerks, lawyers – while only a third was drawn from agriculture (10 per cent) or industry and commerce (22 per cent – a proportion sharply reduced at the leadership level).[16]

The wave of strikes did not quite revive the syndicalist promise (or menace) of 1913, but it demonstrated the frustration that Irish labour shared with its European counterparts in the postwar economic climate. Though the labour movement remained patriotic, and the transport workers (perhaps with some encouragement from the Volunteers) imposed a major embargo on British troops and stores through much of 1920, it was clear that the vague aspirations enshrined in the Democratic Programme were less authentic than de Valera's frank warning 'labour may wait' as an expression of Sinn Féin attitudes. (In 1921 the Dáil Minister for Labour was to be demoted from the Cabinet.) Sinn Féin also took a jaundiced view of the revival of the land war in the west that began with cattle-drives and land seizures in the last year of the Great War. The enforced suspension of emigration during the war inevitably increased the pressure on land, and it was to defuse this explosive potential that the land courts were regularized in 1920. As the Dáil's agriculture director Art O'Connor noted, it was 'a curious anomaly' that the first section of the community to call for the setting up of a judiciary responsible to the Dáil were 'those aggrieved landlords, mostly persons with strong British sympathies and hence opposed to the Republic'.[17]

Sinn Féin was semantically proto-feminist (the 1916 proclamation had summoned 'Irishmen and Irishwomen' as Ireland's 'children' to her flag, though it had gone on to make clear that only 'her manhood' had been trained for combat). It was succesful in mobilizing women, principally through Cumann na mBan, but the very fact of creating a separate organization spoke for itself. In Constance Markievicz the Dáil possessed an emblematic figure – in 1918 she was the first woman to be elected to the British parliament (where of course she never took her seat), and she was already a famous veteran of the Fianna and the Irish Citizen Army, with which she had fought on Stephen's Green in 1916, with an instinct for self-publicization – but her gentry class background perhaps as much as her gender kept her out of the central leadership of the movement. Cumann na mBan itself was, as one historian has said, 'self-professedly ancillary to the Volunteer struggle', and is noticeably absent from the leading general histories of this period. Some of its members did come close to a combat role in the IRA's urban fighting. Exploiting the severe shortage of women in the Crown forces, making it practically impossible for them to search women on the streets, women could act as walking arms caches to enable IRA hit men to carry out assassinations. The proscription of Cumann na mBan alongside Sinn Féin and the Volunteers in 1919 may have shown some perspicacity on the British side, since women became steadily more prominent as die-hard upholders of the republican ideal. The most famous of the nationalist women, Maud Gonne and Constance Markievicz, came to seem moderate in comparison with the widows and sisters of dead national heroes, such as Kathleen Clarke, Hanna Sheehy-Skeffington and Mary MacSwiney.

The question of national unity became most problematic with the re-eruption of sectarian conflict in Belfast in mid-1920. Anti-Catholic riots began in the shipyards and turned into the mass terrorization of Catholic neighbourhoods; for once nationalist propaganda scarcely exaggerated in branding this a 'pogrom'. This was bad enough, but the nationalist reaction set the seal on the virtual partition of Ireland. A boycott of firms accused of discriminating against Catholics gradually widened into a general boycott of Belfast goods. The alarming popularity of this collective action showed how deep-seated were the resentments it mobilized. Seán MacEntee gave comparatively moderate expression to this when he said that although 'they could not reduce Belfast by force of arms, they could bring her to reason by economic force'. A more menacing tone appeared in P. J. Little's independent separatist journal *Old Ireland*, which threatened as early as February 1920 that Sinn Féin could 'smash Belfast in a month' if need be, and in early 1921 was still fulminating, 'When she has learnt by painful experience that Belfast depended on Ireland for its existence, when she has come to see that the English connection only means financial loss and isolation, then it will be time enough to deal with her'. Unfortunately for nationalists, the painful experience was not going to be confined to Belfast.[18]

The British response: reform and counter-terror

Britain observed the early unfolding of the Sinn Féin counter-state with bafflement rather than hostility. Walter Long was unusual in taking Sinn Féin seriously. To this steely Unionist, who had as he said 'watched the rise and fall of every political party in Ireland for the last forty years', this was 'much the most difficult and dangerous of any the government have had to deal with'. Its leaders were 'brave and fanatical and do not fear imprisonment or death', nor could they be suborned by the traditional devices of patronage or private negotiations with the Hierarchy.[19] Long still had influence on Irish policy, both through his friend the Viceroy, Lord French, and as chairman of the Cabinet committee on Ireland, charged with drawing up another – the final – Home Rule Bill. But he could not get his colleagues to share his sense of alarm and urgency. The assembly of Dáil Éireann was dismissed as a charade; *The Times* and the *Manchester Guardian* concurred in calling it a 'stage play', mere 'theatricalism'. When one MP demanded that the abstentionists be compelled to attend the House of Commons, he was told by Bonar Law that the government 'did not propose to take any action in the matter'. In retrospect this inaction was dangerous, maybe fatal, but it was in line with a belief that time was on the side of moderation, coupled with a fear that action could go wrong. As the Chief Secretary, Ian Macpherson, pathetically put it in May 1919, 'we did not and do not know how to act'. When the Dáil was finally banned in September, he explained that 'we had to allow these members to sit together *in consultation* if they wished', but when they 'conspired by executive acts to overthrow the duly constituted authority, then we could act'.

The action they eventually took included, as we have seen, banning not only the Dáil but also a raft of nationalist organizations including the Sinn Féin party, demonstrating how different Ireland remained in British eyes. The head of the civil service, Sir Warren Fisher, later condemned this with only slight exaggeration: it was, he said, as if reactionary Tory backwoodsmen had banned the Labour party. Thus the government fell back naturally into the familiar mixture of coercion and conciliation. The conciliatory line, intended to appeal to moderate nationalist opinion, was the Home Rule Bill that Long's committee drafted at a very leisurely pace through 1919. Asquith's undertaking that Ulster would be given special treatment hardened into a parallel Home Rule structure, with equally empowered parliaments in both Dublin and Belfast, and a more shadowy federal dimension in the form of a Council of Ireland. Not until February 1920, shortly before the Bill was presented to parliament, was the decision finalized that Northern Ireland would consist of six, not all nine counties of Ulster. To advertise the conciliatory policy, a new Chief Secretary, Hamar Greenwood, was appointed, signalling the eclipse of Lord French.

But along with the bid for moderate support went a growing effort to eliminate extremists – 'thugs', 'gunmen' and 'terrorists' in government terminology. Before Greenwood arrived in Ireland, the Dublin Castle administration was shaken out in an attempt to import some British efficiency. A new Military Commander, General Macready, who had made his reputation in internal security work, also arrived, followed by a Chief of Police whose mission was to save the embattled RIC. During the winter of 1919–20 the intensification of IRA attacks had forced the police to retreat into stronger barracks, and by doing so they had surrendered control of much of the country. In the summer of 1920 the police were rearmed and motorized to increase their striking power. A seismic change in the nature of the RIC occurred when, for the first time, non-Irish recruits were sought. Most of these 'Black and Tans' – a shortage of uniform led to a temporary issue of khaki together with RIC dark green – were ex-soldiers, jobless victims of postwar recession whose aptitude for police work was variable. Standards of recruitment (which had been very tightly monitored in the old RIC with careful investigation of every applicant) were certainly relaxed, with damaging results. Out of the several thousand non-Irish recruits, probably only a handful had criminal records, but these were enough to provide a gift for republican propaganda, which branded the Black and Tans generally as 'the sweepings of English gaols'. The militarization process culminated in the creation of the Auxiliary Division, elite motorized companies of ex-officers, 'Temporary Cadets' in official parlance, to spearhead the counter-insurgency campaign.

But they faced the same problem as the rest of the police and troops – lack of reliable information about the guerrilla forces. Increased legal powers, like the Restoration of Order Act in August, which brought back courts-martial on the lines of the wartime Defence of the Realm Act, proved unable to change this. When the IRA responded by forming flying columns and increasing the scale of its attacks, the result was retaliation. The police disciplinary code, whose ultimate sanction was dismissal with loss of pension rights, was simply inadequate to control armed forces cooped up in isolated posts under intense provocation. The first reprisals were possibly spontaneous, but the Chief of Police came to encourage them. Even before the end of August, one of the new Castle officials noted in his diary, 'We are being urged quietly and persistently that Reprisals are the only thing to put down the gun men and hearten the police, and I begin to believe it'.[20]

Ultimately, however, reprisals were a colossal public relations disaster for the government. The 'sack of Balbriggan', the 'notorious looting of Trim', and the burning of Cork in December were only the most highly publicized instances of a lawlessness that shocked liberal opinion in Britain as well as abroad. The alienation of moderate Irish opinion can be read in an angry catalogue of protest issued by a meeting of the Hierarchy in the autumn:

> On a scale truly appalling have to be reckoned countless indiscriminate raids and arrests in the darkness of the night, prolonged imprisonments without trial, savage sentences from tribunals that command and deserve no confidence, the burning of houses, town-halls, creameries and crops, the destruction of industries to pave the way for want and famine – by men maddened by drink and bent on loot – the flogging and massacre of civilians, all perpetrated by the force of the Crown, who have established a reign of frightfulness which has a parallel only in the horrors of the Turkish atrocities or the outrages of the Red Army in Bolshevik Russia.[21]

The events of Bloody Sunday (p. 94 above) were shocking at several levels. After the IRA assassinations, a botched search operation at Croke Park stadium turned into a massacre as Auxiliaries opened fire into the crowd at the all-Ireland final. Eleven people were killed in what looked to many people like a reprisal – the worst yet. The shock effect of the IRA attacks on the security forces triggered a shift of gear in the counter-insurgency campaign; search operations and arrests were stepped up, and for the first time the army was put on an active service footing. By the time the Government of Ireland Act was finally passed in December, martial law was being imposed in south-west Ireland as much to get control of the police as to intimidate the rebels. It did not do either, but it made it all too clear that the situation in

Ireland had got beyond the decorous fiction of 'military aid to the civil power'. Ireland was a war zone.

Partition and truce

When Eamon de Valera returned to Ireland two days before Christmas he found a situation in which triumphs and dangers were mixed. The Dáil government was under intense pressure from British military action, and though the IRA had scored some successes, it too was finding it difficult to widen and intensify its campaign. De Valera took the view that it had lost direction and drifted into insignificant guerrilla fighting. He found too that the influence of Michael Collins had been greatly magnified since he left. When Griffith was arrested by an overzealous military unit after Bloody Sunday it was Collins, not Brugha, who replaced him as Acting President. Over the previous 18 months, Collins had brushed aside Brugha's attempts to exert control over the IRA, and by this time relations between the two men – or two groups, as Collins and Mulcahy found themselves in conflict with Brugha and Stack – were distinctly strained. De Valera had no doubt that the IRA should move to the kind of military actions that would demonstrate its status as the army of a legitimate state, and eventually he got his way. In May 1921 the IRA seized and burned the Custom House in Dublin. In the process over 100 men of the Dublin Brigade were captured, a blow so severe that Collins saw the operation as a disaster. It certainly conflicted with his preference for getting the maximum return for the minimum risk. Yet its public impact was probably greater than Collins was prepared to concede. It came in the same month as the first elections held under the Government of Ireland Act. The two parliaments, Northern and Southern, established by the Act were elected by proportional representation (using the single transferable vote system, an English invention). First introduced for the 1920 local elections, this was a revolutionary departure in British political culture, accepted because of the need to demonstrate the protection of minorities. Sinn Féin (already committed to proportional representation in principle) opted to participate in the election, using the British machinery to elect a second Dáil. Its crushing victory demonstrated that the Southern parliament created by the 1920 Act was never going to function, and forced the British government to face the fact that two years of repression had got nowhere in political terms. If Britain was to avoid being forced into concessions, it would have to step up its military campaign.

In a purely military sense, the IRA was nowhere near defeating Britain. Mulcahy, who admittedly had an axe to grind (as a supporter of the Treaty), later reminded republican die-hards that so far from driving the British out of Ireland, they had not been able to drive them from anything bigger than a medium-sized police station. Mulcahy's own efforts to raise the scale of the campaign in the spring of 1921 by grouping brigades into divisions failed to produced the bigger battles that republican propaganda needed. The British forces were belatedly developing some expertise and dynamism in search operations, and were putting severe pressure on the counter-state administration and IRA GHQ in Dublin. Mulcahy and Collins, acutely conscious of this pressure, were beginning to feel that the IRA might even begin to break up over the summer – the best campaigning season for the motorized British forces. In May de Valera summoned local IRA commanders to Dublin to assess the prospects, and got a mixed response. Only the most advanced, and now really professionalized fighters of the south-west believed (or said) that they could 'keep the field' for several years.[22] Recent research makes it clear that most of the IRA's fighting units were in serious trouble by this time – one historian concludes that the position of most flying columns was 'untenable'.[23]

Both sides could thus see grounds for apprehension. The crucial first steps towards negotiation were harder for the British to take, partly because on the republican side few realized that – as Collins later berated them – the idea of negotiation involved compromise. The British government had denounced their terrorist opponents in terms that made it hard to explain how they could be treated as possible fellow-statesmen. At the same time, Lloyd George had always kept open a few channels of communication with Sinn Féin, and had deliberately restricted the military campaign – for instance, refusing to permit martial law in Dublin – to leave some space for negotiation. When the Catholic Archbishop of Perth (whose son had been mistakenly arrested and killed allegedly 'attempting to escape', in the Dublin Castle guardroom on Bloody Sunday) went to Dublin as an intermediary in December, the possibility of serious discussions opened up, only to founder on the Prime Minister's cautious insistence that the IRA surrender its weapons as a precondition of any talks. By June 1921 the hardline Conservatives in his Cabinet were at least aware of the likely costs of pressing on; it was Lord Birkenhead who first publicly recognized that 'it is a small war that is going on' in Ireland, and admitted 'the failure of our military methods to keep pace with, and to overcome, the military methods which have been taken by our opponents'.[24]

The event which was widely believed to have triggered the negotiation process, and which certainly gave the British government the sense that it had got the Ulster problem out of the way, was the opening of the first Northern Ireland parliament. Whereas the Government of Ireland Act was a dead letter in the rest of Ireland, in the six counties devolution was carried through with exemplary precision. The irony that the fiercest opponents of Home Rule were in the end the only people to accept it has not been lost on historians. Accepted first in a spirit of self-sacrifice, the benefits of special Home Rule status became apparent quite rapidly. A separate administration in Belfast was established well before the Act was passed. In September 1920 an Assistant Under-Secretary, Sir Ernest Clark, was appointed, who, after a brief culture shock on meeting the Ulster Unionist leaders, became a doughty fighter for the maximum transfer of functions to Belfast.[25] The most crucial of these were in the sphere of public order. In October, as the sectarian conflict went on, a new Special Constabulary was established. Theoretically it was to be recruited throughout Ireland, but in practice recruits were found only in Ulster, and in large part from the old UVF. At the elections in May 1921 the Ulster Unionist Party (UUP) secured the comfortable victory (40 out of 52 seats) that the six-county area had been engineered to ensure. On 9 June the head of the Dublin Castle administration, Sir John Anderson, wrote, 'The ship has been launched in the North, and we must hope she will prove seaworthy'.[26]

When King George V opened the Northern parliament in Belfast on 22 June 1921, he called on Irish 'peoples, whatever their race or creed' to 'stretch out the hand of forbearance and conciliation, to forgive and forget'. This plea provided the necessary cover for the risk of restarting talks in Dublin, and within a fortnight a formal truce was agreed. This in itself was a remarkable British concession, since most of the Cabinet had all along insisted that a truce would be tantamount to recognizing the IRA's claim to belligerent status. Churchill had proposed an informal cease-fire – 'we should choke off our people and they theirs'. Instead there were public discussions, signatures, and the appointment of liaison officers between the Crown forces and the IRA. The key point in the truce terms was that neither side should reinforce or expand its forces, but this proved impossible to monitor or adjudicate. Over the next few months, as political negotiations started and stalled several times, there were countless breaches of the truce, but the mutual desire to maintain the cease-fire prevented them from getting out of hand.

Negotiating the Treaty

In retrospect the famous and fatal compromises of the Anglo-Irish Treaty take on an air of inevitability. The difficulties in finding a verbal formula on which talks could begin were, in view of the high symbolic charge built up in terms like the Republic, the Crown and Empire, real enough. So were the substantive issues to be negotiated. Yet a tacit belief that the war was over seems to have pervaded Ireland in the summer of 1921. The IRA was flooded with 'sunshine soldiers', sometimes called 'Trucileers', who like most people probably had no wish to see a return to the grim autumn and winter of 1920–21. The real IRA veterans also became visible – the West Cork flying column commander Tom Barry, for instance, was a senior liaison officer – in ways that made a return to guerrilla action problematic. The brightest visibility, of course, settled on Michael Collins, whose carefully crafted anonymity over the previous three years was one of the great legends of the war. When de Valera selected Collins to accompany Arthur Griffith at the head of the Irish delegation to London in October, he more or less ensured that pragmatism would prevail.

The London negotiations from 11 October to 6 December contained the stuff of real drama amidst a deadening mass of convoluted detail. The key questions were those of status and security. As was clear from the start of the first round of talks immediately after the truce, when de Valera had four summit meetings with Lloyd George over a 10-day period, Britain was prepared to offer 'Dominion status' for Ireland, but with some crucial conditions which would make that status rather different from that of the supposed model, Canada. British security required a limitation on the size of Ireland's military and especially its naval forces, and retention of several bases by Britain. Britain also regarded the question of Ulster as having been essentially settled by the Government of Ireland Act; in other words, partition would have to be accepted by any new Irish state. De Valera went back to Dublin and advised the second Dáil, now able to meet in the open for the first time, to reject these terms, which it did in August. At the same time, it renamed de Valera President of the Irish Republic (a title informally used for some time, though his official title had been President of Dáil Éireann). The Dáil further raised the stakes by taking an oath of allegiance to 'the Irish Republic and the Government of the Irish Republic which is Dáil Éireann'. On this basis, de Valera began to work out his original idea of 'external association' – the voluntary binding of a free Irish state to Britain for defence purposes. Lloyd George still refused the demand that Irish independence be recognized before this 'treaty of free association' be negotiated, but in late September came up with the formula which at last permitted talks to start – 'with a view to ascertaining how the association of Ireland with the community of nations known as the British empire may best be reconciled with Irish national aspirations'.[27]

De Valera had proved a match for the finely honed negotiating skills of Lloyd George. He was in the process of articulating a plausible alternative to the British model of Dominion status. He seemed to have within sight a compromise that both the British and the purist republicans might accept. His decision not to lead the negotiating team – astonishing to most eyes – has never been satisfactorily explained. Cathal Brugha and Austin Stack refused to go. Sending Collins with Griffith has been seen by some of de Valera's biographers as an attempt to ensure that the IRB would not resist the outcome. But since the real resistance was to come from Brugha and Stack, it is hard to avoid the sense that de Valera was watching his republican flank too carefully. The argument that he expected to exert an indirect pressure on the British negotiators cannot be dismissed, and the allegation that he deliberately set Collins up for the inevitable odium of compromise is perhaps too extravagant.[28]

Critics have also suggested that de Valera deliberately engineered the delegation to be split, but this seems both unlikely and unnecessary. If Collins and Griffith could agree, their combined prestige was almost overwhelming. During the course of the negotiations, if not at the outset, Collins came to accept the inevitability of compromise. As the discussions went on it became clear that everything hinged on the symbolic issue of Ireland's status. Financial issues were slowly worked out, the defence question was resolved, and even partition was shelved. Griffith and Collins, like the rest of the delegation, remained implacably hostile to partition, but they accepted the device of a boundary commission to follow the signing of a treaty. The exact size of the northern sub-state had been a matter for debate ever since the first proposal of a four-county exclusion, and the idea of a commission sprang naturally from British political culture. Griffith accepted it because he believed, as did Collins and the rest (including all the nationalists who took part in the Belfast boycott), that Northern Ireland would be economically unviable, and that its fate would be sealed if a plebiscite were held. On 12 November Griffith unilaterally gave Lloyd George an assurance that 'while he was fighting the "Ulster" crowd we would not help them by repudiating him'. Lloyd George interpreted this as an undertaking that Sinn Féin would not break off the negotiations on the partition issue.[29]

The status issue remained intractable, however. One crucial hurdle was got over by dropping the unacceptable title 'republic' in favour of the semantically analogous but less anti-monarchical 'free state'. But still nationalists hung desperately on to the hope that sovereign status would be conceded in principle. As late as 4 December, Gavan Duffy caused the British negotiators to storm out by saying 'Our difficulty is to come into the empire, looking at all that has happened in the past'. Britain insisted that the ultimate sovereignty of the Crown be recognized in the form of an oath of allegiance to the King, to be taken by all members of the Irish parliament. The delegates fought to retain de Valera's wording ('allegiance to the constitution of the Irish Free State ...'), but in the end, under immense pressure, accepted Lloyd George's final proposal on 5 December – pledging allegiance to the King 'in virtue of the common citizenship of Ireland with Great Britain and her adherence to and membership of the British Commonwealth of Nations'. Lloyd George put on an impressive show of exasperation in threatening that unless the delegates signed that night, he would break off negotiations and reopen hostilities. In a break over allegiance to the Crown, British public opinion would back the government as it might not over partition; yet Griffith had (as he now ruefully accepted) foreclosed the other option. At 2.10 a.m. on the 6th the Irish delegation signed the first Anglo-Irish Treaty since Limerick in 1691.

|7|

Civil war and nation-building, 1922–1932

The 1920s were a defining moment in Irish history. The construction of the Irish Free State on the basis of the 1921 Anglo-Irish Treaty was a demanding, often dangerous, and largely thankless task. The Treaty lacked glamour, as did many of its defenders. (Tom Garvin has drawn our attention to the fact that Arthur Griffith is the only face missing from the portrait gallery of prime ministers in Leinster House; he was likewise relegated to a walk-on part in Neil Jordan's avowedly pro-Treaty 1996 film *Michael Collins*.) In 1922 Griffith worked himself to an early death by cerebral haemorrhage, Collins – who famously said, on signing the Treaty, that he had just signed his own death warrant – was shot in an ambush by anti-Treaty forces, and five years later their most dynamic successor, Kevin O'Higgins, was to be assassinated. But the mixture of initiatives and compromises the 'Treatyites' pushed through under intense pressure effectively defined the structure of modern Irish political life. The disaster of civil war froze the development of party politics in a unique mould, and cemented the process of partition which made Irish unity an increasingly distant prospect. Amidst these storms, however, a working democracy was built – an enduring achievement and, in the global perspective, an impressive one.

The Treaty debate

Dáil Éireann began to debate the Treaty on 14 December. As an assembly, it was desperately inexperienced in dealing with major political issues. Its meetings had been infrequent, and often perfunctory. Not only was it a one-party assembly without any genuine opposition, but a large proportion of its members had been elected unopposed for their military credentials rather than their political acumen. In spite of all this, the Treaty debate became a powerful and moving testament to the anguish of an idealist national movement up against hard reality. The debate shattered the unity of what Richard Mulcahy called 'the crowd', the tightly knit (as they had supposed) Sinn Féin revolutionary cohort. The internecine struggle became bitter. How far the fierce passions unleashed in the Dáil reflected the national mood, however, is not altogether clear. Mulcahy, with typical thoroughness, set up a small bureau to study public opinion through the crisis. Its reports reflected general uncertainty, though they showed that this stemmed less from any popular dislike of the Treaty terms – even 'the Oath' – than from a widespread fear that the republicans would reject them and restart the war.[1]

In a private session of the Dáil, de Valera charged the delegates with failing to consult the Cabinet before signing the Treaty, and set out his alternative of external association in the belief that it would unite the Dáil. It did not. De Valera's compromise, as Griffith pointed out, had already been rejected by the British, and did not satisfy the committed republicans either. The main defence of the Treaty was that it was the best available compromise. Mulcahy put the pragmatic argument most clearly, saying that it was the only 'solid spot of ground upon which the Irish people can put its political feet'. Collins, as always, was less pedestrian, coining a famous phrase that demonstrated (if any doubt still existed) his political gifts. The Treaty, he urged, 'gives us freedom – not the ultimate freedom that all nations desire and develop to, but the freedom to achieve it'. Collins tenaciously argued not only the concrete achievements of the Treaty, above all the removal of British military occupation, but even that its acceptance of partition, together with the boundary commission, offered the best prospect of reconciling the north and paving the way for unification. All this was squarely rejected by opponents of the Treaty, who maintained, like Erskine Childers, that it gave Ireland nothing like the real freedom of other Dominions such as Canada, and that the Dáil had no power to surrender the nation's independence. De Valera menacingly warned that the Treaty would bring neither freedom nor peace; Austin Stack denounced the oath of allegiance and charged that the signatories of the Treaty had been corrupted by the British, a re-eruption of deep-rooted Fenian paranoia that was venomously amplified by Cathal Brugha.

The virtual disappearance of the partition issue from the Treaty debate can be simply demonstrated, as F. S. L. Lyons did, on the basis of a simple page count – nine pages out of 338 in the Dáil record. This is certainly significant, but it does not really mean that the issue was unimportant, rather that even the fiercest opponents of the Treaty could not imagine that partition would last. Like Collins they believed it was doomed by the forces of history, culture and economics. Unlike Collins, though, they saw no conflict between the demand for republican status and the possibility of reunification. Indeed nothing could, in their view, stand against the claim to outright independence. To them, the oath of allegiance was a monstrous betrayal of their principles. Mary MacSwiney (sister and mentor of the dead Terence) tersely explained what that meant: 'those who stand for expediency could yield to those who stand for right, but those who stand for principle could not yield to those who stand for expediency'. And principle was backed by a still more potent emotional force: 'I stand here', she declared, 'in the name of the dead'. (In her mind, surely, this had a capital D.)

Treatyite arguments like those of the future Free State leaders William T. Cosgrave and Kevin O'Higgins, that the Treaty would bring real improvements in the quality of Irish life, and that in any case the Irish people should be allowed to decide the matter, were swept aside just as peremptorily. Liam Mellows, thought by some to be a socialist, said that 'You could point out to me the material advantages to be gained under this Treaty and it would remind me very much of what I have read about our Saviour ...'. De Valera made one of his most characteristic interventions when he invoked a Rousseauan notion of the general will: 'whenever I wanted to know what the Irish people wanted, I had only to examine my own heart and it told me straight off what the Irish wanted'. This point was only to be settled with considerable loss of life.

The Dáil at last came to its historic vote, on 7 January 1922, ratifying the Treaty by 64 votes to 57. This was not a resounding majority, and the pro-Treaty vote did not express enthusiasm for the Treaty as such. But the fact that there was enough dour realism around to work the compromise had a formative effect on the new Irish state. As did the fact that, after de Valera lost the Presidency (by only two votes, 60–58), he and his defeated minority walked out of the Dáil.

The Provisional Government and the Split

Under the terms of the Treaty a Provisional Government was to be elected by the Southern parliament. This body had, of course, been defunct since the May 1921 elections, when only the four Unionist

MPs for Trinity College, Dublin, had turned up to inaugurate it. Now, a week after the Treaty vote, the pro-Treaty TDs met with these four in the Mansion House to appoint Michael Collins as Chairman of the Provisional Government. Arthur Griffith as President of Dáil Eireann simultaneously appointed a new Cabinet, including Collins in his old job as Minister for Finance. So two governments coexisted in Dublin, an elaborate fiction designed to fulfil the Treaty terms without alienating the anti-Treaty republicans. This was understandable – and politic – but it did not work.

The Provisional Government included Cosgrave (local government), Edmund Duggan (home affairs), Patrick Hogan (agriculture), Kevin O'Higgins (economic affairs), Fionan Lynch (education), Joe McGrath (labour), and J. J. Walsh (post). O'Higgins (30 years old in 1922) later memorably evoked its situation:

> simply eight young men in the City Hall standing amidst the ruins of one administration, with the foundations of another not yet laid, and with wild men screaming through the keyhole. No police force was functioning throughout the country, no system of justice was operating, the wheels of administration hung idle, battered out of recognition by rival jurisdictions.[2]

The 'wild men' had reverted to Fenian contempt for politics as soon as the Dáil vote was counted. 'Nearly all the members of the Dail became overnight in my eyes "politicians"', as a Dublin Brigade officer put it.[3] The first move was to hold an Army Convention to keep the army together and 'out of politics', but the Provisional Government saw this as an attempt to subvert the forces it was already enlisting to replace the old IRA. On 15 March it proscribed the Army Convention; a week later, Rory O'Connor repudiated the IRA's allegiance to all oath-breakers. On 26 March the illegal Convention met, attended by 223 delegates representing 16 IRA divisions (on paper 112,250 men). On 13 April O'Connor led a force into the Four Courts, the remaining architectural masterpiece on the Liffey after the destruction of the Custom House. Gradually, in agonizing slow motion, Sinn Féin was breaking up. Though splits have happened before and since in Irish political history, this was the one that would always be 'the Split'. As Harry Boland wrote from the Dublin hills in July, 'Can you imagine me on the run from Mick Collins? Well, I am.'[4] The split sundered friendships and families, often permanently, and sometimes fatally. Boland was to be killed that month, Collins the next.

The last effort to hold the movement together was the electoral pact between Collins and de Valera in June – an agreement that in the first

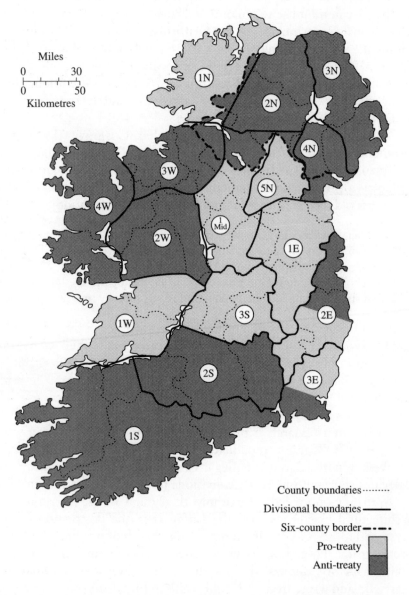

Miles

0   30

0   50

Kilometres

County boundaries ·········

Divisional boundaries ———

Six-county border —·—·—·

Pro-treaty

Anti-treaty

Fig. 7.1 The pro-treaty/anti-treaty split in the IRA, 1922 (circled figures and numbers identify the IRA division in each area)
Source: Based on F. O'Donoghue, *No Other Law* (Dublin 1954)

general election to the Free State parliament the proportion of pro- and anti-Treaty members would remain the same as in the 64–57 January vote. This blatant election-rigging outraged the British government, and was disavowed at the last moment by Collins. The election produced 36 anti-Treaty seats out of a total of 128. Alongside the 58 pro-Treaty Sinn Féiners, the balance of Labour, farmer and independent TDs could be taken as broadly accepting the Treaty, indicating a substantial majority of public opinion in its favour – or at least in favour of not rejecting it.

Most crucially, the IRA itself split. Collins used every device available to the head of the IRB to hold the army to his line, but (though de Valera blamed it for the Treaty) the old secret organization was no longer the nerve centre of the national movement. Still, Collins had immense influence. Many people trusted him implicitly: 'What's good enough for Mick is good enough for me.' But his rivals also had their following. Significantly, the IRA tended to split by units rather than individuals; sometimes whole divisions followed their commanders for or against the Treaty. The pro-Treaty side laid most of the blame for the split on de Valera. Without his political prestige, the anti-Treaty side would have lacked credibility. Yet de Valera himself was acutely conscious of how little the military leaders, first O'Connor and then Liam Lynch, deferred to him. Lynch found de Valera's 'external association' meaningless: 'we have declared for an Irish Republic, and will not live under any other law'.[5] The most notorious off-the-cuff press statement issued by Rory O'Connor, when he replied to a journalist's question whether the IRA was establishing a military dictatorship, 'you can take it that way if you like', was a propaganda gift to the Provisional Government, and must have shaken de Valera himself. But he too stoked the flames of war with his notorious speech threatening to 'wade through Irish blood'. His political bankruptcy was painfully revealed in a private letter he wrote to the Clan na Gael leader Joseph McGarrity in September: 'I have often taken myself to task, but I do not see what I could have done which would have averted this war... I am convinced that there is the will for peace on both sides, but no basis is discoverable on which it can be made'.[6]

Civil war

The split left the anti-Treaty IRA looking numerically the stronger side: by the time open hostilities began with the bombardment of the Four Courts at the end of June, the government estimated republican

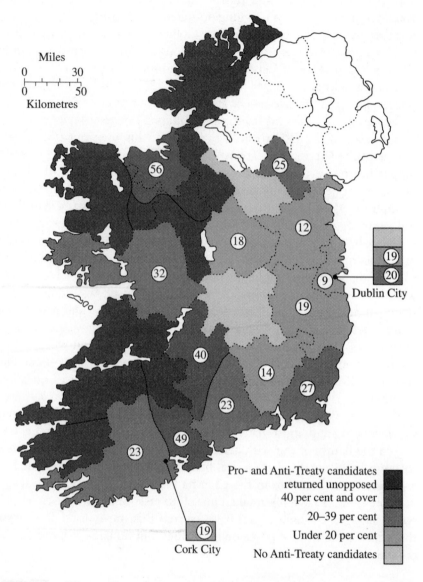

Fig. 7.2 The anti-treaty vote in the 1922 general election (% of 1st-preference votes for Republican candidates)

Source: Based on E. Rumpf and A. Hepburn, *Nationalism and Socialism in Twentieth-Century Ireland* (Liverpool 1977), p.59

strength at 12,900 as against less than 9000 semi-trained recruits in the newly established Free State Army. With nearly 7000 rifles, the anti-Treaty forces were outwardly more impressive than the IRA as a whole had been at the height of the Anglo-Irish war. In spite of this, there is general agreement that the outcome of the civil war was militarily a foregone conclusion, because the republicans rapidly lapsed into a passive strategy.[7] As in 1916, the seizure of big buildings did not trigger a popular uprising in favour of the rebels, the provincial IRA forces failed to act in concert with the capital, and after some hesitation the government decided to use artillery (borrowed from the British army) to crush its opponents. On 28 June the shelling began; two days later the battered defenders surrendered and blew the remains of the building up. Cathal Brugha was killed fighting his way out of the anti-Treaty headquarters in O'Connell Street. The rest of the anti-Treaty fighters in Dublin surrendered or abandoned the city.

Once the capital was lost, the republicans might have been expected to revert to guerrilla strategy, capitalizing on the expertise they had built up against the British. Instead they steadily let go of any military advantage by doggedly sticking to the defence of fixed lines, while abandoning the cities they controlled – Sligo, Waterford, Limerick and Cork – almost without a fight. They were making a gesture, more like ritual combat than modern war. One reason was the very human one that they found it hard to treat their former comrades as an enemy. 'We never tried to kill', as George Gilmore said. Their opponents did not reciprocate the compunction: they eventually turned out to be far more ruthless than the British had been. Admittedly Collins tried for weeks to avoid full-scale hostilities, but after he was killed on 22 August, in an oddly ill-planned attempt to negotiate with Lynch in his home county of Cork, his surviving colleagues pulled out all the stops in orchestrating a struggle of democracy against militarism. Symptomatically they insisted, as Ronan Fanning has shown, that press coverage should reflect the legitimacy of the new state; reports must refer to 'the government' rather than the Provisional Government, and its troops must be described as the 'Irish Army' or 'national troops', whereas the anti-Treaty forces were 'irregulars', 'bands' or 'bodies of men'. The Catholic Church provided vital support when the bishops, in a joint pastoral letter on 10 October, denounced 'A section of the community, refusing to acknowledge the government set up by the nation', who had 'chosen to attack their own country as if she were a foreign power. … They carry on what they call a war, but which … is morally only a system of murder and assassination of the national forces'.[8]

The Provisional Government exploited to the full – and beyond – the democratic mandate it had won in the Pact election. To counter the idealized Irish people invoked by republicans, ministers insistently branded their opponents as enemies of 'the nation'. Week after week, O'Higgins as Minister for Justice reiterated the message that the basic issue was whether Ireland was to be 'a nation governed by constitutional principles, or a mob dictated to by an armed minority'.[9] To vindicate the rule of law he was prepared to take ruthless action. The assassination of a pro-Treaty TD, Sean Hales, on 7 December 1922 produced a truly draconian response. On the insistence of O'Higgins, four leading republican prisoners, O'Connor, Liam Mellows, Dick Barrett and Joe McKelvey, were shot without trial at dawn the next day. This was the most shocking, but not the only example of a policy of counter-terrorism that was semi-officially implemented throughout the war zone, leading the pious Liam Lynch to think that his enemies had become possessed by the Devil (a poignant illustration of his approach to political analysis). In March 1923 a group of republican prisoners in Kerry were forced to stand on an IRA landmine and blown up.

On 10 April Lynch was mortally wounded in a skirmish in the Knockmealdown Mountains of Tipperary. The heart went out of the republican resistance, and on 27 April de Valera issued his famous order to cease operations:

> Soldiers of the Republic, Legion of the Rearguard: The republic can no longer be defended successfully by your arms. ... Military victory must be allowed to rest for the moment with those who have destroyed the republic. Other means must be sought to safeguard the nation's right.

This rhetorical flourish may not have reached the dispersed and bedraggled ranks of the anti-Treaty forces. On 24 May the IRA Chief of Staff, Frank Aiken, issued the final command to dump arms. There were no negotiations, and no truce; the civil war was over in a military sense only. Though some historians have suggested that less than 700 people had died in it, the government listed 800 military deaths. If the total of 4000–5000 fatalities suggested by other historians may be too high, there is no doubt that the death toll exceeded that for 1916–21. The moral and political impact was certainly tremendous. The Free State had executed more 'rebels' in 10 months than the British in the six years of the Anglo-Irish war. Over 10,000 people were interned without trial. The cleavage it marked would endure.

The Free State: constituted authority

Victories in civil wars are usually Pyrrhic, and the Irish Free State (Saorstát Éireann) was almost mortally wounded at birth. Its survival owed as much to popular disenchantment with the republicans as to any enthusiasm for the new state. The Provisional Government was only too well aware that 'the state' in Ireland was an institution which would have to struggle to achieve public endorsement. It exploited its narrow windows of opportunity with skill and judgement. A few crucial policies secured it a decisive advantage: foremost amongst them the decision taken during the summer to recruit a new, unarmed civil police force. The Civic Guard, or Garda Síochána, was modelled in several respects on the old RIC (many of whose qualities Collins admired), in particular its centralized structure. But it immediately secured the vital legitimacy, in the form of public acceptance, that its predecessor had always lacked. It had been noticeable that the IRA had left the unarmed Dublin Metropolitan Police alone during the Anglo-Irish war, and the same tolerance was extended to the new Garda as long as it stuck to non-political duties. This proved to be a fatal mistake, since, as Collins and O'Higgins clearly saw, the policing function was the keystone of the state-building process.[10]

The Provisional Government also established, in unpropitious circumstances, an essentially democratic political system. The basis of this was the constitution, published in June 1922 after some abrasive negotiations with Britain, and adopted in October. Collins tried to use the drafting of the constitution to specify the essential independence of Ireland, and even though he was forced to modify the original draft, the final version retained what one distinguished legal commentator called 'essentially republican' qualities.[11] Collins as usual took a no-nonsense line on what he called 'unnecessary sentiment', which 'might be laughed at' – thus he never even tried to incorporate the kind of symbols so dear to his republican opponents. Unlike many Sinn Féiners he thought that mixing Gaelic and English languages in a single document would be 'grotesque'. But he believed that his constitution contained 'the essence of a Gaelic polity ... without the trappings'.[12] This was to be a crucial issue for the Free State in the long term. Could it satisfy the visionary idealism of the revolutionary movement in the real world of the 1920s?

The Free State constitution itself went some way to doing this. It is possible to argue, as one social scientist has, that it failed to achieve the 'symbolic integration' of the Irish people because it abandoned some important 'Gaelic-Romantic' ideas about the political nature of the community in favour of 'Irish-Enlightenment' views of the state. Prager's cultural analysis is interesting, but the form of statism that emerged in Ireland after 1922 commanded a fair degree of support. The strength of the constitutional tradition in Ireland, which Prager tends to ignore, combined with the peculiar legacy of the Parnellite party to generate a unique balance between centralism and localism.[13] And for all its limits, the mere fact of having a written constitution which entrenched individual freedom was quite revolutionary in the British context. Moreover the constitution contained some highly original ideas for enhancing public participation in decision-making, notably the possibility of a popular initiative (allowing legislation to be initiated by petition or referendum), and the idea of 'extern' ministers to bring in expertise from outside parliament.[14] Proportional representation was maintained for the 153-member Dáil, while a Senate half elected by the Dáil, half appointed by the President of the Executive Council (i.e. the prime minister), advertised the protection of 'minorities or interests not adequately represented in the Dáil' (in a word, Protestants).

Though the political system can be said to have been essentially democratic, it was not, as many critics have since pointed out, abundantly so. When the Free State formally replaced the Provisional Government in December 1922, it embarked on some experiments which might have led to a radically different political system. Over time, though, most of these gradually gave way to the dominant British model. The bicameral system followed the British rather than the American path, as the Senate steadily lost power to the Dáil. The unelected extern ministers, who would be drawn from the professional sphere, would have led to some weakening of Cabinet power, whereas the tendency here, as in Britain, was towards the concentration of power. Their fate was perhaps predictable. Likewise there was never sufficient will to make other novelties like the popular initiative and referendum provisions work, and they were eventually ditched. Most striking of all was the Provisional Government's precipitate decision to scrap the revolutionary legal system in the summer of 1922, when it was arguably working better than the British system it had defeated. On 11 July the circuit judges were recalled in mid-circuit, and two days later the Supreme Court was abolished. Shortly afterwards the Cabinet took the extraordinary step of formally rescinding the Decree of 29 June 1920 that had established the system – the only Dáil decree ever to be rescinded. The result was a degree of chaos that baffled

Michael Collins himself, and belied Kevin O'Higgins's claim that the old British judicial system was sounder and more experienced than its republican rival.[15]

The emergence of modern party politics was stunted by civil war and its aftermath. With the anti-Treatyites back in the abstentionist fold, denouncing the Free State as a British puppet, the role of opposition once again devolved on the Labour party and a handful of independents. Labour, the oldest surviving Irish party, had voluntarily marginalized itself by standing aside in 1918 and once again during the Split. Shorn of charismatic leadership, the patriotic loyalty of the worthy Thomas Johnson and William O'Brien failed to reap much reward in public esteem. As Ronan Fanning has noted, the coming of independence did little to change Labour's situation – 'the radical impulse in Irish politics remained republican' rather than socialist. One delegate at the 1925 party congress lamented that in spite of the fact that workers had 'suffered untold miseries' at the hands of Sinn Féin, 'the electors returned 127 of those [Sinn Féin] parties and 14 Labour representatives'.[16] The situation seemed to improve in 1927, but this was yet another false dawn for Labour. More surprisingly, perhaps, despite the solidification of the Irish Farmers' Union during the troubles, no major farmer party emerged to challenge the pro-Treaty grouping.

The government itself was seemingly uninterested in constructing a grass-roots party organization to support the pro-Treaty line. Only as the Free State's first general election approached in the summer of 1923 did its supporters start the process of establishing local branches, reviving the name of Arthur Griffith's first political group, Cumann na nGaedheal. The August election gave this loosely focused party 63 seats, as against 16 independents, 15 Farmers party, and 14 Labour. Cumann na nGaedheal's dominance did not reflect any clear ideological stance, apart from the hard realism already ingrained into the government by the Treaty struggle. Assailed by fanatics, straitjacketed by the Treaty, and burdened by impossible popular hopes, the government stressed the limits of the possible.

The economy: agriculture or industry?

The conservatism which became the hallmark of Cumann na nGaedheal – 'solid, frugal and unimaginative' – was overwhelmingly evident in the sphere of economic policy.[17] Cosgrave's administration took it further than they needed to, continually overstressing Ireland's economic weakness and the need for sound finance. The long-established power of British 'treasury thinking' was directly transmitted into Irish administration via the Department of Finance, overwhelmingly staffed by former British civil servants. Budgets must balance, at the lowest possible level; borrowing should be avoided, and where unavoidable should be met as far as possible from current revenue; public expenditure should be cut to a bare minimum; state intervention should be shunned, and free trade generally maintained in the face of demands for protectionism.

In 1923 a Fiscal Inquiry Committee delivered a comprehensive argument against protection in general and in particular.[18] Though Cosgrave came up with the term 'selective protection' (determined by an advisory Tariff Commission), the selection was rigorous in the extreme. The Commission operated like a judicial inquiry and took evidence on a generous time-scale, though its deliberations were not shaped by any overall economic policy. In 1927 it granted protection to two commodities, margarine and rosary beads. (Certainly a mark of Ireland's special economic situation.) While it deliberated the fate of other industries – its report on paper and packaging took three years, and was by no means the longest-drawn-out – several applicants went under. The government's claim that by 1929 it had imposed tariffs on 60 per cent of non-agricultural imports, thus creating 15,000 jobs, has been politely described by a recent economic historian as 'somewhat optimistic'.[19]

In essence, the Cosgrave government had only a vestigial economic policy. It accepted a set of British assumptions about the necessity of free trade and minimal state intervention, which by the 1920s were no longer appropriate even for Britain, and were certainly unsuited to the regeneration of the Irish economy. The underlying belief was that Ireland must remain an agricultural country until the volume of exports earned enough capital to make industrial investment possible. Patrick Hogan, the Minister of Agriculture throughout Cosgrave's decade in power, took the view that agriculture 'was and would remain by far the most important industry', and the prosperity of farmers was 'the touchstone by which every economic measure must be judged'.[20] The spirit of the administration was the simple incrementalism of the slogan 'one more cow, one more sow, one more acre under the plough'. Yet despite radical efforts to improve quality and marketing methods, agricultural exports never recovered to wartime levels. The result was persistent unemployment and emigration.

Although Irish (and other) economists at the time endorsed the Free State's agrarian policy, economic historians have stressed its negative aspect: 'the government was stronger in its determination to avoid placing burdens on agriculture than in undertaking active measures'.[21] Industry stagnated; growth was a receding phantom. Arthur Griffith's venerable Listian belief that economic self-sufficiency (autarchy defended by tariffs) would generate growth was dropped by his colleagues, to be taken up a few years later by their principal opponents. All this austere orthodoxy was summed up in the infamous decisions to reduce teachers' salaries by 10 per cent in 1923 and to reduce the old age pension from 10 to 9 shillings a week in 1924 (the Finance Department had called for double this cut). Ireland, as ministers never tired of reminding it, was a poor country. Unfortunately for their political survival, they could not – unlike de Valera – manage to portray this as a virtue.

The bureaucracy as a whole was entrenched and strengthened by the civil war. William Pitt's conservative adage that you do not mend your roof in a thunderstorm was firmly endorsed by the beleaguered Staters. Sinn Féin had undoubtedly committed itself to replacing the British administrative structure. Shortly before his death Michael Collins denounced the 'alien and cumbersome administration', but noted that 'We have to begin the upbuilding of the nation with foreign tools'. More ominously, perhaps, he warned that 'before we can scrap them we must first forge fresh Gaelic ones in their place'.[22] Far from being scrapped, over 98 per cent of the Free State's civil servants had transferred from UK departments. On 1 April 1922, only 131 officials out of 20,500 had worked for the Dáil government. Here, at the heart of the state, the idea of revolution had no place: as Ronan Fanning put it, 'theirs was no brave new world envisioning independence as an opportunity for change'. The near-siege conditions in Merrion Street forged a conservative elite. 'The passion for order and stability which so characterised the government of the Irish Free State in its early years was a product of that shared experience.'[23] The most characteristic, or at least the most permanent keystone of the independent administration was the Ministers and Secretaries Act of 1924, which enshrined British mechanisms of departmental responsibility. 'Successive generations of civil servants rose to the challenge of attempting to convey as little as possible when drafting a Dáil answer.'[24] The result was a pervasive culture of official secrecy which exceeded even that of its British parent, and which would be still very much alive at the end of the century.[25]

The Boundary Commission

Amidst a number of disappointments in the Free State's early years, undoubtedly the heaviest was the persistence, and indeed the entrenchment of partition. Whilst partition had been sidelined in the Treaty debate, its impact was magnified after the civil war. (Ronan Fanning's history of independent Ireland accurately reflects this in devoting seven pages to the civil war, 16 to partition.) The assumption that the Boundary Commission would make Northern Ireland unviable had been crucial to the pro-Treaty argument. (Nobody seems to have asked why Northern Ireland needed to be 'viable' in any conventional sense, since it was not – in theory – going to be a state.) But the disaster of the civil war, together with the fall of Lloyd George, shifted the ground. When the Commission was eventually established in 1924, its remit vitally modified the original plebiscitary assumption; the border would be drawn 'in accordance with the wishes of the inhabitants, so far as may be compatible with economic and geographic conditions'. Northern Ireland refused to appoint a commissioner, but this did not prove damaging to it. Lloyd George's promise to put pressure on the Unionists had perished along with his ministerial career in 1922. The South African judge who chaired the Commission consistently favoured the status quo, and used the economic-geographic criterion to offset the undoubted wish of most northern Catholic/nationalist people for unification. Whether this dogged defence of the arbitrary six-county border was really in Northern Ireland's best interests was a question never raised.[26]

The damaging effect of the Commission was aggravated by the secrecy of its proceedings, and the odd reticence of the Free State's representative, Eoin MacNeill, who had agreed that the commissioners should not say anything in public until they had agreed a report.[27] After months of ineffectual resistance, he resigned when it became clear that the outcome would actually award some Free State territory to the North. (The border was to be shortened from 280 to 229 miles; 183,200 acres with a population of 31,319 would be transferred to the Free State, 49,242 acres with 7594 people, of whom 2764 were Catholics, would go to Northern Ireland.) This was politically unthinkable. The recommendations were finally shelved in return for a fiscal adjustment, a rather grubby bargain which set the seal on a quiet disaster.

Without a boundary revision, the Free State's northern policy did not amount to much more than non-recognition. A more constructive *démarche* had begun before the civil war, with the Craig–Collins Pact (21 January 1922), envisaging an end to the boycott and to anti-Catholic discrimination, and the replacement of the Council of Ireland by a more suitable mechanism. Craig offered regular joint Cabinet meetings, but Collins demanded a wider assembly, more like a joint parliament. In the end he got nothing at all. This was also more or less the outcome of the non-recognition policy, which survived the powerfully reasoned objections of Ernest Blythe, and was taken as far as offering financial support for Catholic schools which refused to work with the new Northern Ireland education laws. Collins evidently considered going further still, encouraging civil resistance to the Northern government, 'a scheme making it impossible for them to carry on'. But non-recognition was a futile form of provocation. Unsurprisingly the Northern reaction was to move ever further from any thought of accommodation with Dublin.[28]

In spite of these body blows, the post-Collins Free State proved to be punctilious in its obligations as a member of the British Commonwealth, and played a dynamic role in the evolution of its fellow Dominions, Canada, Australia, New Zealand and South Africa, towards undisguised independence. The Free State's ability to exploit the ambiguities in Dominion status was shown in its unilateral decision to register the Anglo-Irish Treaty with the League of Nations at Geneva in July 1924. After sitting on the sidelines during the Imperial Conference of 1923, the Irish delegation to the 1926 Conference took the lead by preparing a paper calling for the removal of all inequalities between Britain and other Dominions. Ultimately this process was ratified in 1931 by the Statute of Westminster. In 1927, when the first Governor-General of the Free State, Tim Healy, was suceeded by Eoin MacNeill's brother James, the principle of autonomy was further (if still quietly) underlined.

Nation-building: education, language and religion

In dramatic contrast to its staid and conservative administrative and economic policy, the Free State embarked on a cultural policy that was quite revolutionary. As Collins had said, 'the essence of a Gaelic state' could only be reached by recovering the Gaelic outlook, formed and expressed in the Irish language. The attempt to recover the Irish language has been cynically dismissed by some writers as a cheap compensation for the all too obvious compromises in the hard political world. But this was not a cheap project, in any sense. It sprang from the powerful idealism of the Irish revival, and was widely believed to offer the only path towards real independence. The Gaelic League pioneer Eoin MacNeill, the Free State's first Minister of Education, reiterated in 1925 that 'if Irish nationality were not to mean a distinctive Irish civilization, I would attach no very great value to Irish national independence'.[29] This belief in the emancipatory power of authenticity was saved – at least in the minds of its exponents – from the threat of exclusivism by what Terence Brown has called 'the very powerful myth of Ireland's assimilative capacities'. The possibility that state-driven language revival might alienate Protestants and reinforce partition was never entertained. The idea that the essence of Gaelic society could provide a way of life for the twentieth century, capable of integrating all Irish people, had been a crucial theme in Sinn Féin writings like Darrell Figgis's *Gaelic State* and Terence MacSwiney's *Principles of Freedom*.

It was linked, too, to a humane vision of education grounded in real experience, and the call for a literary culture that would reflect, as Daniel Corkery put it, 'what happens in the neighbourhood of an Irish boy's [*sic*] home – the fair, the hurling match, the land grabbing, the priesting, the mission, the Mass'. But in the process of state-building a fateful change took place in the wider nation-building project. The spontaneous enthusiasm for the language which the Gaelic League had focused was replaced by an assumption that the 'building up of an Irish civilization' (MacNeill) could be done by the schools. The number of League branches suddenly plummeted, from 819 in 1922 to 139 in 1924. At the same time, from April 1922 the school curriculum was radically revised to incorporate Irish as a teaching language. All teachers and school inspectors were to have a knowledge of Irish; the language became compulsory for the 1924 Intermediate and Leaving Certificates; and at primary level it drove out drawing, elementary science, hygiene, nature study and other minor subjects. By 1928 teaching was partly conducted in Irish in 3570 schools, and exclusively so in 1240. Less than 400 schools taught in English alone. This had a massive (many said crushing) effect on the learning experience of generations of Irish children, but surprisingly little effect on the use of Irish in the wider community. In retrospect this was perhaps less remarkable than the assumption of educational experts like the Jesuit Professor Corcoran, that the damage inflicted (as he believed) on the national culture by the national schools under British control could be simply reversed by the same process.[30]

The opposite view was bleakly put by another educationist, a member of the 1925 Commission for the Preservation of the Gaeltacht: 'The task of reviving a language with no large neighbouring population which speaks even a distantly related dialect, and with one of the great world-languages to contend against, is one that has never been accomplished anywhere'. Language imposition policies had only worked in cases where the peasantry still spoke the language (as with Flemish, Czech or the Baltic languages), or where immigrants were learning the language of the host community, as in the USA. Professor Tierney doubted if it was in any case 'possible to impose a language on a people as its ordinary speech by means of the schools alone'. By 1928 the Department of Education's annual report was warning that 'it may well be that the revival of the language may prove to be beyond their powers'.[31]

The difficulty of the language project contrasted with the simplicity of bringing other, more familiar, aspects of the national spirit to full flower. 'The priesting, the mission, the Mass', in Corkery's mantra, formed the texture of Irish daily life, and Catholicism naturally informed the public life of the Free State. Indeed, as Gearóid Ó Tuathaigh has observed, after 1922 'the decisive ethos within Nationalist Ireland was Catholic rather than Gaelic; the ethos pervading its social legislation, its educational system, its delineation of individual and collective rights; its social mores, its public culture'.[32] Cosgrave's administration was careful to avoid establishing what Protestants most feared, a 'Catholic state'. But notions of what constituted a Catholic state inevitably differed. The government would not involve the Hierarchy directly in the policy-making process, certainly; but being Catholics – and good Catholics – they were unlikely to initiate policies that would meet with clerical disapproval. The imbrication of Catholicism and nationalism was so intimate as to be practically invisible to Catholics themselves, but it was none the less blindingly obvious to Protestants. The first meeting of Dáil Éireann, as we have seen, had opened with a Catholic prayer. When the bitter feud between de Valera and Judge Cohalan in the USA was at last composed in March 1920, their pact was 'ratified in a most solemn manner – all present kneeling and receiving the blessing of Bishop Turner of Buffalo'.[33] Equally, it was inevitable that the annual state-of-the-nation address would come to be given on St Patrick's Day. This sense of appropriateness was, and remains, a vital aspect of nationality. By 1938 the Minister for Education could confidently claim 'that in no country in the world does a national system of education approach the Catholic ideal system as in the Free State'.[34]

The Free State's policies on divorce and contraception were as eminently natural to Catholics as they were profoundly dismaying to
Protestants. On divorce, 'The bishops of Ireland have to say that it
would be entirely unworthy of an Irish legislative body to sanction
concession of ... divorce, no matter who the petitioners may be'
(Pastoral, 9 October 1923). The Dáil followed this line. And if the
state's education policy was less of a shock, it was only because
Catholic control had already been achieved under the British system.
Protestantism as a religious persuasion was of course assiduously pro-
tected – freedom of conscience was enshrined in the constitution – and
Protestants continued to be over-represented in the higher professions. But in terms of active political citizenship Protestants became
an ever more insignificant minority. Their enhanced representation in
the Senate counted for less and less as the Senate itself was inexorably
eclipsed by the Dáil. The raw edge of Protestant defensiveness was
sharply displayed by W. B. Yeats in his Senate speech ('an astonishing
outburst', in the view of Lyons) denouncing the divorce prohibition in
1925:

> If you show that this country is going to be governed by Catholic ideas,
> and by Catholic ideas alone, you will never get the North ... you will put
> a wedge into the midst of this nation. ... it is tragic that within three years
> of this country gaining its independence we should be discussing a
> measure which a minority of this nation considers to be grossly oppressive.
> ... We against whom you have done this thing are no petty people. We are
> one of the great stocks of Europe.[35]

The bitter defensive tone was ominous. According to the 1926 census,
almost a third of Protestants in the Free State had emigrated since
1911 (nearly all of these, almost certainly, in the last five years). It was
this fact, rather than the fact that as late as 1936 some 25 per cent of
top businessmen, 38 per cent of lawyers, and no less than 53 per cent
of bank officials were Protestants, that was noticed by their co-reli-
gionists in the North.

    Protestants also saw the creation of the Censorship Board in 1930
(under the 1928 Censorship Act) as another deadly manifestation of
Catholic control, and it can hardly be doubted that the central ethos
of this measure was the rejection of materialism and modern (i.e.
Anglo-Saxon) decadence that had been championed by the Catholic
Church for decades before independence. Even though probably few
Protestants were burning with a desire to read most of the 'indecent
or obscene' books blacklisted (even under the capacious categorization

used by the Board), or indeed the books on birth control likewise prohibited, they still felt that censorship was wrong. Once again it was the assumption of rectitude behind this assault on freedom of expression that revealed the gulf between the two outlooks. Elsewhere, more naked sectarian arguments broke through, as when Mayo County Council vetoed the appointment of a Trinity-educated Protestant, Letitia Dunbar-Harrison, as county librarian in 1930. The reason publicly given was Miss Dunbar-Harrison's ignorance of Irish, but in his sardonic account of the debate Lee notes that the eventual appointee, a Catholic, was herself of dubious competence in the language. The most telling argument, he suggests, was that 'Trinity culture is not the culture of the Gael', and the open repudiation of pluralism: 'Tolerance is synonymous with slavishness'.[36]

State security: law, order and political violence

The enduring image of the Free State is a chilly one: flintily austere in finance, dour in public morality, flat in tone. This was the worthy but uninspiring palette from which William T. Cosgrave painted his public self-portrait. Eamon de Valera scathingly (and prematurely) wrote off the Treatyite leadership after the death of Griffith and Collins: 'the personnel of the Provisional Government is very weak. Cosgrave is a ninny' – though he respected MacNeill, and acknowledged Mulcahy as 'tactful'. Weakness, however, was the wrong term, or at least it mistook the quiet qualities which proved central to the state-building process. The decision to establish an unarmed police in midst of civil war remains one of the Provisional Government's most impressive achievements, evidence of the depth of their commitment to the regularization and internalization of liberal-democratic norms. What men like Cosgrave, Mulcahy, Ernest Blythe (the tight-fisted Minister of Finance) or Attorney-general Hugh Kennedy lacked was not strength but charisma. (Blythe, the only northern Protestant to hold high office in the Free State, was inhibited in expressing to the full the tough-mindedness that marks his cabinet correspondence.) The striking exception was Kevin O'Higgins, who rose to the challenge of chaos by invoking with vigour and even relish the fundamental principles of political power. O'Higgins was that odd thing, a realist zealot. As a crusader for law and order he could seem more British than the British themselves. To Irish ears there was a hefty dose of irony in his assertion that 'the ceasing of the bailiff to function is the first sign of a crumbling civilization'.[37] It may be that he was too aware of the fragility of past allegiance to the state, and compensated by hammering home the elementary principle that 'There will never be stability here until it is established beyond question that the arm of the state is longer and stronger than the arm of any combination of individuals within the state'. More menacingly yet, he insisted that 'the eyes and ears of the state must be keen in proportion to the dangers which menace its existence'. The outcome of this was a battery of state security legislation going dangerously far, in the opinion of his critics, towards establishing a kind of 'strong state' or 'security state'.

Crucial to the establishment of liberal democracy was what may be called the demilitarization of Ireland after the civil war. The prospect of a politicized army was a very real threat in circumstances of such intense ideological conflict. The original decision of Collins and Mulcahy to recruit an entirely new army, which seemed to put the Provisional Government at something of a military disadvantage in the early weeks of the civil war, signalled their determination to eliminate the ambiguity that had plagued civil-military relations between the Dáil and the IRA in 1919–22. It also built up a head of resentment amongst the old IRA officers whose expectation of future leadership of an Irish army was thwarted. At the end of the civil war, Mulcahy embarked on a radical restructuring of the army, slashing the officer corps from 3000 to 1300 and the rank and file from 52,000 to 30,000. He made it clear that even the most famous gunmen could not expect senior positions in a regular army unless they could demonstrate the professional skills he believed necessary. This provoked a murky crisis known as the 'army mutiny' of 1924, which one historian has billed as 'almost a rebellion'.[38] It was indeed threatening, not so much because of the number of disgruntled officers, as their ability to appeal to alternative sources of legitimacy. The charge brought by the so-called 'IRA Organization', or 'Old IRA', led by former stars of Collins's squad like Charles Dalton, Liam Tobin and Tom Cullen, was that the IRB had been revived and was being used as a secret mechanism – from which they were excluded – for reshaping the army. But they also held over the Free State government the menacing allegation that it was failing to be sufficiently republican. Their complaints acted as a magnet for other discontented members of the administration like the Posts Minister Joe McGrath, and polarized the Cabinet.

This crisis spotlit the vital qualities that Mulcahy contributed to the new Irish state. His icy anger at the Old IRA challenge to his reforms was typically couched in terms of the international standards he was determined to achieve: 'I do not think that in any country in the world four officers would come in uniform and sit down in front of the Commander-in-Chief and read in his presence that document'.[39] When Kevin O'Higgins used the Old IRA allegations to charge Mulcahy himself with failing to subordinate the military to the civil power, Mulcahy displayed impressive restraint, and eventually resigned rather than intensify the crisis. The paradoxical result was that civil supremacy appeared to be vindicated through the triumph of O'Higgins over the Commander-in-Chief, though it was the soldier rather than the lawyer who had identified and resisted the threat of military intervention.

The queasy balancing act maintained by O'Higgins was ended by his assassination in July 1927, which might have tilted the state finally into institutionalized repression. Eventually it would move some way in this direction with the notorious 1931 Constitution (Amendment No. 17) Act. In 1927, however, Cosgrave's instinctive parliamentarianism created a vital escape route. Along with a new but predictable Public Safety Act providing wide powers of search and arrest, and creating special juryless courts with enlarged sentencing powers, came an Electoral Amendment Act requiring all parliamentary candidates to testify that if elected they would take their seat – in other words, take the oath of allegiance. The hallowed abstentionist policy on which Sinn Féin had been founded became illegal. Historians differ over whether this was Cosgrave's finest hour – forcing his principal opponent, de Valera's Fianna Fáil party, to become a potential government – or a mistaken attempt to eliminate them from politics. (Joseph Lee has cruelly said that Cosgrave did not refuse to stoop to subterfuge, he was merely an inept subterfugist.[40]) Either way, the outcome was the ending of the virtual one-party rule of Cumann na nGaedheal.

Fianna Fáil and the normalization of politics

De Valera in a sense had been preparing for the challenge of the 1927 electoral amendment for years. As early as June 1923 he said that it was 'only by political means that we can hope for any measure of success in the near future'. Instinctively he was adopting a different time-scale from the republican idealists, and offering a way out for others who chafed against the impasse. He became increasingly out of tune with the 'will-o-the-wisp' virtual world of the 'Second Dáil' (the handful of anti-Treaty survivors of the 1921 election) which continued to claim to be the government of the republic.[41] In March 1926 he caused a second Sinn Féin split by proposing at an extraordinary Ard-fheis that if the oath of allegiance were to be removed 'it becomes a question not of principle but of policy whether or not republican representatives' entered the Dáil. This redefinition of republican principles outraged the 'Faithful Survivors', and led to his resignation as President of Sinn Féin. He set up a new party with the somewhat obfuscatory name Fianna Fáil, a title originally used on the belt-buckles of the 1916 Irish Volunteer uniform, and variously rendered in English as 'Soldiers of Destiny', or less fancifully 'Warriors of Ireland'. The party was given a more substantial English tag by de Valera's hard-headed lieutenant Seán Lemass, who saw the chance to include the most appealing part of its platform by naming it 'the Republican Party'.

Even before its formal launch, the party's aims were codified in a six-point agenda: 1) to secure the unity and independence of Ireland as a Republic; 2) to restore the Irish language as the spoken language of the people and to develop a distinctive national life in accordance with Irish traditions and ideals; 3) to make the resources and wealth of Ireland subservient to the needs and welfare of the people of Ireland; 4) to make Ireland as far as possible economically self-contained and self-sufficing; 5) to establish as many families as practicable on the land; 6) by suitable distribution of power to promote the ruralization of essential industries as opposed to their concentration in cities.[42] This rural-populist manifesto was vague enough to strike a widely resonant chord in an electorate which certainly identified Cumann na nGaedheal as a party of the wealthy bourgeoisie. Fianna Fáil contested the June 1927 election, the month before the assassination of O'Higgins, and won 44 seats (nearly doubling the 25 previously held by the abstentionist Sinn Féin), reducing Cumann na nGaedheal from 63 to 47, and still more decisively swamping the unreconstructed Sinn Féiners, only 5 of whom survived. On 11 August, de Valera at last entered the Free State Dáil by taking the oath without taking it – 'signing the book' without reading, repeating, or listening to the words of the oath of allegiance, and especially without the presence of a Bible. In the end he did what Collins had always said he could, while protesting that he had done nothing; and the spectacle had its unedifying side, as even his sympathizers admitted. But it transformed Irish politics.

Fianna Fáil was not an entirely 'normal' political party, but in re-entering constitutional politics it immediately created a meaningful two-party system. Sean Lemass artfully described his party as 'slightly constitutional', maximizing its republican credentials as well as its freedom of action. Unlike Cumann na nGaedheal, it immediately sank roots in the countryside, partly by the sheer energy with which local branches were set up, and partly by the adoption of bread-and-butter causes like the abolition of the land annuities, first proposed by the left-wing republican Peadar O'Donnell. The land annuities, the remaining payments due to Britain for the loans issued under the Land Acts which had enabled tenants to buy their farms, were a perfect electoral weapon, because they combined individual economic reality with collective symbolism. And Fianna Fáil's policies were skilfully marketed. De Valera set out to counter the monopoly of established opinion on the government side by setting up his own newspaper, the *Irish Press*, which first reached the streets in September 1931. The 1932 election offered the first real possibility of a change of government for 10 years. Cumann na nGaedheal's decade in power was unique amongst elected governments in the interwar period. In a sense, the anti-Treatyite abstention had permitted the Treaty to work, even if it had allowed the Treatyites to place too firm a conservative stamp on the identity of the new state. Irish governments from now on would face the world from a position of more secure authority.

|8|

The dominion of Eamon de Valera, 1932–1948

When Eamon de Valera returned to political primacy at the age of 49, after 10 years out of office, most observers thought that his hold on power would be tenuous at best. Wishful thinking predicted a rapid revival of Cosgrave's party. In the event, Cumann na nGaedheal went into a seemingly irreversible decline, unarrested by its reinvention as Fine Gael in 1934. In spite of the obstacles created by proportional representation, Fianna Fáil achieved an electoral dominance that no other party began to rival until the 1980s.[1] With a couple of three-year intermissions, de Valera was in power from 1932 until his retirement in 1959. In his first 15-year administration he placed an indelible stamp on the self-image of twentieth-century Ireland. Only Michael Collins, had he lived, could have contested this iconic role. De Valera's ascendancy, which Owen Dudley Edwards has puckishly likened to that of a biblical priest-king – 'the reign of Melchisedech' – stemmed from his unique capacity to invest all his actions with high symbolic force, whilst negotiating a path through reality by means of subtle semantic formulations.[2] Typical of his ability to fuse pragmatism with unflinching principle was a statement he made at the time of Fianna Fáil's first attempt to enter the Dáil without taking the oath of allegiance in 1927: 'We must of course recognize existing facts, but it does not follow that we must acquiesce in them'. The same tension marked his electrifying charge in 1929 that Cosgrave's government had 'secured a *de facto* position' but had 'not come by that position legitimately. You brought off a coup d'etat in the summer of 1922.' At that point he implied that the so-called Second Dáil still had a title to rule the country; two years later, however, he told the Free

State Dáil that 'If there is no authority in this House to rule, then there is no authority in any part of the country to rule'.[3]

The transfer of power

After its entry into the Dáil in 1927, Fianna Fáil had a four-and-a-half year apprenticeship in opposition while the Cumann na nGaedheal government dug its own political grave. As Fianna Fáil's programme became more sophisticated, Cosgrave's government became increasingly alarmist, branding the opposition as a pawn of IRA militarism and international communism. However implausible this combination may now look, it mesmerized the comfortable professional class that provided the government's main leadership constituency – what the disgruntled Richard Mulcahy called the 'Ballsbridge complex'.[4] In an atmosphere of 'red scares', the repressive legislation that had followed the assassination of O'Higgins in 1927 was followed by a still more draconian Constitution (Amendment No. 17) Act in October 1931, outlawing the IRA and 11 other organizations, and establishing a Military Tribunal with sweeping powers to punish political crime. Irish public opinion seems to have instinctively rejected this as unconstitutional, despite the undoubted increase in republican political violence. Finally, in an almost reckless display of insensitivity, the authorities arrested the editor of de Valera's newspaper the *Irish Press* and prosecuted him for seditious libel (for reporting fairly widespread stories of police brutality) in the week before the general election. The threat to press freedom was a gift to the opposition. Along with this extremely unpopular judicial repression went another instalment of fiscal austerity.

By contrast, de Valera had, as one of his earliest biographers, Seán O'Faoláin put it, 'hit upon a most powerful form of appeal to the electorate in the rural areas, in other words the mass of the people'. He picked up from the most thoughtful of the IRA irreconcilables, Peadar O'Donnell, the idea of suspending payment of the land annuities. But whereas O'Donnell had aimed to rouse the west with a land-war style rent strike – or more accurately a refusal to pay annuity arrears – de Valera merely proposed to divert the annuities from London to Dublin. Fianna Fáil election campaigning did not stress this point, and 'the farmers saw a picture of a land without rents'.[5] Alongside this, Fianna Fáil picked up and ran with the old Sinn Féin commitment to economic autarchy, which had been abandoned by the Cosgrave government. The symbolic headline of the Fianna Fáil programme was the commitment to abolish the oath of allegiance. Altogether Fianna Fáil promised to kick-start the nation-building process by strengthening Ireland internally and asserting its independence externally.

The result of the February 1932 election did not at first seem quite so decisive as it ultimately came to appear. Fianna Fáil won 44.5 per cent of the vote, and 72 seats; Cumann na nGaedheal took 57 seats, independents 11 and Labour 7. De Valera was dependent on Labour for his working majority, but Labour had already tamely endorsed the Fianna Fáil programme and did not demand any concessions. More remarkably, the old governing party stepped down peacefully. For years it had denounced de Valera as an IRA and communist stooge, and even as an anti-Catholic. (The Hierarchy were certainly suspicious of him, but Cosgrave's attempt to secure a direct clerical intervention against Fianna Fáil during the election campaign had misfired badly.) To the Treatyites, this was the man who had plunged the country into civil war and undermined the new state's legitimacy. To say he was distrusted would be to put it mildly. Many Free State officials feared for their jobs, or even their liberty, if de Valera came to power. But the expectation of a peaceful transfer of power was practically universal.

This was the ultimate test of democratic 'normalization'. Yet as some scholars have pointed out, it was far from normal amongst new states in interwar Europe. While others have suggested that Ireland's apparently instinctive operation of a multi-party system was a predictable result of its British legacy, most agree that the achievement could not be taken for granted.[6] One study of the transfer of power, by Frank Munger, suggested four essential elements in the political culture that accepted the legitimacy of opposition: the long-established Irish parliamentary tradition, the existence of a local government system based on a broad franchise, the continuity (in the eyes of Treatyites if not their opponents) between the independent Dáil and the Free State assembly, and the close association of the Catholic Church with parliamentary methods. Not all these are fully convincing – the democratic credentials of the Church have certainly been questioned. Perhaps the most crucial factor was the unequivocal docility of the Free State's army and police. Both forces, but the army in particular, were closely identified with the extremism of the civil war. Politicization of the army, or the militarization of politics, were very real dangers; indeed it has been suggested that Michael Collins, had he survived, would have found such a process congenial. It was

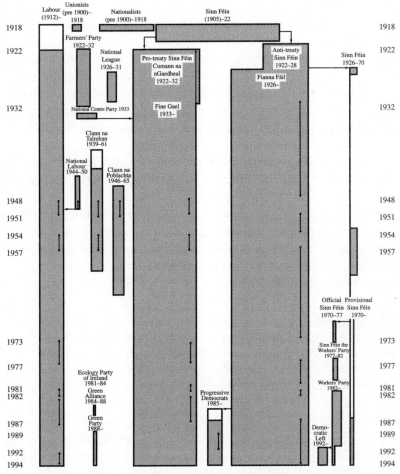

Note Shaded columns are proportional to the size of each party as measured by share of the first preference vote in all elections contested. Vertical rules within columns indicate that the party was in government in the period in question.

Fig. 8.1 Development, approximate size and participation in government of political parties in the Irish Republic, 1918–1994
Source: Based on Richard Sinnott, *Irish Voters Decide* (Manchester 1995)

Mulcahy's determination to build a professional army with a democratic social base which was the ultimate key to the survival of
democracy in Ireland.

Autarchy: symbol and substance

If Fianna Fáil was a 'slightly constitutional' party, it was also only slightly
revolutionary. It did not set out to purge or overwhelm the existing
administrative system. There was no Irish *Gleichschaltung*, as civil servants found to their palpable relief. The most dramatic changes were at
the symbolic level. Unsurprisingly, de Valera's accession to power triggered a protracted crisis in Anglo-Irish relations. Without ever acknowl-
edging the patient groundwork of his predecessors that made his policy
possible, he took a sequence of steps to assert Ireland's sovereignty. With
a rudeness at odds with his generally diplomatic public persona, he
snubbed the Governor-General (Eoin MacNeill's brother James) and
drove him into resignation. After an abortive attempt to appoint the
Chief Justice to the post, he took up an idea originally proposed by a
senior British minister – that the Governor-Generalship should be 'conducted as a purely formal office by a man residing in an ordinary residence' (so as to stop the 're-creating of the old sham [i.e. Viceregal]
court, gathering around it all the hovering sycophants and certain social
types alien to the National life of the country and the rotting effect of
this on social life generally by creating false social values …').[7]

The man chosen was ordinary indeed: Dónal O Buachalla (more
commonly known as Daniel Buckley), a doctrinaire Irish speaker and
anti-Treaty veteran who had lost his seat in the Dáil in the 1932
election after four years of near-silent membership. He took up his
official residence in his brother's house (108 Rock Road, Booterstown)
instead of the Viceregal Lodge. He was told to 'just do what the
Executive Council told him to do, and nothing more and nothing
less'.[8] With the Governor-General reduced to a cipher, de Valera went
on to strip the office of its (theoretical) power to withhold the royal
assent to legislation. After that he was prepared to wait until the
opportunity provided by the royal abdication crisis in 1936 to push
through legislation 'to delete from the constitution all mention of the
king and of the representative of the crown whether under that title or
under the title of governor-general'.

On other symbolic issues too, de Valera moved with brio and skill.
Fianna Fáil's commitment to abolish the oath of allegiance precipitated

a serious confrontation with the Senate, which returned the Removal of Oath Bill to the Dáil soon after its first passage of the lower house in May 1932. When it returned it with amendments a second time, the Senate probably sealed its own fate and guaranteed the ultimate dismantling of the bicameral parliamentary system. De Valera went to the country in January 1933 and Fianna Fáil nearly won the first absolute majority in the state's history (an elusive objective that the party seldom achieved thereafter), with exactly half the Dáil seats. The Bill was presented a third time, and became law in May 1933.

He went on to remove another crucial symbol of the British connection, the right of appeal to the Judicial Committee of the Privy Council. All of this provoked an almost hysterical reaction from the coalition National Government in London. The Colonial Secretary, labour leader J. H. Thomas, gave the impression that the entire Treaty settlement was being overthrown by republican fanatics. After early discussions, he came to the conclusion that de Valera was a hopeless case – 'A complete dreamer with no grasp of realities' – which, as Tim Pat Coogan has remarked, was a symptomatically 'monumental misjudgement'.[9] The Prime Minister, Ramsay MacDonald, came away from his one-to-one meeting with de Valera denouncing him as a dangerous obsessive:

> He begins somewhere about the birth of Christ and wants a commission of four to explore the past centuries, and all he demands is a document … a judgment as from God himself as to how the world, and more particularly Ireland, should have been ruled when they were cutting each others' throats and writing beautiful missives at the same time. It makes one sick. Behind it all is the romance of force and of arms … the fool put into a china shop in hobnail boots with liberty to smash.[10]

With British ministers – even those of Celtic origin – posing as rationalists baffled by wild Celts, there was no meeting of minds at this stage.

The most serious breakdown of Anglo-Irish relations followed from de Valera's commitment to suspend payment of the land annuities. The outraged British government responded with a battery of import duties on Irish goods, and against the advice of both his leading ministers and the Finance Department officials, de Valera insisted on Irish retaliation. The result was the 'Economic War', which was to drag on throughout the mid-1930s, casting a cloud over the regeneration promised in the Fianna Fáil electoral campaigns. A vital question for Ireland was whether the government could deliver the promise of real economic benefits through its vocal repudiation of the Free State's *laissez-faire* policy. It could not, in the event, resolve the tension between agricultural and industrial priorities; in fact the two weightiest ministers in de Valera's Cabinet, Seán MacEntee and Seán Lemass, took opposite sides on this. But the energy and determination of Lemass did have visible results in terms of industrial protection. His department, Industry and Commerce, broke the stranglehold over economic policy previously exerted by the Department of Finance. Cumann na nGaedheal's hesitant steps towards a tariff system – mainly under Fianna Fáil pressure after 1927 – were dramatically extended. Although the independent Tariff Commission remained in being, most new tariffs were imposed by ministerial order after a brief departmental investigation. Lemass characteristically said he 'preferred to take the risk of making mistakes in proceeding [this] way than to take the risk of producing the results that the late Government produced by inactivity'.[11] Most economic historians have concluded that mistakes were indeed made; the rapid new procedures did not allow thorough assessment of either the potential of the industries that applied for protection, or the impact of import duties on the economy as a whole.[12] The scale of the protection enterprise can be exaggerated. The number of tariffs certainly increased; while it had been possible in the late 1920s to list Irish tariff regulations in 10 pages, the schedules a decade later ran to over 100 pages. But as one economic historian has pointed out, Irish policies after 1929 'were hardly extreme by international standards' – in 1937 according to League of Nations calculations 17 per cent of Irish imports were subject to restrictions (licence or quota), as compared with 24 per cent in Belgium, 52 per cent in Switzerland, and 58 per cent in France.[13]

The agricultural flank of Fianna Fáil's drive to autarchy was spearheaded by the aim to expand tillage and reduce Ireland's reliance on livestock. The government was able to claim that between 1932 and 1936 the area under wheat had risen from 24,000 to 254,000 acres, but this gratifying headline disguised recalcitrant details: 147,000 of these acres were in the richest farming area, Leinster, and only 18,000 in the poorest, Connacht; and the expansion of wheat production did not signal a major increase in the total acreage under tillage, which rose only from 1.4 to 1.6 million, and later fell back below 1.5 million by 1939.[14] Rural unemployment remained endemic, and the growth of the industrial sector was too weak to absorb it. Ireland escaped the destabilizing shock of the great depression, but Fianna Fáil's economic programme was more effective at the symbolic level than in substance. It remained perhaps true that in Ireland, as was often said, political economy was

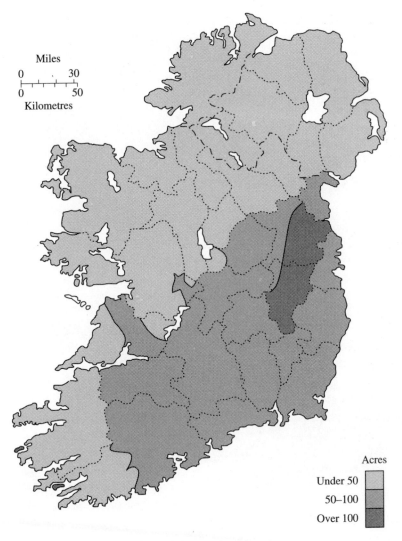

Fig. 8.2 The average size of farms, 1936
Source: Based on T. W. Freeman, *Ireland* (London 1972)

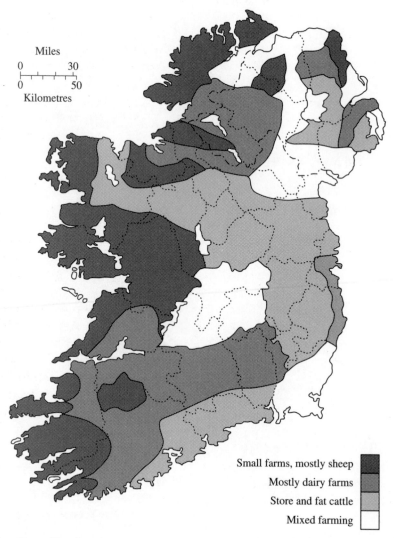

Miles
0   30
0   50
Kilometres

Small farms, mostly sheep
Mostly dairy farms
Store and fat cattle
Mixed farming

Fig. 8.3   Predominant type of farming
Source: Based on T. W. Freeman, *Ireland* (London 1972)

spelt with a capital P and a small E.[15] Certainly this priority determined the intensity of the 'Economic War', which de Valera raised to the level of the highest political stakes: 'If the British Government should succeed in beating us in this fight, then you could have no freedom, because at every step they could threaten you again and force you to obey the British'. Yet it is important to register that despite the hardship it caused, the 'war' was supported by public opinion. Joseph Lee, generally a sharp critic of Ireland's economic performance after independence, suggests that overall 'Fianna Fáil's social and economic achievement 1932–6 was in the circumstances impressive'. Despite the self-inflicted wounds of the economic war, they 'halted the slide into the economic abyss that appeared to threaten in 1931, and thus blunted the potential appeal of political extremism'.[16]

Political extremism: left, right and centre

The threat of extremism in the early 1930s was quite real, and the atmosphere was tense. The 1933 election probably generated more intimidation, and certainly more open violence, than those conducted during the Anglo-Irish war and the civil war. Notwithstanding the unobstructed transfer of power, deep suspicions and resentments persisted. Cumann na nGaedheal's charge that de Valera was an IRA pawn seemed to be borne out by the resurgence of extreme republicanism immediately after Fianna Fáil's 1932 triumph. The Military Tribunal was abolished, and in March 1932 all IRA prisoners were released. The ban on the IRA newspaper *An Phoblacht* was rescinded, as were the proscriptions of the IRA itself and its socialist offshoot Saor Éire. At a big Dublin public rally to greet the released prisoners on 13 March, the members of the Cumann na nGaedheal ministry were denounced as 'a menace to society and the independence of Ireland' – 'it behoved all Republicans to unite and wipe out that menace at all costs'. This incitement was only the beginning of a fierce IRA assault on their old enemies. As Frank Ryan put it in answer to de Valera's appeals for moderation, 'while we have fists, hands and boots to use, and guns if necessary, we will not allow freedom of speech to Irish traitors'.[17]

In response to this robust approach, the losers of the 1932 contest formed an organization that carried some disquieting echoes of continental fascism. The Army Comrades Association (ACA), founded by Dr Tom O'Higgins (the late Kevin's brother) in the spring of 1931, opened membership to the public in August 1932, and within weeks had 30,000 members. By the end of next year it claimed 100,000. In April 1933 it adopted the blue shirt as its uniform, and in July renamed itself the National Guard, though its members were always called Blueshirts. The question whether this was 'really' a fascist movement still puzzles historians, though a good deal of the problem stems from the difficulty of defining generic European fascism itself. It combined both ultra-nationalism and 'the extremism of the centre'. The ACA's founders themselves were not afraid to admit or even exaggerate the fascist connection. Its leading theoreticians, Professors James Hogan and Michael Tierney (Professor of Greek at University College, Dublin), argued that Italian Fascism was the most effective response to the crisis of political liberalism. It was, Tierney wrote, 'a scheme of social and political organization which is quite certain as time goes by to be adapted to the needs of every civilized country'. Hogan specifically insisted that 'it was the growing menace of the Communist IRA that called forth the Blueshirts as inevitably as Communist anarchy called forth the Blackshirts in Italy'.[18] And the Cumann na nGaedheal journal *United Ireland* sometimes struck quite authentic fascist notes in denouncing individualism and *laissez-faire* liberalism, and trumpeting the primacy of action – 'the man in the blue shirt and a beret is psychologically compelled to be for ever planning and doing, persuading and compelling'.[19] At its height, the movement spawned sub-groups not unlike those of its European fascist counterparts, including a (male) youth wing and girls' sections (dedicated to Irish dancing); it mounted big torchlight processions – sometimes totalling 15,000 people – plainly designed to impress and intimidate. What has been called the 'liturgical' face of fascism was certainly visible in all this.[20]

The fascistic impulse was most visible in the man who briefly led the movement, Eoin O'Duffy. Until February 1933, General O'Duffy was Commissioner of the Garda Síochána, and formally outside politics, though he had issued a stream of increasingly dire warnings about the threat of communism to the security of the state. Eventually he goaded de Valera into dismissing him, an action which further magnified the alarm of the ACA. O'Duffy became the linchpin of an alliance between the National Guard, Cumann na nGaedheal, and the Centre Party led by Frank MacDermott. Though he inspired devotion amongst his followers in the National Guard, he was an erratic public speaker, and his clearly fascist leanings – 'party politics has served its period of usefulness', he said – quickly antagonized the politicians around him. Few Blueshirt leaders openly criticized democracy. Even O'Duffy's own rhetoric never matched the cult of violence that made fascism and Nazism so deadly.

Nor could he emulate their capacity to mobilize a wide social spectrum. Ultimately, as one of the most thoughtful accounts of the movement argues, Blueshirtism remained a movement of the middle class and the big farmers, and it foundered because of its narrow social base.[21]

But the flirtation with fascism left behind a hardier legacy in the shape of corporativism. Tierney's praise of fascist Italy had specifically discounted the role of dictatorship in the new society, and praised the corporate state as 'a new and more intelligent because more subtly organised democracy'. The key figure in this programme was not Mussolini but Pope Pius XI, whose encyclical *Quadragesimo Anno* (1931), with its condemnation of materialistic capitalism, was the foundation of modern 'social Catholicism'. Corporativism, or corporatism, seemed in the 1930s to offer an authentically Catholic path of modernization, avoiding the dangers of materialism which the Church had been denouncing so strenuously for two generations. As such it appealed to all nationalists, almost as strongly as it repelled socialists. It was not a special preserve of the Blueshirts; de Valera later went on to establish a Commission on Vocational Organisation to explore the possibility of institutionalizing corporativist principles.

The final reason why Irish nationalism did not turn into fascism was the absence, whatever Professor Hogan said, of a real threat of communism. The 'Communist IRA' was not entirely a figment of his imagination, but it certainly did not begin to resemble the formidable proletarian mobilization in northern Italy that had been the target of the *squadristi*. The most radical organization created by Irish republicans, Saor Éire, was also the most transient. It was the brainchild of one of the most intellectual leaders the republican movement ever produced, Peadar O'Donnell. While de Valera was trying to shift Sinn Féin back into constitutionalism, O'Donnell was trying to move it on into the kind of socialism he believed lay at the root of republicanism. Launching the land annuities agitation in 1926, he hoped that the land struggle would restore momentum to the becalmed republican movement. The annuities issue was, as we have seen, hijacked by Fianna Fáil, but O'Donnell continued to urge the IRA – invoking its patron saint – 'to recognize with Tone that the movement of freedom must be based on that large and respectable section of the community, the men of no property and their allies who are being crushed into misery in the land'.[22] This somewhat tendentious argument – certainly exaggerating the political potential of the dispossessed masses – was hesitantly accepted by the IRA in 1930. Saor Éire (Free Ireland) was launched at a national republican congress in September 1931, with the aim of 'achieving an independent revolutionary leadership for the working class and working farmers towards the overthrow of British imperialism and its ally, Irish capitalism'. The awkward wording reflected a compromise between the IRA's traditional elitist van-guardism and the faint hope of mass mobilization. The latter was an illusion. Even before it was proscribed by Cosgrave's government under the Public Safety Act, it had run into the familiar and fatal counter: as the Saor Éire activist Sheila Humphreys ruefully recog-nized, 'we are introducing class warfare into holy Ireland'.[23]

Even the cautious agrarian 'communism' of Saor Éire went beyond what the real Irish 'masses' actually wanted – a pious peasant propri-etary. O'Donnell's unique talents were ground down between the mill-stones of IRA militarism and peasant conservatism. The independent Communist Party of Ireland, established in 1933, was if anything more marginal still. In retrospect it is easy enough to answer the question posed in the title of Professor Hogan's famous pamphlet *Could Ireland become Communist?* (1933). Even if Saor Éire had not been, as its co-founder George Gilmore later concluded, a mistake, the IRA was rapidly disabused of any idea that Fianna Fáil would create a favourable environment for republican activity. Hogan, like many others including the IRA itself, failed to see how carefully de Valera was establishing a new position of hostility to the old physical force idea, long before his accession to power. In 1926 he held that 'a [free] nation ought to be able to settle its polity so that all occasion of civil conflict between its members may be obviated'; by 1929 his repeated stress on the 'rule of order' was becoming increasingly gov-ernmental. And the crucial fact for the IRA was that although he released republican prisoners after he came to power, de Valera did not repeal the bitterly criticized Public Safety Act. It was used first against the Blueshirts, but ultimately and decisively against the IRA. Indeed, Ronan Fanning has gone so far as to suggest that 'the principal con-tribution of the Blueshirts to Irish history was to postpone the moment when de Valera came to grips with the IRA'.[24] The fateful moment arrived in June 1936, when the organization was proscribed.

Éire: the 1937 constitution

The attack on the Senate, the Governor-Generalship and other trap-pings of the imperial connection were a prelude to de Valera's crowning work, the new constitution. This was his vindication, demonstrating that his old idea of 'external association' had been both meaningful and workable. Very few modern constitutions can have been so completely identified with – indeed composed by – a single statesman. Even though he lifted large swathes from the uncontentious parts of the 1922 constitution, hundreds of hours not only of drafting but also of negotiation went into the process over a period of two years.[25] The constitution, called Bunreacht na hÉireann – literally Ireland's 'basic law', like the German *Grundgesetz* – was adopted by referendum (685,105 for, 526,945 against) on 1 July 1937.

The institutional changes wrought by the new constitution were relatively slight. The Governor-Generalship (finally abolished in June 1937) was replaced by a Presidency. The President, elected for up to two seven-year terms, became head of state, but very much a constitutional monarch in terms of political power. Real power remained in the hands of the Prime Minister, now given the historic (and histrionic) title Taoiseach – 'Chief' – in place of President of the Executive Council. Indeed the steady growth of prime ministerial power, common to both Britain and Ireland, was confirmed in the constitution's description of the Taoiseach's role. The new post of Deputy Prime Minister (Tánaiste) – a position then unknown to British politics – was added. The system of proportional representation for Dáil Éireann was unchanged, though the gradual process of reducing the number of constituencies with more than three TDs went on. The already abolished Free State Senate was replaced by a vocationally selected Senate with greatly reduced powers, in line with the fighting talk of Seán Lemass – 'if there is to be a Second House let it be a Second House under our thumb'. The popular referendum power was retained, but again reduced. The legal system went on unchanged, finally removing any prospect of significant de-Anglicization.

The real force of de Valera's constitution was declaratory and symbolic. The name of the state was changed to 'Éire, or in the English language Ireland'. Article 1 declared national sovereignty in resonant terms: 'The Irish nation hereby affirms its inalienable, indefeasible and sovereign right to choose its own form of government, ... and to develop its life, political, economic and cultural, in accordance with its own genius and traditions'. But though the constitution effectively made Éire a republic, the word was withheld – less for fear of British or Unionist reactions than because the 26-county state did not seem worthy of the aspirations that the word enshrined. The territorial jurisdiction of the state was declared (Article 2) to be the whole island of Ireland, but (Article 3) 'pending the re-integration of the national territory' to be the 26 counties of the former Saorstat. Article 8 declared that Irish was 'the national language', and 'the first official language'; English was 'recognized' as a second official language. De Valera did not try to avoid the absurdities that Michael Collins thought would be produced by mixing the languages in one document, but he delivered the constitution itself in both. Oddly, however, the original draft was in English, but the Irish translation was made the binding version. Linguistic slippage was almost built into the new state rhetoric. Thus although the presidential palace – the old Viceregal Lodge – became known as Aras an Uachtarain, the presidential title was habitually given in English. (Likewise although the English versions of Taoiseach, Tánaiste and Oireachtas (parliament) were completely dropped, few people would ever use the Irish titles for the Chief Justice or the Supreme Court.)

An equally crucial set of declaratory articles (40–44) dealt with 'fundamental rights' and 'directive principles of social policy'. Article 40 was a declaration of the liberty of the individual in continental style, but it was balanced – some said offset – by some remarkable declarations concerning the family, education and religion. Article 41 announced that 'the State recognizes the Family as the natural primary and fundamental unit group of society, and as a moral institution possessing inalienable and imprescriptible rights'. This committed the state to ban divorce, and to 'endeavour to ensure that mothers shall not be obliged by economic necessity to engage in labour to the neglect of their duties in the home'. Article 42 amplified the role of the family by declaring it to be 'the primary and natural educator' of children, relegating the state's function to defining minimum standards and giving some aid to private and corporate educational institutions. Any state initiatives were explicitly subordinated to parental rights 'especially in the matter of religious and moral education'.

The declaration which perhaps above all has been seen as stamping the 1937 constitution with a character fundamentally different from the 1922 original was clause 2 of Article 44, declaring that 'the State recognizes the special position of the Holy Catholic Apostolic and Roman Church as the guardian of the faith professed by the great majority of the citizens'. Too much emphasis can be, and certainly has been, laid on this clause, which by no means turned Ireland into a 'Catholic state' in the sense feared by many Protestants. Clause 3 went on to add that 'the State also recognizes ... the other religious denominations existing in Ireland ... as the guardians of the faith of their respective communities', and clause 4 was an unequivocal guarantee of religious toleration. This article was in one sense, as has often been said, merely a statement of fact. Clearly, however, its significance was bigger than this. After all, not every fact of Irish life was recognized in the constitution. In symbolic terms this clause carefully reversed the studied neutrality that the secular British state had adopted after it disestablished the Church of Ireland in 1869. Nobody in Ireland could doubt that it was also intended, and understood, as reversing the historic subordination of the Catholic Church. The fact that the Catholic flock was the great majority of the Irish people was not just a statistic: it said something special about the Irish people. In that sense Article 44 did identify Catholicism with the Irish nation.

De Valera's constitution was a coping-stone for the irregular edifice of the nation-building process after 1922. F. S. L. Lyons delivered a historian's carefully balanced assessment of it, stressing its essentially benign conservative intent, and the value of even its vague 'principles of social policy' not so much as programmes of action as guiding ideals for succeeding governments. Despite the lukewarm commitment of the people as measured in the referendum, he suggested that in its social provisions 'the state committed itself publicly to upholding a pattern of life that the majority of its citizens felt to be the right pattern for them'. Writing in 1970, Lyons was inclined to play down its divisive potential, though he could not but be acutely conscious of it. In validating one dominant version of nationality, it inevitably excluded the minority for which both the Irish language and the Catholic Church were the opposite of integrative symbols. The combination of Catholic social values and the territorial claim to the whole island cemented the alienation of the northern Protestant Unionists, so that the very success of the nation-building process ensured the frustration of the desire for unification. De Valera may not have accepted this, or even recognized that there might be a contradiction. Still, as Lyons concluded, the 1937 constitution was necessary: 'what it did for Ireland can be summed up in a single sentence. It brought stability'.[26] After a generation of conflict, this was crucial. The risk that it might bring too much stability, that stability might become stasis, hardly weighed at the time.

Church and nation

The question whether Ireland was (and is) a 'Catholic state', for good or ill, has haunted the country since independence. For many

Catholics it was entirely right that it should be one. Ireland was not only overwhelmingly Catholic, but since the nineteenth century it had possessed an especially observant flock. The adjective 'devout' is routinely attached to the personal beliefs of Irish Catholics, in particular leaders like Cosgrave and de Valera. The public character of the country is deeply marked by this. But there has also been a robust tradition of Catholic anticlericalism, insisting on the exclusion of priests from politics. And while a radical anticlerical like Peadar O'Donnell might denounce 'a yahoo-ridden church', few devout Catholics wanted to create a Catholic state of the kind conjured up in some northern Protestant imaginations, where political power would be directly exerted by priests. Plainly this did not happen. Southern Protestants, as Lyons charmingly put it, 'gratefully experienced' the tolerance of both state and society. In another famous phrase he put the issue a little more darkly, however, speaking of 'almost repressive tolerance'. This touches the essence of the minority problem in any powerfully cohesive society. The majority naturally exercise the right to express their sense of collective identity. Legislation may not be directly dictated by priests, but legislators are believers and accept the propriety of clerical guidance. Owen Dudley Edwards has pointed out that the 1937 constitution went so far in legislating Catholic social thought that it was used to illustrate the concept 'Catholicism' in a leading analysis of European social and political doctrines in 1939, and the term 'Catholic state' has continued to be wielded by contestants in more recent debates over divorce and abortion law reform.[27]

Careful studies by John Whyte and Dermot Keogh have demonstrated the complexity and subtlety of the relationship between episcopal and political leaders. Keogh finds that while 'the values and culture of the major political parties in the 1920s and 1930s reflected the dominant Catholic ethos', Cosgrave and de Valera were both meticulous in observing liberal proprieties.[28] But an event like the Eucharistic Congress, which took place in Ireland in 1932, could not fail to demonstrate the centrality of Catholicism in the Irish world-picture. In the weeks before the event, the whole country seemed to be festooned with gold-and-white papal colours. The period of the Congress became a national holiday; not only the banks, but even the law courts stopped work. The addresses to the Congress underlined the global missionary role of Ireland and its special spiritual virtue. One of the Canadian delegation spoke of 'the resurrection of the Catholic nation' as 'proof that there is a Divine Providence'. Cardinal Lauri, the Papal Legate, delivered a message from the Pope voicing an interpretation of Irishness that would have pleased D. P. Moran: 'rightly did the whole Catholic world unite today in the rejoicing of the Irish people whose ancestors carried forth the religion of their fathers and widely diffused it …'.[29]

De Valera consistently returned to the special spiritual quality of the Irish people and its role in the world. Opening the Athlone broadcasting station in 1933, he declared that 'the Irish genius has always stressed spiritual and intellectual rather than material values'. This 'characteristic fits the Irish people in a special manner for the task, now a vital one, of helping to save western civilisation'.[30] He was careful to call this spirituality Christian rather than specifically Catholic, but the spiritual-material antagonism was so salient in Catholic discourse that its origins could not be mistaken. Likewise the headlining of spiritual values in Article 1 of the 1937 constitution – whose Preamble opens with the invocation 'In the name of the Most Holy Trinity …' – would hardly have been likely in a secular liberal state. It is true that de Valera resisted clerical pressure on a number of major issues. He maintained the economic war in the face of clerical protests about the hardship inflicted on farmers, and during the Spanish civil war he refused to withdraw Irish recognition of the Republican government. John Whyte concluded rather grudgingly that the Fianna Fáil leadership's independence of judgement 'had not been altogether abandoned'.[31] In a more positive sense, what is striking is de Valera's capacity to project a symbolic image that was quite variably implemented in reality. (Dermot Keogh has pointed out, for instance, that the 1931 report of the Committee on the Criminal Law Amendment Act and on Juvenile Prostitution presented a picture of Ireland which was the reverse of the pious land of the Eucharistic Congress: the report found striking unanimity among its witnesses that 'degeneration in the standard of social conduct has taken place in recent years'.)[32] This mythopoeic power, or capacity for self-deception, was evident also in other vital symbolic zones of policy – the language question and external relations.

External relations and the Anglo-Irish settlement

Ireland's international posture was profoundly influenced by two major events in de Valera's first administration, the 'economic war' and the Second World War. Although these were utterly incommensurable in global terms, they were both vital stages in the slow and uneasy process of emerging from the smothering weight of British power. British-Irish relations inevitably dominated Ireland's external outlook, but they did not monopolize it. By the time de Valera took office, the Cosgrave government had already established Ireland's credentials as a leader in the evolution of the British Empire into the 'Commonwealth' through the steady enlargement of Dominion status. The 'restless Dominion', as David Harkness labelled it, played a pivotal role in the tough confrontation at the 1930 Imperial Conference which led to the 1931 Statute of Westminster, finally recognizing effective Dominion sovereignty. This was the vindication of the Treaty, as Patrick McGilligan told the Dáil: 'when this country accepted the status of Canada ... the status then accepted was not a stereotyed legal formula'.[33] Not that de Valera was likely to concede this, or the Free State's achievement in establishing a different global role in the League of Nations. But he reaped the full benefit of this in 1932 when Ireland assumed the League Council Presidency immediately after he took office. (He took the External Affairs portfolio throughout his administration.) He was given a world platform and a real international problem to deal with – the imposition of sanctions on Italy after the invasion of Abyssinia.

In this role, his insistence on defending 'the sovereignty of even the weakest state amongst us' provided a *leitmotiv* for his confrontational stance towards Britain. De Valera was the first Irish head of government to exploit the domestic political advantages of foreign policy.[34] Despite the economic costs and dislocation of the trade war, the ultimate political achievement was clear. The confrontation was resolved by a combination of a more flexible British attitude (after an incontrovertible demonstration of de Valera's support in the 1935 election, when Fianna Fáil won 49.7 per cent of the vote, 76 seats), the realization that he was a skilful pragmatist rather than a fanatic, and Britain's own royal crisis. On 25 April 1938 an Anglo-Irish agreement stabilized future relations on the basis of a lump sum payment (£10 million) by Ireland to settle the land annuities, and the return to Ireland of the 'Treaty ports' that had remained under British control (Berehaven, Cobh, Belfast Lough, and Lough Swilly, with depots at Rathmullen and Haulbowline). This was crucial for two reasons. First, it was the result of a fundamental British re-assessment of Irish policy. During extensive discussions by the Joint Chiefs of Staff it became clear that retention of the ports was no use to Britain without Irish goodwill, because the use of military force against Ireland was not a credible option. The formal abandonment of the vaguely retained option of 'reconquest' (which certainly haunted Irish minds) was a pivotal moment in British history.[35] The second crucial point about the recovery of the Treaty ports was that it made a policy of neutrality feasible. Not much more than a year later, this became a defining national issue.

De Valera's sure-footedness across a wide range of policy deserted him in one sphere, however. When he had secured the ports and heralded the policy of neutrality, he declared (on 6 June 1938) 'I have far greater hope of seeing in my lifetime a united Ireland than I had in 1932'. This was no doubt in part a piece of electioneering, but it was more than that. Ever since the issue of partition had arisen, de Valera had instinctively attributed it to British interference ('the play of English interest') rather than deep-seated Unionist resistance to Dublin rule. His attitude towards the recalcitrant loyalists was incoherent; while he often followed the conventional nationalist view that the natural Irishness of the northerners (because 'Gaelic blood' predominated in nearly all of them) would blossom as soon as British mischief-making ended, at other times he could speak of them with undisguised hostility as aliens. He declared in the *Gaelic American* in 1920 that once the British were gone 'we'll put a South of Ireland Catholic on a platform in Ulster and an Ulsterman on a platform in the South, and in ten words they will have dispelled the bogy-illusion of religious differences'. But he dismissed Ulster's case as that of 'the robber coming into another man's house, and claiming a room as his'. In essence, de Valera rejected the right of northern Protestants to recognition as a community; for him, as for most Irish nationalists, the only legitimate unit for self-determination was the island of Ireland as a whole. The impact of his attitudes was wholly negative. It is clear that after 1932 the gulf between North and South was widening rather than narrowing, and that de Valera's confrontational policies played into the hands of irreconcilable Unionist politicians whose all-too-rich stock in trade was the northern 'siege mentality'.[36]

The Emergency and neutrality

The preservation of Irish neutrality during the most terrible of the twentieth century's global wars was not only the capstone of de Valera's assertion of independence, but also the outgrowth of deeply etched beliefs about Ireland's place in the world. Sinn Féin had carried a potent idealistic message about Ireland's role – 'we shall rouse the world from a wicked dream of material greed, of tyrannical power, of corrupt and callous politics'.[37] Neutrality was not an easy policy to maintain. The nature of the Nazi regime made the Second World War a 'good war' which was hard to dismiss as another exercise in British imperialism, though naturally most republicans instinctively did so, and there was generally little public eagerness to grasp the growing evidence of Nazi atrocities. From the Irish standpoint, Britain remained a bigger problem. As the veteran guerrilla fighter Dan Breen put it, 'the Germans and Italians are not the people that murdered and robbed my people for 700 years'. At the beginning of the war, most people probably thought that a German victory would be beneficial to Ireland. The British Prime Minister, Churchill, never accepted Ireland's neutrality ('at war but skulking' was his typically brutal verdict; 'a most grievous and heavy burden that we cannot use the south and west coast of Ireland' his assessment of its impact). After Pearl Harbor he made an gnomic offer of Irish unity as a reward for Irish belligerency – 'Now is your chance. Now or Never. 'A nation once again"', he telegraphed de Valera in December 1941 – but few people believed he could deliver. And de Valera had already rejected a similar invitation from Neville Chamberlain with the argument that 'a neutral Irish Free State would serve Britain's interests better than an allied one'.

Churchill's charge that Ireland was 'at war but skulking' has been endorsed (in less offensive terms) by some modern scholars, who have pointed out that Ireland enjoyed neutrality on the cheap, neglecting to provide anything like realistic defence forces because of its confidence that it could shelter behind Britain.[38] Uniquely in Europe, Irish defence expenditure actually fell during the war. With a navy consisting of two armed trawlers, and no coastal defences or minefields, Ireland was incapable of maintaining strict neutrality, and did not do so. Irish neutrality was distinctly pro-Allied; strict neutrality was compromised by the open acknowledgement of British security concerns, on the basis of the 1938 agreement. More substantial breaches of neutrality included differential treatment of German and Allied aircrew who came down in Irish territory – the former were interned, the latter returned home, on the basis of a conveniently invented distinction between 'operational' and 'non-operational' flights. All this was not enough for some. Churchill, in particular, who was the only leading British politician to have opposed the 1938 settlement, still thought that the loss of the 'Treaty ports' was a deadly threat to Britain's security, and encouraged military planning to recover them. The USA's entry into the war at the end of 1941 imposed a further strain on the neutrality policy. The US ambassador in Dublin, David Gray, was if possible more hostile to Irish neutrality than Churchill, and believed that America was entitled to demand Irish support.

The possibility of a major breakdown in Anglo-Irish relations was averted by the tactful presence of Sir John Maffey as British Representative to (not 'in') Ireland. De Valera's careful choice of preposition reflected the unresolved ambiguity of Éire's status even after the 1938 agreement. This kind of pedantry still annoyed many British officials, but Maffey respected the skill with which de Valera managed a potentially explosive situation. He wisely advised London that 'A show of resentment on our part merely stirs the old passions. ... A friendly and reasoned approach will serve us best ...'. Such an approach survived even the abrasive attitude of Ambassador Gray, who thought de Valera was living in 'a dream-wish world', and that American military action might be needed to force Ireland to co-operate.

In Ireland the war was officially known as 'the Emergency', but this euphemism did not inhibit a very noticeable expansion of government powers of the kind usually witnessed in belligerent states. In June 1939 de Valera finally repealed the once-hated Public Safety laws of the Cosgrave administration, but only to replace them with a new Offences Against the State Act. The main target of this was now the IRA, which had launched a bombing campaign in Britain at the beginning of the year. De Valera was plainly determined to vindicate constitutional authority in Ireland, and challenge the persistent republican claim to superior legitimacy. The Ministry of Justice, true to its O'Higginsite pedigree, lectured de Valera on the need for draconian action because Ireland could not depend, as Britain did, on 'a long tradition of cooperation between the public and the police'. It warned almost melodramatically that 'a small country cannot afford to invite attacks from without by a seeming inability to keep order within its own territory', and suggested that this danger would be acute when 'unlawful organisations' launched operations in 'other states' using Ireland as a base.[39] De Valera took the point. But facing down the IRA was provocative; IRA men detained without trial under the new emergency powers went on hunger strike, and the internal tension reinforced de Valera's belief that neutrality was the only possible war policy.

The wartime state of emergency also generated a regime of censorship that was unusual in a non-belligerent state. Frank Aiken (the anti-Treaty IRA commander who had issued the cease-fire order ending the civil war) became Minister for the Co-ordination of Defensive Measures in a reconstructed Cabinet. Aiken's irregular background perhaps showed through in his announcement that when the 'fundamental basis of democracy' was threatened, 'peacetime liberalistic trimmings' such as freedom of speech and information had to be discarded.[40] Although the broad principle was defensible, the relish with which censorship was applied seemed to go beyond reluctance. Any trace of content which might elicit sympathy for any belligerent was, for instance, enough to get a film banned: this included not only obvious cases like *Target for Tonight*, but even Chaplin's *Great Dictator*. Some films were so savagely cut as to be reduced to a series of disconnected images. Censorship was not limited to suspicious modern media such as film. The Bishop of Achonry's 1941 Lenten pastoral, asking 'Can Catholics view with easy minds the possibility of a victory which would give brute force the power to control Europe?', was kept out of the newspapers.[41] Press censorship became more comprehensive than many people felt to be justified by the public danger Ireland faced, while the military intelligence service (G2) extended its field of surveillance through postal and telegraph interception, and even phone-tapping.[42] Informed or thoughtful public discussion of the world war and the issues at stake was minimized.

All of this contributed to the somewhat strange character of public life in wartime Ireland. Neutrality had costs in further economic paralysis; by 1942 fuel rationing had brought private motoring to a halt, even for doctors; railway services were also drastically reduced. In 1941 a wage freeze was imposed, and trade union rights were cut back. Although the policy of neutrality was to all intents inevitable, it has been quizzically reassessed by a number of writers in recent years. Dermot Keogh, for example, has suggested that after displaying fine political judgement for many years, de Valera made a major error in May 1945 when he sent condolences to the German legation on the news of Hitler's death. De Valera himself portrayed this as a technical matter of neutral protocol, and defended himself in a dignified way against the intemperately sardonic attack launched by Churchill. (Britain had 'left the Dublin government to frolic with the Germans and later with the Japanese representatives to their hearts' content'.) In Ireland de Valera's restrained reply was hailed as the triumphant vindication of neutrality, but in fact no other neutral states paid last respects to Hitler. Ireland was also unusual in not declaring that it would refuse asylum to Axis war criminals. The depth of American annoyance with Ireland can be read in the measured diplomatic language of Cordell Hull's memoirs. The

USA 'did not consider Ireland's response satisfactory': 'we pointed out to the Irish government that we failed to understand how that government could feel that charity, justice, or the interest or honour of Ireland could make necessary the admission of war criminals. We did not, however, obtain better assurances'.[43]

All this tends to sustain the view that Ireland marginalized itself to an excessive degree during the Emergency – a view most vividly put by Lyons in his metaphor of Plato's cave, suggesting that the Irish relegated themselves to a shadow world. This celebrated image has been criticized by J. J. Lee, though Lee goes on to suggest that a brief Nazi occupation of Ireland would have been beneficial – 'It would have allowed experience to at last satisfy the insatiable appetite for grievance. And it would have told us so much more than we can know about ourselves.' Lee has, in turn, offered his own remarkable critique of neutrality. It was 'one more experience from which the Irish would choose not to learn'; a delusion which reinforced a collective self-deception about the power of words.[44]

Education and the national self-image

In the middle of the world war, de Valera made one of his most resonant statements about Irish national aspirations. His annual St Patrick's Day radio address in 1943 has been frequently quoted, more often in mockery than admiration nowadays, but it expressed with real force his unwavering insistence that the fundamental social goal was the quality of life. National independence, as he later said, was not an end in itself, but 'the enabling condition for the gradual building up of a community' which, by 'cultivation of the things of the mind and spirit', could 'have the happiness of a full life'.[45] In 1943 he tried to fix the national self-image of the Irish as:

> a people who valued material wealth only as the basis of right living, a people who were satisfied with frugal comfort and devoted their leisure to things of the spirit – a land whose countryside would be bright with cosy homesteads, whose fields and villages would be joyous with the sound of industry, with the romping of sturdy children, the contests of athletic youths and the laughter of comely maidens ... in a word, the home of a people living the life that God desires that man should live.[46]

The problem, as historians have pointed out, was that the gap between ideal and reality increasingly imperilled the credibility of this image.

The root of the problem, from de Valera's point of view, was the language question. Like many nationalists, he assumed that language was not just the primary badge of nationality, but that it offered the only vehicle through which the nation's essential spirit could shape its everyday life. De Valera once went as far as to say that 'Ireland with its language and without freedom is preferable to Ireland with freedom and without its language'. The revival of the Gaelic language (by this time habitually referred to as the 'Irish language' – a more politically loaded description) was even more vital for the Fianna Fáil project than it had been for Cosgrave's party. But it brought no new thinking to the recalcitrant question of how the language should be revived. It inherited from Cosgrave not only the institutional structure of the school system – the British structure which the Free State had itself preserved – but also the assumption that the language revival would be achieved in the elementary schools. This would be done if necessary at the expense of other educational goals. Indeed, the language issue dominated political ideas about education for decades. The presidential address to the 1947 annual congress of secondary teachers lamented that scarcely any minister or public figure ever mentioned education except in connection with the revival of the Irish language.[47]

Fianna Fáil's main contribution to the education issue was to step up the level of exhortation. Thomas Derrig, de Valera's appointee as Minister for Education, was an uncharismatic minister with a tendency to hector rather than inspire Irish teachers. In June 1934 he summoned representatives of the Irish National Teachers' Organization (INTO) to express his dissatisfaction with their progress in the language revival, and later that year he directed that standards in other subjects could be reduced in order to prioritize the use of Irish. Amongst the subjects that disappeared from infant teaching were rural science and English. In the mid-1930s Derrig raised the proportion of preparatory college places (for primary teachers) reserved for fluent Irish speakers from 50 to 80 per cent. The pressure to increase teaching through the medium of Irish in secondary schools mounted during the 1930s; a bonus scheme offered up to 25 per cent of the capitation grant for schools in Class A (teaching all subjects except languages) through Irish.

The problem was that, as a leading historian of the Irish education system has pointed out, the language was given priority not for educational but for political reasons. Attempts to establish whether education through Irish was beneficial for children were held up for many years. Even as late as 1954, in the first major inquiry into primary education since 1926, no concrete evidence was brought forward. 'No scientific research to prove or disprove this assertion [that teaching through two languages is detrimental] has been carried out in this country.' The INTO itself conducted an investigation in the late 1930s, and found that 345 out of 390 teachers who offered an opinion on this issue thought that their pupils did not learn as much through Irish as they would have learned through English. These teachers thought that the shock of saturation teaching in Irish was confusing for many children, making the infant school a repressive environment, and the experience of education baffling for all but the brightest.[48] Nor did governments attempt to find out what parents thought of the language policy in schools. Again, the only substantial evidence was collected by the INTO, and suggested that the official exclusion of English teaching was consistently fought against by parents throughout the country. Parental, or in other words social disengagement from the language revival explains why, despite all these efforts, the language continued to decline as a means of everyday communication. In 1937, when the new constitution declared it to be the official language, one senior civil servant pointed out that less than 15 per cent of officials even knew the language, and far fewer used it. The *Gaeltacht* areas in the west, officially classified as Irish-speaking, continued to shrink.

By the end of the Emergency a combination of frustration and underpayment had turned Ireland's teachers into a disaffected group, opening the first rift in de Valera's nation-building project. The wage freeze hit them particularly hard, and they resented exclusion from the flexible cost of living bonus granted to civil servants in 1944. The state plainly did not regard the morale or status of teachers as a significant issue. In March 1946, after negotiations over its pay claim had dragged on for well over a year, the INTO took strike action. All the Dublin schools were closed (140 schools with 1200 teachers and 40,000 pupils) and strike pay was contributed from the provinces. De Valera's response was unbending; Derrig called the strike 'a definite challenge to the authority of the state', and even Seán Lemass uncharacteristically assaulted the action as 'reckless and irresponsible', aimed at 'undermining the authority and influence of the government'. This was especially remarkable in that the teachers had for many years been regarded as a mainstay of Fianna Fáil's constituency. The government succeeded in driving the teachers back to work at the end of October without any pay increase, but at the cost of some political damage. Most significantly, the Church had espoused the teachers' cause as

|9|

The second republic and
modernization, 1948–1968

*I*f de Valera's accession to power in 1932 was a crucial test of democratic political culture in Ireland, his loss of it in 1948 was also
vital to the maintenance of pluralism. The fact that Fianna Fáil
was ousted by an improbable coalition of conservative and radical
groups whose main aim was simply to get de Valera out, mattered less
than the demonstration that power was revocable. Towards the end of
its 18-year rule, the governing party was showing signs of arrogance,
and there was a sense that its hegemony was turning Ireland into a
one-party state. This was not, as it had been in the 1920s, because of
the abstention of the opposition, but because political opposition
appeared to be in terminal decline.

The paralysis of political opposition

For 15 years after its creation, Fine Gael's election performance was
linear: in 1937 it got 34.8 per cent of the vote, in 1938 33.3, in 1943
23.1, and in 1944, the last and most successful of de Valera's snap elections, a near-catastrophic 20.1 per cent. The Labour party did better
for a while. In 1943 it looked as though it might take over as the principal opposition party, winning 15.7 per cent (easily its best performance since 1922). But a struggle between the staid William O'Brien
and the newly returned Jim Larkin opened up another split in the
party, and in 1944 Labour fell back below 9 per cent; the breakaway
National Labour party barely secured 2 per cent. Moreover, even the
new parties that emerged in this period were unlikely to prove

formidable rivals. The most dynamic of them, initially, was a new farmers' party, Clann na Talmhan ('Sons of the Soil' was the suitably romantic English version of the title), founded in Co. Galway in June 1939. The Clann claimed to be 'not just land-minded', seeking 'fair play and social justice' for all classes. In 1943 it won 13 seats with 9 per cent of the vote (mainly in the west), and in 1944 its vote increased although it lost seats. After that it went into continuous decline: its vote was halved in 1948, and the party eventually petered out in the 1960s. In retrospect it can be seen to have been crippled from the start by its dependence on a declining occupational constituency, the independent agricultural sector. A smaller party still, Ailtirí na hAiséirighe (Architects of the Resurrection), founded in the early 1940s, never really established a significant constituency for its pure Catholic idealism. Its demand for corporativism, and exclusive use of the Irish language 'to drive English and the godless modernistic culture for which it stands out of Ireland for once and for all', did not secure it a single seat in 1943 or 1944. On the basis of the 1944 result, Fianna Fáil looked impregnable.

The erosion of Fianna Fáil hegemony

From 1944 onwards there were a number of signs that Fianna Fáil's exercise of this power was becoming rather unresponsive. The first was the quite remarkable silence with which it greeted the long-awaited report of the Commission on Vocational Organization which was published in August 1944. Whether or not there was much public support for corporatism (and the failure of the Aiséirighe suggests there was not), the Commission was an important public undertaking, chaired by the Bishop of Galway, whose deliberations over four years had produced a 500-page report, and it might have been expected that the government would give – or at least appear to give – serious consideration to the issue. Instead it ignored it for three months, until the head of one of the departments criticized in the report (Agriculture) obliquely rebutted the charges of bureaucratism which the Commission had made. Some weeks after that, Seán Lemass as Minister for Industry and Commerce confirmed that the government took a wholly negative view of the 'querulous, nagging, propagandist' report. Lemass roundly condemned it as 'slovenly' in its factual basis. The Bishop of Galway's reaction was predictably outraged, and an acrimonious controversy followed.[1]

The government gave still shorter shrift to an independent study drawn up by the Bishop of Clonfert under the title *Social Security: Outlines of a Scheme of National Health Insurance*, published in October 1944. The bishop, Dr Dignan, argued on Christian principles for a thoroughgoing restructuring of the health service, and other social services. He condemned the system inherited from the British poor law administration as both degrading and inadequate, and argued for a comprehensive insurance-based system. But he did not work up detailed financial projections for his scheme, and Seán MacEntee as Minister for Local Government refused even to acknowledge the plan as a contribution to public debate. The government's almost contemptuously dismissive attitude to these attempts at intervention in its sphere of authority was possibly sharpened by the habits of control and suppression induced by the Emergency. But it was regrettable, since whatever its manifest failings the Commission of Vocational Organization was, as one historian has noted, the only inquiry 'that consciously took the whole organisation of Irish social and economic life as its field, and attempted to elaborate a new philosophy and structure of governance'.[2]

By 1945 Fianna Fáil had become more statist than its populist rhetoric might have suggested. The process may have been boosted by the Emergency, but it represented a long-term centralizing trend that has been noted by many observers. It originated with the Provisional Government's overcompensation for what it saw as the historic public delegitimation of the state in Ireland. Despite de Valera's idyllic vision of the self-reliant rural Christian community, the process of centralization continued inexorably under his aegis: in Lee's judgement 'there was a glaring gap between the platform cult of the self-reliant community and the stern realities of the centralising state'.[3] The high-handed manner evident in 1944 was, as we have seen, maintained during the 1946 teachers' strike. In between, the government showed that it was prepared to take the process further still at the institutional level. The Public Health Bill introduced in December 1945 represented a dramatic shift towards the creation of a welfare state of the kind familiar in several European countries, as well as Australia and New Zealand. The underlying cause was the parlous state of the Irish health services, as identified by Dr Dignan, but Ireland faced a more immediate public health crisis in the form of rising tuberculosis and infant mortality rates. It was in fact the only European country where the steady decline in these rates was reversed during the war period.

The reform was pressed by a junior minister, Dr Conn Ward, who had been Parliamentary Secretary to the Minister for Local Government and Public Health ever since 1932, but whose control over health policy increased when Seán MacEntee became Minister in 1941. He was spurred on by a newly appointed Chief Medical Adviser, Dr James Deeny, and probably influenced by the immense favourable publicity given to the 'Beveridge plan' for postwar reconstruction in Britain, which promised liberation from the 'giants' of want and disease. They came up with legislation which was remarkable, by European standards, in the extent of the centralization it proposed for the health service, and also the extent of compulsion (in tests for infectious diseases), and the denial of choice of doctor.

Time would show that these were potentially contentious, indeed explosive issues, but in 1946 as the Bill went through the Dáil it did not provoke widespread public debate. In parliament it was fiercely and persistently opposed by Fine Gael, who put down some 500 out of 642 amendments during the committee stage in March–April. Their target was, as John Whyte's lucid analysis shows, its 'centralising and bureaucratic spirit'. Fine Gael's leader, Richard Mulcahy, denounced the bill as 'an unprecedented series of attacks on public liberty', but the party took its stand not so much on liberal principles as on Catholic belief in family values. Patrick McGilligan specifically identified it as a 'Christian tradition' (rather than a liberal principle) 'that there are individual rights which no State can take away'.[4] Interestingly, though, in the light of the crisis that broke five years later, neither the doctors' organization, the Medical Association of Éire, nor the Catholic Hierarchy, manifested any substantial hostility to the Bill, which would have become law in 1946 but for the eruption of a sleaze charge against Ward (connected with a business enterprise, not the health service) which forced him to resign in July. The government allowed the Bill to fall, and waited almost a year before reintroducing the reform, because the ministry was being restructured.

In December 1946 the Health Ministry was separated from Local Government, and taken over by the former Agriculture Minister James Ryan. The Public Health Bill had to be adapted, and was reintroduced in May 1947. At this point, in spite of Ryan's well-known emollience, the proposal began to attract wider hostility than it had in the hands of the more abrasive Ward. The focus of opposition shifted from the Dáil, where Fine Gael rather oddly greeted the proposal they had fought so relentlessly in 1946 as 'non-controversial', to the doctors and the bishops. It seems that the full import of the reform only began to sink in after several months. As it did, the Bishop of Limerick publicly endorsed (with the tacit approval of the Hierarchy) the objections raised by Catholic doctors in his diocese: the Bill was 'a menace to the rights and duties of doctors ... and a threat to the fundamental rights of parents'. Fianna Fáil was on course for an unprecedented confrontation, when its grip on power was at last prised open in the general election of February 1948.

New republicanism: Clann na Poblachta

The widening disillusionment with de Valera found its most potent focus in the creation of a new political party, more directly threatening to Fianna Fáil than any to have appeared so far. Clann na Poblachta, founded in July 1946 in Dublin, was an outgrowth of the unreconciled IRA. It set out to provide a truly 'republican' alternative to Fianna Fáil. Seán MacBride, the son of Maud Gonne, and a former IRA Chief of Staff, emerged as its leader. Though this republican shift into constitutionalism might have echoed that of de Valera 20 years before, it retained a large part of the idealistic – some would say impossibilistic – rhetoric of the irreconcilables. Clann na Poblachta campaigned for the purification of the state and the nation, the restoration of 'public morality', the elimination of political patronage and corruption, and the curbing of bureaucracy. Its comprehensive design to use planning to end 'the wasteful and harmful system whereby those who are unable to secure employment have to exist on doles and public charity, while essential work remains undone', was probably inspired more by Pearse than by Keynes. The Clann shared the common aspiration to defend and revive Irish cultural authenticity, and though it did not offer any means towards the restoration of the Irish language beyond the already familiar exhortation and education, it at least proposed an expanded free education system – something Ireland would not get until the 1960s.

The urban social-nationalist appeal of Clann na Poblachta was heightened by the charisma of its leader, whose exotic background marked him out from the familiar political crowd against which he so sharply inveighed. MacBride had fought against the Treaty, had helped to found Saor Éire early in the 1930s, and after a year as IRA Chief of Staff he left the organization (arguing that the 1937 constitution essentially fulfilled republican ideals) and made another reputation as a barrister defending IRA prisoners. His striking clipped accent a (perhaps deliberately cultivated) legacy of his French childhood, was a public reminder of his dynastic credentials. He also attracted to the Clann a number of talented young idealists, the most notable of whom was Dr Noel Browne, a leading tuberculosis campaigner. The party grew fast, indeed too fast for its own good. In October 1947 it won two by-elections, and MacBride entered the Dáil for Co. Dublin. In the midst of its steady growth surge, de Valera once again called a snap election. In the 1948 election, Clann na Poblachta put up more candidates than any party except Fianna Fáil itself – at least two per constituency – but this heroic effort 'stretched slender resources and an untried organization to breaking point'.[5] It won 13.2 per cent of the poll, the highest ever secured by a new party, but the proportional representation system did not run in its favour. It hoped for 20 seats, and should mathematically have got 19, but in fact ended up with only 10. This proved to be enough – just.

The new republic: the inter-party government

Ireland's first coalition government was an unlikely mixture. Fianna Fáil had lost its overall majority, but was still too strong to be unseated by anything less than a combination of all the other parties – an improbable eventuality. But the desire to break the apparently permanent Fianna Fáil grip on power, assisted by social links and temperamental affinities, proved enough for the conservative Fine Gael (with its worst-ever electoral performance) to join with the Labour party (up from 8 to 14 seats), as well as the National Labour grouping (5 seats) which had recently split from it, Clann na Talmhan (7 seats), and Clann na Poblachta as well as the independents. The crux of the deal was that Fine Gael's leader, Mulcahy, did not take the position of Taoiseach. His civil war record was too much for MacBride to swallow. Instead a figurehead, John A. Costello, untainted by the civil war – or indeed the 1916 rising – and untried as a minister (but a fellow-barrister of MacBride's) was agreed. In this the past very directly influenced the future. Mulcahy took the Ministry of Education, and Fine Gael took four other Cabinet posts (Finance, Justice, Defence, and Industry), Labour supplied the Tánaiste/Social Welfare Minister and the Minister for Local Government, and MacBride and Browne of Clann na Poblachta took External Affairs and Health – the latter becoming a minister only days after first arriving in the Dáil.

At its first Cabinet meeting the inter-party government addressed a message to the Pope: 'we desire to repose at the feet of your Holiness the assurance of our filial loyalty and of our devotion to your August Person, as well as our firm resolve to be guided in all our work by the teaching of Christ, and to strive for the attainment of a social order in Ireland based on Christian principles'.[6] This continued what seems to have been felt to be an appropriate national tradition, and its heightened tone (compared with de Valera's 1932 message) reflected both the well-known commitment of Fine Gael and the Clann to vocationalist ideas, and a degree of political necessity. There were a number of signs that Irish public culture was moving steadily towards Catholic 'integralism': one landmark on this route was the judgment of the President of the High Court in 1950 holding that the papal decree on mixed marriages, *Ne Temere*, had binding legal force. Protestant parents could not go back on their marital undertaking that their children be raised as Catholics. This was not only a crucial judgment for mixed marriages, but it also had much wider ramifications. As John Whyte has pointed out, Judge Gavan Duffy was shifting the foundations of common law, with the argument that while English and Irish common law generally coincided, 'it is now recognised that they are not necessarily the same; in particular, the customs and public opinion of the two countries diverge on matters touching religion'.[7]

The new government's Catholic stance certainly reflected the concerns of its most high-profile member. MacBride believed that the international situation was critical; the threat of communist takeover in Italy was acute, but there was also a threat to Ireland itself. (This was an idea shared, unsurprisingly, by the Irish secret intelligence service.) If the new administration looked stronger on deals than issues, MacBride at least seemed to know where he wanted to go. He intended to face up to Britain, repeal the External Relations Act, and end partition. He was intensely suspicious of officialdom, and had long held the view that most senior civil servants were 'merely British secret service agents'. This made for an awkward life at his ministry, and he was not an easy Cabinet colleague.

Oddly, in the end, it was not MacBride but Costello who initiated the government's most dramatic gesture in redefining Ireland's international position. On a trip to Canada in September 1948, the Taoiseach departed from his official script at an Ottawa press conference and declared that Ireland would become a republic. When his Cabinet colleagues recovered from the shock, a Bill was duly drafted. The Republic of Ireland Act came into effect on Easter Monday 1949. Although it aroused something less than public euphoria, it did in a sense fulfil one of MacBride's prime policy goals. But it did so at the expense of another, equally cherished aim – the fostering of North–South unity. The declaration was seen by Britain as effectively renouncing the possibility of reunification, and the Labour government's response, the Ireland Act 1949, issued the famous guarantee that Northern Ireland would not cease to be part of the United Kingdom 'without the consent of the parliament of Northern Ireland'. Clement Attlee's view that 'the government of Éire considered the cutting of the last tie ... as a more important objective than ending partition' contained a hint of pique. Roy Foster suggests that, objectively, the Prime Minister spoke no more than the truth, and Dermot Keogh pronounces the declaration of the republic as a 'hollow victory'. But it must be doubtful whether there remained, even without it, any realistic prospect of unification. The declaration was of a piece with the nation-building policies of the previous quarter-century, accepting that it was better to get on with what could be done, rather than to wait endlessly for what could not. The ultimate symbol of independence was a positive and necessary one for national confidence and self-respect.

The mother and child crisis

If Seán MacBride's radicalism proved somewhat hollow in effect, his party colleague Noel Browne was a reformer with impressive potential for public service. This potential was, however, crushed by a political culture which broke his promising career. Browne worked hard at the Health Ministry for three years, concentrating on the endemic tuberculosis which he himself had survived (though several members of his family had not). By July 1950 his emergency bed programme had nearly doubled the provision for tuberculosis patients in two years. Together with the provision of new drugs, this had a dramatic effect on the death rate – down from 124 per 100,000 in 1947 to 73 in 1951. Eventually he moved on to the bigger social problem that had been identified in the 1945 and 1947 reform proposals, and revived the plan to provide free ante- and post-natal care for mothers, and free health care for children up to the age of 16.

To head off the charges of bureaucratic dictation that had been levelled at Fianna Fáil's health reform proposal, Brown set up a Consultative Child Health Council to advise on the framing of the measure. The new 'mother and child scheme', unlike the 1945 plan, was voluntary, but it immediately ran into formidable resistance from the clergy and the medical profession. For the latter, the sticking point was Browne's refusal to consider means-testing to pay for the scheme. Clerical opposition was much more extensive: the whole scheme was faulty, as the Hierarchy wrote to Costello in October 1950: 'the powers taken by the state are in direct opposition to the rights of the family and are liable to very great abuse'. The Church did not flinch from an implicit comparison between Dr Browne and Hitler or Stalin – the proposed powers 'would constitute a ready-made instrument for future totalitarian aggression'. The state could help indigent or negligent parents – at most 10 per cent, the bishops thought – but it could not deprive good parents of their rights. Moreover, the field of gynaecology was not neutral medicine: dealing with the creation of life, it directly involved matters of faith. The proposal opened up the possibility that Catholics might have to be treated by Protestant doctors. 'We have no guarantee that State officials will respect Catholic principle in regard to these matters.'[8]

The direct approach to Costello was the key to the unravelling of Browne's political position when he finally published the mother and child scheme in March 1951. He was rapidly isolated in the Cabinet; MacBride, who might have been thought a natural ally, had turned against him. Still more seriously, Browne had failed to guard his flank by consulting Archbishop McQuaid, who had come to expect such courtesy where there was any official business in which the Church might be interested. When Browne circulated copies of the plan to all the bishops, he received an absolute condemnation from McQuaid. Costello issued a public reassurance that his government 'would not be a party to any proposals affecting moral questions which might come into conflict with the definite teaching of the Catholic Church'.

In spite of ditching Browne, the inter-party government did not survive the crisis. Dermot Keogh is probably right to say that this should not be called a crisis of Church–state relations, but it was certainly a political crisis. In the election of May 1951, Fianna Fáil narrowly failed to reclaim its hegemonic position (winning 46.3 per cent of the poll). But the Clann na Talmhan vote was practically halved, and Clann na Poblachta went into a decline nearly as vertiginous as its rise had been – from 13.2 to 4.1 per cent. Significantly, its older coalition partners, Labour (thanks to its reunification) and Fine Gael, both improved on their 1948 showing. The latter at last reached the end of its seemingly interminable downward path, with a six point recovery that in the circumstances was almost dramatic. The result was a degree of fluidity over the next decade, with two changes of government –

hardly wild instability by continental standards, but certainly a different political environment from the state's first quarter century.

Mid-century Ireland

Ireland in the postwar decade does not form a very attractive prospect in the view of modern historians; Keogh heads his account of the 1950s 'the politics of drift', Brown 'stagnation and crisis', while Lee is at his gloomiest, under the one-word title 'morass'. For him the central and crushing fact of Irish life was emigration; he blames 'a defeatist political and professional elite, spiritual collaborators in the mass eviction process that drove out more than half a million between 1945 and 1960'.[9] Of course there was no eviction process as such, but an economic paralysis that generated virtually no capacity to absorb population growth. The Irish state stuck to its belief that agriculture was the core of Ireland's economic life. In this there was a fundamental continuity between Fianna Fáil and the inter-party government, which failed to deliver on its vague aura of innovation. Its closest approach to Keynesian initiative was its 1950 budget, which committed a proportion of expenditure to capital projects. But it still fell short of a coherent policy of facilitating growth – indeed Brian Girvin suggests that Ireland was distinguished by its lack of interest in the 'ideology of growth' that was a crucial trend in western Europe after the war.

Ireland had had governmental economic management since the 1930s, but 'by the 1940s it was being utilised to preserve stability rather than to generate a modern industrial economy'.[10] The combination of low growth – amongst the lowest in Europe – and record emigration levels produced a corrosive public demoralization, almost a loss of faith in independence itself. When the second inter-party government discussed the possibility of joining the European Free Trade Area in 1957, a special report by senior staff of five departments forecast a gloomy future for the economy whether Ireland went in or stayed out. Ireland's only sociological journal, *Christus Rex*, expressed doubts 'whether the predominantly agricultural economy will permit of urban absorption of rural population [overflow] even in the next fifty years'.

Emigration rose from an estimated 187,000 in the decade 1936–46, to 197,000 in the first half of the 1950s and 212,000 in the second. Four out of every five of the children born in the 1930s emigrated in the 1950s. By 1961 the population had fallen to 2.8 million. This signalled a final crisis of the traditional agrarian society. 'The countryman's determination to stay on the land seemed to have broken', as Hugh Brody put it in his anthropological study of 'change and decline in the west of Ireland', *Inishkillane*.[11] The corrosive psychological impact of rural decline through to the 1970s was explored in another anthropological analysis of a western community, which found the people 'infused with a spirit of anomie and despair'. The decline of traditional agricultural and fishing industries, the virtual dependence of the small communities of the west on welfare schemes, the flight of young people, drinking patterns among the stay-at-home class of bachelor farmers, the low interest in sexuality and procreation were all signs of cultural stagnation. The willingness of young, single farmers to be incarcerated in the county mental hospital as schizophrenics was grim testimony, in the view of Professor Scheper-Hughes, that 'one of the oldest continually settled human communities in Europe is in a virtual state of psycho-cultural decline'. Only 41 of the 138 households in her 'Ballybran' (Ballyquin and Cloghane on the Dingle peninsula in western Kerry) were fully conjugal and had '*any* possibility of replicating themselves in the coming generation'.[12] The inner structure of rural life began to crumble; the extended family pattern made famous by the anthropologists Arensberg and Kimball in the 1930s began to shrivel. Girvin identifies the halving of the number of 'relatives assisting' on farms in the decade after 1945 as crucial testimony to the 'collapse of the old social system'. By the 1960s there was widespread public alarm, taking the form of a 'Save the West' campaign in which conservative clerics formed an unlikely alliance with veteran radicals like Peadar O'Donnell; to no effect. As O'Donnell raged, 'The West of today is a version of the 'Irish Towns' outside the walls of garrison cities in the darkest days of the conquest'. If there was no actual squalor, it was only because 'the disowned people of today are free to fly the country and they know where to go'.[13]

The exodus was not driven merely by the desperation familiar from the nineteenth century, but by a newer and more positive attraction of modern city life. Although the proportion of industrial workers in Ireland remained low (rising only from 4.6 per cent in the mid-1920s to 14.3 per cent by 1960), a real shift was slowly happening. It is worth noting that in the mid-50s, horse-drawn ploughs disappeared from agricultural shows; the age of the tractor had at last arrived. But for the time being, Ireland remained 'between two worlds'. An observant and sympathetic American journalist contrasted the intense conservatism and apparent indifference of Irish small farmers with their Danish counterparts: Irish farms were frankly a mess, lacking 'purposefulness', and 'it almost seems as if the farmer does not take farming seriously'; 'He is afraid to specialise, fearful of getting into debt, suspicious of new ideas, and full of excuses for not doing better at the business to which he was born and bred'.[14]

The apparent paralysis of the labour movement in Ireland was another index of stagnation. Whereas the fragmented Labour parties had been able to reunite to fight the 1948 election and join the inter-party government (without being able to make much impression on policy), the rupture in the trade union movement was more enduring. It sprang from a personality clash, between Larkin and O'Brien, that reflected sharply different beliefs about the movement's role. Larkin remained a revolutionary syndicalist, O'Brien was a cautious reformist and a nationalist. O'Brien had reacted to de Valera's restrictive Trade Union Act of 1941 almost with relief. What looked to many like a plan to control the union movement by forcing smaller unions to merge into officially recognized (and Irish-based) organisations seemed to the ITGWU a heaven-sent opportunity to dispose of the 'superfluous unions which we all want to see eliminated'. The war also provided O'Brien with the means of breaking the tenuous 'internationalism' that survived in the links between Irish and British unions. The Irish Trades Union Congress (ITUC) refused to attend a world trades union conference organized by the British TUC in London on the specious ground that it would breach neutrality. The ITGWU and other Irish-based unions went on to create the Congress of Irish Trade Unions (CIU) in opposition to British domination. The split left the old ITUC with about 145,000 members to the CIU's 77,000; by the late 1950s the figures were 250,000 and 188,000. Only after protracted negotiations did the two eventually reunite as the Irish Congress of Trade Unions in 1959.

The creation of an Industrial Development Authority by the inter-party government did not represent a break with Fianna Fáil's long-established policy of self sufficiency. MacBride criticized Fianna Fáil for its failure to achieve autarchy, but not for setting that objective. The most industrially minded of Fianna Fáil's ministers, Seán Lemass – an urban politician in a party long committed to ruralist ideology – did not quarrel with the notion of autarchy, but only with the primacy of agriculture in the vision of upholders of strict finance like his party rival Seán MacEntee. The IDA represented an important perceptual change by identifying export-led industrialization as the only way of developing the Irish economy, and in the 1950s the climate of thought gradually inched in this direction. The dismal state of Irish exports reflected the uncompetitiveness of the industrial base. From 1950 to 1961 the annual growth rate for exports was 3.7 per cent – a quarter of the rate for Greece.

Seán Lemass and economic development

The most consistent pressure for a recasting of Irish economic policy came from Seán Lemass within Fianna Fáil. For a quarter of a century he contested the role of de Valera's lieutenant with Seán MacEntee; by the time Fianna Fáil returned to power in 1957 – at the start of another 16-year period in office – he was Tánaiste, and clearly de Valera's anointed successor. When at last the father of the nation stepped aside in June 1959 to take the Presidency, Lemass became Taoiseach a month before his 60th birthday. He had endured the long wait with remarkable equanimity (unlike the similarly baulked Anthony Eden in Britain), and though it may have blunted his reforming energy, it seems likely that his natural caution would have been dominant even if he had come to power sooner.

Lemass's workmanlike style betokened a distinctly more modern approach. In Brian Farrell's words, 'he was determined to direct the government and the country to its overdue rendezvous with the realities of the later twentieth-century world'.[15] Though his early Cabinets were not (contrary to the assiduously promoted legend) notable for a dramatic influx of young talent, they were conducted differently. Lemass had always been distinguished from many if not most politicians by his readiness to accept that mistakes would sometimes be made in government, and he was clear that the fear of making mistakes led to paralysis and sterility. Likewise the impulse to avoid dissent. His own account of de Valera's prime-ministerial style is instructive. 'He always wanted to get unanimity and he sought this by the simple process of keeping the debate going – often till the small hours of the morning, until those who were in the minority, out of sheer exhaustion, conceded the case of the majority.'[16] This was an almost mechanical working out of the romantic nationalist need to believe in a single national will. For Lemass, if there was to be a new direction, dissent was inevitable.

Lemass's concrete achievements have been disputed. His reputation rests mainly on the policy signalled in the title of the famous report drawn up by the Secretary of the Finance Department, T. K.

Whitaker, in 1958: *Economic Development*. The thinking behind this had originally been generated in the late 1940s by Ireland's application for Marshall Aid, which required the concoction of a Keynesian 'recovery programme' (though Whitaker himself testified that the officials who drew it up regarded it as more of a cosmetic exercise than a true development programme). The key perception was that Ireland had become disastrously detached from European economic growth, and had to be reintegrated. Lemass put it with typical bluntness: 'our standards must approximate to British standards, or our people will go'. Whitaker's ideas remained at variance with those of Lemass, which he characterized as a 'simple Keynesianism'. Lemass was moving away from the straightforward protectionism, but he remained an economic nationalist. He hovered between *dirigisme* and faith in market forces (or Irish entrepreneurial spirit), but the mere adoption of planning was important in establishing a coherent economic policy. The distinctive feature of the policy he developed in the 1958 White Paper *A Programme for Economic Expansion* was the stimulation of industrial exports through the fostering of foreign investment.

In the 1960s this policy began to flower: over 350 new foreign companies were established in Ireland during the decade. By 1974 foreign firms produced 40 per cent of manufacturing exports. The five years of the first Programme for Economic Expansion (1958–63) saw a growth rate of 4 per cent, and this continued through the Second Programme (1963–70). This was hardly spectacular, but it was adequate. Agriculture, which remained central to both Programmes, failed to respond to planning stimuli, and while employment in manufacturing rose steadily, it was never to equal the service industry's share. In 1966 there was the first population growth to be recorded since the Famine; by 1971 the growth had reached 100,000. Overall, Ireland reached an epochal moment. The point of intersection in the balance between agricultural and industrial workforce was crossed in the 1960s: in 1961 the balance was 379,000/257,000, in 1971 273,000/323,000.

Ireland and the world

This was a key point, theoretically, in the modernization process. And undoubtedly Ireland was modernizing, albeit quirkily. Perhaps the key change was one of attitude: the gradual erosion of insularity. In the economic sphere this was, as we have seen, the result of hard necessity – self-sufficiency was seen to have failed. But there was a more positive, if diffuse, opening up to a world that offered opportunities as well as threats. It worked at many levels: the development of tourism aided by the increasingly successful Bord Fáilte (or Tourist Board, set up in 1952) led to a growth that became 'almost phenomenal' during the 1960s.[17] Mass air travel not only boosted tourism, but radically transformed Ireland's sense of place. Ireland's own airline, Aer Lingus, developed rapidly in the 1950s (guided by its star economist, Garret FitzGerald). The first scheduled transatlantic service into the new Shannon airport began in June 1960. From this point on, even the west of Ireland was no longer at the farthest extremity of Europe, 'an island behind an island', it was practically in the mid-Atlantic.

Television, of course, both symbolized and transmitted the possibility of a new openness and accessibility. Indeed it was the impossibility of stopping television, as much as any positive official enthusiasm for it, that drove the process of expansion. When the BBC built a new transmitter in Belfast in 1955, reception improved dramatically in eastern Ireland, and sales of television sets in Dublin took off. By September, some newspapers were carrying reviews of BBC programmes. Unless Irish people were to end up watching British televison, they had to be provided with their own service. As Donald Connery noted, Telefís Éireann 'began almost in self-defence'. The Broadcasting Authority Act 1960 established Radio Telefís Éireann (RTÉ) as a public authority, obliged to report news 'in an objective and impartial manner and without any expression of [its] own views' – a fairly clear echo of the BBC's mission, though with the distinctive additional obligation to 'bear constantly in mind the national aims of restoring the Irish language and preserving and developing the national culture'.[18]

RTÉ was kept for some time under a degree of state control that was obviously different from normal western practice, but at the same time the formerly strict censorship regime was very slowly easing up. In 1955 the avant-garde Pike Theatre in Dublin staged the first performance of Samuel Beckett's *Waiting for Godot,* the masterpiece of an exile who (like Joyce) had resisted being 'Irish' as strenuously as mainstream Ireland resisted him, but who was, over the next generation, gradually (like Joyce) to be reincorporated into the national canon. Another sign of a new openness came in 1956 when Seán O'Faoláin, an inveterate critic of censorship, agreed to serve on the recently established Arts Council. O'Faoláin, as the writer John Banville has said, had 'stayed, holding on tenaciously, with wit and style through the narrow years, when greater writers such as Joyce and Beckett, who took so much from this impoverished little bit of rock on the edge of Europe, had shaken the dust of Ireland from their heels and never looked back. Irish intellectual life would be very much poorer had he not been there at a crucial time.[19] Still, things moved slowly enough. Edna O'Brien's first novel was banned in 1960, as was the film version of her *The Girl with Green Eyes* in 1964.

The complex process of social evolution is not often marked by unambiguous 'turning-points', but in the 1960s Ireland was coming to such a defining shift. One television programme in particular, the *Late, Late Show*, and its celebrated presenter Gay Byrne, acted as a focus of collective self-analysis, and perhaps even an accelerator of change. As Joseph Lee says, 'the very expression of a variety of views has in itself been revolutionary'.[20] The famous episode of 'the Bishop and the nightie' in February 1966 was a classic case. When a suburban housewife, taking part in a jokey quiz testing the convergence of married couples' memories, was asked what colour nightdress she wore on her wedding night, she found she had forgotten – or, as she roguishly added, thought she might not have worn one at all. Instantly the Bishop of Clonfert fired off a telegram to RTÉ denouncing the show, and next day preached a sermon in Loughrea cathedral branding it as 'objectionable'. Something of a national storm followed, with the Loughrea town commissioners weighing in on the bishop's side ('a dirty programme that should be abolished') and even the *Irish Times* agreeing that the transmission was a 'lapse of taste', though suggesting that the bishop had over-reacted. Subsequent opinion agreed that this was the roar of an episcopal dinosaur, yet, as Mary Kenny has pointed out, that opinion was itself the product of the process of change that the bishop recognized: he knew 'instinctively that the new outspoken mode of the television talk show would eventually remove all modesty from discussion about physical matters – as indeed it has'. This was truly a showdown for the Church's teaching authority.[21]

The quiet but definite defiance of formal religious doctrine, possibly accelerated by the liberalization heralded by the Second Vatican Council in 1962, took significant shape over the papal encyclical *Humanae Vitae* of 1968, which unambiguously reiterated the Catholic Church's ban on artificial contraception. State law continued to uphold this – contraceptives remained illegal – yet a rapid decline in family sizes demonstrated that many people were choosing to act differently. By the late 1960s tradition itself was beginning to lose its sacrosanct quality, and the battle to make reality publicly acceptable (lost in the time of J. M. Synge) began to be waged again. The extent of the floodgate-opening over the next generation can be roughly measured by the fact that, whereas in 1965 John McGahern's banned novel *The Dark* caused a sensation (and cost McGahern his teaching post) by its single f-word, Roddy Doyle's *The Van* (1990) had three thousand of them (according to one brave computation). In this it did no more than follow long-established real-life usage, but simply doing that in print was remarkable enough. So, indeed, was Doyle's eventual incorporation into the school syllabus. And in 1967 the Irish State finally undertook to provide free secondary education for all.

A conscious shift also took place in Ireland's international outlook, in the wake of its long-delayed entry into the United Nations (UN) in 1955. Ireland was kept out of the UN for a decade partly through Soviet hostility, ostensibly in revenge for wartime neutrality. Ireland did not possess 'the qualities required by the Charter'; 'Eire did not help to lay the foundations of the organisation ... Even in the most critical period of the war Eire was expressing open sympathy with the Axis and Franco Spain'.[22] Until the early 1950s, Irish external policy was distorted by the persistence of strident demands for the ending of partition, sharpened by de Valera's vocal campaigning in support of the Anti-Partition League after he lost power in 1948. This ensured that the inter-party government, whose vociferous anti-communism might well have led it to join the North Atlantic Treaty Organisation, adhered to the policy of neutrality. The historic enemy, Britain, remained more threatening than international communism. Ireland's posture in the European organizations that it joined (the Council of Europe and the Organisation for Economic Co-operation and Development) was rather negative. In the view of an outstanding young diplomat, 'Ireland had been isolated from the world for too long and the mental atmosphere in our country had become uncomfortably musty and close'.[23] By the mid-1950s this introversion was moderating – de Valera sharply toned down his anti-partition rhetoric on his return to office in 1951. Ireland's eventual accession to the UN took place in a more benign atmosphere, and was obviously a potent symbol of convergence with the global mainstream. As with the League of Nations in the interwar period, Ireland soon took up a significant role. Its Representative, F. H. Boland, became President of the General Assembly in 1960, and the next year Ireland supplied its first and probably most famous peacekeeping contingent for the UN in the Congo. Special legislation was passed to allow the Irish army to serve abroad, and the Irish contingent's commander acted as

Commander-in-Chief of the UN forces. Awareness of overseas issues was almost too dramatically heightened when 10 Irish soldiers were killed in an ambush; their funeral procession in Dublin on 22 November was a great public event. But Ireland's global profile was probably raised most sharply by Conor Cruise O'Brien's brilliant account of his mission as UN commissioner in the breakaway Republic of Katanga, *To Katanga and Back* (1962), an international best-seller.

South and North

Another event – or perhaps non-event – which seemed at the time to mark a significant stage in the evolution of a more open engagement with the world was the IRA's abandonment of its border campaign in 1962. Since enduring persecution at the hands of de Valera during the Emergency, the IRA was embittered and marginalized. The experience of arrest and internment in camps like 'Tintown University' (the Curragh) once again – as in 1916 – produced a tough and cohesive core organization, but for Sinn Féin this time there was to be no miraculous 1917. The closest the republican irreconcilables came to a revival of popular support was at the time the IRA launched its campaign against the North in 1956. The rationale for this was that the Ireland Act prevented the border issue from being reopened constitutionally, and there was 'no movement to organize a campaign of civil disobedience and passive resistance in the North'. Sinn Féin also went back to contesting elections in the Republic (which remained in its view the 'Free State'), and in 1957 won 5.3 per cent of the poll – more than Clann na Poblachta and Clann na Talmhan combined. But republican hopes gradually declined again, as 'Operation Harvest' failed to live up to its optimistic name. Sporadic attacks on police stations and government installations in Northern Ireland never created sufficient public impact. The abandonment of the campaign in 1962 seemed, like the cessation of the civil war in 1923, a recognition that the republican view was out of touch with the people. (Though in the republican view the blame lay with the people, 'whose minds have been deliberately distracted from the supreme issue'.[24])

In the next few years, indeed, an extraordinary atmosphere of North–South *détente* was generated. Lemass had not shown much sign of subtlety in his attitude to partition in the past, and his embrace of normalization at this stage testified to the general sense of change. The symbolic culmination came with his meetings with the Prime

Minister of Northern Ireland, Terence O'Neill, in 1965. O'Neill was making liberal noises that sounded, in the context of Unionist politics in the North, quite radical. The idea that Lemass made a distinctive contribution to the evolution of thinking about the North has been vigorously scouted by critics like Paul Bew, Ellen Hazelkorn and Henry Patterson. In their view, Lemass never said anything that de Valera had not said before, and proved equally reluctant to 'substitute reality for fantasy'.[25] Still, his assertion that 'unity means bringing the people together. It is not a matter of territorial acquisition', was a sensible line taken at the right moment. And the implicit recognition of Northern Ireland involved in meeting O'Neill was surely, as Foster notes, a potentially damaging concession on Lemass's part. But characteristically, by contrast with O'Neill, 'he had covered his flank far more effectively'.[26] The underlying assumption of the natural and inevitable unity of Ireland was not questioned, and the 1965 *démarche* was followed the next year by an innocently cheerful celebration of the 50th anniversary of the 1916 rebellion. The young Fintan O'Toole, later to become one of Ireland's most acute commentators, took part, like thousands of other schoolchildren, in a breezily daft pageant. Based on the old republican ballad 'The Black and Tan gun': the production quickly fell apart and, with the audience in hysterics, 'land, nationality and religion became a glorious farce'.[27] The IRA's destruction of Nelson's Pillar in O'Connell Street seemed like an unthreatening historical oddity, though it radically transformed the view from where Pearse had stood on the steps of the General Post Office – as if completing the work of the gunboat *Helga* in 1916.

|10|

The Stormont regime: Northern Ireland, 1920–1969

T he partition of Ireland in 1920–21 was the unintended by-product of the Irish national revival. Not for the first, or the last time, the emergence of an assertive nationalist movement, Sinn Féin, intensified the determination of Unionists to resist incorporation into a single autonomous Irish state. And at the height of the Anglo-Irish war, in 1920, the power of Ulster Unionists to give effect to their determination was dramatically enhanced by the Government of Ireland Act's transfer of devolved powers to a Northern parliament. But well before devolution was imposed, the logic of partition had become inescapable.

Partition

In 1914, when the Home Rule Act was pushed through, Asquith had promised special treatment for an unspecified north-eastern part of Ireland. At that time the government still hoped that this would mean no more than a temporary opt-out, or some form of 'home rule within home rule'. But even then, Carson had made absolutely clear that Ulster Unionists rejected the latter altogether, and would accept nothing less than permanent exclusion. Southern Unionists still tried to hold the Unionist movement together, but the Ulster Unionists insisted that 'we should be in a better position to help Unionists in any part of Ireland if we are excluded than if we formed a permanent minority in a Dublin parliament'.[1] The 1916 rising set this determination in stone. Asquith deputed his wiliest negotiator, Lloyd George, to make a final search for compromise, but he could not get further than the dubious stratagem of giving contradictory promises to the two sides. He tried to persuade the nationalists that Ulster would be offered only temporary exclusion, but as one leading Ulster Unionist, Hugh Montgomery, noted in June 1916, 'Carson holds a letter from Lloyd George stating that the proposed Amendment of the Government of Ireland Act is to be a definitive one'. And at the same time the excluded area was unambiguously fixed: 'it was quite clearly understood that the six counties was the minimum'.

So when the Cabinet Irish committee set to work to draft another Home Rule Bill at the end of the war, its room for manoeuvre had already been sharply curtailed. Nobody seriously resisted the inevitability of partition. The vital new development was the decision to give the excluded area its own parliament, on an equal footing with the Dublin legislature. Hence the ultimate irony that the only part of Ireland to be given 'Home Rule' as understood by Gladstone and Asquith was the part that had mobilized so fiercely against it. Home Rule as such never operated in the rest of Ireland; the 'Southern parliament' never met, and the powers of the Irish Free State went significantly beyond Home Rule. Ulster Unionists always portrayed their acceptance of devolution as a heroic sacrifice in the public interest, and it is probably true that they would rather have preserved full UK integration. But they acted decisively to maximize their power as the Government of Ireland Bill took shape. In February 1920 James Craig, then a junior minister in the Admiralty, headed off a belated move to detach *en bloc* all the nine counties of 'historic Ulster', which some ministers thought would look better in the eyes of the world. (Though the counties themselves were English administrative units which had no connection with pre-Norman 'Ulster'.) Craig made brutally clear that the purpose of Northern Ireland was not aesthetic, but functional – to guarantee the survival of Protestant power. He and Carson both assumed that the new state would need to be economically as well as politically viable. (Exactly the same assumption, of course, allowed Collins and Griffith to convince themselves that a boundary commission would inevitably lead to the collapse of a separate Northern state.) It needed a guaranteed Unionist majority and a defensible frontier. So the intelligent argument put forward by St Loe Strachey, editor of the *Spectator*, that ethnic homogeneity was more important than geographical tidiness – so they should 'cast out as many Catholic districts, unions and parishes as possible' even if that created a 'jigsaw' border – was sidelined.[2]

The crisis of birth

As we have seen [pp. 104], the establishment of a separate Northern administrative apparatus began several months before the Government of Ireland Act became law, almost a year before the Northern parliament could establish a responsible government. The key element in this process was public security. In July 1920 attacks on Catholic shipyard workers, beginning in Belfast's smaller yard (Workman Clark) and spreading to Harland & Wolff's, triggered the worst sectarian conflict since the 1880s. Within a week 5000 Catholics had been driven out of their jobs, and many of their families were burned out of their homes over the next month. Violence continued to flare up repeatedly for two years, during which 428 people were killed and over 1700 wounded – totals exceeding all nineteenth-century riots put together. This urban warfare, described not altogether fancifully by nationalists as a 'pogrom', was a traumatic experience for both communities. As always, the Protestants who unleashed it believed that they were defending themselves against the threat of an imminent nationalist takeover. (As the Protestant *Boilermakers' Monthly Report* insisted, the shipyard expulsions were a response to the IRA's killing of RIC District Inspector Swanzy.) The fragile unity of Protestant and Catholic works shown in the '44-hour strike' of 1919 could not survive the intensification of the republican political and military campaign in the spring and summer of 1920. Even those historians who argue that sectarian conflict was essentially a struggle for jobs, recognize (as does David Fitzpatrick) its political edge: 'Loyalists often believed that the expelled Catholic workers were Sinn Féin infiltrators who had migrated from the south to undermine Protestant security'.[3]

The sense of insecurity fuelled a new grass-roots paramilitary mobilization. Already by June the old UVF was reconstituting itself, and in the summer it demanded official recognition. A senior Dublin Castle bureaucrat noted that while the Chief Secretary, Sir Hamar Greenwood, was keen to 'enrol loyal men in the North as Special Constables', both the Under-Secretary and the Commander-in-Chief were aghast at the prospect – in effect the official recognition of civil war.[4] All but one of the local police and military commanders agreed that 'to arm one side and not the other in civil war of this sort is madness'. This resistance was kept up for a week or two, but at the end of August Belfast was festooned with placards announcing that the UVF was to be recognized. The scheme for creating a special constabulary had the crucial backing of Winston Churchill, and in October it went ahead. A last-minute effort to constitute it as an all-Ireland force was dismissed as unrealistic, and it became the Ulster Special Constabulary (USC) – the first public recognition of the six counties' new status and identity. (It would still be two months before the Government of Ireland Act was passed.) The cutting edge of the USC was intended to be the full-time (Class 'A') Special force. The rank and file of the UVF enrolled *en masse* in the part-time ('B') Specials, which, despite some official efforts to recruit Catholics, became in effect a Protestant militia.

A second vital development came in September when a separate Under-Secretary was appointed to begin the process of creating a six-county administraion. Sir Ernest Clark, a Treasury official who had created the income tax system for Cape Colony, appeared to have no obvious credentials for the job – he had no Irish experience, and found the political attitudes of the Ulster Unionists very strange at first. But he quickly allowed himself to be impressed by the seriousness of the threat to Ulster and became an outright partisan of the prospective Northern Ireland government, arguing for a bigger transfer of powers than the Government of Ireland Act envisaged. In particular, the need for customs powers was underlined by the nationalist response to the 'pogrom' of 1920, the Belfast boycott.

Northern Ireland was born in a crisis, and the fears generated by this crisis effectively determined its future. Loyalist fears may have been exaggerated, but they were hardly groundless. Historians have recently clarified the extent of sectarian violence during the IRA campaign – easily enough to trigger Protestant memories of historic massacres. Most telling perhaps are Peter Hart's researches into the assassinations carried out by the IRA as 'executions of spies and informers'. Hart demonstrates that the great majority of these victims were Protestants, who by definition could not have been the true source of the increasingly damaging information leakage from within the IRA.[5] The pattern was unmistakable, and was certainly not going to be mistaken by the ingrainedly neurotic loyalists. In the months before the Irish civil war, the situation worsened as the IRA stepped up its operations in the border zone. In February 1922 a party of 'A' Specials on a train from the USC depot in Newtownards to Enniskillen got into a fight with an IRA detachment as they changed trains at Clones (the line passed through Co. Monaghan – Free State territory). Five were killed and nine wounded in what loyalists instantly denounced as a 'massacre' (though the IRA claimed that the

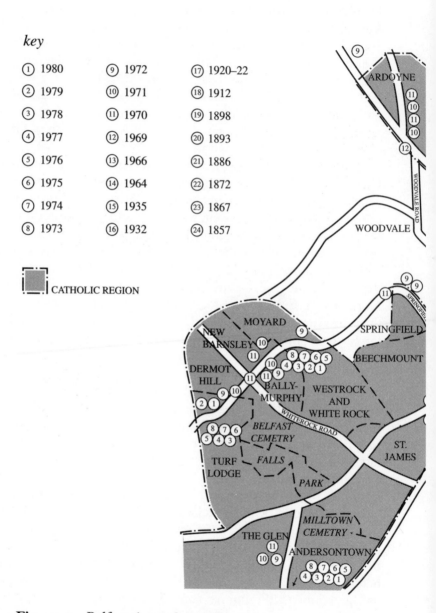

Fig. 10.1 Belfast riots, 1857–1980
Source: Based on T. Downing (ed.) *The Troubles* (London 1980)

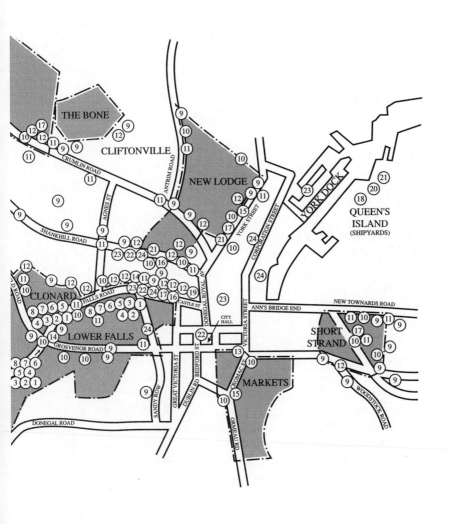

Specials fired first). In response the 'B' Specials waged what they saw as a war for survival. By early 1922 there were around 4000 'A' and 20,000 'B' Specials, and Craig's government decided to increase these to 5800 and 22,000, besides making 'a serious effort to develop' the 'C' Specials, a force that had not yet really taken off.[6] These were quite formidable totals, but the Northern government was in an odd position: the old police force, the RIC, was about to be disbanded, and its replacement was still being decided. (The Royal Ulster Constabulary (RUC) was launched in March 1922, and by mid-summer only 1000 constables had been recruited, out of a planned force of 3000.) The British government was extremely reluctant to allow troops to be used for internal security operations – in fact a number of Craig's requests for military intervention were turned down. In such a situation, the hasty expansion of the USC led to several serious problems of indiscipline and violence.

A couple of episodes may help to explain much that followed. On the night of 23 March 1922 four members of a Catholic family in Belfast were killed by gunmen identified by neighbours as Specials. Though this charge was officially denied, the MacMahon killings had a disastrous impact on Catholic perceptions of the new Northern Ireland state and its police. At the same time, Protestant fears of Free State collusion in the IRA's Northern offensive were becoming ever more acute. In May 1922 a group of anti-Treaty IRA staged an armed demonstration in one of the quirkiest parts of the six-county border, the so-called 'triangle' of Co. Fermanagh on the west bank of Loch Erne. Pro-Treaty forces having occupied Pettigo, a Protestant village in Free State territory, the irregulars seized the Catholic village of Belleek, which was in Northern Ireland, though accessible only by a road passing through the Free State. Sixty-four men of the USC, under the Co. Fermanagh commander Sir Basil Brooke, crossed the lake in boats to 'defend' the triangle. A supporting column was sent along the road, but was ambushed and routed, with the loss of a Lancia armoured car and three trucks. Brooke's force in turn retreated by boat to the safety of the opposite shore. Eventually the area was occupied by British troops, who stayed there until 1924. This débâcle, while demonstrating the military limitations of the USC, fuelled Unionist fears of invasion, and severely bruised the pride of the USC Commandant – who would go on to become Prime Minister of Northern Ireland for over 20 years.[7]

The key expression of the Northern state's insecurity was the Special Powers Act, passed on 7 April 1922, just before the anti-Treaty

IRA occupied the Four Courts in Dublin. It gave the government, in the person of the Minister for Home Affairs, sweeping powers to impose regulations to 'preserve the peace and maintain order'. Though it did not suspend habeas corpus, as was widely believed, it resurrected the special courts of two or three resident magistrates. A torrent of regulations followed, running to 34 pages after a decade. By that time, the Act, originally temporary, had first been extended to five years, and then made permanent. Amidst its very wide-ranging and loosely defined powers, probably the most notorious was Section 5, which provided that on conviction for explosives or firearms offences, or for larceny, arson or malicious damage, a person 'if male, may be once privately whipped' in addition to the standard sentence specified in earlier laws. In the eyes of Catholic nationalists, who instantly christened it the 'Flogging Bill', this was a mark of their permanent subjugation.

Fixing the border

Even after the waning of any direct threat of republican military action in the summer of 1922, a more general insecurity persisted. The Irish civil war itself probably generated some grim satisfaction amongst Unionists who had always insisted that the Irish masses were unfit for self-government, but any such *schadenfreude* was mixed with apprehension. Throughout this time the possibility of border revision remained real. While Michael Collins directed Free State policy, he kept up an unremitting pressure on the Northern state. He almost certainly shared the hope expressed in one IRA GHQ directive that 'Belfast can be brought to ruin' by a general military offensive. He reacted with outrage to the 'pogrom' against Catholics, and authorized the assassination of Sir Henry Wilson. During the Treaty negotiations Collins had repeatedly insisted on the unacceptability of the six-county border, which would consign a large Catholic minority to exclusion from the Irish state. In early 1922 he had a series of meetings with Craig in an effort to link all these issues in a general settlement: the 'Craig–Collins pact' traded the cessation of the Belfast boycott and the choking-off of IRA activity for the return of Catholics to their homes and jobs. Instead of a formal Boundary Commission as envisaged in the Anglo-Irish Treaty, there would be a joint working party. But Collins clearly still expected large-scale transfers of population to the Free State, and in May Craig used the announcement of the electoral pact between Collins and de Valera (a prelude, in his view, to a republican takeover of the Free State) as the basis for a final rejection of any border adjustment. 'What we have now we hold, and we will hold against all combinations'.[8]

This remained his attitude when the Free State, after the death of Collins, moved gradually towards a formal demand for the establishment of the Boundary Commission. Cosgrave moved cautiously, as he was well aware of the impact of the civil war on both Ulster and British perceptions of the Free State's stability. Kevin O'Shiel, who was given responsibility for setting up a North-eastern Boundary Bureau to prepare the Free State's case, invited his colleagues to 'imagine the flamboyant contrast that would be drawn between the chaos and horror of the South and the peaceful and law-abiding conditions in the North'.[9] But Cosgrave foregrounded the demand for boundary revision in the August 1923 election campaign, in order to head off republican criticism, and the demand was accepted by Ramsay MacDonald's new Labour government in January 1924. Craig simply refused to nominate a representative, forcing the British government to bring in legislation to allow it to appoint one (J. R. Fisher) on Northern Ireland's behalf. The Free State representative was Eoin MacNeill. The most crucial appointment, however, was the Commission's Chairman, Richard Feetham. Considering his decisive contribution to Irish history, Feetham's own history has remained oddly obscure; most historians, like Lyons, have described him as 'neutral', by virtue of the fact that he was a Justice of the Supreme Court of South Africa. The implication that he was out of the same stable as that icon of imperial responsibility General Smuts may well have played a part in his appointment (as did his old friend Lionel Curtis), but Feetham was in fact English, and a Milnerite imperialist who had been a prime mover in the policy of Union for South Africa.

The Commission's remit, specified in Article XII of the Anglo-Irish Treaty, was to determine the boundary of Northern Ireland 'in accordance with the wishes of the inhabitants'. The framers of the Treaty undoubtedly had in mind the plebiscites then being carried out in several disputed territories in central Europe. It is still not clear whether Feetham ever entertained the theoretical possibility of major transfers of territory to the Free State; what is clear is that his narrow enforcement of the proviso 'so far as may be compatible with economic and geographic conditions' ensured that the transfers would be (as Craig had often been assured) minimal. In the end, after practically a year of evidence-taking, the minimal nature of the adjustments was leaked to the press, and MacNeill was panicked into resignation, belatedly announcing that his interpretation of Article XII was radically different from Feetham's. An embarrassing fiasco for the Free State was a quiet triumph for Northern Ireland. From that point on, no serious political effort to revise the border would ever be made.[10]

Fixing the political system

The political history of Northern Ireland for nearly half a century after 1921 was preternaturally uneventful. Normal political events did not occur, because there was no political process as the concept is usually understood in western Europe. Though Northern Ireland was in formal terms a democracy – a point that the UUP never ceased to reiterate – it was a one-party state. The minority was consigned to permanent opposition. From time to time, by way of protest, it abandoned constitutional politics altogether. Governments displayed a fixity that made even the British political system appear unstable: from 1921 to 1963, Northern Ireland had just three prime ministers, two of them serving 20-year terms. When Craig (by then Lord Craigavon) died in office in 1940, five out of his seven Cabinet ministers had been in place continuously since 1921.

The essential reason for this immobility was the state's Protestant character. The *raison d'être* of partition was to preserve the Protestant 'way of life'. Protestantism had provided the mobilizing force of resistance to Home Rule ('Rome Rule') since the 1880s and the political vocabulary of the 1911 Ulster Covenant. Protestant dominance was asserted still more strongly after 1921 as the Catholic character of the Free State became more distinct. In the 1930s, James Craig unblinkingly praised the parliament, by then magnificently rehoused in Stormont Castle, as 'a Protestant parliament for a Protestant people'. The idea – especially strong amongst Presbyterians – of the Protestant people was a key political belief underpinning the nature of the state. The Protestant tradition valorized endurance, self-reliance, and the public testifying of faith, rather than pragmatism and compromise.[11] As the sociologist Steve Bruce has pointed out, Protestantism and Catholicism are not merely two different denominations. Protestantism defined itself in opposition to Catholicism, and many Protestants remain profoundly suspicious of ecumenical efforts to resolve the antagonism. Fear and dislike of the Papacy was more than a fertile source of sloganeering ('No popery', 'Kick the Pope', 'the

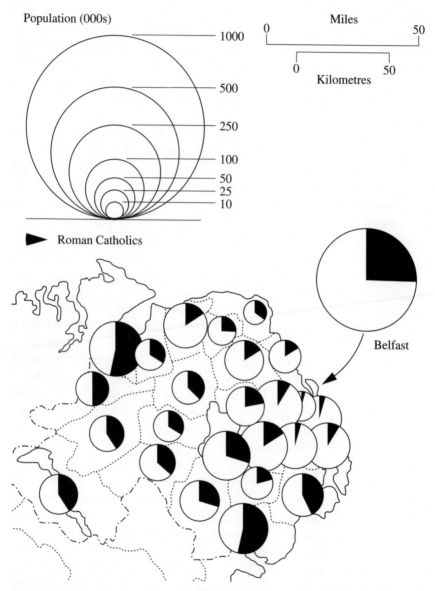

Fig. 10.2 The proportion and distribution of Catholics in Northern Ireland
Source: O'Leary and McGarry (1981) Northern Ireland Census

whore of Babylon'). It mirrored, and mutually reinforced, Catholic fears of conversion by trickery and force. For Ulster Protestants, Catholics are always 'Roman Catholics'. The result is a textbook case of what political scientists have labelled 'zero-sum' reasoning: the alternative to total victory is total defeat, concession or compromise is fatal. There is no middle way. The 'siege mentality' often attributed to loyalists is a perfect metaphor for this, and the siege of Derry has been preserved as a defining political trauma.[12] The unfortunate Governor Lundy, burned in effigy every December to commemorate the last-minute closing of the city gates in face of King James II's Catholic army, has become an immortal symbol of the fear of betrayal.

Thus two unassuageable fears debilitated the Northern Ireland state: the fear of Catholic irredentism, and the fear of British betrayal. Both these fears were quite well founded. The result was a pervasive lack of civic trust, the vital spark of democratic political culture. In these circumstances, the Ulster Unionist governments had a powerful incentive to construct a hegemonic system. This was not a foregone conclusion. The original constitution for Northern Ireland, laid out in the Government of Ireland Act, was quite pluralistic: a bicameral parliament (a 52-seat House of Commons and a 26-seat Senate), proportional representation, a direct British presence in the form of a Governor-General, and the federalistic possibility of the Council of Ireland. Minority protection was (the British government believed) built in by the requirement that the Northern Ireland parliament 'shall not make a law so as either directly or indirectly to give a preference, privilege or advantage, or impose any disability or disadvantage, on account of religious belief'. But this assumed a spirit of pluralism which never materialized. Sir James Craig, Prime Minister from 1921 to 1940, saw his main task as overcoming the fissiparous tendencies that had disrupted Protestant unity before the war. It was fear of Unionist splinter groups as much as fear of nationalists that led to the most significant political change of the 1920s, the abolition of proportional representation, first for local elections (in 1922) and finally for elections to Stormont (1929).

This was certainly perceived by Catholics as a deliberate step towards disempowering them. (In 1923 seven bishops of north-eastern Ireland would protest that there was no parallel 'in modern times ... for the way in which the Catholic minority in the North of Ireland is being systematically wronged under the laws of the Northern Parliament'.[13]) It was a vital test of Britain's preparedness to intervene to maintain its Irish Settlement. In 1922 the Westminster government did indeed try to withhold the royal assent, but this attempt at control was countered by a blunt threat that Craig's entire Cabinet would resign. The prospect of trying to impose a government on Northern Ireland rapidly undermined Britain's will. On this issue, of course, Britain was in a weak position to insist on an electoral system that it rejected for itself. From this point onwards, no real attempt was ever made to limit the actions of the Northern Ireland government except by the indirect route of financial restrictions. Even parliamentary inquiry was choked off by the Speaker's ruling that Northern Ireland issues could not be debated at Westminster. By the 1930s, Northern Ireland was being treated as a virtual Dominion, rather than a subordinate part of the UK.

Left to its own devices, the Unionist majority at local council level went on to elaborate a complex system of dominance. Along with the abolition of proportional representation came the restoration of a property-based franchise giving many people multiple votes, and this together with the careful redrawing of constituency boundaries (usually known as 'gerrymandering') could produce spectacular results like the Unionist control of Derry council. A large nationalist majority on the ground was turned into a 12–8 Unionist majority on the council. Unionist gerrymandering was aided by the nationalists themselves, who boycotted the committees established to redraw constituency boundaries, in protest against the 1922 reform. Indeed widespread nationalist refusal to recognize or co-operate with the new Northern Ireland state (especially prominent in the education system) provided Unionists with not only the opportunity, but also the justification for stacking the system in favour of 'loyal' people and against

Table 10.1: Wards and local-government election results, Derry/Londonderry, 1967

Ward	Anti-Unionist			Unionist		
	No. of votes	No. of councillors	Ratio, votes : councillors	No. of votes	No. of councillors	Ratio, votes : councillors
South	10,047	8		1,138	0	
North	2,530	0		3,946	8	
Waterside	1,852	0		3,697	4	
Total	14,429	8	1,804.1	7,781	12	732.1

Source: Cameron Committee (1969, para. 134)

those who repudiated it. Catholic nationalists in the six counties found themselves in a vicious cycle: their outrage at their involuntary exclusion from the Irish state led them to exclude themselves from Northern Ireland institutions, and that exclusion became the basis for discrimination against them. The inequalities produced by this could only be rectified by political participation, but until the 1960s Catholic political action always carried a demand for 'reunification' that automatically antagonized Unionist opinion. Throughout its life, the Stormont political system was marked by deepset pre-modern characteristics, the most salient of which were clientelism and localism. Politicians in Northern Ireland, as in the Republic, tended – and still tend – to represent the constituencies in which they were born and live. This was an 'essentially rural political culture' that was, even in the north-east, 'largely unaffected by urbanisation'.[14]

The limits of devolution

There was a sharp contrast between Westminster's evident relief at being able to wash its hands of Irish complications, and Whitehall's steady insistence on enforcing Northern Ireland's economic subordination. The financial terms of the Government of Ireland Act set the only real limits to the political power of Stormont, but these were exerted in a way that was more annoying than effective. For a brief period, in 1921, Lloyd George tried to use fiscal threats to urge Northern Ireland into closer co-operation with the Free State: Northern Ireland could escape from its liability to pay an imperial contribution, and thus reduce the rate of income tax, if it subordinated itself to an all-Ireland dominion. Craig was predictably 'shocked and embittered' by this imputation of naked materialism.[15] The Treasury proceeded to exact an imperial contribution that in 1923 exceeded the cost of the 'transferred services', and over the next decade it became painfully clear that Northern Ireland, however indomitable its spirit of self-reliance, could not 'pay her own way'. Northern Ireland's 'residuary share' of UK revenue was assessed on the basis of its wealth – measured by the revenue it raised – not its population relative to the UK as a whole. Thus economic decline inexorably reduced its entitlement to a level that was manifestly inadequate.[16]

Britain was thus sucked resentfully into a series of emergency subventions, which continued even after the situation had been officially adjusted by an arbitration committee, chaired by Lord Colwyn, in

1924 and 1925. Northern Ireland went on falling behind British expenditure levels until eventually, in 1938, the Treasury accepted that Northern Ireland was entitled to the same level of public services as Britain, and would have to be subsidized accordingly – and permanently. As the Treasury Controller grumbled, 'we have invented a series of *dodges* and *devices* to give them *gifts* and *subventions* within the ambit of the Government of Ireland Act so as to save Northern Ireland from coming openly on the dole'.[17] Still, financial stringency was to remain a severe constraint on government policy throughout the life of Northern Ireland.

Discrimination and the economy

The society shaped by the Stormont system was undoubtedly divided, unequal and discriminatory. The precise effect of discrimination is, as we shall see, not easy to measure, but the divisive intent of Northern Ireland's statesmen was crystal clear. Craig argued at the outset that the division was a political and not a religious one: as he told the Northern Ireland parliament in March 1922, 'I do hope that people will realise that the Ulstermen are up against, not Catholics, but ... rebels, that they are up against murder, Bolshevism, and up against those enemies not only of Ulster, but of the Empire'.[18] In the 1930s, however, Brooke shifted the ground. He instructed the House of Commons that 'there is, in fact, a Catholic political party, which ranges from what I might call benevolent nationalism to the extreme of the extreme'. Contrasting loyalists with 'disloyalists', who were 'scheming and plotting to destroy the country in which they live', he argued that disloyalists should not be given employment. 'Every disloyalist allowed to come in is a potential voter for the destruction of this country.' He frankly identified these as 'Roman Catholics – political Roman Catholics'.[19] This was his reasoned response to the outrage caused by his more colourful public appeal 'to Loyalists ... wherever possible, to employ good Protestant lads and lasses'. He went on to clarify the point for the Derry Unionist Association in 1934: 'I recommend those people who are Loyalists not to employ Roman Catholics, 99 per cent of whom are disloyal. ... You are disenfranchising yourselves in that way.'

Protestant employers, and most notably the public authorities, undoubtedly responded to this call. John Whyte, who made the most careful efforts to measure discrimination during the Stormont period, found a consistent pattern: 'at manual labour levels, Catholics generally received their proportionate share of public employment. But at any level above that, they were seriously under-represented, and the higher one went, the greater the shortfall.' Through to the 1960s, a similar pattern ran across the whole society. Protestants dominated the higher professions and higher-paid occupations; they predominated in superior positions within occupations; and they were concentrated in higher status industries and locations.

Table 10.2: Religion and occupational class, 1971 (%)

Occupational class	Catholic	Protestant	Total
Professional, managerial	12	15	14
Lower-grade non-manual	19	26	24
Skilled manual	17	19	18
Semi-skilled manual	27	25	26
Unskilled, unemployed	25	15	18
Total	100	100	100

Note: Base = economically active men and women
Source: A.E. Aunger, 'Religion and occupational class in Northern Ireland' *Economic and Social Review*, 7, 1 (1975) 1–18

Most decisive of all, perhaps, were the patterns of unemployment: Catholics were always a majority, though they made up less than one-third of the economically active population. They were also significantly over-represented in the statistics of emigration.[20]

The impact of structural discrimination was especially severe because Northern Ireland's economy was shrinking. The optimism of the expansionary prewar years was replaced by persistent gloom. Because it was so tightly integrated into the United Kingdom economy, Northern Ireland had neither the capacity nor the will to reverse the decline of its two crucial industries, shipbuilding and linen production, or to find alternative paths of economic regeneration. The impact of decline in the linen industry was pervasive, because production was so localized. The prevalence of small-scale firms has been blamed for the industry's problems, but the inescapable reality was the global and permanent fall in demand.[21] The most successful sector of the economy was agriculture, where improved quality standards and marketing techniques were consistently promoted (the 1922 Livestock Breeding Act was the cornerstone of an increasingly sophisticated registration system which was to provide ultimate salvation for the beef industry during the BSE disaster of the 1990s). As in the South, however, the average size of farmsteads remained very small – nearly two-thirds of them were still under 30 acres in 1939, while less than 5 per cent were more than 100 acres (the figure for Éire at that time was 9 per cent). Output per capita was only 46 per cent of the British level in 1924. The bottom line for the survival of agriculture, and its 30 per cent of the workforce, was the British market.

The Agriculture Ministry was, Harkness suggests, 'perhaps the most dynamic and successful' of Northern Ireland's six governmental departments – but the competition was not strenuous. More characteristic was the performance of the housing authorities: a mere 2166 council houses were provided in the interwar period, out of a total of 34,312 new houses built. Housing standards were dramatically lower than in Britain. A survey in 1943 showed that nearly three-quarters of the housing stock needed repair, and that at least 100,000 new houses would be required – and another 100,000 if overcrowding was to be tackled.[22] In these circumstances, slum clearance was a non-starter, and a real housing crisis became inevitable. This had crucial political implications, too, since the allocation of housing was a key element in the gerrymandering mechanism. The territorial segregation (or 'ghettoization' in the minority's view) inherited from the nineteenth-century growth patterns of northern cities, especially Belfast, was if anything reinforced rather than reversed. Significantly, it was to be conflict over council housing allocation that precipitated the civil rights agitation of the late 1960s.

On the whole, it is hard to resist the conclusion, suggested by a leading historian of the Stormont system, that it was 'a factory of grievances'. Yet though the system deliberately sharpened discrimination in many sectors, there is some doubt whether it could have substantially eroded communal barriers even if it had tried. In the most vital sphere, of education, the Northern Ireland government did indeed try to establish a non-sectarian school system, and it was defeated by the same forces that had stymied British educational reforms under the Union. Lord Londonderry, the first Education Minister, was one of those rare Ulster Unionists who believed that it was better to try to incorporate the Catholic minority rather than to exclude it. His first action was to establish a wide-ranging consultative commission, with the aim of recasting the whole educational structure, dealing with the severe deficiency of secondary schools, and the absence of teacher training provision in the six counties. (Until Stranmillis College was established in 1922, the only training establishment was St Mary's College, for Catholic women.) But the Lynn

Committee, chaired by a prominent Unionist, immediately ran into the baleful effects of the fierce communal strife raging through the North. It was cold-shouldered by the Catholic Hierarchy; Cardinal Logue professed to believe that the inquiry would be used as a 'pretext for an attack' on the Catholic schools.

This prefigured the eventual fate of the reform package that followed the Lynn Committee's recommendations. The 1923 Education Act set up three categories of schools, with varying degrees of public funding. Fully funded schools were to be under the direct control of local authorities; 'four and two schools' would receive most of their funding and have two representatives of the local authorities alongside four of their original managers; voluntary schools, outside public control, would receive teacher salaries and possibly half their running costs, but no capital grants. The Catholic Church refused to allow Catholic schools to come under outside control, and so consigned them to the lowest funding category – thereby both maintaining segregated education, and creating a new political grievance. Many Protestants were also unenthusiastic about the extension of secular control, but they found it easier to adapt to the new funding principles. The paradoxical result of Londonderry's reforms was in the end to ensure that segregation remained the overwhelming feature of socialization in Northern Ireland.

The most limpid and dispassionate picture of what may be called the consensual apartheid of Ulster life can be found in the fieldwork of the anthropologist Rosemary Harris in a Co. Fermanagh border village (called a 'town', but with a population of only 324 in 1951) in the early 1950s. She documented a 'community' lacking the most vital characteristic that most people expect to find in such a group – a sense of fundamental unity of outlook. Neighbours lived at peace, but it was a peace of coexistence rather than co-operation: essentially they remained 'strangers'. Their whole socialization, and to a remarkable extent their economic life as well, were segregated. Though Harris was careful to stress that there was a 'common culture' at the structural level – such as the intense personalism of social relations, and the resistance to bureaucratic logic – she noted the vast range of topics that were taboo in 'mixed [Protestant–Catholic] company'. This range extended far beyond what are normally seen as political matters, into culturally loaded subjects like sport. Only racing and betting, in fact, were 'really neutral subjects'.[23] The only point during her years of fieldwork at which a definite civic unity appeared was when the County Health Department cast a slur on the cleanliness of the town's water supply; apart from that, Harris found 'no situation in which it could be said that a majority of the inhabitants shared a common viewpoint, still less that they acted together for a common end, no matter how trifling'.[24]

The legacy of the Second World War

The Second World War gave Northern Ireland a new experience to reinforce its special identity and its sense of distinctness from 'the South'. There was never any possibility that it would stand aside from the war. Stormont may have been rather slow to copy Britain's prewar preparations – its 1938 Air Raid Precautions Act came a year after Britain's, for example – and civil defence planning remained rudimentary. But action to complete the national register, the basis for military service and civilian food rationing, was taken within a few weeks of the outbreak of war. Resistance to the application of conscription came not from Craig's government but from Westminster, which saw the issue as politically explosive. Possibly alarmed by the outburst of IRA terrorism in Sean Russell's otherwise ineffective 'mainland' campaign of 1939, Britain decided that the costs of implementing compulsory service would outweigh the benefits. So as in the First World War, recruitment from Ulster remained voluntary – and was not in statistical terms very impressive. Nor did Northern factories become significant munitions producers; many operated at low capacity, or closed down. Recent research (showing that Unionist myths are just as vulnerable as nationalist myths to 'revisionism') has led one historian to conclude that there was no sense of 'war urgency' in Northern Ireland – if anything, the reverse.[25]

But unquestionably Northern Ireland experienced the war in a direct way, both as a vital base for Atlantic convoy protection, and a target of German air attack. The bombing of Belfast in 1941 culminated in an attack by 150 bombers on the night of 15 April, in which 70,000 people were driven from their homes, and 745 killed. Much of the damage was due to the culpable inadequacy of the city's emergency services, as well as to the weight of explosives dropped. Thirteen fire appliances were famously despatched from south of the border to assist. As in some blitzed English cities, public morale plummeted, and in May the Public Security Minister once again urged that conscription be brought in, to allow Northern Ireland to feel fully involved in the war: 'the principle of equality of sacrifice is essential to promote the degree of corporate discipline which a united population must have if it is to withstand the tide of total war'.[26] Churchill, however, was still convinced that it would be 'more trouble than it was worth'.[27]

The most positive effect of this traumatic experience was perhaps the sudden daylight cast on the state of the city slums, whose inhabitants – 'nearly sub-human' in the words of the Home Affairs Minister, Dawson Bates – were evacuated to a rather shocked countryside. The basis for a more consistent effort to bring Northern Ireland's welfare system into line with Britain's after the war was laid. Politically, though, the war experience was more problematic. The British government's attempt to offer Irish unity to persuade de Valera to abandon neutrality revived all the worst Unionist fears of betrayal. In unusually intemperate language Craig professed himself 'profoundly shocked and disgusted' by Chamberlain's initial suggestion of tripartite talks. 'To such treachery to loyal Ulster I will never be a party.'[28] This might have been viewed by British statesmen as a kind of loyalty that elevated self-interest above the common good of the United Kingdom, but in the event the Labour leadership were just as ready as Churchill himself to recognize the vital contribution that Northern Ireland had made to Britain's survival in the war. Thus it was Attlee's government that responded to Ireland's exit from the Commonwealth by issuing the famous constitutional 'guarantee' in the 1949 Ireland Act, that Northern Ireland would remain part of the UK as long as the majority of its citizens wished. In a sense this did no more than state the obvious, and the very fact that it had to be stated attested to Northern Ireland's oddity (no such assertion being made about Yorkshire, for instance), yet the statement became – like Article II of the Éire constitution – another focus of hostility. The ineffectual rhetoric of de Valera's anti-partition campaign at the same time kept fear and suspicion on the boil.

Northern Ireland grew, if possible, even further apart from Ireland after the war. The Labour government, while holding the Union fast, was radically changing its social economy. Conservative Ulster Unionists were intensely suspicious of the 'welfare state' reforms, but this ambitious and expensive programme finally terminated Northern Ireland's semi-detached financial status. If the reforms were to be implemented there, it could only be through massive British subventions. The province's economy was in steady decline. The continuing erosion of its staple industries was underlined in the semi-official 1955 *Economic Survey of Northern Ireland*, which pointed out that the dominance of family businesses in the linen industry (60 per cent) was paralysing reinvestment and expansion. Throughout local industry there was a noticeable concentration on profit margins rather than sales volumes, and a lack of management and marketing expertise. Modernization was stalled.[29] In 1960 Harland and Wolff laid off over a third of its 21,000 workforce, and by the following year almost a half had gone. These were sickening blows, which as in the past did not augur well for intercommunal relations.

The government of Northern Ireland steadfastly denied that discrimination against Catholics was widespread, and about three-quarters of Protestants (according to research in the 1960s) agreed. Only 16 per cent thought that there was discrimination, and only 4 per cent admitted personal knowledge of it.[30] Since the British government's abortive attempt to get information about the issue in the 1930s, academic research has fairly consistently undermined this self-deception. Differentials between Protestants and Catholics did not shrink under Stormont, and may well have widened. For instance, the proportion of Catholics amongst unskilled workers increased.[31] Catholic membership of the RUC fell from 17 per cent in 1936 to 11 per cent in 1969. John Whyte's balanced survey rejected both the extreme Unionist and nationalist versions in favour of a line somewhere in the middle, but stressing the sharp geographical variation in experience. A group of local authorities in the west (Londonderry County Borough, Counties Tyrone and Fermanagh, and parts of Counties Londonderry and Armagh) caused 'a startlingly high proportion of the total number of complaints' – three-quarters, in fact, for an area with a quarter of the province's population. There, discrimination was consistent and unmistakable.[32]

One of the few academic researchers to conclude that discrimination was 'not particularly inequitable' has argued that the minority's sense of disadvantage was heightened, if not indeed created, by its sense of nationality.[33] From a political point of view, of course, it was this perception that was ultimately crucial. During the campaign for 'civil rights' in the 1960s, the same proportion of Catholics (74 per cent) believed that discrimination existed as of Protestants who denied it. Over a third of Catholics said they had personal experience of it. Richard Rose's famous research, carried out just before the civil rights movement began, led him to the conclusion that the failure to achieve legitimacy, or consensus, in Northern Ireland was not due to inequality, but to religious and political consciousness. Others have pointed out that his evidence did not unambiguously support this conclusion, citing the fact that while 55 per cent of his Catholic respondents said they would approve 'if Catholics began protesting very strongly against cases of religious discrimination' (as against 27 per cent who would disapprove), only 32 per cent agreed that nationalists should support the republican cause more actively.[34] But inequality was itself a product of religious-political attitudes; and one-third was to be an ample basis for a more radical movement. What was manifestly missing in Northern Ireland was what would, in later political jargon, come to be called 'parity of esteem'. Perhaps the most characteristic of Stormont laws, apart from the Special Powers Act, was the Flags and Emblems Act of 1954, which went beyond making display of the green-white-orange Irish tricolour illegal (it had been banned since 1922), to oblige the police to protect displays of the Union flag, which in Northern Ireland was inevitably a party banner (and which was employed in ways that were quite unknown in Britain). This law was regarded by the Inspector-General of the RUC as impossible to enforce, and it clearly showed that the government was, as some members of the Northern Ireland Cabinet protested, 'yielding to the agitation of the extremists'. Ultimately, however, that was how the state maintained its position.[35]

The breakdown of the system

Northern Ireland's long political stagnation ended with the belated retirement of the ageing Lord Brookeborough in March 1963. Some change was inevitable, but the pace and nature of change was determined by the UUP's choice of successor. Instead of the political heavyweight who would probably have been elected if there had been an open leadership election – Brian Faulkner – the leader who 'emerged' (like his counterpart in the British Conservative party that year) was Terence O'Neill. On the face of things, O'Neill was a reformer. He politely but firmly rejected the inert style of his predecessor. He announced the need to bring Catholics into the fold of economic progress. Although his blithe remark that 'if you treat Catholics with due consideration and kindness they will live like Protestants in spite of the authoritative nature of their church' is nowadays cited as proof of his hopeless paternalism, it was at the time an astonishing denial of the virtually racist beliefs implicit (and often explicit) in mainstream Protestant prejudices. The possibility of real movement towards integration seemed to open up.

This was in part a response to great changes that were taking place in Catholic attitudes themselves. The 1950s saw a clear movement away from the old posture of non-recognition and abstention towards participation in Northern Ireland's public structures. The herald of this was a new upwardly mobile Catholic middle class. The scale and impact of this change has been disputed; measurement of middle-class status is hampered by the fact the census statistics for Northern Ireland between 1911 and 1971 (i.e. the censuses of 1926, 1937 and 1951) lack the information necessary to correlate occupation with religion. On the basis of the 1911 census data, one group of historians has argued that there was little change; though the proportion of Catholics in professional and managerial jobs increased by slightly more than average, those in lower-grade non-manual jobs actually decreased over the 60 years from 1911 to 1971.[36] Nonetheless, there was a widely felt sense of change. An index of this was the fact that the proportion of Catholic students in Queen's University, Belfast, was rising, to 22 per cent in 1961 and 32 per cent in 1972. New political approaches were signalled by the appearance of the National Unity group in 1959, willing to play the role of a constructive opposition, and to accept that reunification would be conditional on majority support within the province. The Campaign for Social Justice in 1964, the National Democratic Party in 1965 and finally the Northern Ireland Civil Rights Association in 1967 charted a path towards the reform rather than the overthrow of the Stormont system.

Another novel factor was British pressure, which began to reappear as the cost of welfare state subventions led to increasing exasperation at the immobilism of the Brookeborough regime. This exasperation had often cropped up within the civil service, but it got a new political edge after the election of Harold Wilson's Labour government of 1964. O'Neill's reforms were, however, hesitant at the structural level. His emphasis on planning and modernization has been harshly judged by some analysts as a cosmetic use of fashionable political rhetoric primarily designed to fend off the threat of British interference. Even his laudable attempt to encourage a rethinking of social attitudes was vitiated by his own social background. Although he was descended from one of the Gaelic high kings, Niall of the Nine Hostages, and thus had – as Unionists liked to point out – 'a far purer pedigree than President de Valera or any member of the Irish government', his aristocratic style was formed by specifically British experiences (Eton, the brigade of guards), which also weakened his political leverage because he had no local roots in the deeply traditional political system: he had, for instance, to join the Orange Order belatedly in a bid to reassure loyalists of his reliability.

O'Neill's talk about 'building bridges' in 1964 was followed by the decision to put Northern Ireland's new university in the small Protestant town of Coleraine, not the Catholic city of Derry, where most Catholics naturally assumed it would go. By 1967, after his celebrated meetings with Seán Lemass, O'Neill was rapidly losing support on both political extremes.[37] His 1968 package of reforms (under heavier British pressure), which included a promise to ensure impartial allocation of public housing, the appointment of an Ombudsman, reform of the local government system, and repeal of the Special Powers Act, was a perilous departure. It 'simultaneously increased Unionist disunity and minority expectations', thus undermining what Brendan O'Leary and John McGarry label 'the control system'.[38] In the end it was impossible to turn the UUP into a non-sectarian modern party, that would be 'attractive to all citizens willing to identify their interests with membership of the UK'.[39]

The civil rights movement was thus channelled into traditional confrontational politics: to loyalists it was merely a cover for a renewed assault on the state. The slide into open conflict was dismayingly rapid. The first major civil rights march, from Coalisland to Dungannon, took place on 24 August 1968. It was organized by the Campaign for Social Justice and the Northern Ireland Civil Rights Association, and focused on the abuse of local authority housing allocations in the village of Caledon, near Dungannon. A family of Catholic squatters was removed from a council house, which was allocated to a single, 19-year-old Protestant woman employee of a local Unionist councillor. The Nationalist MP Austin Currie led an occupation to publicize the issue, which became the key issue for the march. Tempers ran high as the marchers were confronted by a Unionist counter-demonstration, but they dispersed peacefully on police orders. A few weeks later the outcome was very different, when the next march, in Derry on 5 October, was banned by the Home Affairs Minister and triggered rioting that lasted for two days. The American – indeed international – civil rights anthem 'We shall Overcome' was interpreted in a very specific local way by its Protestant hearers in Northern Ireland. The final catastrophe was precipitated by the march from Belfast to Derry organized by a radical student group, Peoples Democracy, in January 1969. It was ambushed at Burntollet Bridge, not far from Derry, by loyalists with at least tacit police connivance. The 'Battle of Burntollet' was immediately fixed in nationalist mythology: 'from lanes at each side of the road a curtain of bricks and boulders and bottles brought the march to a halt. From the lanes burst hordes of screaming people wielding planks of wood, bottles, laths, iron bars, crowbars, cudgels studded with nails, and they waded into the march ...'.[40] After the bloodied marchers reached Derry, the first serious riots began. Any chance of reconciling the Catholic minority was probably lost by this point.

O'Neill went on trying; he set up a commission of inquiry into the disorders (the Cameron Commission), and pushed 'one man one vote' through his Cabinet – but at the price of the resignation of James Chichester-Clark. The Stormont elections on 28 February revealed his weakening political base, as anti-O'Neill Unionists took 17 per cent of the vote (as against his own Official Unionists' 31 per cent, and the 13 per cent of 'Unofficial Unionists' identified with him). On 28 April O'Neill resigned, in the hope that Chichester-Clark could reunite the party. But public disorder accelerated. The climax was reached, as so often before, during the summer marching season: riots in Derry against the Apprentice Boys' parade on 12 August 1969 dramatically outran Stormont's policing resources; outright sectarian fighting began in the Bogside area, and went on until the British army finally intervened on 15–16 August. Britain's 50-year attempt to resolve its residual Irish problem by ignoring it had spectacularly boomeranged.

automatically the final failure of the Stormont system. The British government's first instinct was to increase the pressure on Northern Ireland to implement real and significant reforms. The Cameron Commission (the first major commission of inquiry since Northern Ireland had been established), which was set up in January 1969 by O'Neill to investigate the 1968 disturbances, eventually produced a comprehensive analysis of the discriminatory structure of Northern Ireland's public authorities. This established a plain agenda for reform. The first and most obvious candidate was the security apparatus that had undoubtedly failed. Cameron found the police guilty of 'misconduct which involved assault and battery, malicious damage to property ... and the use of provocative sectarian and political slogans', amongst other failings. The Scarman inquiry into the August 1969 disturbances, however, while it condemned the use of machine guns as wholly unjustifiable, cleared the RUC of the charge of participation in sectarian assaults. A further inquiry, the Hunt Committee, recommended the disarming of the RUC and the abolition of the Specials.

The first of these actions reflected a deep-set British notion of 'normal' policing, but it quickly wilted when violence escalated in the early 1970s. Perhaps it came 40 years too late, or perhaps it could never have been made to work in the such unBritish circumstances. Nobody in politics would take responsibility for doing anything that might endanger police who were under deadly threat. Here, as so often, policy was determined by terrorists rather than by government. In any case, disarmament was not enough to turn the RUC into a normal police force. So the RUC was rearmed once more, and was never to shed its gendarmerie style. Lord Scarman's conclusion in 1972, that the force had completely lost the confidence of the Catholic community, was not to be satisfactorily addressed.[2] (The issue was still a political minefield in 1998, when reform became a crucial element in the Stormont agreement, and Chris Patten headed another commission of inquiry.) The abolition of the 'B' Specials also followed a historically determined path: these men being too dangerous to put out on the street, as it were, they were given a more formal military structure as the Ulster Defence Regiment (UDR). On paper, the UDR was yet another new start, carrying the renewed hope of enrolling enough Catholics to give it representative legitimacy. In practice, the 20 per cent recruitment of Catholics in the early optimism of April 1970 fell within a year to 8 per cent of the force; by 1975 a bare 2 per cent of the UDR was Catholic.

In 1970, nonetheless, there seemed to be a real possibility of fundamental political change in Northern Ireland. Two new political parties were formed. In August that year a group of independent, nationalist and labour members of Stormont – Ivan Cooper, Austin Currie, Paddy Devlin, John Hume and Paddy O'Hanlon – came together to form the Social Democratic and Labour Party (SDLP), with the former Republican Labour Party MP, Gerry Fitt, as leader. Under the banner of vaguely leftish progressive rhetoric (calling for 'the public ownership and democratic control of such essential industries and services as the common good requires'), the SDLP reconfigured the nationalist commitment to Irish unity on the basis of consent.[3] This meant, in effect, recognition of Northern Ireland as long as a majority supported it. This acceptance of Northern Ireland as a viable political entity was made even more explicit in the other new political grouping, the Alliance Party, which insisted that it had no connection with any 'outside' political organization: 'We are Northern Irishmen'. On the grounds that Britain was a legal and not a cultural nation, it held that there was 'no inconsistency between being culturally Irish and politically British'.[4] The SDLP's participatory outlook opened the way for a more coherent nationalist political strategy than before, even though the party never succeeded in building a mass basis. Its constitutionalist approach, moreover, drew no answering response from the UUP, which persisted in the attempt to preserve its monopoly of power.

But Unionism was also rapidly losing its monolithic cast. The crisis opened up the most dramatic fissures so far seen in the ruling party. The two last prime ministers of Northern Ireland, James Chichester-Clark and Brian Faulkner, struggled – against the odds, as it looks in retrospect – to keep the mainstream of Unionism together on a course of moderate reform. The once unchallengeable Unionist government was now racked by conflicting pressures, with Britain urging faster reform, and the loyalist die-hards fulminating against any concessions to disloyal Catholics. Intense nationalist/civil-rights agitation went on through 1970–71, with frequent demonstrations leading to confrontation and often all-night rioting; the images of burning shops and vehicles, cascades of petrol bombs and rocks raining down on troops and police in riot gear came to dominate outside impressions of Northern Ireland. The loss of traditional Unionist control of the security forces fatally undermined Chichester-Clark's prestige, and in March 1971 he was replaced by Faulkner, a man of very different metal. Faulkner's credentials were impressive; he had earned the reputation of a hardliner when as Home Affairs Minister in 1959 he wielded the weapon of internment against the IRA and presided over the crushing of the border campaign. He resigned from O'Neill's

Cabinet in protest against the establishment of the Cameron Commission, which he saw as a concession to violence. As Minister of Development in 1970, however, he succeeded in demonstrating a businessman's dynamism that looked, at least in economic terms, progressive.

Unfortunately for the success of his mission, to preserve Stormont against the growing threat that Britain would resume direct rule, Faulkner could not make the leap towards the idea of sharing power with the minority. Quite apart from the Unionist rebellion that such a course was bound to provoke, he himself remained a believer like most Unionists in the idea of 'majoritarian democracy' (i.e. the fixed Unionist majority) that underpinned the Stormont system. His Green Paper on reform (October 1971) offered no real scope for nationalist participation in government. For him, the crucial issue was the recovery of public security, without which the state was doomed to fall apart. In July 1971 the situation became critical. After four nights of rioting in Derry, with gunfire added to the usual barrage of rocks and petrol bombs, the army shot two men, and the SDLP demanded a public inquiry. Faulkner, true to form, refused, and the SDLP withdrew from Stormont.

Now, having resisted internment before, Faulkner decided that it offered the only hope of recovering governmental authority. When it had first been discussed, he had argued to Chichester-Clark that the creation of barricaded 'no-go' areas in parts of Belfast and Derry, where the security forces had abandoned the attempt to maintain control, had deprived the police of the information they needed to make internment effective. This argument remained just as cogent in 1971. It was thus likely that the introduction of internment would become the final débâcle for the Stormont system. When the army set out to arrest 452 men in dawn raids on 9 August, it could only pick up 342, and 105 of these had to be released within 48 hours.

Far from crushing the opposition, the arrests triggered a spectacular outburst of protest. In three days 22 people were killed and some 7000 driven from their homes; alongside this traditional communal warfare went an intensification of republican terrorist action. The authorities seemed to have lost control of streets. By 1972 communal conflict was verging into civil war. The army had long since lost the support of moderate Catholics. Two years of the casual brutality inseparable from military action had seen to that, but a crescendo of alienation culminated in the ghastly slaughter of 'Bloody Sunday' on 30 January 1972, when paratroops brought from Belfast to Derry

('One platoon of 1 Para could do what one company of any other battalion could do in Belfast', as one officer noted, 'We hoped their reputation had spread to Londonderry') fired 108 rounds of ammunition into a demonstrating crowd, killing 13.[5] Prime Minister Edward Heath demanded the surrender of all Stormont's security powers – including the Special Powers Act – and when Faulkner refused, Stormont was suspended (24 March) and the Northern Ireland government replaced by a Secretary of State, William Whitelaw.

The rise of paramilitarism

In retrospect, the cautious steps taken towards normalization in the 1960s can be seen to have been dogged from the start by groups dedicated to the use of violence. The loyalist tradition of paramilitary mobilization against any perceived nationalist threat was an ever-present danger to the possibility of gradual reform. The crucial year was 1966, the 50th anniversary of the battle of the Somme and the Easter rebellion. The Reverend Ian Paisley, a veteran street activist against displays of the Irish tricolour flag (illegal in Northern Ireland since 1933), headed an Ulster Constitution Defence Committee and started to form the Ulster Protestant Volunteers, aspiring to act as a revived Ulster Volunteer Force. Paisley had already defied the public order law by organizing street protests against the decision to lower the Union flag as a gesture of respect on the death of Pope John XXIII in 1963. He was prepared to go to any length of rhetorical violence to defend the Protestant ascendancy against the menace of Rome (for him, Catholics were always 'Papists', Irish nationalism a Popish plot).

Inevitably the organizations his confrontational rhetoric inspired took violence beyond the realms of rhetoric, and in 1966 the first of a series of grisly sectarian killings began. In May a group readopting the title of the UVF issued a statement declaring war on the IRA, and in June two Catholics were shot dead in Belfast. Next year the first bombs were set. This was the beginning of a proliferation of loyalist militias of varying size and longevity, with names like the Ulster Citizen Army, Ulster Protestant Action Group, Ulster Service Corps, and of course Ulster Defence Association and Ulster Freedom Fighters (UDA, UFF). The political loading of the province's name was by now irreversible. The UVF was reckoned to have 1500 members by 1972, the UDA maybe 40,000.[6]

The republican paramilitary counter-mobilization was slower but ultimately devastating. When the civil rights crisis broke in 1969 the IRA was still a marginal organization. Since the failure of the border campaign its old physical-force leadership had been superseded by a more articulate, theoretically minded generation, with Marxistic ideas that put aside the voluntarism of the past and looked to leadership of a new working-class mobilization. It was not ready for a situation in which the most primitive of all instincts, those of self-defence and revenge, would suddenly blossom into major political forces. When this happened in the Bogside in 1969, a splinter group, the 'Provisional' IRA, sprang up around the barricades. The motivation of the PIRA was at one crucial level romantic: it upheld a sacred cause. Shane O'Doherty, a 15-year-old at St Columb's College in Derry, was reading the works of Pearse and MacDonagh at the age of nine, and weeping as he read. When he was 10 years old, he put a note under the floorboards of his bedroom (where it was later found by the police): 'When I grow up, I want to fight and, if necessary, die for Ireland's freedom. *Signed*: Shane Paul O'Doherty.' When he was sworn into the PIRA he was exhilarated to be 'part of the heroic tradition of Ireland, but above all at that time, part of the defence of my people'.[7] O'Doherty – educated, middle-class – was not a Bogsider himself (he lived two crucial blocks from it), and was certainly untypical of the Provo rank and file. But he united the simple resentment and anger that mobilized ordinary Catholics with the sense of mission that had kept the Fenian organization in being for over a century.

The PIRA never had enough guns to mount a real defence of Catholic ghettos; even in this role its violence was demonstrative and political rather than strictly military. The chance of creating another 1920-style guerrilla campaign was vanishingly small, for the same reason that the 1920 campaign itself had never caught fire in the north-east. Beyond the borderlands like south Armagh, most northern Catholics were city-dwellers. Liberated spaces like the famous 'no-go' area of 'Free Derry' existed on sufferance, and were eradicated as soon as the government made up its mind to use enough force (as it eventually did with Operation 'Motorman' in July 1972). In fact the defenders brought down more trouble on the people they claimed to be protecting: as one British Army commander pointed out, the mere fact of the PIRA's existence caused the security forces to concentrate their attention on the Catholic community.[8] The real business of the PIRA was not positional defence but psychological aggression, to retaliate against Protestant power and to 'hurt England' as

O'Donovan Rossa had once put it. Shane O'Doherty, for instance, realized that killing soldiers and policemen in Northern Ireland was too indirect a method, and went on to mount a letter-bomb campaign in England (for which he was given 30 life sentences at the Old Bailey in 1976). Most of the Provos did not think so hard about what they were doing. Revelling in their new-found destructive power, 'the teenagers who swelled the IRA's ranks' had no problem with systematically wrecking their own home towns. For most, it was a question of 'blind faith': a common response to objections was 'We know we're right and if you don't lay off we'll shoot ye'.[9]

In the process of arming themselves to bomb Protestant stores and shoot at the security forces, they steadily extended their grip on the Catholic communities in which they were rooted. Paramilitarism became an almost regular, if capricious, system of government – a protection racket, like all governments, enforcing a rough-and-ready rule of law (especially against drug traders and joy-riders), and skilful in exploiting economic opportunities like the construction work which burgeoned in the wake of its own destructive actions. Moderate Catholic opinion disliked the PIRA's offensive methods but reluctantly acknowledged their effect. 'Every blast was a dramatic demonstration of the fact that we, who had been scorned for so long, could now strike out in an unmistakable fashion and make the establishment scream'.[10] But if the violence and destruction were 'unmistakable', the campaign's logic was not. Leaders like Seán MacStíofáin, PIRA Chief of Staff, and Martin McGuinness, commander of the Derry Brigade, advanced the argument that damaging the economic base of the province would drive away investment and force the British to pay compensation, thus driving up the cost of occupying Northern Ireland to the point at which it outweighed the benefits for Britain.[11] Unfortunately, this rational analysis proved to be less well founded than 'blind faith', since it rested on a total misconception of the reasons for the British presence. Northern Ireland was already formidably expensive for Britain before the violence began, and the benefits were of the philosophical kind that tend to thrive (like the IRA's own) on sacrifice. Britain too had its cause, and in an ideological struggle like this – 'law and order' versus 'liberation' – the greater the cost, the more precious the cause comes to seem.

The fall of Stormont looked like a spectacular vindication of the PIRA's methods, and was followed by an intensification of destruction in 1972–73, the most murderous phase of the troubles. In March 1972 the car bomb was introduced, showing that necessity could lead to invention. Shortage of the traditional commercial explosive, gelignite, chimed with the discovery of powerful, though bulky, fertilizer-based explosives such as 'ANFO' (ammonium nitrate fertilizer with fuel oil), that could only be carried to the target in motor vehicles. Using the vehicle as a bomb was a logical step, but it made targeting more imprecise, indeed increasingly indiscriminate. In May the British army recorded 1223 shooting engagements and incidents; next month it suffered more casualties than ever before. In 1972 there were altogether 10,628 shootings, and 467 deaths (as against 174 in 1971, and 250 in 1973). The PIRA's confidence was high; it had effectively crushed its rival Official IRA. In 1972 it declared a cease-fire and on 7 July sent delegates to secret talks in London with the Northern Ireland Secretary – notable among them the young commanders of the Derry and Belfast Brigades, Martin McGuinness and Gerry Adams. The republicans concluded that the British were stalling ('I learned in two hours what Irish politicians still haven't learned', McGuinness said in 1986, 'that the British don't give easily'[12]) and that any future cessation of violence would be conditional on a British declaration of intent to withdraw from Northern Ireland.

Power-sharing: the failed experiment

While William Whitelaw was talking to the Provos – a political error, as he later acknowledged – Heath's government was preparing the most significant constitutional reform of the century. Its method, which echoed through subsequent British administrations, oscillated between consultation and imposition. The search for consensus proved frustrating. In September 1972 a conference on political options for Northern Ireland failed to reach any agreement on a future structure – and even this had taken place without the SDLP, which boycotted it in protest against internment. A few days beforehand, the SDLP issued a policy statement, *Towards a New Ireland*, calling for joint British-Irish sovereignty and a British commitment to try to persuade Unionists to accept Irish unity. This went well beyond what Britain then envisaged, and in October the Northern Ireland Office issued its own Green Paper, *The Future of Northern Ireland*, reiterating Britain's 1949 commitment to the union. But it also proposed a radical new political idea: 'real participation should be achieved by giving minority interests a share in the exercise of political power'. This idea was buried fairly deep in the document

– at paragraph 79 – but it opened up quite novel possibilities. (And some loyalists were accordingly alarmed.) These hardened into the formal White Paper of March 1972 (*Northern Ireland Constitutional Proposals*), announcing an assembly to be elected on a system of proportional representation with multi-member constituencies, as in the Republic. Crucially, the government declared that the Northern Ireland executive could 'no longer be based upon any single party' if it drew 'its support and its elected representation virtually entirely from only one section of a divided community' (paragraph 52). Moreover it wanted the new arrangements to be 'as far as possible acceptable to the Republic of Ireland', a proviso that was sure to intensify loyalist fears, and brought a serious Unionist split closer.

As the new constitutional plans came into operation over the summer, attitudes were hardening. A referendum on the unity question ('Do you want Northern Ireland to remain part of the UK?') held in March was boycotted by nationalists; 57 per cent of the electorate voted Yes. The assembly elections at the end of June saw a high turnout (72.3 per cent), but proportional representation unexpectedly worked in favour of the extremes rather than the centre. The result was an immediate crisis for the old Unionist party. Faulkner only endorsed candidates who pledged to accept the White Paper: these 'Official Unionists' ended up as a bare majority of the Unionist representation (the Official Unionists had 23 seats, the SDLP 19, and Alliance 8). Unionists opposed to the White Paper won 10 seats, and two new hardline splinter parties, the Vanguard and Democratic Unionist parties (VUPP, DUP) led by William Craig and Ian Paisley, won 6 and 9 seats respectively. All these represented the differing paths that Unionism might take: the DUP held fast to UK integration, while the VUPP moved towards an autonomous Ulster. Glen Barr, the political voice of the paramilitary UDA, declared that 'An Ulsterman's first allegiance must be to the state of Ulster'.

In November 1973 the details of the power-sharing executive were worked out, and shortly afterwards the Official Unionists went – poorly prepared, in the view of some critics – to a conference at Sunningdale (the Civil Service Staff College in Berkshire) to flesh out the Irish dimension, the proposed Council of Ireland. This was an epochal moment. Irish government representatives (Taoiseach Liam Cosgrave, Foreign Minister Garret FitzGerald, and Communications Minister Conor Cruise O'Brien) joined British and Northern Ireland leaders – from the SDLP and Alliance – for the first time since 1925. Even the hard-headed Brian Faulkner may have been awed by the significance of the event. When he signed up on 9 December to a Council of Ireland with 'executive and harmonising functions' he knew he would provoke a loyalist revolt; the question was, how big. Over the next few weeks it gathered force.

The eventual disaster was precipitated not by Irish but by British political priorities. The power-sharing Executive took office formally on 1 January 1974, with Faulkner as Chief Executive and Gerry Fitt as Deputy Chief Executive. Unionists filled five principal ministries (Finance, Environment, Education, Agriculture, and Information), the SDLP three (Commerce, Housing and Local Government, Social Security) and the Alliance one. On 4 January the Ulster Unionist Council rejected the Sunningdale Agreement, and Faulkner resigned as leader of the UUP. He gambled heavily on the success of the new Executive to maintain his political position, but the ground was cut from beneath him by his British political allies. Barely a month later, Edward Heath called a general election to force a showdown with British trade union power on the issue 'who governs?'. This meant that voters in Northern Ireland would be turning out for the fourth time in 10 months – something that the new Executive would certainly not have wanted. Its Unionist opponents had formed the United Ulster Unionist Council to orchestrate their campaign, and under the slogan 'Dublin is just a Sunningdale away' won 11 of the 12 Westminster seats, with over 50 per cent of the total poll. (The only Executive member to hold his seat was Gerry Fitt in West Belfast.) The legitimacy of the Executive was severely damaged, and equally seriously Heath's government, which had created it, also fell – for reasons quite unconnected with fears of Irish unity. Finally a province-wide strike organized by the Ulster Workers' Council (UWC) in May brought the whole power-sharing project down.

The UWC was an *ad hoc* body which crystallized the widespread Unionist fear that Sunningdale was a prelude to the abandonment of British sovereignty. It did not help that nationalists also believed this, and said it quite loudly in early 1974. The street-level muscle for the barricade-building and the steadily increasing enforcement of the strike, to the point at which the province was facing paralysis, was supplied by paramilitary groups like the UDA and the Loyalist Defence Volunteers under the aegis of a short-lived Ulster Army Council; but mainstream Unionist opinion was in essence behind the protest. This was the conclusion drawn by the incoming Labour government, whose Northern Ireland Secretary, Merlyn Rees, abandoned the effort to maintain the Executive on 28 May. The army had told the Cabinet that it could not run the vital services that had come to a standstill. Faulkner had already resigned when Rees refused to negotiate with the UWC; British reasoning evidently included a fear that the massive destabilization of Ulster could affect Britain itself. Political analysts have agreed that the Executive was bound to collapse in any case, but the sudden withdrawal of British support caused lasting resentment amongst nationalists.[13]

Loyalism and Paisleyism

At the height of the UWC strike, one of its leaders told a television camera crew, 'it now seems we're running the country'. The UWC were certainly stopping it from running, but that is very different. In terms of its positive political legacy, this formidable loyalist mobilization remained oddly barren. As soon as the threat of Sunningdale was lifted, the protest died away. The Ulster Army Council was followed by the lower-key Ulster Loyalist Central Co-ordinating Committee. Between then and the next attempt at a full-scale loyalist uprising, in protest against the Anglo-Irish Agreement 12 years later, loyalism was searching for a meaningful political direction. The reason for its failure was, of course, that it remained – as it had always been – an essentially negative, reactive movement. It was defined principally, if not exclusively, by what it rejected. Most of its great slogans were negative: 'No home rule', 'No popery', 'No surrender', 'Not an inch', 'Six into twenty-six won't go', and of course 'Ulster says No'. For most of its modern history, at least since the 1880s, this negativity has ensured it a bad press with mainstream opinion, broadly committed to the ethos of compromise and consensual political evolution. Loyalism was routinely dismissed as 'bigotry', and its acute lack of sophisticated political thinkers (or at least writers) did nothing to help its image. The resounding chorus of denunciation only hardened the loyalist sense of isolation, and the siege mentality it so assiduously cultivated. The tendency to caricature loyalist thinking undermined most progressive attempts to formulate 'solutions' to the crisis, as the pseudonymous Frank Burton argued in his pioneering study of a Belfast locality in 1978.[14] Only in the last 20 years or so has a serious attempt been made to grasp the springs of loyalist thought and action.

Sarah Nelson, a research student in the early 1980s, produced the first attempt at a study of loyalist attitudes in depth. The title of the book she published in 1984, *Ulster's Uncertain Defenders*, aptly captured the hollowness that she found behind the defiant bombast of Orange parades and paramilitary pronouncements. The problem was that the simple loyalty to the British Crown that was the historic linchpin of the Union had long been undermined by Britain's evident undependability. Some loyalists remained committed to straight-forward maintenance of the Union, or full integration. Others accepted that this was a political non-starter. Some turned, like Craig's VUPP, to Ulster independence on the basis of the argument that the 'Ulster Scots' were a separate nation. These at least had a positive vision of a future political outcome, however implausible. But they remained a minority; for the majority, all the ideal solutions lay in the past. They faced the future in a spirit of pessimism. This point has been put effectively, if pugnaciously, by the sociologist Steve Bruce. His major study of Protestant paramilitary groups shows the limita-tions of what he labels 'pro-state terrorism'. Because of the essentially reactive nature of most loyalist violence (which looks conclusive from a simple statistical graph), there is no view of a longer-term project beyond defending the status quo – and that itself is a poor substitute for the old Protestant ascendancy. In 1992 Bruce suggested that even Protestants who believed that most loyalist violence was clean, 'mil-itary' action, 'still find it hard to identify a purpose, a direction, or a programme in what they are doing'.[15] In a later study he amplified the 'dismal' and paralysing vision of the future that had eroded many loy-alists' faith in the political process to generate an acceptable outcome. Politics had come to mean continual surrenders to Catholic/nation-alists. A typical paramilitary view was, 'I don't know where this thing is going. It has been going on so long now that I've stopped thinking about it ending. How can it end?'[16]

The most coherent vision of the Ulster Protestant future is the intensely sectarian one usually labelled 'Paisleyism'. Bruce, again, has produced the most careful study of Dr Paisley's role as a symbol of a sense of exceptionalism that runs far wider than the confines of his own church (the Free Presbyterians) or even his political party, the DUP. Ian Richard Kyle Paisley grew out of a deep-rooted tradition of fissiparous and miniscule free churches, and fiercely committed street preaching. The church in which he delivered his first sermon, the Ravenhill Evangelical Mission Church, had itself been formed by people walking out of the Ravenhill Presbyterian Church after a heresy dispute.[17] For such evangelical sects, testifying their faith was inherently bound up with confronting error and sin. Paisley estab-lished his own Free Presbyterian Church in 1951, and soon projected his confrontational style into the political sphere. In 1959 he was fined £5 for disorderly conduct at a public meeting in Ballymena. His first political demonstration in 1963 became the first loyalist march to be banned under the Special Powers Act, and when he was fined £10 for going ahead he characteristically insisted on going to prison rather than paying. (The fine was paid anonymously.) From then on his political style was marked by unblinking opposition to the Roman church, and fierce suspicion of the Irish republic as its agent.

Mainstream Protestant Unionists may have blenched at the 'bigotry' of his convictions, but they gave him the highest personal vote of any Northern Ireland politician (in the European election of June 1979), and seats in three assemblies simultaneously (Northern Ireland, Westminster, and Strasbourg) in the early 1980s. Voting for Paisley did not necessarily equate with 'Paisleyism' exactly; the die-hard grass-roots resistance movement, sometimes called 'Ultra' Protestant, never really recovered its full power after 1974. Paisley's prestige was damaged by the failure of his attempt to stage a repeat of the strike in 1977, and his repeated efforts to create what he called the 'Third Force', a veiled paramilitary organization, did not come to fruition (though it claimed 15,000–20,000 members in 1981).

The reinvented republic

The country that Paisley so vehemently denounced as a front for the imperialism of the Papacy, 'the whore of Babylon', was changing more rapidly during the first decade of the Northern troubles than at any time in its history. One cultural historian has even suggested that the 1970s in Ireland were marked by ostentatious consumption and rapidly rising living standards 'as in no other country in modern history'.[18] The tide of consumer goods and the international culture fostered by the media (by 1978, 83 per cent of all Irish homes, and 92 per cent of those in Dublin, had television) worked an inexorable change in the public attitudes. A symbolic turning-point was the resignation of the ancient Eamon de Valera from the presidency in 1973; more concrete shifts came when Ireland joined the European Community (EC) in 1972, and a new era of coalition governments began in 1973. The May 1972 referendum vote on Europe was decisive – over 1 million for and 211,891 against on a healthy turnout of 71 per cent. The result of the snap election called by Jack Lynch (in traditional de Valera style) in early 1973 was less overwhelming, but significant. The second breaking of Fianna Fáil hegemony followed, and ushered in a generation in which there was a viable alternation of government and opposition.

By 1973 Fianna Fáil had been in power for 16 years. Jack Lynch, Lemass's successor since 1966, was modestly successful in continuing the process of modernization, but the ruling party had once again begun to ossify. One of its less impressive efforts was its attempt to abolish proportional representation in favour of the British first-past-the-post system – ironically, at the time when Northern Ireland was under pressure to abandon that. The Fianna Fáil leadership had long hankered after the security that the British system would give them – over 90 Dáil seats according to the estimates of political scientists. But when the issue was brought to a referendum in 1968 the Yes vote, despite vocal support from Lemass and Seán MacEntee, only reached 423,496, with 657,898 Noes. Broadly, if not overwhelmingly, Irish people seemed to find proportional representation congenial. Fianna Fáil's strength survived this defeat, and Lynch went on to win the 1969 election, thanks in part no doubt to the systematic redrawing of constituency boundaries carried out by Kevin Boland in the wake of the referendum defeat (the Electoral Amendment Act 1969, uncharitably labelled a 'gerrymander' by one of the more acerbic political commentators), in part to his own popularity (helped by his background as a hurling star of the 1940s), and also the failure of the opposition parties to construct a viable alternative.

It fell to Lynch to construct Ireland's response to the Northern crisis. His government was poorly prepared for it: there had been little or no Cabinet discussion of Northern policy since the 1940s. Lynch's famous television address on 13 August 1969, offering cautious support for endangered Northern Catholics – 'the Irish Government can no longer stand by and see innocent people injured and perhaps worse' – chimed with public opinion, as probably did his less public acceptance that the pursuit of reunification offered no immediate solution to the problem, and might well exacerbate it. Some of his senior ministers took a very different view, however. In 1970 the administration was rocked by an 'arms crisis': Neil Blaney, the Agriculture Minister, and Finance Minister Charles Haughey, were dismissed on the night of 5/6 May for their involvement in an illegal attempt to import 500 pistols and 180,000 rounds of ammunition. This looked like an ominous sign that traditional physical-force nationalism still had a respectable constituency. Lynch survived this buffeting with his personal reputation intact: his image remained that of 'the reluctant man of power, doing the minimum, and delaying it for as long as possible'.[19] In terms of concrete achievement, his administration (not unlike some of its predecessors) dealt more successfully with security than with social issues. Although Lemass's educational reform programme was continued – at record cost in the 1968 budget, for instance, when Haughey also raised old age pensions, maternity and unemployment benefits – Lynch presided over a further toughening of de Valera's Offences Against the State Act, allowing the arrest of anyone believed by a senior police officer to be a member of an illegal organization (i.e. the IRA), and the revival of the juryless Special Criminal Courts. These were sharply criticized as undoubted infringements of civil liberties, but the need for demonstrative action against political violence was broadly accepted.

Lynch lost the 1973 election, though only narrowly, because the potential Fine Gael–Labour coalition got its act together, and voters used their transfers in a way that favoured it (as they had not in 1969). The new coalition held real promise. With exceptionally able younger ministers like Garret FitzGerald and Conor Cruise O'Brien, and the experienced Liam Cosgrave presiding, it looked like a world-class administration. Two other events in 1973, Eamon de Valera's retirement from the presidency, and Ireland's admission to the EC, marked a new possibility of change. Entry into Europe, in particular, though its timing was dictated by British rather than Irish policy, was at last to give Ireland the power to move out of Britain's shadow. But the country was immediately hit by the devastating impact of the oil price rise that year, and the new government failed to come up with any miraculous solutions. For Ireland, as for other states, the ultimate message was that the ideal of economic independence was gradually being undermined towards the end of the twentieth century.

The coalition faced up to another, more sensitive, failure of policy when it abolished the Irish language requirement for entry into the civil service and other government jobs, which had been a keystone of the state's language revival project since independence. For advocates of realism this was refreshing, but evolution was not easy. After the premature death of Erskine Childers, who had ideas of making the presidency a more significant political force, the Defence Minister, Patrick Donegan, raised a discreditable storm by insulting the makeshift President, Cearbhall Ó Dalaigh. (The issue of presidential power was buried for the more decorous 14-year term of his successor, Patrick Hillery.) At Foreign Affairs, Garret FitzGerald polished up his political credentials; EC membership transformed the formerly obscure department, as Lee points out, and FitzGerald 'quickly acquired a glowing reputation abroad, which gradually penetrated domestic consciousness'.[20] But he was all too obviously the future Fine Gael leader, and Cosgrave sidelined him accordingly. Had he moved him to Finance – which many saw as FitzGerald's natural role – before the election called in June 1977, nine months before the end of the Dáil term, the coalition might have survived. In the event Fine Gael lost 10 seats, and Fianna Fáil returned to power with a 20-seat majority. It looked like the prelude to another mammoth term of office, but this time the coalition was able to retain its credibility as an alternative government.

Fianna Fáil's vague economic optimism allowed the reins to be taken off public spending once again, and the national debt spiralled. By the time the party suffered a surprise defeat in the European elections of 1979, Lynch's position was being eroded. In December 1979 he was replaced by the ambitious but shady Charles Haughey, who outmanoeuvred Lynch's preferred successor George Colley. Haughey combined daunting force of personality with remarkable lack of clarity about policy issues. Until 1977 he had a reputation as a sort of progressive (certainly by his party's standards). Then as Lynch's Health Minister he moved with almost theatrical caution to deal with what had become one of the most pressing of Ireland's social issues, contraception. After a demonstratively extensive consultation exercise, he introduced a conservative Bill making contraceptives available to married couples on prescription. The Labour party understandably denounced this 'legislative crawl' towards a betrayal of human rights and women's rights. But Haughey could claim that by respecting Irish – that is, the Church's – attitudes he had at least succeeded, where earlier campaigners (including the rising star Labour senator Mary Robinson) had failed, in passing a law. As Taoiseach Haughey, 'the boss', presided over repeated bouts of near-disastrous public spending sprees, yet gradually tightened his grip on his party and the public imagination. The whiff of sulphur hanging about him after the Arms Trials seems to have done him little harm with Fianna Fáil voters. Nor did his conspicuously rich lifestyle (not to be satisfactorily explained until long after his retirement, when large-scale donations from the head of Dunnes Stores came to light), in sharp contrast to the austere tenor of former prime ministers.

Garret FitzGerald, who led Fine Gael from 1978 to 1987, and headed two coalition governments in 1981–82 and 1982–87, could hardly have been more different, and the interplay between the two created (perhaps for the first time in the state's history) a true dynamic of opposition. Where Haughey was the self-made man, the personification of naked ambition, FitzGerald – 'Garret the Good' – was from a political dynasty, son of Desmond FitzGerald, though he was rather untraditional in his intellectualized approach to politics. Meticulous command of detail took the place of rhetoric. His mental austerity was very much in the Cosgrave–Blythe tradition, and he campaigned consistently for two objectives – first, to bring Ireland to a sense of economic reality, and second, to reduce the assertively nationalist-Catholic (indeed, he used the blunt label 'sectarian') elements of the constitution and legal code that he believed were a major obstacle to reconciliation with the North. Haughey's easy populism on these crucial issues was the recipe for a fierce confrontation, which began early on with FitzGerald's dark reference to the new Taoiseach's 'flawed pedigree'. But the tag that stuck best was contributed by another outstanding intellectual in politics, Labour's Conor Cruise O'Brien, who picked up Haughey's description of the arrest of the murderer of a young nurse in the flat of his Attorney-General in July 1982 as 'grotesque, unbelievable, bizarre and unprecedented', and turned the acronym GUBU on the Taoiseach himself. To his opponents, at least, there was always something incredible, and dangerous, about Haughey's power.

In September 1981 FitzGerald launched his constitutional reform campaign, 'Garret's Crusade'. In a television interview he called for 'a republican crusade, to make this a genuine republic on the principles of Tone and Davis' – invoking the venerable United Irish tradition of secular pluralism. A key element in this was the New Ireland Forum, established in 1983 during his second coalition administration. This was the first attempt at systematic public discussion of long-term possibilities, and it gave careful consideration not only to traditional nationalist ideas about reunification but also to possible federal arrangements, and the idea of shared or joint sovereignty between Ireland and Britain in the North. Though all three of these lines of discussion were famously rejected by Margaret Thatcher – 'out! ... out! ... out!' ... – the shape of the discussion marked a real shift away from entrenched positions. Political and moral shibboleths were at least beginning to be interrogated, if often hesitantly and ineffectually. Conor Cruise O'Brien, for instance, launched a sustained campaign to puncture 'nationalist self-delusion, posturing and hypocrisy' over the reunification issue, which required tremendous moral courage out of proportion to its measurable results.[21]

A high-profile example of moral-social agonizing was the series of referenda on reform of the constitutional prohibition on abortion. The first, in September 1983, was on a constitutional amendment framed by Fianna Fáil during the brief 1982 Haughey administration. The precise meaning of the amendment, carried by a two-thirds majority of a low electoral turnout, was disputed: FitzGerald himself argued against it on the grounds that it would open up the possibility of introducing abortion, whereas the Archbishop of Dublin held that it would 'block any attempt to legalise abortion'. The outcome was a fudge. Over the following decade a steady stream of women crossed to Britain for abortions (some 4000 each year, though the figures were speculative). This was a real social problem that neither the government nor, it seemed, the people could bring themselves to confront. When the journalist Mary Holland wrote an article (about homosexuality), in which she mentioned that she herself had had an abortion, she was made to feel – and still felt 10 years afterwards – that she was 'apparently the only woman in Ireland who has had an abortion'.[22]

At last the issue erupted with the particularly grim 'X case' in 1992, when the family of a 14-year-old rape victim were prohibited from taking her to England for an abortion. Under great public pressure (and pressure of time) the Supreme Court ruled that she should be allowed to leave Ireland. In the process it not only overturned the High Court ruling to the contrary, but condemned 'the failure of the legislature to enact appropriate legislation' in the years since the referendum. Another complex referendum was framed, and on 25 November 1992 the right to information about abortion, and to travel to secure one, were publicly endorsed. (The eventual result of this was the 1995 Abortion Information Act.) The amendment permitting termination of pregnancy where there was 'a real and substantial risk' to the mother's life, however, was rejected by a majority of 65.4 per cent.

It was hardly surprising that opinion remained agonizingly undecided on this most intensely sensitive of moral-political issues. Even the issue of divorce hung in the balance for year after year during which it was becoming ever more obvious that modern Irish society was moving away from the old belief in the permanence of marriage. An increasing rate of marital breakdown without the possibility of divorce was a previously unknown social problem, but although public opinion surveys consistently indicated majority support for a constitutional amendment, the first referendum (26 June 1986) produced a negative vote after a rather feeble governmental campaign. Another nine years passed before the issue was finally resolved, and then only by the narrowest possible margin. By the time of the second referendum (24 November 1995), the rate of births outside marriage in Ireland was one of the highest in Europe (20.3 per cent), and high rates of income tax and of unemployment made traditional marriage an economically impossible luxury for many, especially in Dublin. The knife-edge outcome – a majority of 9000 votes for reform on a turnout of 1.5 million voters – surely expressed a profound public ambivalence about the future direction of social evolution. The shift from a powerfully ordered traditional society to the instability of late twentieth-century individualism is not easy. Ireland remained, for instance, the only western country to continue limiting the availability of condoms to licensed clinics and chemists, even in face of the danger of AIDS. In 1990 the Irish Family Planning Association was fined for selling them in the Dublin Virgin Megastore.

What was undoubtedly clear, though, was that Ireland had become a very different society. Secularization (like pluralism) is a somewhat imprecise concept, which has as much to do with atmosphere as with hard power balances, but the referendum campaign reflected an Ireland that was unmistakably more secular than at any time earlier in the century. Episcopal pronouncements no longer carried the awesome weight they once had; indeed the Hierarchy's intervention in the campaign – threatening divorcees with refusal of all sacraments – was condemned even by Catholic conservatives such as the law professor William Binchy, who declared on television that the tone of Bishop Flynn's warning was lacking in 'sympathy, support and solidarity with people living their lives'. Suggestions that the Church was failing the people were made with a frequency hardly imaginable in the past, and a series of sex scandals, including serious cases of child abuse, undermined its moral authority. The subversive irreverence of the TV comedy *Father Ted* (whose Church bears a disturbing resemblance to the mafia) may still have been shocking for many people, but it was one of many signs that the traditional Church might be coming to be seen as something of an oddity at the end of the twentieth century.

Other signals of edging towards the western canon of emancipation were given by the emergence in 1985 of a new party, the Progressive Democrats (founded by Desmond O'Malley and Mary Harney, Fianna Fáil frontbenchers who had fallen foul of Charles Haughey) specifically embracing European-style political rhetoric and repudiating the ossified civil-war division of Irish politics); and the election of

Ireland's first woman President in November 1990. Mary Robinson was a veteran campaigner for contraception and divorce, and former head of the single-parent association, Cherish. Although the fact that as President she became easily the most popular political figure in Ireland did not imply wholesale endorsement of the causes with which she was identified, it clearly reflected a new kind of public self-image. Gender equality was at least a recognizable aspiration, even if the reality still fell lamentably short: even now only some 12 per cent of TDs are women, and in the commercial sphere the proportion in senior management is still less. The situation in the North was not noticeably better in structural terms, although the greater politicization generated by the conflict led to the emergence of more self-conscious women's groups.[23] President Robinson was a distinguished academic (at Trinity College) as was her successor, Mary McAleese (at Queen's University, Belfast). But even Robinson was unable to propel the presidency into a real political role; she went on to take a UN job rather than stand for a second term.

Mary Robinson's presidential candidacy was backed by Labour, and the Labour party itself became a far more secure element in the country's political structure. In the 1992 election campaign, its leader Dick Spring even suggested that he might head a government, and the party secured no less than 33 seats (compared with 45 for Fine Gael). Spring went on to confound traditional assumptions by forming a coalition not with Fine Gael but with Fianna Fáil, which had at last jettisoned Haughey in favour of the more straightforward former dance-hall manager Albert Reynolds. Politics may still have been a narrow, almost closed system, dominated by clientelism and provoking increasing criticism of the 'democratic deficit', but Ireland seemed at last to have made its escape from the lines of political conflict laid down in 1922.

Its greatest escape, however, was economic; the 1990s witnessed growth rates that finally ended the long period of uncertain and often demoralizing transition out of the traditional economy. In the late 1980s, when the Fianna Fáil-led boom had been followed by a crushing slump, the outlook still seemed doubtful. The pattern shifted decisively in the early 1990s, when Ireland began to outperform the EC average: after 1993 an astonishing 7 per cent growth rate was maintained, until in 1997 Ireland topped the European table for per capita gross national product. From a very modest level, standards of living began to rocket; they looked likely to reach the European Union (EU) average between 2005 and 2010. The 'Celtic tiger'

became a world leader in the exploitation of *i*
and – equally important – a skilful exploite*i*
development policy. Though this was a wo*i*
Gaelic vision of simple comfort, and brought*i*
severe postmodern social problems, it was ex*i*
ation, psychological as well as material. Ir*i*
transformed. Above all, perhaps, the sense of*i*
could be expunged, on the back of a dramati*i*
relationship: where before 1973, 61 per cent of Irish exports went to
the UK and only 9 per cent to other EU countries, by 1996 these
figures were 26 and 48 per cent.[24]

The dirty war

For 20 years after the collapse of the Sunningdale settlement the
republican movement pursued its war against Britain and Ulster loyalism. Their rationale for this remained all too straightforward: as
Sinn Féin's publicity director Danny Morrison said in 1985, 'The
Loyalists will only fight in proportion to the amount of hope Britain
can give them', so the question was how to persuade the British to give
up. A very simple cost/benefit analysis was applied, so that, as
Morrison put it (as late as 1989), 'When it is politically costly for the
British to remain in Ireland, they'll go', adding 'it won't be triggered
until a large number of British soldiers are killed'.[25] The statistics of
death and destruction gradually levelled out in the later 1970s after the
bloody peaks of 1972–76. British soldiers, however, were seldom a
majority amongst the casualties. In 1979 (statistically a fairly typical
year), the PIRA carried out a few high-profile operations. Airey
Neave, the Conservative spokesman on Northern Ireland and a close
ally of Mrs Thatcher, was blown up in his car at the House of
Commons. The Queen's cousin Lord Mountbatten was killed on his
boat in western Ireland, and on the same day 18 paratroopers were
killed in an ambush at Warrenpoint in Co. Down. But alongside such
headline-grabbing spectaculars that trumpeted the 'Brits out' campaign, went a more extensive street-level struggle for control of local
communities, and systematic vendettas against the opposing paramilitaries. Most of the victims in this grim struggle were defenceless
people, attacked on simple sectarian grounds. (Nationalist paramilitaries killed about 20 times as many civilians as they did identifiable
loyalist paramilitaries, loyalists 25 times as many.) The shooting up of

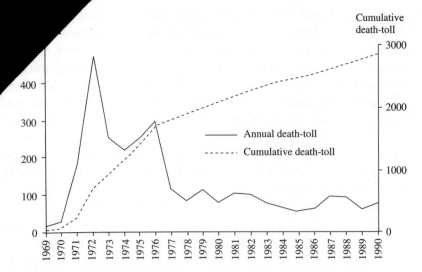

Fig. 11.1 The annual and cumulative death-toll from political violence, 1969–1990
Source: B. O'Leary and J. McGarry *The Politics of Antagonism* (London 1993)

Protestant or Catholic bars became perhaps the most resonant emblem of this hopeless civil war. The PIRA enforced its rules by a fairly capricious system of rough justice – punishment beatings, kneecappings and so on – handed down by kangaroo courts.

'Kangaroo court' is of course an emotive epithet, and the legitimacy of justice systems is a complex issue. The official response to what the government almost inevitably labelled 'terrorism' tended to confirm nationalist distrust of the Stormont/British system. Although the Special Powers Act was repealed, it was replaced by emergency powers that were still obviously unBritish. Under the 1973 Emergency Provisions Act 'Diplock courts' (as recommended by Lord Diplock's inquiry in 1972) superseded jury trial. Such adaptation of British legal culture has hardly caused a ripple of concern in Britain itself, but as an American observer saw in the late 1980s, 'the result of years of life under the Diplock rules is entirely predictable: no one in the Catholic ghettos believes that a fair trial is possible in the special courts'.[26] This has a corrosive effect on public life generally. The 1974 Prevention of Terrorism Act, yet another temporary law that was to be renewed annually from then on, introduced the outlandish idea of 'internal exile', whereby people could be excluded from Great Britain and confined to Northern Ireland. All this time the European Commission on Human Rights was assessing the case brought

by the Irish Republic in 1971, that Briti[...]
torture in the interrogation of terrorist su[...]
niques', which had been imported direct[...]
gency action in Aden, were curtailed [...]
intervention, and ultimately judged by [...]
and degrading treatment' – though no[...]
mittees (Compton and Gardiner) wr[...]
force was appropriate in anti-te[...]
success.[27] Meanwhile the RUC w[...]
International described (in a June 1978 report) a[...]
gation of terrorist suspects.[28]

The ending of internment in 1976 was followed by bitter strugg[...]
republican prisoners against the withdrawal of 'political status', leading
to the so-called 'dirty protest' in Long Kesh internment camp (renamed
Maze Prison) – in which republican prisoners 'went on the blanket',
refusing to wear prison clothes, and smearing the walls of their H-blocks
with their excrement – and culminating in the hunger strikes of 1981.
These were an awesome confrontation between the apparently inde-
structible republican faith in Terence MacSwiney's belief that victory
would rest with 'those who could endure the most', and the deadly
simple refusal of Margaret Thatcher to take any notice of the protest.[29]
Victory in one sense rested with Thatcher's iron determination: after the
death of Bobby Sands and nine others the hunger strike was abandoned
without any direct governmental concessions (though indirect adjustments gradually followed, until by the 1990s the Maze was practically
run by its inmates: even guns were brought in, and in December 1997 a
leading loyalist prisoner, Billy Wright, was shot dead within the prison
by republicans). But the victory was bought at a fearsome price not only
in lives but also in traumatic realignment of the Catholic community, in
whose view there was no question that the strikers had earned the right
to respect. The political results were dramatic: by June 1983 Sinn Féin
was securing over 13 per cent of the vote, within striking distance of the
SDLP's 18 per cent. Though this was mainly due to the electoral mobilization of previously non-voting Catholics, rather than to the transfer of
votes from the SDLP, it was a danger signal that rang alarm bells in
London as well as Dublin, with ultimately momentous consequences.

At the same time British anti-terrorist policy was also evolving in a
potentially dangerous way. After the well-meaning Merlyn Rees was
replaced by the cultivated toughness of Roy Mason in the later 1970s,
the attempt to make Northern Ireland less obviously dependent on the
British army – the policy of 'Ulsterization' – led to the use of smaller,

ven more aggressive security forces. The deployment
Air Service regiment in the mid-1970s was kept secret
but eventually resulted in the publication of many sensa-
unts, and a possibly misconceived glorification of this elite
he new operating methods rested on the use of sophisticated
gence-gathering techniques to forestall IRA operations, but like
older methods these also carried the risk of generating unwelcome
ublicity when they went wrong, as they did in the Gibraltar shootings
of March 1988. Some years earlier the special counter-insurgency unit
developed within the RUC also led to fears of unwarranted (if not
illegal) aggression – labelled the 'shoot to kill policy' by journalists. A
police inquiry into three shooting incidents, in one of which the RUC
had fired no less than 109 bullets into a fleeing car, ran into such resistance within the RUC that its head, John Stalker, resigned.
Altogether, in the early 1980s several aspects of the security system
combined to give an impression that the state was playing fast and
loose with the law, and with the time-honoured idea of 'minimum
force'. The use of 'supergrasses', informers from within terrorist
organizations, as the sole basis for securing convictions, was stoutly
defended by the authorities but to many people looked wrong.

Another story that would not go away easily was the alleged collusion between the security services and loyalist paramilitaries, especially in connection with the 'Force Research Unit' established by the
army in 1986 to 'complement the efforts of' the RUC Special Branch
in the 'exploitation of intelligence'. The problem was once again not
only the inevitable use of dubious methods, but the frustration of the
subsequent inquiry headed by the then Deputy Chief Constable of
Cambridgeshire. Like Stalker before him, John Stevens seems to have
been systematically baulked, even to the extent of the mysterious
destruction of the inquiry team's offices and records by fire on the
night of 10 January 1989. The RUC maintained that this was an
unfortunate accident, after an investigation that Stevens's team
allegedly denounced in private as 'a travesty and a disgrace'.[30]

Peace processes

For 20 years after Sunningdale, as the quasi-war went on, a series of
'political initiatives' were started by successive governments in the
hope of finding a solution. The abandonment of the power-sharing
executive was followed by the first of the attempts to set up all-party

negotiations in Northern Ireland, the Constitutional Convention of 1975–76, based on the belief that (as Merlyn Rees put it) 'the hope of finding a successful solution lies with the Northern Irish people'. Further attempts followed under Humphrey Atkins (the Constitutional Conference, 1980, and the proposed 50-member nominated advisory council of 1981) and James Prior, who brought in 'rolling devolution' in 1982. The October 1982 Assembly was to have its powers gradually increased as it showed more capacity to integrate the communities, but the SDLP boycotted it from the start, and it withered away over the next year. The paralysis of all these initiatives left 'direct rule' as the only viable method of government, virtually turning Northern Ireland into a Crown Colony. The Secretary of State had (and has) immense powers with scant parliamentary accountability.

This power was used to pursue the moderate reformist agenda that Britain had tried to induce Stormont to begin in the 1960s. Housing and community relations were prime candidates for attention, and there was a consistent (but ultimately disappointing) effort to establish 'fair employment', through the Fair Employment (Northern Ireland) Acts of 1976 and 1989. In the civil service, at least, things improved. In 1983 a Fair Employment Agency report showed that there were still only two Catholics among the top 43 officials, and that promotion patterns were still very much like those under Stormont. By 1992, 35 per cent of civil servants at management level, and three out of ten permanent secretaries were Catholics. The Northern Ireland Office announced a goal of 25 per cent Catholic representation in the top 'policy-related posts', to be achieved by the end of 1996. Otherwise the gap within the Catholic community between the conspicuously successful professional elite and the increasingly depressed long-term unemployed was widening, to an extent that might call in question the long-established concept of a single 'community'. Sinn Féin chairman Mitchel McLaughlin and SDLP deputy leader Seamus Mallon, for instance, both denounced the prosperous middle class 'who milked the advances of the civil rights movement dry, and put nothing back into it', as having been enlisted into the British government's project.[31]

The Housing Executive has worked patiently to improve the generally inadequate standard of Northern Irish housing, but without being able to reverse the steady erosion of 'mixed' areas by voluntary or enforced movement, and the consequent entrenchment of segregation. Attempts to revive the Northern economy were also disappointing, or worse, as in the unfortunately unforgettable case of the government grants lavished on the doomed DeLorean sports car enterprise. Northern Ireland conspicuously failed, by contrast with the Republic, to attract outside investment in the growth sectors of manufacturing. After a brief period of expansion, output went into a steady decline. British government industrial subsidies were about twice as high as in other depressed areas; by the mid-1980s Harland and Wolff, for instance, was receiving support equalling its entire wage bill. One economist labelled Northern Ireland a 'workhouse economy'.[32]

The bottom line always seemed, however, to be the paralysis of local political life. Ordinary people, both Unionists and nationalists, were in a real sense disempowered. When Sinn Féin support surged after the 1981 hunger strikes, even Mrs Thatcher was impressed by the need to find new structures – partly to improve security co-operation with the Republic, and partly to bolster the position of the SDLP. In spite of her triple rejection of the New Ireland Forum's ideas, she seems to have made up her mind by 1983 to 'do something about Ireland'. What to do was determined by a group of British ministers and senior civil servants, who persuaded her that tightening the inter-governmental link between London and Dublin would deliver real benefits without the need to tinker with either devolution or power-sharing. (An interesting sign of the drift of establishment thinking about Ireland was provided by the unofficial Kilbrandon Committee Report in November 1984, which favoured a form of joint authority, labelled 'co-operative devolution', in which there would be an executive of five ministers, one British, one Irish, one Northern Ireland nationalist and two Unionists.)

The result was the most substantial and far-reaching political step to be taken since 1921, the Anglo-Irish Agreement signed at Hillsborough Castle (former residence of the Governor-General of Northern Ireland) on 15 November 1985. Its central pillar was the establishment of a 'regular and frequent' intergovernmental conference whose business would 'receive attention at the highest level'. Its key innovation, however, was the creation of a permanent joint governmental secretariat, at Maryfield, Co. Down, in which a number of Irish officials were to represent the interests of the nationalist community. Their role was highly contentious in the loyalist view; while it was not the joint sovereignty envisaged by the Forum report, it looked to be more than merely consultative. The Agreement's formal reiteration of the British view that the status of Northern Ireland as part of the United Kingdom could not be changed without majority consent

– designed to reassure Unionists – in fact reawaken
a sell-out. (The UK government did not make th
obvious about, say, Yorkshire or the Home Coun

The angry Unionist reaction to the Agreem
belief that they had been deliberately kept in
progress of the secret Anglo-Irish negotiations, show
was to achieve compromise in the absence of trust – or, at this
hope. In fact, the Agreement delivered less than most nationalists still
thought essential. Garret FitzGerald, whose acceptance that the Irish
claim to unity had to be shelved was a keystone of the agreement,
thought that he had secured nothing more than responsibility without
power. Technically it was true that, as he said, nothing substantive had
changed, but the Maryfield secretariat was a remarkable adjustment of
British practice (and, to some degree, assumptions). It was a device
that could be used in subtle ways to enhance the aura of co-operation
and, perhaps most importantly, of inevitability. Unionist resistance
never reached the scale hoped for by the organizers of the 'Ulster says
No' campaign; and in the longer run the basis for a major change of
perspective was laid.

When the Agreement was reviewed in May 1989 the balance sheet
for the first few years was reasonably encouraging for the signatories.
The intergovernmental conference had by then met 27 times in
pursuit of its remit, to work 'for the accommodation of the rights and
identities of the two traditions which exist in Northern Ireland', and
'for reconciliation, respect for human rights, co-operation against terrorism and the development of economic, social and cultural co-operation', The Irish government applauded measures like the repeal of
the Flags and Emblems Act, and the 1987 Public Order law giving the
police stronger powers to 'control potentially provocative marches', as
well as the economic development programmes for deprived areas. It
induced the British government to recognize 'the importance of the
Irish language' in the context of 'promoting mutual esteem and understanding between the two traditions', and to 'undertake to support
efforts to enhance awareness and appreciation of this particular strand
of the cultural heritage'. This was a pious and fairly anodyne commitment; on the more concrete – and crucial – point of 'fostering confidence in the system of justice' and 'enhancing respect for the rule of
law', fudging was harder. It is significant that during the summit talks
before the Agreement, FitzGerald had focused on a specific case of a
police officer involved in a machine-gun attack on the Divis Flats, who
had then been promoted to a senior post, to impress on Thatcher how

s the policing issue was.[33] Britain had agreed to more systematic
itoring of the nature and handling of public complaints about the
haviour of the security forces, but the key nationalist demand for
structural reform of the RUC itself was simply not mentioned in the
official review, and there was outright disagreement over the Irish
insistence that the Diplock courts should be abolished.[34]

But the real question was whether the Agreement would achieve
its underlying purposes of strengthening moderate nationalists
against Sinn Féin, and persuading moderate Unionists of the
inevitability of political compromise. The Sinn Féin vote had in fact
already peaked by the time of the Agreement, and stabilized at
around 11 per cent after it. What happened was that instead of being
pushed to the margins, Sinn Féin began a direct dialogue with the
SDLP in the form of the 'Hume–Adams talks'. Hume and the SDLP
had for some time looked to the evolution of European integration
to provide new frameworks for identity and erode the exclusivist
model of national sovereignty. There was no sign that Sinn Féin was
moving in the same direction, and the disagreement over self-determination persisted.[35] But the republican leadership was evidently
ready to experiment with constitutional politics for the first time in
a generation. At the same time, the possibility of a more accommo-
dating Unionist politics was also emerging. The failure of the
original protest against the Agreement to mobilize Unionist opinion
en masse was significant; the most dramatic gesture, the mass resignation of Unionist members from the assembly, only produced a
minor accretion of electoral support. The Agreement was deeply distrusted, but mass militancy was neutralized by a 'debilitating sense of
material dependence on the UK Exchequer', and 'a growing
awareness that the Agreement was a more-or-less permanent
fixture'.[36]

As a result, the renewed effort at negotiations, launched by Peter
Brooke in January 1990, was able to tap into an incipient attitude shift.
Brooke himself entered into the spirit of North–South relations a little
too enthusiastically, ending up politically damaged by an impromptu
sing-song on Irish television. His successor, Sir Patrick Mayhew,
battled gamely against his stage-English patrician mannerisms to carry
the talks further, and was rewarded with a more thoughtful and substantial adjustment of the Unionist position in 1992. This reflected
not simply a Unionist sense of resignation, but a growing confidence
that multi-party talks (involving the SDLP but not Sinn Féin) offered
a real possibility of an acceptable outcome. The broad contours of a

settlement involving a new power-sharing Northern assembly were emerging. Less publicly, a new round of secret negotiations between the British government and the IRA followed from the latter's message, sent via an intermediary, to the effect that 'the war is over; we need your help to end it'.[37] The wording was highly uncharacteristic of the IRA, but the underlying shift of strategy was real. As a result, the Downing Street Declaration, jointly issued in December 1993 by the British and Irish governments, had a surprising effect. In itself the declaration merely reiterated a political truism – that constitutional negotiation was open to those who wanted to use it. It was the IRA's persistent rejection of this option that had been the basis for 20 years of warfare. Now the political path seemed worth following. In 1993 the IRA stepped up the intensity of its campaign, but mainly – it seems – to heighten the impact of the cease-fire it eventually declared in August 1994.

This was, inevitably, a carefully controlled semantic exercise: not the 'unconditional and permanent renunciation of violence' that the British government and the Unionists demanded, but 'a total cessation of operations'. Low-level, internal violence (such as punishment beatings) went on unabated, but the political significance of the suspension of 'military' action was dramatic and unmistakable. It challenged the loyalist paramilitaries to make good their claim that their terrorism was purely reactive, and in August an answering cease-fire was declared by a specially convened 'Combined Loyalist Command'. Suddenly there was 'peace' of a sort: a carnival of normality was unleashed on the streets of Belfast. Just what the IRA thought would follow from this in political terms remained obscure. The basic republican demand for 'self-determination' for the whole island of Ireland was unaltered; but a new belief that all-party roundtable talks could deliver an acceptable version of this had gained ground in the higher echelons of the movement. Republicans expected such talks to begin immediately, but the British government was wary of pushing the Unionists too far too fast. The demand for renunciation of violence, practically demonstrated by 'decommissioning' of IRA weapons, was an essential precondition for any Unionist negotiation with what they insisted on calling 'Sinn Féin–IRA'. In reaction to the cease-fires, the political Unionist movement was less united than ever before, and mainstream Unionism faced a defining moment with the retirement of the long-serving UUP leader James Molyneaux. His replacement by David Trimble seemed to announce a new phase of intransigence. Trimble, though an academic lawyer at Queen's University, Belfast, had been a VUPP activist in the 1970s, and renewed his ultra-Unionist credentials with ostentatious participation in the exceptionally aggressive Orange march in Portadown in 1994. But the sometimes alarming ferocity of Trimble's political style disguised a major adaptation of Unionist thinking. He was perhaps the UUP Unionist leader with the confidence to play the political media game so successfully mastered by John Hume and Gerry Adams, raising his international profile by carefully staged visits to Washington DC, and endorsing the 'Mitchell Principles' set out by the US senator sent to chair the negotiation process after President Clinton's visit to Northern Ireland.

The intervention of Bill Clinton really added a new dimension in the process of peace negotiation. Previous US presidents had maintained a punctilious respect for British sovereignty, enhanced by the myth of the 'special relationship'. The key issue for Clinton, which first arose during his 1992 election campaign, was that of granting a visa to Gerry Adams to visit the USA. In 1993, the President turned Adams down, on the grounds that 'credible evidence exists that Adams remains involved at the highest level in devising IRA strategy'. In 1994, however, Adams was invited along with other Northern leaders (Hume, Molyneaux, Alderdice, Paisley) to a high-profile symposium organized by the unofficial but prestigious National Committee on American Foreign Policy. This time, Clinton issued a 48-hour visa, in the teeth of fierce – and typically misconceived – British hostility. Just as typically, Molyneaux and Paisley immediately withdrew from the symposium. But Adams went.

Clinton's visit to Northern Ireland in November 1995, and the despatch of Senator George Mitchell, exerted a benign external pressure which helped to maintain the public belief that a long-term settlement was now possible. It was this atmosphere of hope (still, perhaps, fragile; and coupled with resignation in the Unionist community) which enabled the momentum of the 'peace process' – a phrase which itself reflected the American dimension – to survive the violent ending of the IRA cease-fire with the Canary Wharf bomb in February 1996. The Mitchell Principles in particular provided an elementary common code that could perform the vital function of disguising fairly substantial differences in assumptions about the preconditions for any formal settlement, the thorniest of which was the issue of 'decommissioning' terrorist weapons. Decommissioning was in fact a rock on which the whole process could have foundered. While Unionists argued that only a substantial step in this direction could show that terrorists were serious about democratic politics, nationalists argued that decommissioning was worthless in itself (since terrorists could re-acquire arms if they chose) – the real need was to remove the causes of violence. Behind this argument was the simple fact that the IRA saw 'decommissioning' as a codeword for 'surrender'.

When all-party talks were finally restarted in 1997, the essential framework of a political structure based on a six-county power-sharing assembly elected by proportional representation, with 'cross-border' institutions with executive powers of some kind, was well established. The structure of the 'Good Friday agreement', when it came, was unsurprising, though the negotiation process was imperilled to the last moment by the threat of paramilitary action, and walk-outs staged by die-hard Unionists. The question was whether republicans would accept the explicit legitimization of partition, which they had abso-lutely rejected in the past, and whether loyalists would see this as a guarantee or a betrayal of the Union. Adams and McGuinness on one side, and Trimble on the other, faced a formidable task in persuading their communities of this, and neither side had complete success. In the early summer of 1998 new republican factions – the Real IRA and the Continuity IRA, linked to the 32-County Sovereignty Committee – emerged, and the official Unionist party splintered. As Trimble put it, with a touch of the old irascibility he was now moderating, 'a number of Unionists are too stupid to realise they have won'. Remarkably, however, the loyalist paramilitary groups provided con-sistent support for the agreement, with their political faces – David Ervine, Billy Hutchinson and Gary MacMichael – often managing to look more statesmanlike than their mainstream counterparts. Trimble himself, who must have been acutely conscious at this stage of Faulkner's fate, came out in the week before the Assembly elections on 26 June with ideas that had not often been heard in the mouths of Unionist leaders: 'We can now get down to the historic and hon-ourable task of this generation: to raise up a new Northern Ireland in which pluralist Unionism and constitutional Nationalism can speak to each other with the civility that is the foundation of freedom'.[38]

Two crucial moments arrived in May and June 1998: the all-Ireland plebiscite on the agreement, and the elections to the new Northern assembly. On both occasions the vital question was not whether there would be a majority for the agreement, but whether the anti-agreement vote would coalesce into a sufficiently powerful grouping to wreck it. The result of the election was certainly not a Trimble landslide, but his party emerged as the largest in the 108-seat assembly

(28 seats, with 21.3 per cent of the vote), and the SDLP won the largest vote share of any party (22.3 per cent, 24 seats); the anti-Agreement DUP achieved roughly the same vote as Sinn Féin (DUP 18.1 per cent, 20 seats; Sinn Féin 17.6 per cent, 18 seats). The process of forming an executive headed by Trimble as first minister, with the SDLP's Seamus Mallon as deputy, could begin, but the question whether a basis for stable administration could be created remained unanswered. The reform of the RUC was an issue that still divided Unionists and nationalists as sharply as decommissioning, and so did the issue of the Irish language. All of these promised serious trouble once the machinery of government began to work. More immediately, the 'marching season' went on, and the first major attempt of the newly established Parades Commission to begin drawing the con-frontational sting from the Portadown Orange Lodge's annual expression of what Orangemen were now calling their (or 'claiming as their') cultural traditions and civil rights led to yet another dramatic confrontation at Drumcree church, between marchers and security forces who entrenched themselves behind massive fortifications to block off the Garvaghy Road. They faced a week-long stand-off with the full repertoire of stone-throwing, petrol bombs, and even gunfire; but unlike the previous year, they held firm. This facing down of the old spectre of a Unionist uprising was an important turning-point. Equally crucial was the reaction to the most destructive explosion of the entire conflict, the Real IRA bomb in Omagh on 11 August. The death toll was 29, but the public reaction isolated the Real IRA, which declared a cease-fire at the end of the month. Only the shadowier Continuity IRA remained at war. Most crucially of all, perhaps, the belief that mainstream Unionists and Nationalists could work together survived. Consensus in Northern Ireland remained a fragile plant, but the number of hands committed to nurturing it seemed to be growing at last.

Notes

Chapter 1 The state of the Union, 1900

1. James Joyce, 'Ireland, Island of Saints and Sages' [1907], in *The Critical Writings of James Joyce*, ed. Ellsworth Mason and Richard Ellmann (London 1959).
2. *The Times*, 5 April 1900.
3. S. A. W. Waters, *Memoirs*, unpublished draft (1924) p. 60 (ed. S. Ball, Cork 1999, forthcoming).
4. R. B. McDowell, *The Irish Administration 1801–1914* (London 1964).
5. F. S. L. Lyons, *Ireland since the Famine* (London 1971), 61.
6. Chief Secretary George Wyndham vehemently denounced it in 1902 as 'an anachronism which serves only to confirm memories of a constitutional division between Britain and Ireland which has long since been abolished and ought never to be revived'. E. O'Halpin, *The Decline of the Union. British Government in Ireland 1892–1920* (Dublin 1987), 6.
7. Charles Townshend, *Political Violence in Ireland* (Oxford 1983), 9.
8. L. Paul-Dubois, *Contemporary Ireland* (originally *L'Irlande contemporaine* (Paris 1907), 199.
9. *Irish Catholic*, 20 January 1906 and 6 November 1909, quoted in Lawrence W. McBride, *The Greening of Dublin Castle* (Washington DC 1991), 36.
10. 'We must fight with all our might until we have laid hands on as much of the power, place and position of this country as our numbers, our ability, and our unabated historical claims entitle us to demand.' *Handbook of the Catholic Association* (Dublin 1902), 42. Senia Paseta, 'The expansion of Catholic Organisation', Irish History Seminar, Oxford 1996. *Before the Revolution* (Cork, forthcoming).
11. R. F. Foster, *Modern Ireland* (London 1988), 291.
12. R. B. MacDowell, 'Administration and the public sevices, 1800–70', in W. E. Vaughan (ed.), *New History of Ireland* vol. V (Oxford 1989), 543.
13. J. J. Lee, *The Modernization of Irish Society 1848–1918* (Dublin 1973), 26. The most persuasive argument for social engineering is Oliver MacDonagh, *Ireland: the Union and its Aftermath* (London 1977), ch. 2 ('The Siamese Twins').

14. D. G. Boyce, *Nineteenth-Century Ireland* (Dublin 1990), 69–71.

15. Daniel Ryan, *The Irish Practical Farmer and Gardener*, quoted in Cormac O'Grada, 'Poverty, population, and agriculture, 1801–45', in Vaughan (ed.), *New History of Ireland* vol. V, 126.

16. Ignatius Murphy, 'Primary education', in P. J. Corish (ed.), *A History of Irish Catholicism* vol. 5 part VI, *Catholic Education* (Dublin 1971), 35.

17. D. H. Akenson, 'Pre-university education, 1782–1870', in Vaughan (ed.), *New History of Ireland* vol. V, 536.

18. Murphy, 'Primary education', 46.

19. Lee, *The Modernization of Irish Society*, 27.

20. Mary Daly, 'The development of the national school system, 1831–40', in A. Cosgrove and D. McCartney (eds), *Studies in Irish History* (Dublin 1979), 159–62.

21. *Dublin Review*, 22 (1874), in A. C. Hepburn (ed.), *The Conflict of Nationality in Modern Ireland* (London 1980), 57.

22. Brian Walker, 'The 1885 and 1886 general elections: a milestone in Irish history', in *Dancing to History's Tune* (Belfast 1996), 15–33.

23. *Daily Express*, 21 August 1895, quoted in Andrew Gailey, *Ireland and the Death of Kindness* (Cork 1987), 20.

24. There is a good contemporary account of the CDB's impact in Stephen Gwynn's essay 'Three Days in the "Granuaile"', in *Today and Tomorrow in Ireland* (Dublin 1903).

25. Its budget originally came not from government but from the interest on part of the Church Temporalities Fund, created after the disestablishment of the Church of Ireland in 1869.

26. O'Halpin, *The Decline of the Union*, 14.

27. Plunkett's diary, 19 June 1895, quoted in Catherine Shannon, *Arthur J. Balfour and Ireland* (Washington DC 1988), 85.

28. Horace Plunkett, *Ireland in the New Century* (London 1904), 81.

Chapter 2 The national question

1. The first and still most thorough evaluation is George Cornewall Lewis, *Local Disturbances in Ireland* (London 1836).

2. R. F. Foster, *Modern Ireland* (London 1988), 292.

3. Nancy Curtin, *The United Irishmen* (Oxford 1994), 13–37.

4. T. W. Moody, 'Thomas Davis and the Irish nation', *Hermathena*, 102 (1966), 16.

5. T. W. Rolleston (ed.), *The Prose Writings of Thomas Davis* (London 1889), 193, 281.

6. Donal A. Kerr, *Peel, Priests and Politics* (Oxford 1982), ch. 7.

7. *The Nation*, 18 November 1843.

8. Croke to Cullen, 25 January 1878, quoted in Mark Tierney, *Croke of Cashel: The Life of Archbishop Thomas William Croke* (Dublin 1976), 91.

9. T. W. Moody, *Davitt and Irish Revolution 1846–82* (Oxford 1981), 292.

10. R. F. Foster, *Charles Stewart Parnell: The Man and his Family* (Hassocks 1979), 260–84. For some other views of the Ladies' League, see Maria Luddy (ed.), *Women in Ireland 1800–1918* (Cork 1995), 260–8.

11. Barbara Solow, *The Land Question and the Irish Economy, 1870–1903* (Cambridge MA 1971); W. E. Vaughan, 'An assessment of the economic performance of Irish

landlords, 1851–81,' in F. S. L. Lyons and R. A. J. Hawkins (eds), *Ireland under the Union* (Oxford 1980), 173–200.

12. Sam Clark, *Social Origins of the Irish Land War* (Princeton 1979); K. T. Hoppen, *Elections, Politics, and Society in Ireland 1832–1885* (Oxford 1984), provides a rich account of local politics.

13. Speech at Liverpool, July 1877, quoted in F. S. L. Lyons, *Charles Stewart Parnell* (London 1977), 63.

14. Paul Bew, *C.S. Parnell* (Dublin 1980), 71.

15. Frank Callanan, *T. M. Healy* (Cork 1996), 378–404.

16. E. Blythe, 'Arthur Griffith', *Administration*, 8 (1960), 37. (Mrs O'Shea was called 'Kitty' only by her enemies.)

17. E. Larkin, 'Church, state and nation in Modern Ireland', *American Historical Review*, 80 (1975), 1244.

18. The term coined by Emmet Larkin, 'The devotional revolution in Ireland, 1850–75', *American Historical Review*, 77 (1972), 625–52.

19. L. Paul-Dubois, *Contemporary Ireland* (London 1908), 492.

20. S. J. Connolly, *Priests and People in Pre-Famine Ireland* (Dublin 1982); D. Keenan, *The Catholic Church in Nineteenth-Century Ireland* (Dublin 1983), ch. 2.

21. Hoppen, *Elections, Politics and Society*, 205–8, is a brilliant survey.

22. Sean Connolly, *Religion and Society in Nineteenth-Century Ireland* (Dublin 1985), 29.

23. K. T. Hoppen, *Ireland since 1800* (London 1989), 147.

24. P. Finlay, 'Religion and civil life', *New Ireland Review*, 14 (1901), 323, quoted in Senia Paseta, 'The expansion of Catholic organisation', Irish History Seminar, Oxford 1996.

25. J. O'Shea, *Priests, Politics and Society in Post-Famine Ireland* (Dublin 1983), provides an acute study of Co. Tipperary.

26. C. J. Woods, 'The general election of 1892: the Catholic clergy and the defeat of the Parnellites', in Lyons and Hawkins (eds), *Ireland under the Union*, 289–319.

27. Oliver MacDonagh, *States of Mind. A Study of Anglo-Irish Conflict 1780–1980* (London 1983), 102.

28. Inspector-General's monthly report, March 1902, Public Record Office (PRO) CO 904 702, quoted in Charles Townshend, *Political Violence in Ireland* (Oxford 1983), 232.

Chapter 3 Cultures and civilizations: the struggle for Ireland's soul

1. R. V. Comerford, 'Nation, nationalism, and the Irish language', in T. E. Hachey and L. McCaffrey (eds), *Perspectives on Irish Nationalism* (Lexington KY 1989), 24.

2. Mark Tierney, *Croke of Cashel: The Life of Archbishop Thomas William Croke* (Dublin 1976), 195.

3. Tom Garvin, *Nationalist Revolutionaries in Ireland 1858–1928* (Oxford 1987), 81.

4. C. C. O'Brien, 'Passion and cunning: an essay on the politics of W.B. Yeats', in A. N. Jeffares and K. Cross (eds), *In Excited Reverie* (London 1965), 217.

5. Roy Foster, 'Anglo-Irish literature, Gaelic nationalism and Irish politics in the 1890s' in Lord Blake (intro.), *Ireland after the Union* (Oxford 1989), 61–82.

6. R. F. Foster, *W.B. Yeats. A Life*, vol. 1 (Oxford 1997), 501.

7. Martin J. Waters, 'Peasants and emigrants: considerations of the Gaelic League as a social movement', in D. J. Casey and R. E. Rhodes (eds), *Views of the Irish Peasantry 1800–1916* (Hamden CT 1977), 160–77.

8. Tom Garvin, 'Priests and patriots: Irish separatism and fear of the modern, 1890–1914', *Irish Historical Studies*, 25 (1986), 72.

9. Eoin MacNeill, *Celtic Ireland* (Dublin 1921), ch. 7.

10. *An Claidheamh Soluis*, 19 November 1904, quoted in Ruth Dudley Edwards, *Patrick Pearse. The Triumph of Failure* (London 1977), 72.

11. Liam O'Flaherty, *Skerrett* (London 1932), ch. 19.

12. Dr Windle to Archbishop Walsh, 14 June 1909.

13. Patrick Maume, *D.P. Moran* (Dublin 1996), 8.

14. *The Leader*, 13 September 1900.

15. *The Leader*, 6 February 1904, quoted in Roy Foster, 'Varieties of Irishness: Culture and Anarchy in Ireland', in *Paddy and Mr Punch* (London 1993), 24.

16. David W. Miller, *Church, State and Nation in Ireland 1898–1921* (Dublin 1973), 111.

17. Alf MacLochlainn, 'Gael and peasant – a case of mistaken identity', in Casey and Rhodes (eds), *Views of the Irish Peasantry*, 17–37.

18. D. G. Boyce, *Nationalism in Ireland* (London 1982), 243.

19. Maume, *Moran*, 23.

20. J. Healy, 'University education in Ireland', *Dublin Review*, 23, (1890), 26.

21. *The Leader*, 24 November 1900.

22. Maurice Goldring, *Pleasant the Scholar's Life. Irish Intellectuals and the Construction of the Nation State* (London 1993), 18–19.

23. Seán O'Faoláin, *The Irish* (London 1947), 129.

24. R. F. Foster, 'Good behaviour: Yeats, Synge, and Anglo-Irish etiquette', in *Paddy and Mr Punch*, 204.

25. Foster, *W. B. Yeats. A Life*, vol. 1, 288.

26. D. G. Boyce, ''One last burial' – culture, counter-revolution, and revolution in Ireland, 1886–1916', in D. G. Boyce (ed.), *The Revolution in Ireland 1879–1923* (London 1988), 125–8.

27. Seán Ó Luing, 'Arthur Griffith and Sinn Féin', in F. X. Martin (ed.), *Leaders and Men of the Easter Rising* (London 1967), 62.

28. Griffith's address to Sinn Féin *árd fheis*, 1905, reported in the *United Irishman*, 9 December 1905.

29. Horace Plunkett, *Ireland in the New Century* (London 1904), 191.

30. Donal McCartney, 'The political use of history in the work of Arthur Griffith', *Journal of Contemporary History*, 8 (1973), 9–12.

31. *An Claidheamh Soluis*, 26 November 1904.

32. *United Irishman*, 2 January 1904, in A. Mitchell and P. Ó Snodaigh (eds), *Irish Political Documents* vol. I (Blackrock 1989), 117.

Chapter 4   Home Rule and the British crisis, 1905–1914

1. Paul Bew, *Conflict and Conciliation in Ireland 1890–1910. Parnellites and Radical Agrarians* (Oxford 1987), 133–43.

2. A. C. Hepburn, 'The Ancient Order of Hibernians in Irish politics, 1905–14,' *Cithora* X (1971), 9.

3. Eamonn Phoenix, 'Northern Nationalists, Ulster Unionists and the Development of Partition', in P. Collins (ed), *Nationalism and Unionism* (Belfast 1994), 109–12.

4. Bulmer Hobson, *Defensive Warfare. A Handbook for Irish Nationalists* (Belfast 1909), 48–9.

5. Patricia Jalland, *The Liberals and Ireland* (London 1980), 46.

6. Alvin Jackson, *The Ulster Party* (Oxford 1989), 284–5.

7. A. T. Q. Stewart, *Edward Carson* (Dublin 1981), 80.

8. Patrick Buckland (ed.), *Irish Unionism 1885–1923. A Documentary History* (Belfast 1973), 224. (Text from the Public Record Office, Northern Ireland, D1496/3.)

9. A. T. Q. Stewart, *The Ulster Crisis* (London 1977), 62–3.

10. *The Times*, 29 July 1912, quoted in Michael Laffan, *The Partition of Ireland 1911–1925* (Dublin 1983), 27.

11. Paul Bew, *John Redmond* (Dundalk 1996), 34.

12. Drilling certificate issued to 2nd Battalion South Down Regiment, UVF, 16 December 1913, in Buckland (ed.), *Irish Unionism*, 237.

13. J. J. Lee, *Ireland 1912–1985* (Cambridge 1989), 18–19.

14. *Éire*, 16 June 1924, quoted in Emmet Larkin, *James Larkin, Irish Labour Leader 1876–1947* (London 1965), 161.

15. Emmet O'Connor, *Syndicalism in Ireland 1917–1923* (Cork 1988), 13.

16. For a sharp analysis see Ruth Dudley Edwards, *James Connolly* (Dublin 1981), 74ff.

17. *Sinn Féin*, 28 November 1908, quoted in Dermot Keogh, *The Rise of the Irish Working Class* (Belfast 1982), 129.

18. Thomas Morrissey, SJ, *William Martin Murphy* (Dublin 1997).

19. C. Desmond Greaves, *The Life and Times of James Connolly* (London 1972), 326–7.

20. Jalland, *The Liberals and Ireland*, 59.

21. UVF Confidential Circular, Public Record Office of Northern Ireland D.1327/4/21, quoted in Charles Townshend, *Political Violence in Ireland* (Oxford 1983), 252.

22. They were not, as some historians have suggested, given the option of resigning their commissions. In fact French made it clear that any officer who tried to resign on this issue would be instantly cashiered. Townshend, *Political Violence*, 271.

23. Memo given to Brig. H. P. Gough, 23 March 1914, in I. F. W. Beckett (ed.), *The Army and the Curragh Incident, 1914* (London 1986), 218.

24. No. 103 in M. and E. Brock (eds), *H. H. Asquith. Letters to Venetia Stanley* (Oxford 1982), 123.

25. Waters, *Memoirs* p. 85.

Chapter 5   *World war and rebellion, 1914–1919*

1. R. F. Foster, *Modern Ireland* (London 1988), 471.

2. David Fitzpatrick, 'The logic of collective sacrifice: Ireland and the British Army 1914–1918', *Historical Journal*, 38, 4 (1995), 1017–30.

3. Paul Bew, *John Redmond* (Dublin 1996), 37.

4. I.V. Provisional Committee announcement, 24 September 1914, quoted in M. Tierney, *Eoin MacNeill* (Oxford 1980), 153–4.

5. George Boyce, *The Sure Confusing Drum: Ireland and the First World War* (Swansea 1993), 7.

6. Paul Bew, *Ideology and the Irish Question* (Oxford 1994), 118–60.

7. United Irish League Standing Committee, *The Irish Party: What it has done for Ireland* (1915), quoted in D. Fitzpatrick, *Politics and Irish Life* (Dublin 1977), 114.

8. Fitzpatrick, *Politics and Irish Life*, 109.

9. Published in Pearse's journal *An Barr Buadh* (The Trumpet of Victory), 16 March 1912. Quoted in Ruth Dudley Edwards, *Patrick Pearse*. (London 1977), 161–2.

10. Edwards, *Patrick Pearse*, 237.

11. MacNeill, Memorandum No. 2, in F. X. Martin, 'Eoin MacNeill on the 1916 Rising', *Irish Historical Studies*, 12 (1961), 247.

12. *Workers' Republic*, 25 December 1915.

13. *Workers' Republic*, 20 November 1915.

14. *Workers' Republic*, 5 February 1916.

15. See Paul Bew, 'James Connolly and Irish Socialism', in Ciaran Brady (ed), *Losers in Irish History* (Dublin 1989), 159–68.

16. HQ General Order, IV and ICA, 28 April 1916, quoted in Edwards, *Patrick Pearse*.

17. Published in the Dublin *Sunday Independent*, 23 April 1916.

18. Though the memoir of Frank Robbins, *Under the Starry Plough. Recollections of the Irish Citizen Army* (Dublin 1977), holds that capture was never intended.

19. Commander-in-Chief's Orders, 3 May 1916, Public Record Office (PRO) WO 35 69/1.

20. Maureen Wall, 'Partition: the Ulster question 1916–1926', in Desmond Williams (ed.), *The Irish Struggle* (London 1966), 80–1.

21. War Cabinet Minutes, 29 July 1918, quoted in D. G. Boyce, *The Irish Question and British Politics* (London 1988), 57.

22. RIC Monthly Confidential Reports, PRO CO 904 102.

23. T. P. Coogan, *Michael Collins* (London 1990), 66–7.

24. *Round Table*, March 1917, 374, quoted in Michael Laffan, 'The unification of Sinn Féin in 1917', *Irish Historical Studies* (1972), 379.

25. *Freeman's Journal*, 19 June 1917; RIC Reports July 1917, PRO CO 904 103.

26. Inspector-General RIC to Under-Secretary, Dublin Castle, 15 June 1918, PRO CO 904 169/2.

27. John Coakley, 'The election that made the first Dáil', in Brian Farrell (ed.), *The Creation of the Dáil* (Tallaght 1994), 31.

28. Memorandum by Colonial Secretary, 31 December 1918, G.T.6574, PRO CAB 24 72/1.

Chapter 6 The first republic and the Anglo-Irish war, 1919–1922

1. Dorothy Macardle, *The Irish Republic* (London 1937, 1968), 253.

2. Michael Laffan, '"Labour must wait": Ireland's Conservative revolution', in P. J. Corish (ed.), *Radicals, Rebels and Establishments* (Belfast 1985), 203–22.

3. T. M. Healy to William O'Brien, 4 November 1918, National Library of Ireland MS 8556, quoted in Frank Callanan, *T.M. Healy* (Cork 1996), 546.

4. Arthur Mitchell, *Revolutionary Government in Ireland. Dáil Éireann 1919–22* (Dublin 1995), Appendix 1, 342.

5. J. Lee, 'The significance of the first Dáil', in Brian Farrell (ed.), *The Creation of the Dáil* (Tallaght 1994), 104.

6. There is a thoughtful assessment in Mitchell, *Revolutionary Government*, 50–2.

7. Collins to Boland, 19 April 1920, quoted in T. P. Coogan, *Michael Collins* (London 1990), 107.

8. Mary Kotsonouris, *Retreat from Revolution: The Dáil Courts 1920–24* (Dublin 1994), ch. 3, 36–50.

9. General Order No. 4, 26 May 1920, University College Dublin Archives (UCDA) P7/A/45 quoted in Maryann Valiulis, *Portrait of a Revolutionary. General Richard Mulcahy and the Founding of the Irish Free State* (Dublin 1992), 53.

10. Peter Hart, *The IRA and its Enemies: Violence and Community in Cork 1916–23* (Oxford 1998), 21–38.

11. Diary of Terence MacSwiney, (UCDA) P48/a, quoted in Francis J. Costello, *Enduring the Most. The Life and Death of Terence MacSwiney* (Dingle 1995), 76.

12. Terence MacSwiney, *Principles of Freedom* (Dublin 1921), 32.

13. On the cult of martyrdom, Richard Kearney, *Myth and Motherland* (Field Day Pamphlet no. 5, Derry 1984), 9–13.

14. Kathleen McKenna, 'The Irish Bulletin', *Capuchin Annual* (1970), 503–27.

15. Memorandum by Officer Commanding Ist Southern Division IRA, 24 November 1921, quoted in Hart, *The IRA*, 229.

16. On Arthur Mitchell's computation of the 'leadership', only 9 per cent were drawn from this category. *Revolutionary Government*, 34.

17. Mitchell, *Revolutionary Government*, 133.

18. D. S. Johnson, 'The Belfast Boycott', in J. M. Goldstrom and L. Clarkson (eds), *Irish Population, Economy and Society* (Oxford 1982).

19. Memo 31 December 1918, GT 6574, Public Record Office (PRO) CAB 24 71/1.

20. Diary of Sir Mark Sturgis, 24 August 1920, PRO 30 59/1.

21. Quoted in Seán O'Faoláin, *De Valera* (Harmondsworth 1939), 78.

22. Tom Barry, *Guerrilla Days in Ireland* (Tralee 1949, 1962), 175.

23. Joost Augustejn, *From Public Defiance to Guerrilla Warfare* (Dublin 1996), 138–9.

24. *House of Lords Debates*, 21 June 1921, 5th series, vol. 45, col. 690.

25. John McColgan, *British Policy and the Irish Administration 1920–22* (London 1983), ch. 4.

26. To Sir Warren Fisher, 9 June 1921, quoted in McColgan, *British Policy*, 58.

27. Dáil Éireann, *Official Correspondence*, 29 September 1921, quoted in J. M. Curran, *The Birth of the Irish Free State* (Alabama 1980), 73.

28. See T. P. Coogan's bitterly critical asssessment in *Michael Collins*, 227–9, and *Eamon de Valera* (London 1993), 255–6. Frank Pakenham's classic account *Peace by Ordeal* (London 1935), and his official biography of de Valera (London 1970), are more forgiving.

29. Curran, *The Birth of the Irish Free State*, 106.

Chapter 7 Civil war and nation-building, 1922–1932

1. Reports of Frank Cremins, Mulcahy papers, University College Dublin Archives (UCDA) P7/A/II 76.
2. Tom Garvin, *1922. The Birth of Irish Democracy* (Dublin 1996), 94.
3. C. S. Andrews, *Dublin Made Me* (Dublin 1979), 208.
4. Boland to McGarrity, 13 July 1922, in S. Cronin (ed.), *The McGarrity Papers* (Tralee 1972), 120.
5. Florence O'Donoghue, *No Other Law* (Dublin 1954), a biography of Liam Lynch, remains an outstanding source on anti-Treaty ideas.
6. De Valera to McGarrity, 10 September 1922, in Cronin (ed.), *The McGarrity Papers*, 124.
7. Michael Hopkinson, *Green Against Green. The Irish Civil War* (Dublin 1988), 128–9.
8. *Irish Catholic Directory* 1923, quoted in Ronan Fanning, *Independent Ireland* (Dublin 1983), 19.
9. T. de Vere White, *Kevin O'Higgins* (London 1948), 125.
10. Garvin, *1922*, ch. 4, suggests that the IRA's militarism blinded it to the significance of the civil police.
11. Leo Kohn, *The Constitution of the Irish Free State* (London 1932), 80.
12. Note by Collins, March 1922, Irish National Archives (INA), Department of the Taoiseach, S.6541.
13. J. Prager, *Building Democracy in Ireland* (Cambridge 1986); cf. Alan J. Ward, *The Irish Constitutional Tradition* (Dublin 1994); David E. Schmitt, *The Irony of Irish Democracy* (Lexington MA 1973).
14. Michael Gallagher, 'The constitution', in J. Coakley and M. Gallagher (eds), *Politics in the Republic of Ireland* (Dublin 1993), 50.
15. Mary Kotsonouris, 'The Courts of Dáil Éireann', in Brian Farrell (ed.), *The Creation of the Dáil* (Tallaght 1994), 96–102.
16. Irish Labour Party *Annual Report* 1925, quoted in E. Rumpf and A. C. Hepburn, *Nationalism and Socialism in Twentieth Century Ireland* (Liverpool 1977), 83.
17. Michael Gallagher, *Political Parties in the Republic of Ireland* (Manchester 1985), 44.
18. Denis Gwynn, *The Irish Free State 1922–7* (London 1928), ch. 16.
19. Mary E. Daly, *Industrial Development and Irish National Identity 1922–1939*, (Dublin 1992), 41–2.
20. George O'Brien, 'Patrick Hogan, Minister for Agriculture 1922–32', *Studies* (1936), 355.
21. Kieran Kennedy, Thomas Giblin and Deirdre McHugh, *The Economic Development of Ireland in the Twentieth Century* (London 1988), 37.
22. Notes by General Michael Collins, August 1922, in *The Path to Freedom* (Cork 1968), 25.
23. Fanning, *Independent Ireland*, 65.
24. Dermot Keogh, 'Ireland and "Emergency" culture: between civil war and normalcy, 1922–1961', *Ireland. A Journal of History and Society*, 1 (1995), 9.
25. Brian Farrell, '"Cagey and secretive": collective responsibility, executive confidentiality and the public interest', in R. J. Hill and M. Marsh (eds), *Modern Irish Democracy* (Dublin 1993), 82–103.
26. The only exception seems to have been St Loe Strachey, editor of the *Spectator*,

writing to Carson in February 1920, quoted in N. Mansergh, *The Unresolved Question: The Anglo-Irish Settlement and its Undoing 1912–72*, 252.

27. G. J. Hand, 'MacNeill and the Boundary Commission', in F. X. Martin and G. J. Byrne (eds), *The Scholar Revolutionary. Eoin MacNeill 1867–1945* (London 1973), 199–276.

28. Clare O'Halloran, *Partition and the Limits of Irish Nationalism* (Dublin 1987), 97–130.

29. Eoin MacNeill, 'Irish education policy', *Irish Statesman* 17 October 1925, quoted in Terence Brown, *Ireland. A Social and Cultural History 1922–79* (London 1981), 58.

30. Seamas Ó Buachalla, *Education Policy in Twentieth Century Ireland* (Dublin 1988), ch. 3; Donald H. Akenson, *A Mirror for Kathleen's Face: Education in Independent Ireland, 1922–1960* (Montreal 1975), ch. 3.

31. Fanning, *Independent Ireland*, 82.

32. G. Ó Tuathaigh, 'The Irish-Ireland idea: rationale and relevance', in Edna Longley (ed.), *Culture in Ireland. Division or Diversity?* (Belfast 1991), 63.

33. National Council, 18 June 1920, Friends of Irish Freedom papers, Irish American Historical Society, New York.

34. *Irish Ecclesiastical Record*, September 1938, quoted in Michael Nolan, 'The Influence of Catholic Nationalism on the Legislature of the Irish Free State', *Irish Jurist*, 10 (1975), 130.

35. D. R. Pearce (ed.), *The Senate Speeches of W.B. Yeats* (London 1960), 92, 99.

36. *Connaught Telegraph*, 3 January 1931, quoted in Lee, *Ireland 1912–1985*, 163.

37. Executive Council 11 April 1924, INA, Department of the Taoiseach, S.3435.

38. Maryann G. Valiulis, *Almost a Rebellion. The Irish Army Mutiny of 1924* (Cork 1985).

39. Tobin Mutiny File, Mulcahy papers P7/B/195, quoted in Maryann Valiulis, *Portrait of a Revolutionary. General Richard Mulcahy and the Founding of the Irish Free State* (Dublin 1992), 204.

40. J. J. Lee, *Ireland 1912–1985* (Cambridge 1989), 171.

41. For a wonderfully deft account of this, see Seán O'Faolain, *De Valera* (Harmondsworth 1939), 111–19.

42. Richard Dunphy, *The Making of Fianna Fáil Power in Ireland 1923–1948* (Oxford 1995), 83.

Chapter 8 The dominion of Eamon de Valera, 1932–1948

1. Richard Sinnott, *Irish Voters Decide* (Manchester 1995), 101.

2. Owen Dudley Edwards, *Eamon de Valera* (Cardiff 1987), ch. 1.

3. Kevin B. Nowlan, 'President Cosgrave's last government', in F. MacManus (ed.), *The Years of the Great Test 1926–39* (Cork 1967), 15–16.

4. Ronan Fanning, *Independent Ireland* (Dublin 1983), 102.

5. Seán O'Faolain, *De Valera* (Harmondsworth 1939), 125.

6. For opposed views, see Frank Munger, *The Legitimacy of Opposition: The Change of Government in Ireland in 1932* (Sage Professional Papers in Contemporary Political Sociology, 1975), and Bill Kissane, 'The not-so-amazing case of Irish democracy', *Irish Political Studies*, 10 (1995).

7. Hugh Kennedy (Chief Justice) to de Valera, 6 October 1932, INA, Department of the Taoiseach S.10550. T. P. Coogan, *Eamon de Valera* (London 1993), 458–9, plausibly suggests that the minister may have been Lord Birkenhead.

8. Dáil Éireann Debates, 14 July 1933, quoted in Brendan Sexton, *Ireland and the Crown 1922-1936. The Governor-Generalship of the Irish Free State* (Dublin 1989), 154.

9. Cabinet Memorandum by Secretaries of State for War and the Dominions, 8 March 1932, Public Record Office CAB 27 525, quoted in Coogan, *Eamon de Valera*, 450.

10. MacDonald to Sir Abe Bailey, 22 July 1932, quoted in Deirdre MacMahon, *Republicans and Imperialists. Anglo-Irish Relations in the 1930s* (London 1984), 68.

11. Mary E. Daly, *Industrial Development and Irish National Identity 1922–1939* (Dublin 1992), 67.

12. David S. Johnson, 'The economic History of Ireland between the Wars', *Irish Economic and Social History*, 1 (1974), 57.

13. Cormac Ó Gráda, *Ireland. A New Economic History 1780–1939* (Oxford 1994), 388.

14. J. F. Meenan, *The Irish Economy since 1922* (Liverpool 1970), 117; Lee gives the original figure as 24,000 acres in *Ireland 1912–1985* (Cambridge 1989), 185.

15. See, for instance, Mary Daly, 'The economic ideals of Irish nationalism: frugal comfort or lavish austerity?', *Eire-Ireland* (1994), 77–100.

16. Lee, *Ireland 1912–1985*, 195.

17. T. P. Coogan, *The I.R.A.* (London 1971), 91.

18. David Thornley, 'The Blueshirts', in MacManus (ed.), *Years of the Great Test*, 45, 49.

19. *United Ireland*, 21 October 1933.

20. Mike Cronin, 'The Blueshirt Movement 1932–5: Ireland's Fascists?', *Journal of Contemporary History*, 30 (1995), 314.

21. Paul Bew, Ellen Hazelkorn and Henry Patterson, *The Dynamics of Irish Politics* (London 1989), 48–67.

22. *An Phoblacht*, 27 June 1931, quoted in Richard English, *Radicals and the Republic. Socialist Republicanism in the Irish Free State 1925–1937* (Oxford 1994), 126.

23. Uinseann MacEoin (ed.), *Survivors* (Dublin 1980), 349.

24. Ronan Fanning, '"The Rule of Order": Eamon de Valera and the I.R.A. 1923–1940', in J. P. O'Carroll and J. A. Murphy (eds), *De Valera and His Times* (Cork 1983), 163.

25. The drafting process is carefully unpicked in Dermot Keogh, 'The constitutional revolution: an analysis of the making of the constitution', *Administration*, 35, 4 (1987), 4–84.

26. F. S. L. Lyons, *Ireland since the Famine* (London 1971), 540, 543.

27. Edwards, *Eamon de Valera*, 121; John Cooney, *The Crozier and the Dáil. Church and State 1922–1986* (Cork and Dublin 1986), ch. 1.

28. Dermot Keogh, *The Vatican, the Bishops and Irish Politics 1919–39* (Cambridge 1986), 227.

29. Dublin *Evening Echo*, 22 June 1932.

30. 'The Values of the Spirit', 6 February 1933, quoted in M. Moynihan (ed.), *Speeches and Statements of Eamon de Valera*, 231.

31. J. Whyte, *Church and State in Modern Ireland* (Dublin 1984), 89.

32. INA, Department of the Taoiseach S.5998, quoted in Dermot Keogh, *Twentieth Century Ireland*, 71.

33. Dáil Éireann Debates, 16 August 1931, quoted in D. Harkness, *The Restless Dominion. The Irish Free State and the British Commonwealth of Nations 1921–31* (London 1969), 245.

34. Dermot Keogh, *Ireland and Europe 1919–1948* (Dublin 1988), 41.

35. Paul Canning, *British Policy Towards Ireland 1921–1941* (Oxford 1985), ch. 9.

36. John Bowman, *De Valera and the Ulster Question 1917–1973* (Oxford 1982), 130.

37. Terence MacSwiney, 'Separation', in *Principles of Freedom* (Dublin 1921), 25.

38. Trevor Salmon, *Unneutral Ireland* (Oxford 1989), ch. 5.

39. Memorandum by Secretary Dept of Justice Jan. 1939, Irish National Archives S10454B, quoted in Lee, *Ireland 1912–1985*, 220.

40. Robert Fisk, *In Time of War* (London 1983), 484–5.

41. Whyte, *Church and State*, 94.

42. Donal Ó Drisceoil, 'Censorship in Ireland during the Second World War', Ph.D. thesis University College, Cork, 1994, 440.

43. Cordell Hull, *Memoirs* (London 1948), 1365.

44. Lee, *Ireland 1912–1985*, 269.

45. M. A. G. Ó Tuathaigh, 'De Valera and Sovereignty: a note on the pedigree of a political idea', in O'Carroll and Murphy (eds), *De Valera and his Times*, 67.

46. Moynihan, *Speeches and Statements of Eamon de Valera*, 466–9.

47. Donald Akenson, *A Mirror to Kathleen's Face: Education in Independent Ireland, 1922–1960* (Montreal 1975), 41.

48. INTO, *Report of Committee of Inquiry into the Use of Irish as a Teaching Medium to Children whose Home Language is English* (Dublin 1941), 28, 42, quoted in Akenson, *A Mirror to Kathleen's Face*, 56–7.

Chapter 9 The second republic and modernization, 1948–1968

1. J. Whyte, *Church and State in Modern Ireland* (Dublin 1984), 106–8.

2. J. J. Lee, 'Aspects of corporatist thought in Ireland: the Commission on Vocational Organisation, 1939–43', in A. Cosgrove and D. McCartney (eds), *Studies in Irish History* (Dublin 1979), 329.

3. J. J. Lee, 'Centralisation and community', in *Ireland: Towards a Sense of Place* (Cork 1985), 84.

4. Dáil Éireann Debates, 3 April 1946, quoted in Whyte, *Church and State*, 136.

5. Ronan Fanning, *Independent Ireland* (Dublin 1983), 163.

6. Whyte, *Church and State*, 158.

7. *Annie Cook v. Thomas Carroll*, 31 July 1945, in *Irish Law Times Reports*, 79, 117.

8. Bishop of Ferns (Secretary to the Hierarchy) to Taoiseach, 10 October 1950, printed in full in Whyte, *Church and State*, Appendix B, 424–5.

9. J. J. Lee, *Ireland 1912–1985* (Cambridge 1989), 384.

10. Brian Girvin, *Between Two Worlds. Politics and Economy in Independent Ireland* (Dublin 1989), 170–1.

11. Hugh Brody, *Inishkillane. Change and Decline in the West of Ireland* (London 1973), 71.

12. Nancy Scheper-Hughes, *Saints, Scholars and Schizophrenics. Mental Illness in Rural Ireland* (Berkeley 1979), 4–5, 35.

13. Peadar O'Donnell, *The Role of the Industrial Workers in the Problems of the West* (Dublin 1965).

14. Donald S. Connery, *The Irish* (London 1968), 67.

15. Brian Farrell, *Seán Lemass* (Dublin 1983), 109.

16. M. Mills, 'Seán Lemass looks back', *Irish Press*, 3 February 1969.

17. Basil Peterson, 'Tourism', in Owen Dudley Edwards (ed.), *Conor Cruise O'Brien Introduces Ireland* (London 1969), 206.

18. Gearóid Ó Tuathaigh, 'The media and Irish culture', in Brian Farrell (ed.), *Communications and Community in Ireland* (Cork 1984), 98.

19. John Banville, 'The Ireland of de Valera and O'Faoláin', *Irish Review* 17/18 (1995), 151.

20. Joseph Lee, 'Dynamics of social and political change in the Irish Republic', in D. Keogh and M. Haltzel (eds), *Northern Ireland and the Politics of Reconciliation* (Cambridge 1993), 121.

21. Mary Kenny, *Goodbye to Catholic Ireland* (London 1997), 267.

22. B. J. O'Connor, *Ireland and the United Nations* (Dublin 1961), 3.

23. Conor Cruise O'Brien, *To Katanga and Back: a U.N. Case History* (London 1962), 14.

24. *United Irishman*, March 1962, quoted in Seán Cronin, *Irish Nationalism* (Dublin 1980), 172.

25. Paul Bew and Henry Patterson, *Seán Lemass and the Making of Modern Ireland* (Dublin 1982), 11.

26. R. F. Foster, *Modern Ireland* (London 1988), 585.

27. Fintan O'Toole, 'The southern question', in Dermot Bolger (ed.), *Letters from the New Island* (Finglas 1991), 17.

Chapter 10 The Stormont regime: Northern Ireland, 1920–1969

1. Hugh de Fellenberg Montgomery to C. H. Montgomery, 22 June 1916, Public Record Office of Northern Ireland (PRONI) D 627/429.

2. Strachey to Carson, 12 February 1920, and reply. PRONI D 1507/1/1920/6, quoted in N. Mansergh, *Unresolved Question: The Anglo-Irish Settlement and Its Undoing 1912–72*, 252–3.

3. David Fitzpatrick, *The Two Irelands* (1998), 97.

4. Diary of Mark Sturgis, 19 August 1920, PRO 30/59/1.

5. See his vividly detailed analysis *The IRA and Its Enemies* (1998), especially chapters 12 and 13.

6. Michael Farrell, *Arming the Protestants. The Formation of the Ulster Special Constabulary and Royal Ulster Constabulary, 1920–27* (1983), 95.

7. Brian Barton, *Brookeborough. The Making of a Prime Minister* (Belfast 1988), 50.

8. Brian Follis, *A State Under Siege*, 101.

9. Memo. to Executive Council, 7 Feb. 1923, UCDA, Mulcahy papers P7/B/101.

10. There is a terse assessment of the repartition option in K. Boyle and T. Hadden, *Northern Ireland* (1985), 34–7.
11. The ramifications of this were thoughtfully explored by Mary McAleese in a series of BBC radio discussions. Radio 4, broadcast in January–February 1995.
12. See Ian McBride, *The Siege of Derry in Ulster Protestant Mythology* (1997).
13. Mary Harris, *The Catholic Church and the Northern Irish State*, 154.
14. Ian McAllister, 'Territorial differentiation in Northern Ireland', in T. Gallagher and J. O'Connell (eds) *Contemporary Irish Studies* (Manchester 1983), 59.
15. Harkness, *Northern Ireland since 1920*, 11.
16. Fitzpatrick, *The Two Irelands*, 145.
17. Sir R. Hopkins to Sir F. Phillips, 8 February 1939, quoted in P. Bew, P. Gibbon and H. Patterson, *Northern Ireland 1921–1994* (London 1995), 62.
18. Northern Ireland House of Commons debates, 23 May 1922, quoted in T. Hennessey, *A History of Northern Ireland* (1997), 31.
19. Northern Ireland House of Commons, 24 April 1934.
20. D. P. Barritt and C. F. Carter, *The Northern Ireland Problem: A Study in Group Relations* (1962), 108.
21. D. S. Johnson, 'The Northern Ireland Economy 1914–39', in Kennedy and Ollerenshaw (eds), *An Economic History of Ulster*, 196.
22. Lawrence, *The Government of Northern Ireland*, 152.
23. Ruth Harris, *Prejudice and Tolerance in Ulster. A Study of Neighbours and 'Strangers' in a Border Community* (1972), 147.
24. Ibid., 9.
25. Brian Barton, *The Blitz: Belfast in the War Years* (Belfast 1989), and *Northern Ireland in the Second World War* (Belfast 1995), 4–21.
26. PRONI CAB 4/475/15, May 1941; Harkness, *Northern Ireland*, 88.
27. J. Blake, *Northern Ireland in the Second World War* (1956), 198.
28. Craigavon to Chamberlain, 27 June 1940, PRO PREM 4/53/2/409; P. Canning, *British Policy toward Ireland*, 285.
29. K. S. Isles and N. Cuthbert, *An Economic Survey of Northern Ireland* (1957), 187–9; Bew, Gibbon and Patterson, *Northern Ireland*, 124–5.
30. Richard Rose, *Governing Without Consensus* (1971), 272–3.
31. R. Osborne and R. Cormack, 'Religion and the Labour Market: Patterns and Profiles', *Discrimination and Public Policy in Northern Ireland* (1991).
32. J. Whyte, 'How much discrimination was there under the unionist regime, 1921–68?', in T. Gallagher and J. O'Connell (eds), *Contemporary Irish Studies* (1983), 31.
33. Christopher Hewitt, 'Catholic grievances, Catholic nationalism and violence in Northern Ireland during the civil rights period: a reconsideration', *British Journal of Sociology*, 32 (1983).
34. D. J. Smith and G. Chambers, *Inequality in Northern Ireland* (Oxford 1991), 56–7.
35. Cabinet minutes, 7 January 1954, in Bew, Gibbon and Patterson, *Northern Ireland*, 105.
36. Bew, Gibbon and Patterson, *Northern Ireland*, 150–1; cf. E. A. Aunger, 'Religion and occupational class in Northern Ireland', *Economic and Social Review*, 7 (1975), for analysis of the 1961–71 decade.
37. Feargal Cochrane, '"Meddling at the crossroads": the decline and fall of Terence O'Neill within the Unionist community', in R. English and G. Walker (eds), *Unionism in Modern Ireland* (1996), 148–68.

38. Brendon O'Leary and John McGarry, *The Politics of Antagonism. Understanding Northern Ireland* (London 1993), 167.
39. Harkness, *Northern Ireland*, 157.
40. Bernadette Devlin, *The Price of My Soul* (1969), 139–41.

Chapter 11 *The thirty years' crisis, 1968–1998*

1. Tom Garvin, 'The North and the rest', in Charles Townshend (ed.), *Consensus in Ireland* (Oxford 1988), 109.
2. *Violence and Civil Disturbances in Northern Ireland in 1969*, Cmd. 566 (1972).
3. Ian McAllister, *The Northern Ireland Social Democratic and Labour Party: Political Opposition in a Divided Society* (London 1977), 40.
4. *Alliance* 1,3 (April 1971), quoted in Thomas Hennessey, *A History of Northern Ireland*, 184.
5. Desmond Hamill, *Pig in the Middle. The army in Northern Ireland 1969–1984* (London 1985), 86–91.
6. W. D. Flackes and S. Elliott, *Northern Ireland. A Political Directory* (4th edn. Belfast 1994), 327, 342.
7. Shane O'Doherty, *The Volunteer* (London 1993), 66.
8. M. L. R. Smith, *Fighting for Ireland? The Military Strategy of the Irish Republican Movement* (London 1995), 99.
9. Kevin Toolis, *Rebel Hearts. Journeys within the IRA's soul* (London 1995), 307–8.
10. Eamonn McCann, *War and an Irish Town* (London 1974), 106.
11. Seán MacStiofain, *Memoirs of a Revolutionary* (1975), 243.
12. Patrick Bishop and Eamon Mallie, *The Provisional IRA* (London 1987), 179.
13. Ian McAllister, 'The legitimacy of opposition: the collapse of the 1974 Northern Ireland Executive', *Éire-Ireland*, 12 (1977), 41–2.
14. F. Burton, *The Politics of Legitimacy. Struggles in a Belfast Community* (London 1978), 155–63.
15. Steve Bruce, *The Red Hand. Protestant Paramilitaries in Northern Ireland* (Oxford 1992), 288.
16. Steve Bruce, *The Edge of the Union. The Ulster Loyalist Political Vision* (Oxford 1994), 109.
17. Steve Bruce, *God Save Ulster! The Religion and Politics of Paisleyism* (Oxford 1986), 30–1.
18. Terence Brown, *Ireland A Social and Cultural History 1922–79* (London 1981).
19. Bruce Arnold, *What Kind of Country? Modern Irish Politics 1968–1983* (London 1984), 91.
20. J. J. Lee, *Ireland 1912–1985* (Cambridge 1989), 476.
21. Ibid., 477–9, is a shrewd evaluation.
22. Edna Longley (ed.), *Culture in Ireland – Division or Diversity?* (Belfast 1991), 41–2.
23. R. L. Miller, R. Wilford and F. Donoghue, *Women and Political Participation in Northern Ireland* (Aldershot 1996), 259–61.
24. Garret FitzGerald, 'Ireland in the next millennium', *Irish Studies Review*, 17 (1996/7), 7.
25. Malachi O'Doherty, *The Trouble with Guns. Republican Strategy and the Provisional IRA* (Belfast 1997), 103–10.

26. John Conroy, *War as a Way of Life. A Belfast Diary* (London 1988), 97–8.

27. Charles Townshend, *Making the Peace. Public Order and Public Security in Modern Britain* (Oxford 1993), 176–9.

28. Peter Taylor, *Beating the Terrorists? Interrogation in Omagh, Gough and Castlereagh* (Harmondsworth 1980), 286–302.

29. Padraig O'Malley, *Biting at the Grave. The Irish Hunger Strikes and the Politics of Despair* (London 1990).

30. 'The army and the death squads', *Sunday Telegraph*, 29 March 1998, 23.

31. Fionnula O'Connor, *In Search of a State. Catholics in Northern Ireland* (Belfast 1993), 15–16, 40–1.

32. Bob Rowthorn, 'Northern Ireland: an economy in crisis', in Paul Teague (ed.), *Beyond the Rhetoric. Politics, the Economy and Social Policy in Northern Ireland* (London 1987), 117–18.

33. Garret FitzGerald, *All in a Life* (London 1991), 549.

34. Tom Hadden and Kevin Boyle, *The Anglo-Irish Agreement: Commentary, Text and Official Review* (London 1989), 83–8.

35. John Hume, 'The Hume–Adams initiative', *Personal Views* (Dublin 1996), 91–6.

36. P. Bew, P. Gibbon and H. Patterson, *Northern Ireland 1921–1994* (London 1995), 218.

37. According to *The Times*, 29 June 1998, the intermediary was Denis Bradley, a Catholic priest turned film-maker.

38. 'At last, Mr Trimble has a Big Idea to sell to Ulster', *Independent*, 24 June 1998.

Biographical notes

Aiken, Frank: b. 1898 in Co. Armagh; farmer, Gaelic Leaguer and Irish Volunteer; commandant general 1st Northern Division IRA 1921; anti-Treaty IRA Chief of Staff in civil war; Sinn Féin TD 1923, Fianna Fáil TD 1927; Cabinet minister 1932–48, 1951–54, 1975–69; Tánaiste 1959–69; d. 1983.

Andrews, John: b. 1871; President of Belfast Chamber of Commerce 1936; Northern Ireland Minister of Labour 1921–37, Minister of Finance 1937–40, Prime Minister 1940–43; d. 1956.

Blythe, Ernest: b. 1889 in Co. Antrim; government clerk and Gaelic Leaguer; Sinn Féin MP 1918; Dáil minister 1919; Free State Minister of Finance 1922; Vice President of the Executive Council 1927–32; lost Dáil seat 1933; Managing Director of the Abbey Theatre 1941–67; d. 1975.

Brooke, Sir Basil (Lord Brookeborough): b. 1888 in Co. Fermanagh; Commandant Fermanagh Ulster Special Constabulary 1922; Northern Ireland MP 1929; Minister of Agriculture 1933; Minister of Commerce 1941; Prime Minister 1943–63; d. 1973.

Carson, Edward (Lord Carson): b. 1854 in Dublin; barrister 1877, QC 1894; Irish Solicitor-General 1892; knighted 1900; Solicitor-General 1900–6; leader of UUP 1910; Attorney-General 1915, First Lord of the Admiralty 1916, in War Cabinet 1917; resigned as leader of UUP 1921; d. 1935.

Collins, Michael: b. 1890 in Co. Cork; post office clerk in London; Captain in HQ Battalion Irish Volunteers, Easter 1916; Sinn Féin MP 1918; Dáil Minister of Finance, Director of Intelligence, Irish Volunteers, and President of the IRB Supreme Council 1919; signatory of Anglo-Irish Treaty 1921; Chairman of the Provisional Government and Commander-in-Chief of the National Army 1922; d. in an ambush, 22 August 1922.

Connolly, James: b. 1868 in Edinburgh; soldier; founder of Irish Socialist Republican Party 1896; founder-editor of *Workers' Republic* 1898; Ulster organizer ITGWU 1910; General Secretary ITGWU and organizer of Irish Citizen Army 1914; Commandant-

General of Irish Volunteers and Irish Citizen Army forces in Dublin, Easter 1916; executed 12 May 1916.

Cosgrave, William T.: b. 1880 in Dublin; Irish Volunteer 1916; Sinn Féin MP 1917; Dáil Minister of Local Government 1919; President of the Executive Council, Irish Free State August 1922; leader of Cumann na nGaedheal 1923–33 and of Fine Gael 1935–44; d. 1965.

Costello, John A.: b. 1981 in Dublin; barrister 1914; Attorney-General 1926–32; TD 1933–43, 1944–69; Taoiseach 1948–51 and 1954–57; d. 1976.

Craig, Sir James (Lord Craigavon): b. 1871 in Belfast; brought up in Edinburgh; MP 1906; Quartermaster-General 36th (Ulster) Division 1914–18; civil servant 1918–21; leader of UUP and Prime Minister of Northern Ireland 1921–40; Viscount Craigavon 1927; d. 1940.

de Valera, Eamon: b. 1882 in New York; brought up in Co. Limerick; mathematics teacher and Gaelic Leaguer; Irish Volunteer commandant Easter 1916; Sinn Féin MP, and President of Sinn Féin, 1917; President of Dáil Éireann 1919; President of the Irish Republic 1921–22; opposed the Treaty and enlisted in IRA, 1922; Sinn Féin TD 1923; resigned from Sinn Féin 1926 and founded Fianna Fáil 1927; President of the Executive Council, Irish Free State 1932, and Taoiseach of Éire 1937–48, 1951–54, 1957–59; President 1959–73; d. 1975.

Devlin, Joseph ('Wee Joe'): b. 1871 in Belfast; journalist; Secretary of United Irish League 1902; President of the Board of Erin, Ancient Order of Hibernians 1905–34; Nationalist MP (Kilkenny North) 1902, (West Belfast) 1906–22 and 1922–29 in Northern Ireland parliament, (Fermanagh and Tyrone) 1929–34 in Westminster parliament; d. 1934.

Dillon, John: b. 1851 in Co. Dublin; MP 1880–83, 1885–1918 (East Mayo); leader of the 'Plan of Campaign' 1886; anti-Parnellite 1891, leader of anti-Parnellite Nationalist Party 1896–1900; Redmond's successor as leader of Nationalist Party 1918; lost E. Mayo to de Valera 1918; d. 1927.

Faulkner, Brian: b. 1921 in Co. Down; worked in family linen factory; Stormont MP 1949–72; Minister of Commerce 1963; resigned from Cabinet January 1969 over decision to appoint Cameron inquiry; Minister of Development 1969; Prime Minister 1971–72; negotiated power-sharing assembly 1973; became Chief Executive 1973–74; resigned from UUP and launched Unionist Party of Northern Ireland 1974; d. 1977.

FitzGerald, Garret: b. 1926 in Dublin; lecturer in Political Economy at University College, Dublin; Fine Gael senator 1965, TD 1969–92; leader of Fine Gael 1977–87; Minister for External Affairs 1973–77; Taoiseach 1981–82 and 1982–87; signed Anglo-Irish Agreement 1985.

Gonne [MacBride], Maud: b. 1866 in Surrey, moved to Ireland 1867; actress, lived in France with Boulangist Lucien Millevoye 1887; founder of Inghinidhe na hÉireann 1900; converted to Catholicism; married John MacBride 1903, separated 1905; adopted his name 1916 after his execution; arrested 1918; Secretary of the Prisoners Defence League 1922; d. 1953.

Griffith, Arthur: b. 1871 in Dublin; printer and journalist, founded the *United Irishman* and *Sinn Féin*; Vice-President of Sinn Féin 1917; Sinn Féin MP 1918; in Dáil Cabinet 1919, Acting President 1919–20; signatory of Anglo-Irish Treaty 1921; President of Dáil 1922; Irish Free State Provisional Government minister; d. 12 August 1922.

Haughey, Charles J.: b. 1925 in Co. Mayo; accountant; Fianna Fáil TD 1957–92; minister 1961–70, 1977–79; leader of Fianna Fáil 1979–92; Taoiseach 1979–81, 1982, 1987–92.

Hobson, Bulmer: b. 1883 in Belfast; Quaker and Gaelic Leaguer, founding secretary of Antrim Gaelic Athletic Association 1901; founded Fianna Éireann 1903; joined IRB 1904; founded Dungannon Clubs and Ulster Literary Theatre 1905; Vice-President of Sinn Féin 1907–10; Secretary of Irish Volunteers 1913; resigned from IRB Supreme Council 1914; Irish Free State civil servant 1922; d. 1969.

Hyde, Douglas: b. 1860 in Co. Roscommon; founder and first President of the Gaelic League 1893–1915; resigned in protest against politicization of League 1915; Free State senator 1925; President of Ireland 1938–45; d. 1949.

Johnson, Thomas: b. 1872 in Liverpool; in Ireland from 1892; commercial traveller; co-founded Irish Labour Party 1912; President of Irish TUC 1915; drafted Dáil Democratic Programme 1919; General Secretary of Irish TUC 1920–28; TD and leader of Labour Party 1922–27; senator 1928–36; d. 1963.

Lemass, Seán: b. 1899 in Dublin; Irish Volunteer in Easter 1916 rising; anti-Treaty IRA 1922–23; Sinn Féin TD 1924, Fianna Fáil TD 1927–69; minister 1932–48, 1951–54, 1957–59; Tánaiste 1945–48, 1951–54, 1957–59; Taoiseach 1959–66; d. 1971.

Lynch, Jack [John]: b. 1917 in Cork; civil servant and barrister; Fianna Fáil TD 1948–81; minister 1955–66; Taoiseach 1966–73, 1977–79.

MacDiarmada, Seán: b. 1884 in Co. Leitrim; gardener, tram conductor, and barman in Belfast; Gaelic Leaguer, Dungannon Clubs organizer 1905; joined IRB 1906; paid organizer for Sinn Féin 1907; crippled by polio 1912; Irish Volunteer Provisional Committee member 1912; signatory of 1916 Proclamation of the Republic; executed 12 May 1916.

MacEntee, Seán: b. 1889 in Belfast; electrical engineer and poet; Irish Volunteer in Easter 1916 rising; Sinn Féin MP 1918–22, Fianna Fáil TD 1927–69; Cabinet minister 1932–48, 1951–54, 1957–65; Tánaiste 1959–65; d. 1984.

MacNeill, Eoin: b. 1867 in Co. Antrim; law clerk; founder of Gaelic League 1893; Chairman of Irish Volunteer Executive 1913; foundation Professor of Early and Medieval Irish History at University College, Dublin, 1908; issued 'countermanding order' to stop Easter 1916 rising; MP 1917; Dáil Minister for Industry 1919; Irish Free State Minister for Education 1922–25; Free State representative on Boundary Commission 1924, resigned 1925; first President of Irish Historical Society 1936; d. 1945.

Markievicz, Constance: b. 1868 in London, family [Gore-Booth] Co. Sligo landowners; married Count Casimir Markievicz 1900; Sinn Féiner; co-founder of Fianna Éireann 1909; labour movement activist; officer in Irish Citizen Army, participant in Easter 1916 rising; President of Cumann na mBan 1917; first woman Westminster MP 1918; Dáil Minister of Labour 1919; anti-Treaty activist and Sinn Féin TD (abstentionist) 1923–27; d. 1927.

Mulcahy, Richard: b. 1886 in Waterford; post office clerk; in 1916 rising with Fingal Volunteers, planned Ashbourne ambush; Chief of Staff 1918; Sinn Féin MP 1918, Dáil TD 1922–43, 1944–61; Senator 1943–44; Commander of National Army 1922–23; Minister for Defence 1923–24; Chairman of Gaeltacht Commission 1935–36; leader of Fine Gael 1944–59; Minister of Education 1948–51, 1954–57; d. 1971.

O'Brien, William: b. 1852 in Co. Cork; editor of *United Ireland* 1881; wrote the 'No Rent Manifesto'; Secretary of National League 1882; MP 1883–1918; founded United Irish League 1898; resigned from Nationalist Party 1903; founded All-for-Ireland League 1910; d. 1928.

O'Brien, William: b. 1881 in Co. Cork; Treasurer of Irish Socialist Republican Party; co-founder of ITGWU 1909; General Secretary of Irish Labour Party 1915; co-drafted Dáil Democratic Programme (with Thomas Johnson) 1919; Labour TD 1922–23, 1927, 1932–38; General Secretary of ITGWU 1923–46; d. 1968.

O'Higgins, Kevin: b. 1892 in Co. Laois; imprisoned for anti-conscription speech 1918; Sinn Féin MP 1918–22; Dáil Assistant Minister for Local Government 1919; Free State Minister for Economic Affairs, Justice 1922–27; Vice-President of the Executive Council 1923–27; assassinated 10 July 1927.

O'Kelly, Seán T.: b. 1882 in Dublin; Gaelic Leaguer; Sinn Féin MP 1918–22; Dáil Ceann Comhairle 1919; Vice-President of the Executive Council 1932–37, Tánaiste 1937–45; President of Ireland 1945–59; d. 1966.

Parnell, Charles Stewart: b. 1846 in Co. Wicklow; MP (Meath) 1875; first President of the Land League 1879; leader of the Irish parliamentary party 1880; imprisoned for incitement to violence Oct. 1881–May 1882; connection with Phoenix Park murders investigated by the *Times* Special Commission 1887–89; co-respondent in O'Shea divorce Dec. 1889; refused to accept defeat as leader of IPP Dec. 1890 and continued campaigning; died of exhaustion Oct. 1991.

Redmond, John: b. 1856 in Co. Wexford; MP 1881; barrister 1886; leader of Parnellite section of Nationalist Party 1891; leader of reunited Party 1900–18; d. 1918.

Reynolds, Albert: b. 1932 in Co. Roscommon; dance-hall manager and pet-food manufacturer; Fianna Fáil TD 1977; minister 1979–81, 1982, 1987–92; Taoiseach 1992–95; issued Downing Street Declaration with John Major December 1993.

Robinson, Mary: b. 1944 in Co. Mayo; Reid Professor of Constitutional and Criminal Law, Trinity College, Dublin; independent senator 1969–76, 1985–89, Labour senator 1976–85; President of Ireland 1990–97.

Yeats, William Butler: b. 1865 in Dublin; co-founder of National Literary Society 1892; wrote *The Celtic Twilight* 1893; *The Countess Cathleen* and *Cathleen ni Houlihan* (with Lady Gregory), performed 1899 and 1902 by Irish National Theatre; co-founder of Abbey Theatre 1904; Irish Free State Senator 1922–28; Nobel Prize for Literature 1923; d. 1939.

Chronology

1782	'Grattan's Parliament'
1798	United Irish rebellion
1801	Act of Union
1803	Robert Emmet's rebellion
1829	Catholic emancipation achieved by O'Connell's Catholic Association
1831	foundation of Irish national education system
1836	Creation of Irish Constabulary (RIC 1867)
1840	Repeal Association founded by O'Connell
1842	first issue of the *Nation* edited by Thomas Davis
1847	death of O'Connell; Young Ireland Confederation formed
1848	Irish famine; Young Ireland rebellion
	William Smith O'Brien's rising at Ballingarry, Co. Tipperary
1850	Paul Cullen becomes Archbishop of Armagh
1858	Irish Republican Brotherhood (IRB) founded by James Stephens
1860	'Deasy's Act'
1866	first Fenian invasion of Canada (second in 1870)
1867	Fenian risings; 'Manchester Martyrs'; Clerkenwell explosion
1869	Disestablishment of Church of Ireland
1870	Gladstone's first Irish Land Act
	Home Government Association founded by Isaac Butt
1876	Society for the Preservation of the Irish Language founded
1877	Charles Stewart Parnell President of Home Rule Confederation
1879	Irish National Land League founded by Michael Davitt
1881	Gladstone's second Irish Land Act
1882	'Kilmainham Treaty'; Phoenix Park murders
1884	Gaelic Athletic Association founded

1885	general election: 86 Parnellite MPs
	Ashbourne's Land Act
	Irish Loyal and Patriotic Union founded
1886	first Home Rule (Government of Ireland) Bill; 'Plan of Campaign'
	Ulster Loyalist Anti-repeal Union founded
1887	Crimes Act (Criminal Law and Procedure (Ireland) Act)
	The Times Special Commission investigation into 'Parnellism and Crime'
1889	Establishment of first co-operative creamery
	Captain O'Shea's divorce petition citing Parnell as co-respondent
1890	Irish parliamentary party split
1891	death of Parnell
	creation of Congested Districts Board
1892	founding of National Literary Society; Douglas Hyde's address 'On the Necessity for de-Anglicizing the Irish People'
	Ulster Convention League
1893	Second Home Rule Bill
	Ulster Defence Union; Unionist Clubs movement
	Gaelic League (Conradh na nGaedhilge) founded
1894–96	Royal Commission on financial relations between Ireland and Britain
1894	Irish Agricultural Organization Society founded
1898	Local Government Act
	United Irish League (UIL) founded by William O'Brien
1899	creation of Department of Agriculture and Technical Instruction
	Irish Literary Theatre's first production
	first performance of W. B. Yeats's *The Countess Cathleen*
	United Irishman founded by Arthur Griffith
	Eoin MacNeill editor of *An Claideamh Soluis*
1900	reunification of parliamentary party under John Redmond; Cumann na nGaedheal founded by Arthur Griffith
	The Leader founded by D. P. Moran
1902	Irish Land Conference
	first performance of Gregory and Yeats's Cathleen ni Houlihan
1903	Wyndham's Land Act
	resignation of O'Brien from UIL; All-For-Ireland League
1904	'devolution crisis'
	Arthur Griffith's *The Resurrection of Hungary* published
	Abbey Theatre opened
1905	Dungannon Clubs founded by Bulmer Hobson
	D. P. Moran's *The Philosophy of Irish Ireland* published
	Ulster Unionist Council

1906	Landslide Liberal victory in general election
	James Bryce succeeded by Augustine Birrell as Chief Secretary
1907	Sinn Féin founded by Arthur Griffith
	J. M. Synge's *Playboy of the Western World* performed
	Irish Council Bill
1908	St Enda's School founded by Patrick Pearse
1908–10	campaign for compulsory Irish at National University of Ireland
1909	Lloyd George's 'People's Budget'
1910	Two general elections. Liberals 272, Conservatives 255, Labour 42, UUP 17, Irish parliamentary party 84
	Edward Carson leader of UUP
1911	Parliament Act
	Cabinet Irish Committee to redraft Home Rule Bill
	August: 'county option' outlined by Birrell
1912	Third Home Rule Bill (1st reading 11 April)
	28 September: 'Ulster Day' – signing of Ulster Covenant
1913	January: Ulster Volunteer Force (UVF) created
	August: ITGWU strike
	November: Irish Citizen Army, Irish Volunteers founded
1914	March: Curragh 'mutiny'
	April: UVF gunrunning at Larne
	July: Buckingham Palace conference; Irish Volunteers gunrunning at Howth; Bachelors Walk affray
	August: outbreak of First World War
	September: Home Rule Act passed; 20 September Redmond's speech at Woodenbridge: Irish Volunteers split – Eoin MacNeill and Bulmer Hobson lead *c.* 2000 Volunteers out of Irish National Volunteers
1915	IRB Military Council (headed by Thomas Clarke and Patrick Pearse) begins planning insurrection; Casement seeks German help in raising Irish Brigade from prisoners of war
1916	February: MacNeill's attempt to head off insurrection ignored by Pearse
	19 April: the 'Castle Document'
	24–29 April: proclamation of Irish Republic; occupation of GPO: 'Easter Week'
	3–12 May: execution of 15 rebel leaders; internment of 1836 men and 5 women
	September: W. B. Yeats wrote (but did not publish) *Easter 1916*
	December: release of internees (including Michael Collins)
1917	January: Count Plunkett stood as Sinn Féin candidate in North Roscommon by-election
	May: Longford by-election: Joseph McGuinness (in Lewes gaol) elected

	July: Irish Convention (chair: Horace Plunkett)
	August: Eamon de Valera won East Clare by-election
	October: Sinn Féin *Ard-Fheis* (national convention)
1918	April: conscription crisis
	May: Lord French as Viceroy; 'German Plot' arrests
	November: end of Great War
	December: general election: Sinn Féin win 73 seats
1919	21 January: first meeting of Dáil Éireann (Chairman/Speaker: Sean T. O'Kelly); Declaration of Independence, Democratic Programme, Constitution of Dáil Éireann; 3rd Tipperary Brigade ambush at Soloheadbeg, Co. Tipperary
	February: escape of Eamon de Valera from Lincoln gaol
	April: elected President (Priomh-Aire)
	June: de Valera's departure for USA; Arthur Griffith Acting President
	23 June: daylight assassination of RIC district inspector in Thurles
	4 July: Sinn Féin, Irish Volunteers, Cumann na mBan and Gaelic League declared illegal in Tipperary
	7 September: North Cork Brigade attack on troops at Fermoy
	10 September: Sinn Féin and Dáil Éireann illegal throughout Ireland
1920	January: municipal elections: Sinn Féin controlled 72 out of 127 councils
	May: rural council elections: Sinn Féin control 28/33 county councils, 182/206 rural councils; transport workers' strike began
	17 May: first Dáil Land Court (at Ballinrobe, Co. Mayo)
	22 May: appointment of General H. H.Tudor as Police Adviser
	28 May: destruction of Kilmallock RIC barrack
	July: riots in Belfast (recurrent until 1922; total deaths 450/500+) 'Belfast Boycott' by nationalists
	August: Restoration of Order in Ireland Act
	September: establishment of Ulster Special Constabulary; appointment of Sir Ernest Clark as Under-Secretary in Belfast
	21 November: 'Bloody Sunday'
	28 November: Kilmichael ambush
	11 December: burning of centre of Cork city
	12 December: declaration of martial law in south-west
	23 December: Government of Ireland Act
1921	February: William Craig (later Lord Craigavon) succeeds Carson as UUP leader
	May: elections to Northern and Southern parliaments
	23 May: burning of Dublin Custom House

1922	22 June: opening of Northern Ireland parliament 9 July: cessation of active operations ('the Truce') 11 October: beginning of negotiations in London 5 December: signing of Anglo-Irish Treaty 7 January: ratification of Anglo-Irish Treaty by Dáil Éireann (majority 64–57) (de Valera lost Presidency 60–58) 14 January: establishment of Provisional Government: Chairman Michael Collins 30 March: Craig–Collins Pact 7 April: Northern Ireland Civil Authorities (Special Powers) Act (temporary, renewed annually until 1928, then for five years; made permanent 1933) 9 April: IRA repudiation of authority of Dáil; establishment of Army Council (Chief of Staff: Liam Lynch) 13 April: occupation of Four Courts, Dublin June: 'Pact General Election' – pro-Treaty Sinn Féin 58, anti-Treaty 36 28 June: artillery attack on 'irregulars' in Four Courts 30 June: destruction of Four Courts; Cathal Brugha killed in O'Connell Street 12 August: death of Arthur Griffith 22 August: Michael Collins killed in west Cork ambush William T. Cosgrave President of Executive Council 11 September: abolition of proportional representation for Northern Ireland local elections 27 September: Special Powers Resolution establishment of unarmed Civic Guard (later Garda Síochána) October: constitution of the Irish Free State (Saorstat Éireann) December: assassination of Sean Hales; execution of four republican prisoners
1923	10 April: Liam Lynch killed in action, Tipperary 27 April: end of republican military campaign announced by de Valera June: Northern Ireland Education Act August: first Free State general election: Cumann na nGaedheal 63, independents 16, Farmers 15, Labour 14
1924	March: 'Army mutiny'
1925	20 November: resignation of Eoin MacNeill from Boundary Commission December: end of Irish Boundary Commission
1926	May: foundation of Fianna Fáil IRA attacks on police barracks; Public Safety Act

1927	June: general election: Fianna Fáil win 44 seats; Cumann na Gaedheal 47; Labour 22
	10 July: assassination of Kevin O'Higgins
	20 July: Public Safety Act
1929	July: Censorship of Publications Act
	abolition of proportional representation for Northern Ireland state elections
1930	Constitution (Amendment No. 17) Act
1932	9 February: foundation of Army Comrades' Association/National Guard
	16 February: general election: Cumann na nGaedheal 56, Fianna Fáil 72, Labour 7, Farmers 5, independents 12
	9 March: Fianna Fáil administration; ministers Seán MacEntee (Finance), Seán Lemass (Industry and Commerce), Frank Aiken (Defence)
	30 June: Eucharistic Congress; withholding of land annuities; beginning of 'economic war'
1933	24 January: general election: Fianna Fáil 76, Cumann na nGaedheal 48, Centre 11, Labour 8, independents 9
	3 May: removal of oath of allegiance and Governor-General's veto power
	22 August: proscription of National Guard ('Blueshirts')
	2 September: formation of Fine Gael
1934	21 December: 'coal-cattle pact'
1935	February: sale and importation of contraceptives becomes illegal
1936	18 June: proscription of IRA
	11 December: removal of Crown and Governor-Generalship from Free State constitution
1937	14 June: referendum on new constitution (Bunreacht na hEireann)
1938	25 April: Anglo-Irish trade agreement; return of Treaty Ports
1939	16 January: beginning of IRA bombing campaign in Britain
	June: Offences Against the State Act
	29 June: formation of Clann na Talmhan (10.3 per cent, 13 seats in 1943 election)
	2 September: announcement of Éire's neutrality
1943	report of Commission on Vocational Organization
	April: Basil Brooke (later Lord Brookeborough) Prime Minister of Northern Ireland
1946	6 July: foundation of Clann na Poblachta by Seán MacBride
1947	Seán MacBride's victory in Dublin by-election

1948	4 February: election: Fianna Fáil retained 41.9 per cent, 67 seats (up 1); Fine Gael 19.1/31 (up 1); Labour 14; Clann na Poblachta 10; Clann na Talmhan 7, National Labour 5
	'inter-party' (coalition) government: Taoiseach John A. Costello, Tánaiste Seán MacBride, Minister for Health Noel Browne
	21 December: Republic of Ireland Act
1949	Ireland Act
1950	September: 'mother and child' health insurance scheme condemned by Hierarchy
1951	April: Noel Browne forced to resign as Health Minister
	May: general election; Clann na Poblachta lost 8 of its 10 seats, share falling from 13 to 4 per cent. Fianna Fáil government
1954	Flags and Emblems Act
1954–57	Costello's second inter-party government
1955	Republic of Ireland admitted to United Nations
1956	IRA border campaign ('Operation Harvest') launched
1957	5 March: general election
1958	July: Industrial Development Act, 'Whitaker plan'
1959	17 June: election of de Valera as President
	23 June: Seán Lemass Taoiseach
1963	March: Terence O'Neill Prime Minister of Northern Ireland
1964	July: Publication of Second Programme for Economic Expansion
	Campaign for Social Justice founded
1965	14 January: meeting of Lemass and O'Neill in Belfast
	9 February: meeting of Lemass and O'Neill in Dublin
1966	8 March: destruction of Nelson's Pillar, Dublin, by IRA
	June: rebirth of UVF: three Catholics killed
	July: Ian Paisley convicted of unlawful assembly and breach of the peace
	10 November: Seán Lemass succeeded by Jack Lynch
1967	January: Northern Ireland Civil Rights Association (NICRA) founded
	announcement of free second-level education in Éire
1968	24 August: NICRA Coalisland-Dungannon march
	October: emergence of People's Democracy (PD)
1969	January: PD Belfast–Derry march; 'Battle of Burntollet'
	15 January: Cameron Commission announced
	April: two loyalist bombs damage Belfast water pipelines
	19 April: riots in Derry
	28 April: resignation of O'Neill
	12 August: serious disorder following Apprentice Boys' parade
	13 August: 'Battle of the Bogside'

15 August: British army intervention

29 August: Scarman inquiry into August disturbances

10 October: abolition of USC and disarmament of RUC recommended by Hunt Committee

1970 1 January: USC replaced by Ulster Defence Regiment (UDR)

January: IRA split: creation of Provisional IRA (PIRA)

21 August: founding of Social Democratic and Labour Party (SDLP)

1971 20 March: Brian Faulkner Prime Minister of Northern Ireland

9 August: introduction of internment (until 1976)

5 October: foundation of Ian Paisley's Democratic Unionist Party (DUP)

1972 30 January: 'Bloody Sunday' in Derry: 13 killed by paratroops

9 February: launch of William Craig's Ulster Vanguard (VUPP)

24 March: suspension of Northern Ireland parliament: 'direct rule'

22 June: Provisional IRA cease-fire

7 July: secret Government–PIRA meeting in London

21 July: 'Bloody Friday': 22 IRA bombs, 9 killed

31 July: Operation Motorman: ending of 'no-go areas'

21 November: 19 killed in Birmingham pub bombings

29 November: Prevention of Terrorism (Temporary Provisions) Act

1973 8 March: 'Border Poll': 591,000 (57.5 per cent of electorate) pro-Union

November: Erskine Childers elected president of Ireland after retirement of de Valera

6 December: Sunningdale conference

1974 1 January: installation of 'power-sharing' Northern Ireland Executive headed by Brian Faulkner

28 February: UK general election: Harold Wilson Prime Minister, Merlyn Rees Secretary of State for Northern Ireland

15 May: Ulster Workers Council strike

17 May: 22 killed by car bombs in Dublin

28 May: collapse of power-sharing executive

16 July: contraception Bill defeated in Dáil Éireann

20 December: PIRA temporary cease-fire (to 17 January)

1975 30 January: Gardiner Report

9 February: PIRA indefinite cease-fire

12 October: split in VUPP: Craig (and David Trimble) support coalition

1976 January: first deployment of SAS in Northern Ireland

12 August: launch of Peace People movement

10 September: Roy Mason Secretary of State for Northern Ireland

1 December: Fair Employment Act

1977	3 May: United Unionist Action Council strike
1978	17 February: 12 killed by IRA incendiary bomb at La Mon House
1979	16 March: Bennett Report on interrogation of terrorist suspects
	30 March: assassination of Airey Neave at Westminster Palace
	3 May: UK general election: Margaret Thatcher Prime Minister, Humphrey Atkins Secretary of State for Northern Ireland
	7 June: European Parliament elections: Ian Paisley heads poll (170,688 first preference votes)
1980	8 December: first Anglo-Irish summit meeting in Dublin
1981	5 May: death of Bobby Sands on hunger strike
	20 August: death of tenth hunger striker, Michael Devine
	27 September: launch of Garret FitzGerald's constitutional 'crusade'
1982	19 February: failure of DeLorean motor company ('one of the gravest cases of the misuse of public funds in many years' – Commons Public Accounts Cttee, 18 July 1984)
	5 April: White Paper *A Framework for Devolution* (Cmnd 8541)
	20 October: Northern Ireland Assembly elections (Single transferable vote): UUP 29.7 per cent, DUP 23 per cent, SDLP 18.8 per cent, Sinn Féin 10.1 per cent, Alliance 9.3 per cent
1983	9 June: UK general election: Sinn Féin poll 102,701 votes, SDLP 137,012
	7 September: abortion referendum in Irish Republic: pro-life amendment to constitution
	17 December: 6 killed by bomb outside Harrods, London
1984	29 March: Haagerup report adopted by European Parliament
	2 May: New Ireland Forum report
	12 October: 5 killed in IRA bombing of Grand Hotel, Brighton
1985	15 November: Anglo-Irish Agreement (Hillsborough, Co. Down): ratified by Dáil 21 Nov. (88–75), Commons 28 Nov. (473–47)
1986	3 March: Unionist 'Day of Action' against Anglo-Irish Agreement
	26 June: Irish constitutional referendum: ban on divorce upheld
	6–15 July: Orange Order – police clashes in Portadown, Co. Armagh
1987	8 May: 8 IRA killed in SAS ambush at Loughgall RUC station
	11 June: UK general election: UUP 37.8 per cent, DUP 11.7 per cent, SF 11.4 per cent, Alliance 10 per cent
1988	11 January: beginning of Hume-Adams talks
	25 January: announcement that no prosecutions will arise from Stalker–Sampson Report
	6 March: 3 members of IRA Active Service Unit killed by SAS in Gibraltar

19 March: death of 2 soldiers at funeral of Kevin Brady

19 October: 'broadcasting ban' announced by Home Secretary

15 December: new Fair Employment Bill

1989 12 February: shooting of Patrick Finucane (a month after Douglas Hogg spoke in parliament of 'solicitors unduly sympathetic to the cause of the IRA')

1990 9 November: election of Mary Robinson as President of Irish Republic

1991 7 February: IRA mortar attack on 10 Downing Street

1992 6 February: Charles Haughey succeeded by Albert Reynolds as leader of Fianna Fáil and Taoiseach

10 April: Baltic exchange bombing

1 July: UDR merged into Royal Irish Regiment

September–November: failure of Brooke–Mayhew talks

25 November: Irish republic general election: Labour vote doubled

1993 15 December: Downing Street Declaration

1994 July: Portadown disturbances after RUC attempt to ban Orange march

31 August: PIRA cease-fire

13 October: loyalist cease-fire

1995 22 February: publication of Anglo-Irish 'Framework document'

9 September: election of David Trimble as leader of UUP

1996 9 February: Canary Wharf bombing

18 February: Aldwych bus bomb

15 June: Manchester bombing

12 July: Drumcree (Portadown) confrontation; riots – 600 families driven from their homes

1997 Autumn: all-party talks at Stormont

12 December: Gerry Adams visits 10 Downing Street

1998 10 April: signature of Stormont Agreement

Select bibliography

General histories

J. Bardon, *A History of Ulster* (Belfast 1992)

T. Brown, *Ireland: a Social and Cultural History 1922–79* (London 1981)

D.G. Boyce, *Nationalism in Ireland* (London 1982, 1995)

D.G. Boyce, *The Irish Question and British Politics 1868–1986* (London 1988)

L.M. Cullen, *An Economic History of Ireland since 1660* (London 1972)

M.E. Daly, *Social and Economic History of Ireland since 1800* (Dublin 1981)

D. Fitzpatrick, *The Two Irelands 1912–1939* (Oxford 1998)

R.F. Foster, *Modern Ireland 1600–1972* (London 1988)

K.T. Hoppen, *Ireland since 1800* (London 1989)

D. Keogh, *Twentieth-century Ireland. Nation and State* (Dublin 1994)

J.J. Lee, *The Modernisation of Irish Society 1848–1918* (Dublin 1973)

J.J. Lee, *Ireland 1912–85* (Cambridge 1989)

F.S.L. Lyons, *Ireland since the Famine* (London 1971)

J.A. Murphy, *Ireland in the Twentieth Century* (Dublin 1975)

C. O'Grada, *Ireland: A New Economic History 1780–1939* (Oxford 1994)

C. O'Grada, *A Rocky Road: The Irish Economy since the 1920s* (Manchester 1997)

Thematic analyses

D.H. Akenson, *A Mirror to Kathleen's Face: Education in Independent Ireland 1922–60* (Montreal 1975)

P. Bew, E. Hazelkorn and H. Patterson, *The Dynamics of Irish Politics* (London 1989)

C. Coulter, *The Hidden Tradition. Feminism, Women and Nationalism in Ireland* (1993)

L.P. Curtis, Jr., 'Moral and physical force: the language of violence in Irish nationalism', *Journal of British Studies* 27 (1988), 150–89

M. Hechter, *Internal Colonialism. The Celtic Fringe in British National Development 1536–1966* (London 1975)

T. Inglis, *Moral Monopoly. The Catholic Church in Modern Irish Society* (Dublin 1987)

K. Kennedy, T. Giblin, D. McHugh, *The Economic Development of Ireland in the Twentieth Century* (London 1988)

E. Larkin, 'Church, state and nation in modern Ireland', *American Historical Review* 80 (1975), 1244–76.

O. MacDonagh, *States of Mind: A Study of Anglo-Irish Conflict 1780–1980* (London 1983)

N. Mansergh, *The Unresolved Question. The Anglo-Irish Settlement and its Undoing 1912–72* (New Haven 1992)

C. O'Halloran, *Partition and the Limits of Irish Nationalism* (Dublin 1987)

E. Rumpf and A.C. Hepburn, *Nationalism and Socialism in Twentieth-Century Ireland* (Liverpool 1977)

R. Sinnott, *Irish Voters Decide. Voting Behaviour in Elections and Referendums since 1918* (Manchester 1995)

A.T.Q. Stewart, *The Narrow Ground. Aspects of Ulster 1609–1969*

C. Townshend, *Political Violence in Ireland. Government and Resistance since 1848* (1983)

A.J. Ward, *The Irish Constitutional Tradition. Responsible Government in Modern Ireland 1782–1992* (1994)

M. Ward, *Unmanageable Revolutionaries: Women and Irish Nationalism* (Dingle 1983)

Historiography

C. Brady (ed.), *Interpreting Irish History. The Debate on Historical Revisionism* (Dublin 1994)

D.G. Boyce and A. O'Day (eds), *Modern Irish History. Revisionism and the Revisionist Controversy* (London 1996)

N.J. Curtin, 'Varieties of Irishness: historical revisionism, Irish style', *Journal of British Studies* 35 (April 1996), 195–219

J. Ruane, 'Colonialism and the interpretation of Irish historical development' in M. Silverman and P.H. Gulliver (eds), *Approaching the Past. Historical Anthropology through Irish Case Studies* (London 1992)

C. Townshend, 'Modernization and nationalism: perspectives in recent Irish history', *History* 66 (1981)

C. Townshend, 'The making of modern Irish public culture', *Journal of Modern History* 61, 3 (1989), 535–54

C. Townshend, 'Contesting the history of modern Ireland', *Journal of British Studies* 34, 4 (1995), 546–54

Chapter 1 The state of the Union, 1900

V. Crossman, *Local Government in Nineteenth-Century Ireland* (Belfast 1994)

L.P. Curtis, *Coercion and Conciliation in Ireland* (Princeton 1963)

A. Gailey, *Ireland and the Death of Kindness. The Experience of Constructive Unionism 1890–1905* (Cork 1987)

J. Kendle, *Ireland and the Federal Solution. The Debate over the UK Constitution 1870–1921* (Kingston 1989)

L.W. McBride, *The Greening of Dublin Castle: The Transformation of Bureaucratic and Judicial Personnel 1892–1922* (Washington DC 1991)

R.B. McDowell, *The Irish Administration 1801–1914* (London 1964)

M. O'Callaghan, *British High Politics and a Nationalist Ireland* (Cork 1994)

E. O'Halpin, *The Decline of the Union. British Government in Ireland 1892–1920* (1987)

C.P. Shannon, *Arthur J. Balfour and Ireland* (Washington DC 1989)

W.E. Vaughan (ed.), *Ireland under the Union I. 1801–70; II. 1870–1921* (New History of Ireland vol.V, Oxford 1989, 1996)

T. West, *Horace Plunkett, Co-operation and Politics* (1986)

Chapter 2 The national question

P. Bew, *C.S. Parnell* (Dublin 1980)

P. Bew, *Conflict and Conciliation in Ireland 1890–1910. Parnellites and Radical Agrarians* (Oxford 1987)

S. Clark, *Social Origins of the Irish Land War* (Princeton 1979)

B. Farrell (ed.), *The Irish Parliamentary Tradition* (Dublin 1973)

T. Garvin, *The Evolution of Irish Nationalist Politics* (Dublin 1981)

T. Garvin, *Nationalist Revolutionaries in Ireland* (Oxford 1987)

F.S.L. Lyons, *The Irish Parliamentary Party 1890–1910* (London 1951)

F.S.L. Lyons, *John Dillon: a Biography* (London 1968)

F.S.L. Lyons, *Charles Stewart Parnell* (London 1977)

D.W. Miller, *Church, State and Nation in Ireland 1898–1921* (Dublin 1973)

T.W. Moody, *Michael Davitt and Irish Revolution 1846–82* (Oxford 1981)

C. Cruise O'Brien, *Parnell and His Party* (Oxford 1957)

J.V. O'Brien, *William O'Brien and the Course of Irish Politics 1881–1918* (Berkeley 1975)

L. O'Broin, *Revolutionary Underground: The Story of the Irish Republican Brotherhood 1858–1924* (Dublin 1976)

Chapter 3 Cultures and civilizations: the struggle for Ireland's soul

D.G. Boyce '"One last burial": culture, counter-revolution and revolution in Ireland 1886–1916', in *The Revolution in Ireland*

M. Cullen, 'How radical was Irish feminism between 1860 and 1920?', in P.J. Corish (ed.), *Radicals, Rebels and Establishments*

R. Davis, *Arthur Griffith and Non-Violent Sinn Fein* (Dublin 1974)

R. Dudley Edwards, *Patrick Pearse: the Triumph of Failure* (London 1977)

R.F. Foster, 'Anglo-Irish literature, Gaelic nationalism and Irish politics in the 1890s', in Blake (intr.) *Ireland after the Union*

J. Hutchinson, *The Dynamics of Cultural Nationalism: the Gaelic Revival and the Creation of the Irish Nation State* (Allen & Unwin, London 1987)

F.S.L. Lyons, *Culture and Anarchy in Ireland* (Oxford 1979)

P. O'Leary, 'Uneasy alliance: the Gaelic League looks at the 'Irish' renaissance', in Eyler and Garratt (eds), *Uses of the Past*, 144–60

J. Sheehy, *The Rediscovery of Ireland's Past* (London 1980)
W. I. Thompson *The Imagination of an Insurrection: Dublin, Easter 1916. A Study of an Ideological Movement* (New York 1967)
M. Tierney, *Eoin MacNeill* (Oxford 1980)

Chapter 4 Home Rule and the British crisis, 1905–1914

P. Buckland, *Ulster Unionism and the Origins of Northern Ireland 1886–1922* (1973)
P. Buckland, 'Carson, Craig and Partition' in Collins (ed) *Nationalism & Unionism*
I. Budge and C. O'Leary, *Belfast: Approach to Crisis. A Study of Belfast Politics 1613–1970* (London 1973)
A. Jackson, *The Ulster Party* (Oxford 1989)
P. Jalland, *The Liberals and Ireland* (London 1980)
J. Kendle, *Walter Long, Ireland and the Union 1905–1920* (Montreal and Kingston 1992)
D.W. Miller, *Queen's Rebels: Ulster Loyalism in Historical Perspective* (Dublin 1978)
A. Mitchell, *Labour in Irish Politics 1890–1930* (Dublin 1974)
J.V. O'Brien, *'Dear, Dirty Dublin'. A City in Distress 1899–1916* (Berkeley 1982)
L. O'Broin, *The Chief Secretary. Augustine Birrell in Ireland* (London 1969)
H. Patterson, *Class Conflict and Sectarianism. The Protestant Working Class and the Belfast Labour Movement 1868–1920* (Belfast 1980)
E. Phoenix, *Northern Nationalism: Nationalist Politics, Partition and the Catholic Minority in Northern Ireland, 1890–1940* (Belfast 1994)
A.T.Q. Stewart, *The Ulster Crisis* (London 1967)

Chapter 5 World war and rebellion, 1914–1919

P. Bew, *Ideology and the Irish Question* (Oxford 1994)
D.G. Boyce, *The Sure Confusing Drum: Ireland and the First World War* (Swansea 1993)
O. Dudley Edwards and F. Pyle (eds), *1916. The Easter Rising* (1968)
D. Fitzpatrick, *Politics and Irish Life 1913–21: Provincial Experience of War and Revolution* (Dublin 1977, Cork 1997)
S. Hartley, *The Irish Question as a Problem in British Foreign Policy 1914–18* (1987)
M. Laffan, 'The unification of Sinn Féin in 1917', *Irish History Studies* (March 1971)
M. Laffan, *The Partition of Ireland, 1911–25* (Dublin 1983)
F.X. Martin (ed.), *Leaders and Men of the Easter Rising: Dublin 1916* (London 1967)
K.B. Nowlan (ed.), *The Making of 1916* (London 1969)
L. O'Broin, *Dublin Castle and the 1916 Rising* (London 1966)
D. Ryan, *The Rising* (Dublin 1957)
C. Townshend, 'The suppression of the Easter Rising' *Bullán: an Irish Studies Journal* 1 (1994), 27–39.
T.D. Williams (ed.), *The Irish Struggle 1916–26* (London 1966)

Chapter 6 The first republic and the Anglo-Irish War, 1919–1922

J. Augustejn, *From Public Defiance to Guerrilla Warfare* (Dublin 1996)

D.G. Boyce, *Englishmen and Irish Troubles: British Public Opinion and the Making of Irish Policy 1918–22* (London 1972)

T.P. Coogan, *Michael Collins* (London 1990)

G. Doherty and D. Keogh (eds), *Michael Collins and the Making of the Irish State* (Cork 1998)

B. Farrell, *The Founding of Dáil Éireann* (Dublin 1971)

B. Farrell (ed), *The Creation of the Dáil* (Dublin 1994)

D. Fitzpatrick, *Politics and Irish Life 1913–21: Provincial Experience of War and Revolution* (Dublin 1977, Cork 1997)

P. Hart, *The IRA and its Enemies. Violence and Community in Cork 1916–23* (Oxford 1998)

A. Mitchell, *Revolutionary Government in Ireland: Dail Eireann 1919–1922* (Dublin 1994)

C. Townshend, *The British Campaign in Ireland 1919–1921* (Oxford 1975)

M.G. Valiulis, *Portrait of a Revolutionary. General Richard Mulcahy and the Founding of the Irish Free State* (Dublin 1992)

J. Van Voris, *Constance de Markievicz in the Cause of Ireland* (1967)

C. Younger, *Arthur Griffith* (Dublin 1981)

Chapter 7 Civil war and nation-building, 1922–1932

J.M. Curran, *The Birth of the Irish Free State 1921–1923* (Alabama 1980)

M.E. Daly, *Industrial Development and Irish National Identity 1922–1939* (Dublin 1992)

R. English, *Radicals and the Republic. Socialist Republicanism in the Irish Free State 1925–1937* (Oxford 1994)

R. Fanning, *The Irish Department of Finance* (Dublin 1978)

R. Fanning, *Independent Ireland* (Dublin 1983)

T. Garvin, *1922: The Birth of Irish Democracy* (Dublin 1996)

D. Harkness, *The Restless Dominion. The Irish Free State in the British Commonwealth 1921–31* (London 1969)

M. Hopkinson, *Green Against Green: The Irish Civil War* (Dublin 1988)

T. Inglis, *Moral Monopoly. The Catholic Church in Modern Irish Society* (Dublin 1987)

D. Keogh, *The Vatican, the Bishops and Irish Politics 1919–1939* (Cambridge 1986)

J. Prager, *Building Democracy in Ireland* (Cambridge 1986)

J. Whyte, *Church and State in Modern Ireland 1823–79* (Dublin 1984)

Chapter 8 The dominion of Eamon de Valera, 1932–1948

J. Bowman, *De Valera and the Ulster Question 1917–1973* (Oxford 1982)

T.P. Coogan, *De Valera: Long Fellow, Long Shadow* (London 1993)

O. Dudley Edwards, *Eamon de Valera* (Cardiff 1987)

R. Dunphy, *The Making of Fianna Fáil Power in Ireland 1923–1948* (Oxford 1995)

D. Keogh, *The Vatican, the Bishops and Irish Politics 1919–39* (Cambridge 1986)

Lord Longford and T.P. O'Neill, *Eamon de Valera* (1970)

T.J. McElligott, *Education in Ireland* (Dublin 1966)

D. MacMahon, *Republicans and Imperialists: Anglo-Irish Relations in the 1930s* (New Haven 1984)

M. Moynihan (ed.), *Speeches and Statements of Eamon de Valera 1917–73* (1980)

S. O'Faolain, *De Valera* (Harmondsworth 1939)

T. Salmon, *Unneutral Ireland* (Oxford 1989)

Chapter 9 The second republic and modernization, 1948–1968

M. Bax, *Harpstrings and Confessions: Machine-Style Politics in the Irish Republic* (Assen 1976)

P. Bew and H. Patterson, *Sean Lemass and the Making of Modern Ireland 1945–66* (Dublin 1982)

R. Carty, *Party and Parish Pump: Electoral Politics in Ireland* (Dingle 1983)

J. Coakley and M. Gallagher (eds), *Politics in the Republic of Ireland* (Dublin 1992)

B. Farrell, *Seán Lemass* (Dublin 1983)

B. Girvin, *Between Two Worlds: Politics and Economy in Contemporary Ireland* (Dublin 1989)

J. Horgan, *Seán Lemass. The Enigmatic Patriot* (Dublin 1997)

J.K. Jacobsen, *Chasing Progress in the Irish Republic. Ideology, Democracy and Dependent Development* (Cambridge 1994)

K. Kennedy, *Productivity and Industrial Growth: The Irish Experience* (Oxford 1971)

J. Lee (ed.), *Ireland 1945–70* (Dublin 1979)

J. Meenan, *The Irish Economy since 1922* (Liverpool 1970)

P. O'Malley, *Irish Industry: Structure and Performance* (Dublin 1971)

Chapter 10 The Stormont regime: Northern Ireland, 1920–1969

D.H. Akenson, *Education and Enmity. The Control of Schooling in Northern Ireland 1920–50* (Newton Abbot 1973)

P. Arthur, *Government and Politics of Northern Ireland* (London 1980)

P. Bew, P. Gibbon and H. Patterson, *Northern Ireland 1921–1994: Political Forces and Social Classes* (London 1994)

P. Buckland, *The Factory of Grievances: Devolved Government in Northern Ireland 1921–39* (Dublin 1979)

B.A. Follis, *A State under Siege. The Establishment of Northern Ireland 1920–1925* (Oxford 1995)

D. Harkness, *Northern Ireland since 1920* (Dublin 1983)

R. Harris, *Prejudice and Tolerance in Ulster* (London 1972)

D.S. Johnson, 'The Northern Ireland economy 1914–39' in L. Kennedy and P. Ollereshaw (eds), *An Economic History of Ulster, 1820–1940* (1985)

D. Kennedy, *The Widening Gulf: Northern Attitudes to the Independent Irish State 1919–49* (1988)

R. Rose, *Governing Without Consensus* (London 1971)

J. Todd, 'Unionist political thought 1920–72' in Boyce *et al.* (eds) *Political Thought in Ireland* (London 1993)

J. Whyte, 'How much discrimination was there under the Unionist regime 1921-68?', in T. Gallagher and J. O'Connell (eds), *Contemporary Irish Studies* (Manchester 1983)

Chapter 11 The thirty years' crisis, 1968–1998

A. Aughey, *Under Siege. Ulster Unionism and the Anglo-Irish Agreement* (London 1989)

J. Bowyer Bell, *The Irish Troubles. A Generation of Violence 1967–1992* (Dublin 1993)

P. Bew and G. Gillespie, *Northern Ireland. A Chronology of the Troubles* (Dublin 1993)

P. Bew and H. Patterson, *The British State and the Ulster Crisis* (London 1985)

P. Bishop and E. Mallie, *The Provisional IRA* (London 1987)

S. Bruce, *God Save Ulster! The Religion and Politics of Paisleyism* (Oxford 1986)

S. Bruce, *The Red Hand. Protestant Paramilitaries in Northern Ireland* (Oxford 1992)

S. Bruce, *The Edge of the Union. The Ulster Loyalist Political Vision* (Oxford 1994)

G. Hussey, *Ireland Today* (London 1994)

D. Keogh and M. Haltzel (eds) *Northern Ireland and the Politics of Reconciliation* (Cambridge 1993)

A. Morgan and B. Purdie (eds), *Ireland: Divided Nation, Divided Class* (London 1980)

B. O'Leary and J. McGarry, *The Politics of Antagonism. Understanding Northern Ireland* (London 1993)

P. O'Malley, *Biting at the Grave. The Irish Hunger Strikes and the Politics of Despair* (Boston 1990)

C. Townshend (ed.) *Consensus in Ireland: Approaches and Recessions* (Oxford 1988)

Appendix 1

Population and Social Indicators, 1841–1991

Year	Population	Urban population %	Dublin population %	Males in agriculture %	Catholics %	Other de-nominations %	Irish-speakers %
1841	6,528,799	16.7	3.7	74.3	·	·	·
1851	5,111,557	22.0	5.8	68.8	·	·	29.1
1861	4,402,111	22.2	6.7	64.6	89.3	10.7	24.5
1871	4,053,187	22.8	7.4	63.1	89.2	10.8	19.8
1881	3,870,020	23.9	8.4	62.6	89.5	10.5	23.9
1891	3,468,694	25.3	9.6	61.4	89.3	10.7	19.2
1901	3,221,823	28.0	11.2	61.7	89.3	10.7	19.2
1911	3,139,688	29.7	12.3	59.5	89.6	10.4	17.6
1926	2,971,992	31.8	13.7	58.9	92.6	7.4	19.3
1936	2,968,420	35.5	15.9	55.9	93.4	6.6	23.7
1946	2,955,107	39.3	17.1	54.1	94.3	5.7	21.2
1961	2,818,341	46.4	19.1	43.1	94.9	4.9	27.2
1971	2,978,248	52.2	26.9	31.9	93.9	4.3	28.3
1981	3,443,405	55.6	29.1	21.7	93.1	3.7	31.6
1991	3,523,401	57.0	29.1	19.0	·	·	(31.1)

Notes: All data refer to the present area of the Republic of Ireland. Urban areas are defined as those with a population of 1,500 or more, but figures for these and for Dublin are difficult to compare over time due to changes in boundary definition criteria. The data on involvement in agriculture are also difficult to compare over time due to varying classification criteria, and it has been possible to compute comparable data for men only. Data on religion are expressed as percentages of the total population (which includes those refusing to give information on this matter). Data on Irish speakers from 1926 onwards refer to the population aged over three years. The figure for Irish speakers in brackets in the bottom row refers to 1986

Source: Calculated from *Census of Ireland* and *Statistical Yearbook of Ireland*, various dates, from *Labour Force Survey*, 1992, and from David Fitzpatrick, 'The disappearance of the Irish agricultural labourer, 1841–1912', *Irish Economic and Social History*, 7 (1980), 66–92

Appendix 2

Strength of the Parties in the Dáil after each General Election 1922–1992

Election	Total	Republican/ Fianna Fáil	Cumann na nGaedheal/ Fine Gael	Labour
1922	128	35	58	17
1923	153	44	63	14
1927(1)	153	44	47	22
1927(2)	153	57	62	13
1932	153	72	57	7
1933	153	77	48	8
1937	138	69	48	13
1938	138	77	45	9
1943	138	67	32	17
1944	138	76	30	8
1948	147	68	31	19
1951	147	69	40	16
1954	147	65	50	19
1957	147	78	40	13
1961	144	70	47	16
1965	144	72	47	22
1969	144	75	50	18
1973	144	69	54	19
1977	148	84	43	17
1981	166	78	65	15
1982(1)	166	81	63	15
1982(2)	166	75	70	16
1987	166	81	51	12
1989	166	77	55	15
1992	166	68	45	33

Note: *Details of the strengths of other parties are as follows:

1927(1)	National League 8; Sinn Féin 5
1927(2)	National League 2
1933	Centre Party 11
1944	National Labour 4
1948	Clann na Poblachta 10
1951	Clann na Poblachta 2
1954	Clann na Poblachta 3
1957	Sinn Féin 4; Clann na Poblachta 1
1961	National Progressive Democrats 2; Clann na Poblachta 1

Farmers Clann na Talmhan	Progressive Democrats	Other Parties*	Independents
7	•	•	11
15	•	•	17
11	•	13	16
6	•	2	13
4	•	•	13
•	•	11	9
•	•	•	8
•	•	•	7
14	•	•	8
11	•	4	9
7	•	10	12
6	•	2	14
5	•	3	5
3	•	5	8
2	•	3	6
•	•	•	3
•	•	•	1
•	•	•	2
•	•	•	4
•	•	5	3
•	•	3	4
•	•	2	3
•	14	5	3
•	6	9	4
•	10	5	5

1981	H-Block 2; Ind. FF 1; SLP 1
1982(1)	Workers Party 3
1982(2)	Workers Party 2
1987	Workers Party 4; Democratic Socialist Party 1
1989	Workers Party 7; Democratic Socialist Party 1; Green Party 1
1992	Democratic Left 4; Green Party 1

Index

Page numbers in bold refer to figures

Abbey Theatre 46–7
Abortion Information Act (1995) 220
Act of Union (1801) 3
Adams, Gerry 210, 230, 232, 233
Aer Lingus 173
'agrarian' action 20
Agriculture, department 120
Aiken, Frank 116, 153–4, biog. 250
Akenson, D.H. 12
Alliance Party 205
Amnesty International 225
Ancient Order of Hibernians 55
Anderson, Sir John 104
Andrews, J.H. biog. 250
Anglo-Irish Agreement
    (1938) x, 150
    (1985) 228–30
Anglo-Irish Treaty (1921) 105–10,
        137, 185
    oath of allegiance 107, 109, 130,
        134, 136–7
Army Comrades' Association 141–2
Ashe, Thomas 80, 83–4
Asquith, H.H. 53, 56, 57, 65, 67,
        70, 178, 179
Attkins, Humphrey 227

Attlee, Clement 166, 197
autarchy 50, 133, 138, 170

Bachelors Walk, Dublin 67
Balfour, Arthur James 5, 7, 13,
        14–15
Balfour, Gerald 5, 15
Barr, Glen 211
Bates, R. Dawson 197
Beckett, Samuel 173, 174
Belfast 58, 104
    44-hour strike (1919) 180
    air raids 196
    riots 180, 182–3
    shipyards 180
Belfast boycott 98–9, 122, 181, 185
Bew, Paul 31, 177
Biggar, Joseph 29
Birkenhead, Earl of 103–4
Birrell, Augustine 53, 65, 67, 70, 77
'Black and Tans' – *see* RIC
Blaney, Neil 216
Blanqui, Auguste 25
'Bloody Sunday' (1920) 94, 101;
        (1972) 206–7
Blueshirts 142–3

Blythe, Ernest 31, 123, 128, biog. 250
Boer War 2, 41
Boland, Harry 85, 87, 91, 111
Boland, Kevin 216
Bonar Law, Andrew 59, 99
Booterstown, Co. Dublin 136
Bord Fáilte 173
Boundary Commission 106, 122–3, 185–7
Brehon law 21
British army 202, 206–7, 225–6
  SAS regiment 226
Brooke, Sir Basil (Viscount Brookeborough) 184, 192, 199, biog. 250
Brooke, Peter 230
Browne, Noel 164, 166–7
Bruce, Steve 187, 214
Brugha [Burgess], Cathal 88, 89, 102, 106, 109, 115
Bryce, James 46, 53
Burntollet, 'Battle' of 201–2
Burton Frank, 214
Butt, Isaac 29
Byrne, Gabriel (Gay) 174

Campbell-Bannerman, Sir Henry 53
Cameron Commission 202, 204
Carson, Sir Edward 58–9, 65, 70, 178, 179, biog. 250
Casement, Sir Roger 75
Catholic Association 3, 19
Catholic church 32–4, 42, 45–6, 83, 115, 125–6, 146–9, 174
  the 'Catholic state' 125–6, 146–9
  Eucharistic Congress (1932) 148–9
  Hierarchy 34, 84, 99, 101, 125, 134, 162–3, 167, 221
Catholic Emancipation 3, 32
cattle-driving [ranch war] 54
Censorship Board 127, 173–4
Centre Party 142

Chichester-Clark, James 202, 205, 206
Childers, Erskine 67, 96, 109
Childers, Erskine (President of the Republic) 217
Christian Brothers schools 12
Churchill, Winston S. 65, 104, 152, 153, 154, 197
Civic Guard [see Garda Síochana]
Civil Authorities (Special Powers) Act (Northern Ireland), 1922, *see* Special Powers Act
Clan na Gael 26
Clann na Poblachta 163–4, 167, 176
Clann na Talmhan 160, 164, 167, 176
Clark, Sir Ernest 104, 181
Clinton, Bill (US President) 232
Cohalan, Daniel F. (Clan na Gael co-president) 125
Collins, Michael 76, 81–2, 83, 85, 87, 89, 91, 93, 94, 102–3, 105, 106, 107, 109, 111–13, 115, 117, 119, 121, 124, 127, 128, 132, 134, 146, 185, biog. 250
Collins-de Valera pact [1922 election] 111–13, 115, 186
Commission on Vocational Organisation 143, 160
Congested Districts Board 14–15, 54
Connolly, James 61, 62, 64–5, 73, 74, 76, biog. 250
Constructive Unionism 14–17
contraception 174–5, 218
Coogan, T.P. 137
Co-operative movement 16
Corcoran, Fr T.J. 124
Corkery, Daniel 124, 125
Cosgrave, Liam 211, 217
Cosgrave, William T. 90, 110, 111, 120, 128, 129, 133, 148, 150, 186, biog. 251
Costello, John A. 164, 165, 167, biog. 251

Council of Europe 175
Craig, Sir James [Lord Craigavon]
    58, 179, 185, 186, 187, 189,
    190, 191, 192, 196, 197, biog.
    251
Craig, William 211, 214
Craig-Collins Pact 185
Crimes Act (1887) 7
Croke, Thomas (Archbishop of
    Cashel) 39
Cullen, Cardinal Paul 26, 33, 34
Cumann na mBan 77, 90, 98
Cumann na nGaedheal 119, 129,
    130, 131, 132, 133, 134, 141–2
Currie, Austin 201, 201

Dáil Éireann (1st) 87–92, 97, 99
    (2nd) 102, 105–6, 108–9, 110,
    111, 130, 132
    arbitration courts 91–3, 118
    Declaration of Independence 87,
        90
    Democratic Programme 88, 97
    Free State 118, 126, 130, 133,
        137
Davis, Thomas 21, 40, 46
Davitt, Michael 27–8
Democratic Unionist Party 211
Department of Agriculture and
    Technical Instruction 15–16
Derrig, Thomas 156–7
Derry city 190, 201, 202, 206
de Valera, Eamon 82, 87, 89, 90,
    102, 103, 105–6, 107, 110, 113,
    116, 126, 130, 132–58, 159,
    161, 171, 197, 215, biog. 251
'devolution crisis' (1904) 17, 52
Devlin, Joseph 55, 85, biog. 251
Devoy, John 27
Dignan, John (Bishop of Clonfert)
    161
Dillon, John 35, biog. 251
'Diplock courts' 224, 230
Disraeli, Benjamin 5, 19

divorce, prohibition 125–6; (1937
    constitution) 146; (1986, 1995
    referenda) 220–1
Downing Street Declaration (1993)
    231
Doyle, Roddy 175
Dublin 51, 67, 72
    1913 lockout 61, 63–4
    Custom House burning 102
    Easter rising 74, 76–80
    Four Courts 111, 113–14
Dublin Castle (Irish Government)
    5–6
    Local Government Board 91
Dublin Metropolitan Police 93
Duke, H.E. 81
Dunbar-Harrison, Letitia 127
Dungannon Clubs 55

Easter rebellion (1916) x, 40, 68
'Economic War' 137, 141
education 11–13, 124–6, 155–8, 163
    Northern Ireland 194–5
Edwards, Owen Dudley 132, 148
Éire 1937 consitution 144–7
Emergency [the Second World
    War] 151–5, 161
Emergency Provisions Act
    (Northern Ireland) 1973 224
Emigration 11, 168–9
Ervine, David 233
European Community 215
European Union 222, 223

Fanning, Ronan 115, 121, 122, 144
Farrell, Brian 171
Father Ted 221
Faulkner, Brian 199, 205–7, 211,
    212, biog. 251
Feetham, Richard 186–7
Fenians [see also Irish Republican
    Brotherhood]
    1867 rising 7
Fianna Éireann 55

Fianna Fáil 129, 130–1, 132–41, 143, 149, 156, 157, 159, 216, 218, 222
Figgis, Darrell 89, 124
Finance, department 120, 121, 138
Fine Gael 132, 159, 162, 164, 167, 218
Fiscal Inquiry Committee [1923] 120
Fisher, J.R. 186
Fitt, Gerry 205, 212
FitzGerald, Desmond 96
FitzGerald, Garret 173, 211, 217, 218–19, 220, 229, biog. 251
Fitzpatrick, David 180
Flags and Emblems Act (Northern Ireland) 199, 229
Foster, Roy 8, 40, 41, 68, 166, 177, 203
Free Presbyterian Church 215
French, Field Marshal Viscount 84, 99–100

Garda Síochána 117, 127, 133, 134, 142
Gaelic Athletic Association 39, 43
Gaelic League 40–3, 90, 124
Gaeltacht, Commission for the Protection of 125, 157
Garvin, Tom 108, 203
George V, King 66, 104
'gerrymandering' 190
Gilmore, George 115
Girvin, Brian 168, 169
Gladstone, William Ewart x, 6, 11, 13, 14
Gonne, Maud [MacBride] 2, 46, 47, 98, 163, biog. 251
Government of Ireland Act (1920) 101, 102, 104, 105, 179, 189, 190, 191, 192
Gregory, Augusta 46, 47, 48
Greenwood, Sir Hamar 180
Griffith, Arthur 2, 48–51, 62, 66, 76,

83, 88, 91, 97, 102, 105–7, 108, 109, 111, 121, 127, biog. 252

Harland and Wolff shipyard, Belfast 18, 180, 228
Harney, Mary 221
Harris, Rosemary 195
Haughey, Charles 216, 218–220, 221, biog. 252
Healy, T.M. 31, 35, 55, 88, 123
Heath, Edward 207, 210, 212, 225
Hillsborough [see Anglo-Irish Agreement 1985]
Hobson, Bulmer 55–6, 71, 75, 84, biog. 252
Hogan, Professor James 142, 143, 144
Hogan, Patrick 120
Holland, Mary 220
Home Rule [Government of Ireland] bills 13–14
(1911) 56–7, 178
(1920) 100–2, 104, 179, 189, 190
housing 194
Hull, Cordell 154–5
Hume, John 201, 230
Hume–Adams talks 230
Hyde, Douglas 39–40, biog. 252

Industrial Development Authority 170
Inghinídhe na hÉireann 2
Inter-Party Government 164–7
Irish Bulletin 96–7
Irish Citizen Army 61, 65, 68, 98
Irish Convention 81, 84
Irish dancing 142
Irish Free State 107, 116
1922 constitution 117–18
British Commonwealth 150
Constitution (Amendment No.17) Act 129, 133
creation 118
Governor-generalship 136, 145

Irish Literary Theatre 46
Irish National Teachers'
    Organisation 156–8
Irish Nationalist [Parliamentary]
    Party 30, 54–5, 68–9, 81, 83–4,
    85
Irish Patriotic Children's Treat
    Committee 2
Irish Press 131, 133
Irish Republican Army [see also
    Provisional IRA] 87, 89, 91,
    94–8, 101, 102, 103, 105,
    111–13, 116, 133, 141, 143–4,
    176, 177, 181, 184, 208–10
    Army Convention (1922) 111
    border campaign 176
    Continuity IRA 233, 234
    'IRA Organization' 128–9
    Real IRA 233, 234
Irish Republican Brotherhood
    24–7, 35, 55, 71–2, 83, 106,
    113, 128
Irish Trades Union Congress 170
Irish Transport and General
    Workers' Union 62–3, 170
Irish Volunteers [see also Irish
    Republican Army] 60–1, 66–7,
    68, 69, 88, 93
    Active Service Units ('flying
        columns') 94
    Dublin Brigade 94, 102
    in Easter rebellion 76–80
    GHQ 93
    Irish Republican Army 89
    North Cork Brigade 93, 97
    Soloheadbeg ambush 87

Johnson, Thomas 88, 119, biog. 252
Jordan, Neil 108
Joyce, James 1–2, 173, 174

Keogh, Dermot 148, 149, 154, 166,
    167, 168
Kennedy, Hugh 128

Kettle, Thomas 55
Kickham, Charles J 26
Kilbrandon Committee 28

Labour party [Ireland] 85, 113, 119,
    134, 159, 170, 218
Land Acts **18**
    (1870) 6,11
    (1881) 13
    (1903) 17, 54
    land annuities 133
Land Conference 17
Land League 27–8, 31
language, Irish 21–2, **22**, 38, 40–3,
    123–5, 156–7, 217, 229
    'the national language' 146
Larkin, James 61–4, 159, 170
Liberal party 52–4, 56
The Leader 43
League of Nations 123
Lee, J.J. 12, 61, 127, 129, 155, 168,
    174, 218
Lemass, Seán 130, 138, 157, 160,
    170, 171–2, 176–7, 201, 216,
    biog. 252
Livestock Breeding Act (Northern
    Ireland) 193
Lloyd George, David 56, 81,
    105–6, 107, 122, 178–9, 191
Local Government Act (1898) 16
Londonderry, Marquess of 194–5
Long, Walter 58, 66, 86, 99
Longford, county (by-election
    1917) 82
Lynch, Jack 203, 215–17
Lynch, Liam 113, 115, 116
Lyons, F.S.L. 109, 126, 147, 155,
    186

McAleese, Mary (President of the
    Republic) 228
MacBride, John 48
MacBride, Seán 163–4, 166, 167,
    170

MacCurtain, Tomás 96
MacDermott [MacDiarmada], Seán
    55, 71, biog. 252
MacDonald, J. Ramsay 186
MacDonnell, Sir Antony 17
MacEntee, Seán 98, 138, 161, 162,
    170, 171, 216, biog. 252
McGahern, John 175
McGarrity, Joseph 113
McGuinness, Martin 209, 210
McLaughlin, Mitchel 227
MacMichael, Gary 233
MacNeill, Eoin 41, 43, 60–1, 69,
    75, 76, 84, 122, 124, 186–7,
    biog. 252
MacNeill, James 123, 136
Macready, General Sir Nevil 100
McQuaid, John Charles (Archbishop
    of Dublin) 158, 167
MacStíofáin, Seán 209
MacSwiney, Mary 110
MacSwiney, Terence 95–6, 124, 225
Maffey, Sir John 153
Mahaffy, John 43
Mallin, Michael 75
Mallon, Seamus 227, 234
Manchester Guardian 99
Markievicz, Constance 62, 77, 90,
    98, biog. 252
Mason, Roy 225
Mayhew, Sir Patrick 230
Mayo County Council 127
Mazzini, Giuseppe 21, 39–40
Mellows, Liam 110, 116
Ministers and Secretaries Act (1924)
    121
Mitchell, US Senator George 232
Moran, D.P. 43–5, 46, 48, 49, 51
Morrison, Danny 223
Mountbatten, Earl 223
Mulcahy, Richard 80, 93, 103, 109,
    127, 128, 129, 133, 162, 164
Munger, Frank 134
Murphy, William Martin 63

The Nation 38
National Army [Irish Free State]
    113–16, 128, 135–6
National Guard [see Blueshirts]
National Schools 11–12
Neave, Airey 223
Nelson, Sarah 213
neutrality 152–4
New Ireland Forum 219, 228
New University of Ulster 201
Northern Ireland 122
    discrimination 192–3, 198–9
    parliament 102, 104, 178, 179,
        187, 189
    power-sharing Executive 212
    welfare system 197
Northern Ireland Civil Rights
    Association 200, 201
Northern Ireland Office 227

oath of allegiance [see Anglo-Irish
    Treaty]
O'Brien, Conor Cruise 31, 40, 176,
    203, 211, 217, 219
O'Brien, Edna 174
O'Brien, William 35, 43, biog. 253
O'Brien, William 88, 119, 159,
    biog. 253
O Buachalla, Dónal 136
O'Connell, Daniel 3, 4, 19, 23, 24,
    32
O'Connell, J.J. ('Ginger') 71, 75
O'Connor, Rory 111, 113, 116
O'Doherty, Shane Paul 208, 209
O'Donnell, Peadar 131, 133, 143–4,
    169
O'Duffy, Eoin 142–3
O'Faoláin, Seán 47, 133, 173–4
Offences Against the State Act
    (1939) 153
O'Flaherty, Liam 42
O'Higgins, Kevin 108, 109, 111,
    115–16, 119, 128, 129, biog.
    253

O'Higgins, Thomas 141
O'Kelly, Seán T. biog. 253
O'Malley, Desmond 221
Omagh, Co. Tyrone, IRA bombing 1998 234
O'Neill, Terence 177, 199–202, 204
O'Toole, Fintan 177
O Tuathaigh, Gearóid 125
Orange Order 7, 200

Paisley, the Rev. I.R.K. 207, 211, 214–15
Parliament Act (1911) 56
Parnell, Anna 28
Parnell, Charles Stewart 2, 13, 27–32, 40, 41
Parnell, John 2
Parnell, William 4
Pearse, Patrick 41–2, 50, 60, 71–2, 73, 74, 76, 80
Peel, Sir Robert 5,7
Phoenix Park, Dublin 2
Pius XI, Pope 143
Plan of Campaign 35
Plunkett, Count 82
Plunkett, Horace 16–17, 50, 81
Plunkett, Joseph 76
Poor Law (1838) 10
Portadown 232, 234
Prager, Jeffrey 117
Prevention of Terrorism Act (1974) 224
Prior, James 227
Programme for Economic Expansion 172
Progressive Democratic party 221
Protestants
    emigration from Free State 126
    victimization by IRA 181
Provisional Government [Irish Free State] 110–18, 128
Provisional IRA 208–10, 221–6, 231, 232
Public health 161–3, 166–7

Quadragesimo Anno (1931 Papal Encyclical) 143
Queen's Colleges 12–13
Queen's University, Belfast 200, 231

Radio Telefís Éireann 173, 174
Ravenhill Evangelical Mission Church 214
Redmond, John 36, 53–4, 57, 59–60, 68–70, 84, biog. 253
Rees, Merlyn 212–13, 225, 227
Republic of Ireland Act (1949) 165
Restoration of Order in Ireland Act 94, 100
Reynolds, Albert 222, biog. 253
Ribbonmen 20
Robinson, Mary 218, 222, biog. 253
Rose, Richard 198
Royal Irish Constabulary 7, 36
    Auxiliary Division 94, 100–1
    'Black and Tans' 87, 100
Royal Ulster Constabulary 184, 199, 204, 225, 229–30, 234
Russell, Lord John 10
Russell, George (AE) 16
Russell, Seán 197

Salisbury, Earl of 14, 52
Sands, Bobby 225
Saor Éire 141, 143–4, 163
Scarman Inquiry 204
Senate [Seanad Éireann] 118, 126, 137, 145
Sheehy-Skeffington, Frank 42, 77
Sheehy-Skeffington, Hanna 98
shipbuilding industry 193, 228
Sinn Féin 37, 51, 55–6, 81–6, 87, 88, 89, 97–9, 102, 103, 109, 111, 113, 119, 121, 124, 129, 130, 176, 225, 227, 228, 230
Smuts, Jan 186
Social Democratic and Labour Party 205, 206, 210, 212, 225, 230, 234

Society for the Preservation of the
Irish Language 38
Special Powers Act (1922) 184, 199,
201, 207, 215, 224
Spring, Dick 222
Stack, Austin 92, 106
Stalker, John (Assistant Chief
Constable, Manchester police)
226
Stephens, James 25
Stevens, John (Deputy Chief
Constable, Cambridgeshire
police) 226
Stormont Agreement (1998) 233
Stormont Castle [see also NI
Parliament] 187
Sunningdale Conference (1972)
211–12, 222, 226
syndicalism 61–4
Synge, J.M. 47, 48, 175

Tariff Commission 120, 138
Thatcher, Margaret 219, 228, 229
Tierney, Professor Michael 125, 142
The Times 2, 31, 66, 81, 99
Trimble, David 231, 233, 234
Trinity College, Dublin 45–6

Ulster Army Council 212, 213
Ulster Covenant (1911) 59, 60, 187
Ulster Defence Association 207,
211, 212

Ulster Defence Regiment 204
Ulster Freedom Fighters 207
Ulster Special Constabulary 180–4
Ulster Unionism 13, 57–60
Ulster Unionist Council 58
Ulster Unionist Party 104, 199,
205, 211, 231
Ulster Volunteer Force 60, 65–7,
180, 207
Ulster Workers' Council 212–13
United Nations 175–6
United Irish League 2, 17, 30,
34–6
University College, Dublin 41, 42

Victoria, Queen 1–2

Walsh, William Joseph (Archbishop
of Dublin) 44
Warrenpoint ambush 223
Whitaker, T.K. 171
Whiteboyism 6, 20
Whitelaw, William 207, 210
Whyte, John 148, 162, 165, 192,
198
Wolfe Tone, Theobald ix, 20, 21,
43
Wyndham, George 17

Yeats, W.B. 36, 40, 46–8, 68, biog.
253
Young Ireland 23–4, 32